I0796524

This book is dedicated to Friends of the High Line in gratitude for their pioneering efforts in conceiving this unique public space, for their courage and tenacity in realizing it, and for their ongoing hard work to fund, manage, curate, maintain, and protect the High Line into the future.

THE HIGH LINE

THE HIGH LINE

FORESEEN . UNFORESEEN

JAMES CORNER FIELD OPERATIONS • DILLER SCOFIDIO + RENFRO

00_INTRODUCTION

The High Line is a one-and-a-half-mile-long (2.4 km) public park in New York City. It rests on an elevated stretch of obsolete freight railway that serviced the West Side of Manhattan for nearly fifty years. When first built in 1934, the project was celebrated as one of the most important works of infrastructure in the history of Manhattan. As manufacturing businesses fled the area in the 1970s, the industrial neighborhood surrounding the railway dissolved into a sea of open parking lots, and the booming trucking industry eclipsed railroads as the primary means of freight transportation to and from the city. The last train ran in 1980, and the abandoned tracks soon became rusted and overgrown.

In 1999, two local residents formed an activist group, Friends of the High Line, to fight for the preservation of the derelict structure. In December 2001, under pressure from neighborhood property owners, the outgoing mayor signed an executive agreement to demolish the structure. A lawsuit temporarily halted this plan, and within a few months, the incoming Bloomberg administration had rescinded the demolition order and announced its support of the project. In 2003, a competition was launched to find a team of designers with a vision for the next chapter of the abandoned rail line.

There are so many extraordinary stories surrounding the High Line: its history; the activism of the Friends of the High Line; the economic development strategy of the politicians who supported it; its influence within a broader cultural context. This book captures many of these stories, but focuses on the design, development, and construction of the High Line. Narrated from the perspective of James Corner Field Operations and Diller Scofidio + Renfro, together with Piet Oudolf and other members of the team, this is the story of New York's park in the sky as experienced by those who designed it.

HUDSON RIVER
HUDSON
YARDS
MEATPACKING
DISTRICT
CHELSEA
MANHATTAN

CENTRAL PARK

CORE DESIGN TEAM

Lisa Switkin
James Corner Field Operations

Ricardo Scofidio
Diller Scofidio + Renfro

James Corner
James Corner Field Operations

Elizabeth Diller
Diller Scofidio + Renfro

Matthew Johnson
Diller Scofidio + Renfro

After the final section of the High Line opened in fall of 2014, the principal designers met to discuss the decade-long collaboration. The conversation was recorded, transcribed, and is printed in these pages in three installments: Forethoughts, Process, and Afterthoughts.

CONVERSATION PART ONE: FORETHOUGHTS

MODERATOR: It's been ten years since you began designing the High Line, a good distance from which to reflect on the process that resulted in a very successful public work. What did you know about the High Line before the design competition?

JAMES CORNER (JC): Before the design competition in 2004, I did not know a lot about the High Line. I initially learned about it through architecture studios that Steven Holl taught at Columbia University. I would see the structure when I went to bars and galleries in the neighborhood, but it never registered as something that was a mile-and-a-half (2.4 km) long with a secret green meadow above.

RICARDO SCOFIDIO (RS): I was teaching at the Cooper Union School of Architecture when I realized that this obsolete piece of infrastructure could be a great site for architectural speculation. After seeing Steven's hypothetical project, Bridge of Houses, for the High Line, I thought this could be fertile ground for students to challenge the status quo.

ELIZABETH DILLER (ED): At that time, rumors swirled about Steven buying the High Line from the city for one dollar. It seems to have been an urban legend.

RS: The High Line was a great pedagogical tool. It naturally made its way to schools all over the country.

ED: It provided two juicy conceptual issues: the obsolescence of one program stimulating the invention of another, and the dismantling of the distinction between architecture and urbanism.

LISA SWITKIN (LS): The High Line was the site of my final landscape architectural design studio at the University of Pennsylvania, so I had already spent a lot of time thinking about it. The studio class aimed to create strategic scenarios for the High Line's future by exploring the relationship between forces of preservation and those of globalization. My project focused on ways to engage the surrounding neighborhood, specifically the two large public housing developments in the area. But as a landscape architecture student, thinking of the High Line as a prospective landscape was something that captured my imagination and stayed with me.

MATTHEW JOHNSON (MJ): For me it was a mystery, but I remember hearing about it constantly. Walking through Chelsea, I never saw it, because I didn't know what I was looking for. It was buried midblock, and there was always a billboard or a large tree in front of it. You walked into a shadow and didn't realize you had just walked under the High Line.

JC: In a quiet way, it seemed almost mythical — it split through buildings and blocks, and you never had a clue as to its actual scale or significance. You couldn't get on top of it, so you only caught glimpses, fragments, bits and pieces from the street below. It seemed discarded, silent, and obsolete.

ED: None of us actually trespassed onto the High Line before 2004, right?

LS: No, but I did photograph it from the street below and from the rooftop of the Kitchen above.

RS: There weren't a lot of residential buildings in the area at the time. It was filled mostly with industrial warehouses. If there had been more eyes looking down on it and witnessing the formation of the wild landscape that flourished after the trains stopped running, there might have been a greater awareness.

ED: Before 1999, the High Line wasn't discussed much outside of academia. The next time I remember thinking about it was when Friends of the High Line launched the ideas competition to bring public attention to the preservation effort. At that point, the prospect of saving the High Line still seemed so improbable. The culminating exhibition at Grand Central seemed like a tribute to the extinction of a dying species.

Did any of you spend time in the area?

LS: I went to Florent!

MJ: Same here, after many late nights out. It really didn't matter where we were in the city; we'd always end up at Florent before the sun came up.

ED: Come on, nobody went to the leather bars? I had an architectural motivation for going to the neighborhood. In 1999, I was a jury member for a design competition to reimagine the West Side Rail Yards, which was the last large undeveloped tract of real estate in Manhattan — twelve city blocks bordered by the High Line on three sides. My strongest memory was that, while most of the celebrity architects competing filled the site with buildings, Cedric Price proposed to leave the West Side Rail Yards totally vacant as the "lungs of the city." He was intoxicated when he made his presentation, but he was incredibly lucid. The competition was run by the Canadian Center for Architecture, and the final exhibition, in 2000, included photographs by Joel Sternfeld, who had been commissioned by Friends of the High Line to shoot large-format photographs of the High Line across the seasons. These were the images that were later published in *The New Yorker* to great acclaim.

RS: Those Sternfeld photos were key to saving the High Line.

ED: Yes; the political power of the photographs was palpable. But the Sternfeld photos were very romantic and didn't really capture the illicit quality of the place.

RS: It was an industrial relic, and it seemed inevitable that it would get torn down. Unlike the razing of Penn Station, no one would get upset about losing obsolete industrial infrastructure. In fact, the sentiment was more like, "Get rid of it: let's make way for progress!"

JC: Not only the High Line, but the entire neighborhood appeared forlorn. Through our research, we found amazing photographs documenting the decades-long decline of this overlooked, postindustrial neighborhood — graffiti, darkness, and shadows, a seductive aesthetic with an undeniable authenticity.

ED: When the Dia Art Foundation arrived on 22nd Street in 1987, change was in the air.

MJ: The Dia certainly brought a wave of interest from the New York cultural elite, but the big cultural shift was in the '70s, when all these queer subcultures started to emerge in the neighborhood. In 1975, the city neared bankruptcy, and the manufacturing industry had all but evaporated, leaving vacant warehouses and lofts for new communities to take root. Artists, sex workers, and cross-dressing kids shared the street with meatpacking workers and longtime tenement residents. The Dia opening fit within this larger cultural chain reaction, a postindustrial urban narrative by now very familiar to New Yorkers and urbanites all over the world.

ED: Right. The progression was almost inevitable. Space in the neighborhood was so cheap to rent, and so, by the 1990s, the art scene had migrated from SoHo to TriBeCa to Chelsea.

RS: The neighborhood was physically changing, too. Another elevated structure, the West Side Highway, was built at the same time as the High Line, but permanently closed after a section of the highway collapsed. The highway was torn down in 1989, which made everyone think that the High Line was the next to go.

ED: The very notion that the High Line could add value to this decaying context eluded mostly everyone. Giuliani, the mayor of New York at the time, was under great pressure from local developers who believed the High Line was devaluing their properties. But there was a quiet movement under way led by a couple of citizen activists who had the foresight to know that the High Line could make a positive impact.

LS: It's interesting, thinking back. When the West Side Improvement Project was proposed in the late '20s and completed in 1934, the High Line was branded as the "Life Line of New York," providing food, milk, and meat to the vibrant industrial West Side. It was hailed in its time as transformative, but would later be seen as a blight. The city faced the same general question again in the late 1990s: how to re-envision the West Side. The transformation of the abandoned rail tracks into an elevated park was a new phase in the city's ambition to reinvent the neighborhood.

ED: This had been a site of reinvention for a long time. When the street-level railroad tracks along the West Side were first built in the 1850s, Manhattan had only just recently grown past Canal Street. Huge swaths of West Chelsea had only just been created through infill development — before 1830, the ground that the High Line stands on was in the Hudson River! In the Victorian era, all of this changed rapidly — the population of the city nearly tripled, and New York established itself as the largest manufacturing hub in the U.S. and one of the great cities of the world. The area surrounding what is now the High Line quickly became crowded with factories, warehouses, and rows of tenements. What had been countryside was suddenly a dense industrial and residential neighborhood, and public protest about the traffic accidents caused by the railroad tracks eventually convinced the city and the railroad company to do something about it. That's why the High Line exists. Of course, money was important, too—the city thought the elevated track would bring even more business to the neighborhood. But the local activism was also essential. When the Friends of the High Line came along to advocate for their cause, they inherited a site that had already been the site of contentious civic engagement for over a century.

RS: I've always been amazed by the Friends of the High Line origin story: Joshua David and Robert Hammond just happened to sit next to one another at a community board meeting. What was the spark that made them decide it was their calling to save the High Line for the good of the neighborhood and the city?

LS: I think their passion, their entrepreneurial and pioneering spirit, combined with an innocent naïveté about how exactly to enact their plan, are what actually allowed them to be successful.

MJ: It started as a preservation project, but there was momentum growing that shifted priorities toward a broader transformation.

JC: There were people living in the neighborhood back then who had elevated views of the old High Line and who saw something none of us could ever see—a continuous ribbon of emergent green meadow running silently through the city, above the streets. They saw a certain romance and potential in this green corridor and thought it was worth preserving without knowing exactly what it would become.

LS: Robert told me that one of the hardest problems in the beginning was convincing people that the High Line was worth saving without taking them up there to see it with their own eyes. Once he took people to see it for themselves, they were sold.

ED: Anyone with an imagination might have thought of preserving the High Line and transforming it into a great park; the creative leap in saving it was constructing a story about its potential as a catalyst for development in this forgotten area of Manhattan. It's not a new strategy: 150 years ago, advocates for Central Park argued its merits as an economic catalyst for the northward growth of Manhattan.

RS: But wasn't the catalyst argument used by Giuliani as a reason to tear it down?

ED: Yes. He reversed the argument: demolition would spur development.

LS: In 2002, the Design Trust for Public Space published a study, "Reclaiming the High Line." The story is that Robert and Josh pitched it to the office of the mayor, and the administration asked for an economic assessment because its merits of public space alone were insufficient to save it. The Friends of the High Line hired HR&A, an economic development consulting firm, to prove that the tax revenue generated by the project would outweigh the capital costs and therefore warrant city support. Without the economic argument, the project fell into the "improbable" category.

JC: The HR&A report turned out to be a conservative underestimation, but at that time no one could have anticipated the speed of growth we have seen. Bloomberg was a smart businessman: he saw an underachieving, deteriorating section of the city that held a huge amount of untapped economic potential. In order to unlock that potential and stimulate reinvestment, he brought the No.7 subway line west, rezoned the district for new development, and retained the High Line as a magnet that would bring a special identity and charm to the area. The revitalized High Line as new public space would help catalyze the development that followed. It was very farsighted, strategic, and ambitious.

ED: Amanda Burden played a key role in the project when she became commissioner of city planning. She is one of the heroes of the project alongside Josh and Robert.

RS: Though I heard it started off poorly—Josh and Robert made an appointment to take her up for a walk on the High Line but forgot and stood her up. She arrived, and nobody showed. Fortunately, she agreed to reschedule the tour.

What was Ms. Burden's role in the process?

JC: Under her watch, City Planning created an urban design strategy for West Chelsea that allowed developers to build taller on the outer avenues while preserving light and air immediately around the High Line. This incentivized development, but also protected space for the High Line. Amanda was also an important advocate for the quality of design; she paid significant attention to all the details and supported many of our ideas.

ED: A decade before, we might have publicly criticized a rezoning strategy that allowed developers to build at the water's edge. But given the overall intent to save the High Line from the canyon effect, it seemed like the right trade-off. Even though lots of new towers are now shooting up around the park, the space immediately around it continues to be protected by her vision.

So the park was economically driven?

ED: Altruism alone rarely drives civic and public architecture; but if there's an economic incentive, it can move mountains.

How did the *Promenade Plantée* factor into your project?

ED: Having a predecessor helped us make our case to city authorities. When the design team and the Friends of the High Line took a field trip to Paris to visit the *Promenade Plantée*, we made it clear that the High Line would be different and distinctly New York — gritty, not pretty. When you fast-forward to today, it's interesting that the High Line is the reference for new infrastructural parks being planned across the globe. The great irony is that the *Petite Ceinture*, a new park on the elevated railway encircling Paris, references the High Line as much as their own predecessor, the *Promenade Plantée*.

MJ: That visit helped us clarify what we didn't want to do. The *Promenade Plantée* was incredibly formal and rigid — the design didn't take advantage of its urban context or the fact that it was an elevated park. There seemed to be no references to its previous life as a viaduct except at ground level.

LS: It felt like it could have been anywhere. It blocked out the city.

RS: It was deserted when we first visited. I walked the entire length and saw only one person, and I realized it was more pleasurable to walk on the city sidewalks of Paris. I was told that the park's gardens were designed by each neighborhood it passed through, so it did not have strong continuity along its length.

JC: The *Promenade Plantée* has a bit of a Parisian-bourgeois finish to it: limestone masonry with quite formal plantings similar to a garden in the tradition of enclosure. We all felt very strongly that the High Line should have a much different aura, set within a broader field of urban conditions. This was a postindustrial ruin, a melancholic steel structure with an emergent green meadow and a silence so palpably strange in the context of Manhattan. These characteristics suggested a design approach that might seek to amplify these conditions rather than erase them. In a sense, the *Promenade Plantée* was the antithesis of what we wanted to do: it was too beautiful, too scripted, too clean, and too cut off from its urban context.

RS: But it was still a very noteworthy first.

ED: The High Line's beauty came from its abjectness as a ruin. In the competition phase, the best adjective we could find to describe the experience was "otherworldly."

RS: But our most important argument was not an aesthetic one. It was an appeal to revitalization: here is an elevated piece of urban infrastructure that can be given a second life.

JC: At first, it wasn't obvious that the High Line would be a park: options ranged from light transit to open space, from building to outright demolition. Even if defined as a park, would it be a recreational corridor, a linear promenade, or a series of gardens? And for any conversion of the High Line to a park, the constraints were significant and overwhelming. It was up in the sky — how do you get people up there? The structure had a very shallow cross section, which meant there was very little room for soil and plant root systems. It's quite narrow, so it was difficult to imagine how you could have a lot of people up there without it losing its wild character. Of course, there were all sorts of safety, policing, and fire concerns as well.

ED: And security, maintenance, drainage, garbage, snow removal — all of those sundry support systems you take for granted in a park. How do you navigate the web of New York City codes, legalities, and approval processes for a city park in the air? These constraints necessitated that everyone rethink what a park meant. For the idea to have traction, we had to convince skeptics that this would not only be a beautiful destination for the public but also logistically achievable.

MJ: It took a long time for the city to even understand what agency had jurisdiction over the High Line. The Department of Buildings didn't consider it relevant to their purview, the Parks Department had no experience with precedents for elevated structures like this, and the Department of Transportation only had standards relevant to highway overpasses and pedestrian bridges that were specifically about transportation concerns, not recreation and leisure.

LS: If it was not an overpass, a bridge, a street, a sidewalk, a building, or a typical street-level park, what rules would apply?

JC: I remember our first visit on the High Line. To get up there we had to take a freight elevator in a warehouse that was completely dark inside. Then, all of a sudden, the huge doors opened and we stepped into a magical garden of green. It was such a delightful surprise.

ED: As I remember, we had to sign safety waivers accepting that we wouldn't sue the rail company, CSX, if we got hurt because there was so much debris in the way.

RS: I remember that the building we entered for elevator access was an abattoir. It smelled of beef carcasses and fat, and there were blood splatters everywhere.

JC: Everything around the High Line was tough. The structure itself is steel with a concrete bed, stone ballast, wood ties, and steel tracks. In its first life, there was nothing organic up there at all. When the trains stopped running in 1980, the wood ties began to rot and accumulate moisture, and the first seeds, brought in by birds and breezes, grew into plants. As those plants died, they formed the first organic material, allowing for more growth and diversity to emerge. Over the next years, nature started to take over, in terms of soil-making, plant growth, and biodiversification. The resulting contrast was stunning: this benevolent, melancholic garden, alone and quiet, doing its own thing next to the tough and unforgiving city.

ED: There was this overwhelming sense of the unintended. You saw the backs of things, the party walls, castaway furniture, broken toys, and torn fences. You could practically see that the soil was toxic; there was broken glass everywhere and heroin needles. You really didn't want to touch anything. The views of New York were dramatic, but not like any postcard you would find in a gift shop. In a way, it was a blind spot in real estate-crazed Manhattan.

LS: People living next to the High Line had a very personal way of interacting with it — a real secret garden with makeshift drawbridges made of wooden planks from their windows to the structure. We found a garden with an irrigation system and a Christmas tree with lights and bows.

JC: There were random findings: a sculptor who created all these steel pieces within one of the tunnels, a bucket filled with used spray cans, a tricycle.

MJ: A row of old turnstiles leading nowhere.

ED: Used condoms.

LS: A strange chair with a face mask.

MJ: There was a Keith Haring Running Man buried under layers of graffiti.

JC: The best part was the effect of the collage: the sense of cut, rupture, splice, and juxtaposition. Because the High Line so ruthlessly cuts through blocks, it produced surprising and unforeseen effects, juxtaposing emergent natural systems with urban leftovers and decay. Also, being thirty feet (9 m) in the sky really changes your perspective. You can see the Statue of Liberty, the Hudson River, and various vistas across Manhattan. It becomes a viewing platform from which to see the city in new and unexpected ways.

ED: It's a New York made up of abruptly changing atmospheres: a deep alley with ghostly smokestacks, fire escapes draped with laundry, massive billboards with underwear ads, an incidental view into a bedroom window, mechanical lifts that park cars in the air, the sweet sound of children playing echoing from the churchyard.

RS: The sound is highly specific up there. There's a drop in noise level when you're thirty feet (9 m) above the street.

ED: Although, strangely, it becomes noisier when it gets dark. In the day, the din of the city disappears as the visual calm absorbs your attention. At night, you can hear every detail of the city — every car and every helicopter or plane flying overhead, as well as distant conversation.

LS: Subtle environmental conditions are palpable up there: slight shifts of wind and sun.

RS: But what affected me most when I stepped onto the High Line was a sense of dread about the near future; like the end of so many science fiction novels where the jungle emerges through the concrete, all signs of civilization completely erased, with the abandoned railway at the center. The plants I saw were robust and survived with almost no soil in unnatural conditions. You could imagine that in another fifty years the plants would consume the High Line structure and then the city. Everything would turn to dust: nothing would be left but primal vegetation. New Yorkers would be gone: only the weeds would survive.

ED: The cycle of decay and rebirth was so palpable, as if plants were born of industry while industry took its last breath. The vegetation took over. Seeds accidentally flew off of train cars or blew in from afar. The mile-and-a-half (2.4 km) stretch became a collection of microecologies, enabled by the variety of urban conditions: areas of shade between tall buildings that bred sumac trees, sun-drenched areas that bred Kentucky bluegrass, windswept areas that spawned asters and goldenrods. For me, the surprise was discovering the logic of what grew where in this perverse urban ecosystem.

RS: There were trees! It's one thing to find weeds; it's another to find self-seeded trees on a man-made structure hovering in midair!

JC: This carpet of self-sown green gave the High Line a sense of unity. It was a linear garden, and each block had its own particular microclimate. The green assumed different textures, heights, and combinations. That observation informed our design approach significantly, because we knew we wanted a unified but also varied experience. We didn't want to go from block to block with different design vocabularies. The design concept emulated the self-similarity of the rail bed landscape: a mile-and-a-half (2.4 km) of something constant and systematic, a ribbon of rail bed with plants that thicken, thin out, ebb, and alter their textures according to different microclimates.

LS: For me, there was a strong sense of opportunity. There was dereliction, but it was also hopeful. There was so much new life: bird eggs, cascading vines, an exotic pear tree likely carried from a seed on a train.

JC: On the one hand, it felt entropic, decaying, but on the other hand, the sense of life was profoundly positive. The feeling was double-edged: sadness and melancholy touched by enthusiasm and optimism. The High Line was built in an extremely repetitive way: the same combination of columns, beams, tracks, rivets, and railings, repeated for a mile-and-a-half (2.4 km). It's absolutely singular, indifferent to the neighborhood buildings that grew up around it. That collage effect I spoke of earlier is about this very contrast: the singularity of the High Line, covered with newly emergent plant life juxtaposed against a myriad of buildings and adjacencies.

ED: When I first walked down the High Line, it was as if I could feel my place in the collective history of the city. There was this deep sense of loss for an irretrievable past.

LS: It's a dual feeling of leaving the city and diving deeper into it at the same time. It's not a complete escape: you're in the city, seeing it in a new way, but at the same time, you feel like you're in a different world.

RS: It wasn't an escape from the city but more like a portal to the city, a way to enter into its unconscious.

How did this affect your design?

JC: The strange autonomy of this structure and its emergent life in the context of the city deeply informed our design approach. We sought to amplify these found conditions.

LS: We had a dilemma: how do we take such an authentic place and make it accessible without destroying it? Our work was a balancing act, and the concept straddled preservation and transformation, hard and soft. We wanted the experience of the High Line to remain informal. Even today, as busy as it is, people still use it in a very casual way, as if it is their backyard. That was the informal spirit that we were trying to hold on to.

ED: Yet the problem was paradoxical: if this otherworldly park was to become a catalyst for development, attracting many people and buildings around it, how could we preserve the very thing that made it an attraction in the first place — its wildness? How do you balance the imprint of the past with the present and an uncertain future?

MJ: From the beginning, I thought that some of the wonder of the place — the feeling of moving off the city grid while still being completely immersed in it, the sensation of meandering alone — might be hard to share with crowds of people. There was an aspect to the experience that would be lost forever no matter what we designed. I'm not a sentimental designer — cities need change, and forcing a piece of architecture to remain strictly frozen in time inevitably compromises the experience of it. Still, there was this strong impulse, after having spent time up there, to keep this place secret. But the competing urge to play with this bizarre sliver of industrial urban space always won out — the opportunities for adaptive reuse were endless.

JC: At the very beginning, we made a diagram that showed a spectrum from maximum preservation to maximum transformation. Among the competition entries, you could see the range of approaches along that spectrum: from Michael Van Valkenburgh's light touch to Zaha Hadid's complete obliteration of the High Line. We found the sweet spot in the middle, perhaps weighted more toward preservation but with an additional layer, recognizing that a park in this unprecedented context demanded a new design vocabulary.

Does that also include rethinking the program of a park?

RS: At the beginning, we felt that the public needed something to do when they visited the High Line — an excuse for going there — so our initial proposal included an amphitheater, an outdoor cinema, and a wetland area that would be an ice-skating pond in the winter and beach in the summer.

JC: These theatrical features were necessary in the competition.

RS: We eliminated many when we realized that the most powerful act of design was to leave it alone. Well, almost.

ED: The design language is minimal. The goal was to focus attention not on the High Line but on everything around it. It's about de-familiarizing the city, altering people's sense of New York by prompting them to look more deeply.

JC: Which brings the actual High Line as well as the unexpected into focus.

LS: Would I have noticed a condom wrapper in the middle of the street? Probably not. On the High Line, everything was hyperpresent. The scale is so intimate that your focus is amplified.

What were your thoughts about the relation of the High Line to the city?

RS: In cities, people act like mice. We come out of holes in our apartment buildings and run along the edges of blocks like rodents clinging to a baseboard, never crossing the center of a room. The High Line allows you to experience the middle of a block. On the street, you cross avenues and streets but you never stand at the center of the intersection for more than a moment. On the High Line, you can occupy the middle of a street intersection without getting run over. You could also walk for a mile-and-a-half (2.4 km) and not stop for a single red light.

ED: In the design we were adamant about not allowing the High Line to become another city street. In fact, we were militant about not bringing cafés, bookstores, and shops — the whole consumer leisure world — up to the level of the structure, as was featured in other schemes. The High Line had to be a nonstreet.

LS: That was a radical idea at the time. Most people thought that since the High Line was elevated, the project should take over adjacent rooftops, expand outward, and physically connect to its surroundings. Make it bigger — why not? Our idea, instead, was about limiting its reach.

MJ: The report published by the Design Trust for Public Space was filled with these ideas. Most of the images envisioned connecting markets at that upper level, like a boardwalk at a popular beach. That was exactly what we were trying to avoid. It had to remain apart from everything, an oasis.

What about the park next door?

LS: At the competition interview, we made the distinction between the Hudson River Park and our vision for the High Line.

ED: Yes, the Hudson River Park is naturally a place for runners, bikers, and rollerbladers, adjacent to high-speed traffic at the river's edge. The High Line would not be a place for wheels, only feet. We wanted the High Line to encourage slow motion and be a place for sitting and strolling.

MJ: And cruising — a place to see and be seen. Given the night life and fashion boutiques that had already become rooted in the neighborhood, we knew this would be part of the High Line experience as much as the appreciation for its landscape.

JC: From the outset, we were very clear about our design philosophy for the High Line: keep it! Keep it wild; keep it slow; keep it quiet; keep it simple! Our philosophy was to do all we could to maintain everything that made the High Line distinct from other spaces in the city: its melancholy and otherworldliness; its autonomy and wildness; and its sense of pace and duration.

IBP
MAG
WHOLESALE BE
PHONE 212 924-7

01_FOUND

In May 2004, alongside other teams vying to convert the abandoned railway into a public park, our design team, comprised of James Corner Field Operations, Diller Scofidio + Renfro, and Piet Oudolf, visited the High Line for the first time. The structure, a property of CSX Transportation Corporation, loomed thirty feet (9 m) above the street, its edges lined with dilapidated fences and topped with barbed wire to keep trespassers out. After signing several safety waivers, we entered the freight elevator of an abandoned warehouse in the Meatpacking District. The steel doors of the elevator shut and the noisy cab slowly ascended to the height of the tracks. The doors opened directly onto the High Line, and we emerged into a field of unexpected wilderness above Gansevoort Street. From this meadow of grasses and concrete, we began the walk uptown along the mile-and-a-half (2.4 km) of rusting, overgrown tracks.

ARCHIVAL VIDEO 05 / 04 / 2004

70 ft. (21 m)

160 ft. (48 m)

275 ft. (83 m)

330 ft. (100 m)

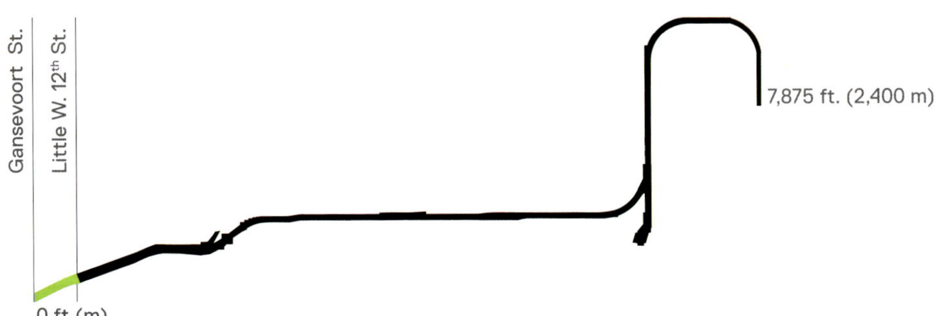

390 ft. (118 m)

455 ft. (139 m)

560 ft. (170 m)

618 ft. (188 m)

SWEET CHERRY
WET®
FLAVORED
LUBRICANT
SUGAR-FREE
NON-STAINING
10 MI

RESK 1
KERN

MEDS

685 ft. (208 m)

755 ft. (230 m)

815 ft. (248 m)

890 ft. (271 m)

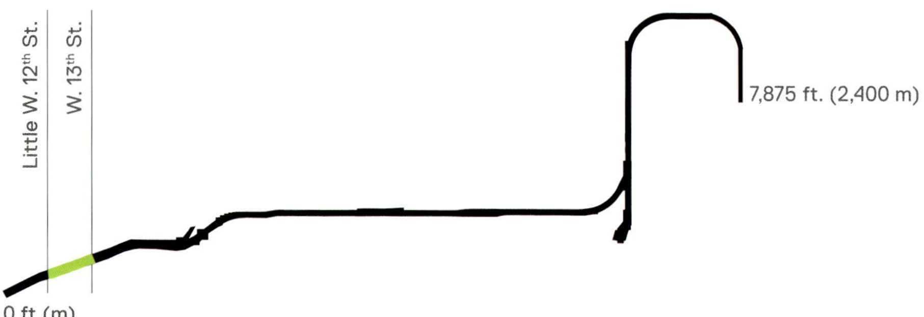

945 ft. (288 m)

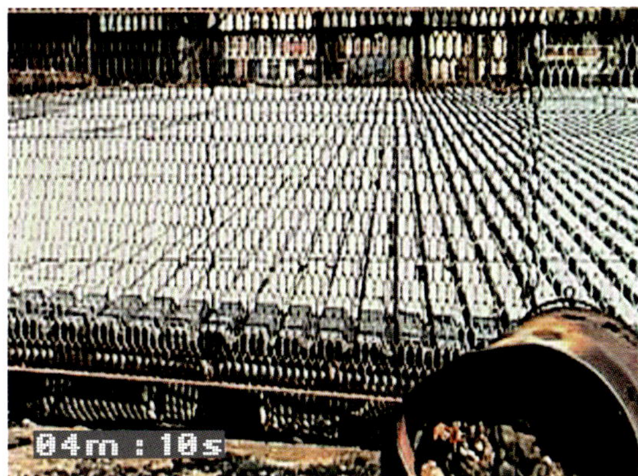

1,040 ft. (316 m)

1,150 ft. (350 m)

1,265 ft. (385 m)

MARINE & A

EXIT
RIDGI

PK

1,475 ft. (449 m)

1,505 ft. (458 m)

1,525 ft. (464 m)

1,540 ft. (469 m)

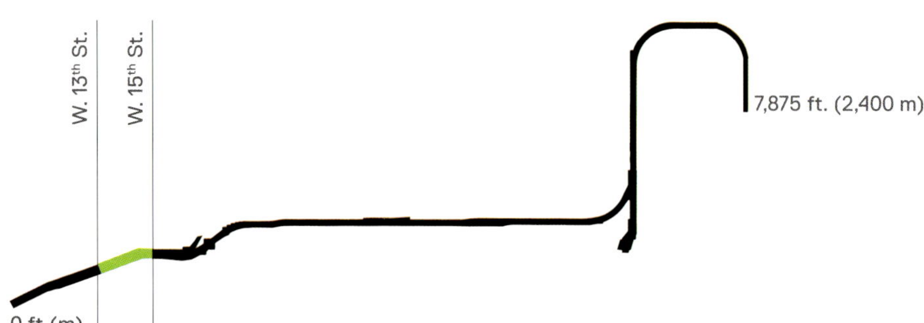

1,550 ft. (472 m)

1,560 ft. (475 m)

1,575 ft. (480 m)

1,585 ft. (483 m)

FLORIAN

CLEAR
FIRE LANE
FOR
EMERGENCY
VEHICLES
SNOW ROUTE
NO STANDING

RESIDENT EVIL

1,690 ft. (515 m)

1,825 ft. (556 m)

1,910 ft. (582 m)

2,080 ft. (633 m)

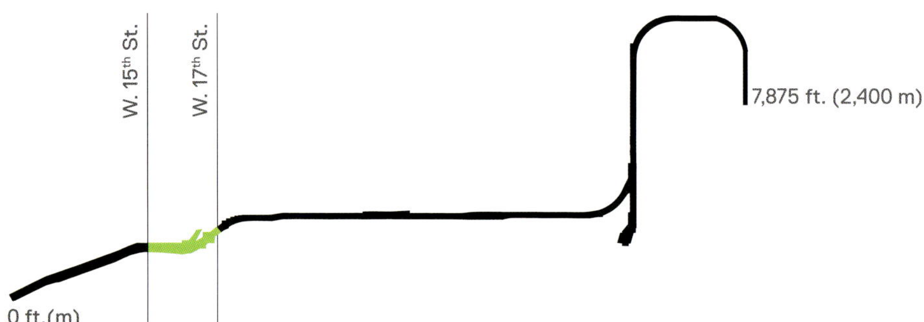

2,205 ft. (685 m)

2,320 ft. (707 m)

2,410 ft. (734 m)

2,530 ft. (771 m)

10 AV
W 17 ST
99
ONE WAY
99 Tenth Avenue

STORAGE USA

XKR
born with: 390 hp
lives for: carpool lanes
THE ENTIRE YELLOW PAGES ONLINE AND ON YOUR CELL? OOH LA LA.
verizon
VERIZON SUPERPAGES
SUPERPAGES.COM

2,690 ft. (819 m)

2,760 ft. (841 m)

2,850 ft. (869 m)

2,945 ft. (898 m)

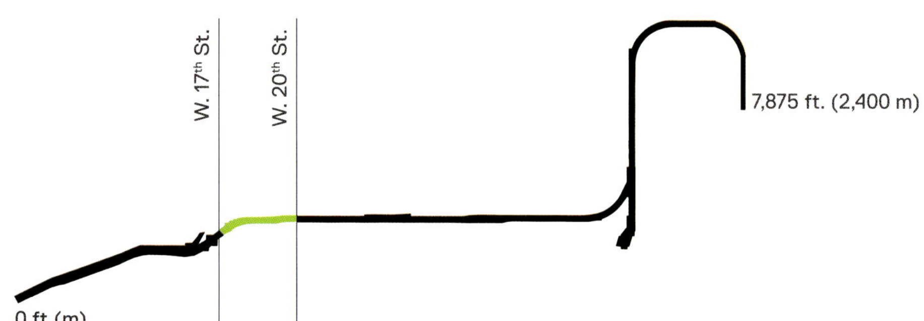

3,055 ft. (931 m)

3,175 ft. (968 m)

3,250 ft. (990 m)

3,365 ft. (1,025 m)

PAINTERS TOUCH

RAMAPO AJAX CORP
No 25
1360

INC
BONDED
AND
COST

3,480 ft. (1,061 m)

3,595 ft. (1,069 m)

4,005 ft. (1,220 m)

4,095 ft. (1,248 m)

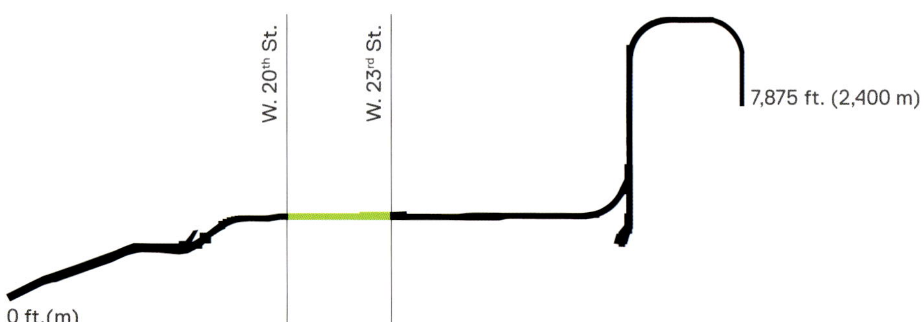

4,145 ft. (1,263 m)

4,250 ft. (1,295 m)

4,335 ft. (1,321 m)

4,415 ft. (1,346 m)

OVERSEAS
HOUSEHOLD & PERSONAL EFFECTS

4,685 ft. (1,428 m)

4,755 ft. (1,449 m)

4,985 ft. (1,519 m)

5,145 ft. (1,568 m)

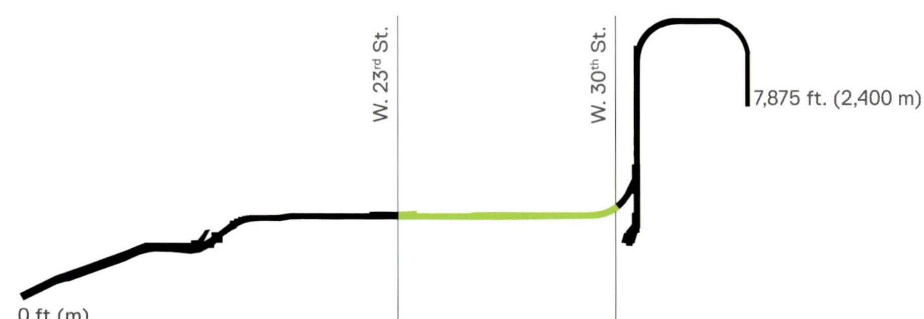

5,215 ft. (1,590 m)

5,275 ft. (1,608 m)

5,355 ft. (1,632 m)

5,530 ft. (1,686 m)

IMPEACH

New Girl

7,185 ft. (2,190 m)

7,305 ft. (2,227 m)

7,365 ft. (2,245 m)

7,395 ft. (2,254 m)

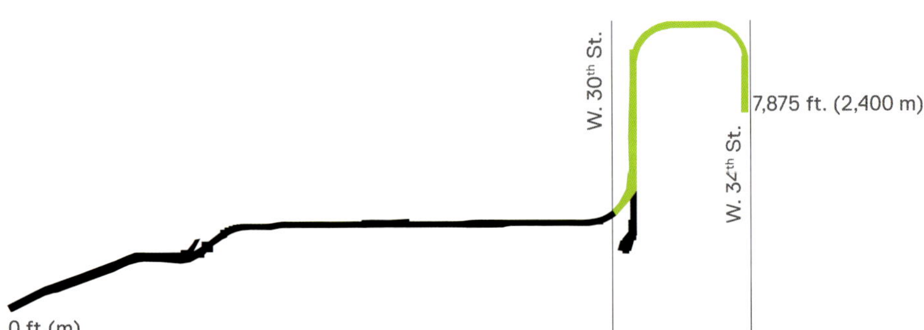

7,415 ft. (2,260 m)

7,440 ft. (2,268 m)

7,500 ft. (2,286 m)

7,525 ft. (2,294 m)

PARK
Save
Tracks

02_ARCHIVE

A collection of archival documents served as the foundational research for our team's creative work. Collected from public libraries, municipal archives, and private collections, the material spans over a century of Manhattan's architectural and cultural development, from the mid-nineteenth century to the new millennium. Over the course of this period, New York grew from a bustling town at the tip of Manhattan to the five-borough behemoth of today. The West Side, once a booming nexus of food markets and light manufacturing, transformed first into a subcultural hotspot for illicit activities, and then a postindustrial haven for culture and commerce. Across this timeline, the High Line evolved from a street-level rail line to an elevated freight viaduct, to a forgotten postindustrial relic, and ultimately to the park we know today. Many of the forces driving the High Line's contemporary reincarnation—community activism, innovative planning, and public-private partnerships—mirrored the original effort to build the railway generations before.

See extended captions on pages 115–119.

1
Specialized markets on the West Side of lower Manhattan served by the New York Central Railroad, 1912

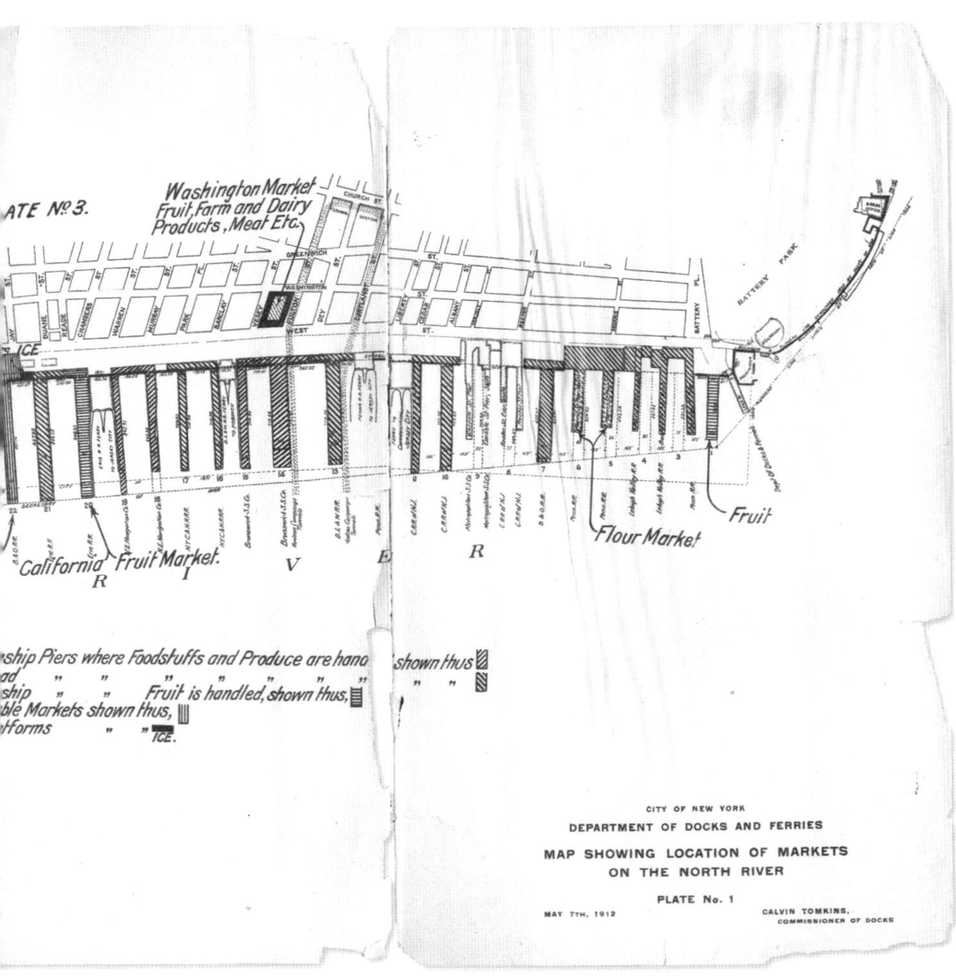

2
Chicken coops, loading docks, and train platforms along Eleventh Avenue, c. 1925

3
Street-level train, carriage, auto, and pedestrian traffic along Eleventh Avenue, c. 1925

F THE CRUISER COLUMBIA.

indictment of Holmes for murder is almost assured.

WANT THE WORLD'S AID.

West Side Citizens Ask for Help in Fighting the N. Y. Central RR. on Eleventh Avenue.

The West Side Citizens' Club, which was organized principly to fight the New York Central and Hudson River Railroad Company in its ocupancy of Eleventh avenue, met last night at No. 557 West Fifty-first street to perfect plans for carrying on its work. The spirited activity of the club just now is due to the fact that the railroad company's franchise to ocupy the avenue will expire next May, and the club is anxious to prevent its renewal.

The railroad company has run freight trains in Eleventh avenue for fifty

Death Avenue Claims Another.

John Langenfeld, aged twenty-one years, telegraph messenger, of No. 93 Vandam street, who was run over by a New York Central train at Tenth avenue and Twenty-sixth street Oct. 7, died at the New York Hospital yesterday.

CHILDREN PARADE AGAINST DEATH AVE.

Five Hundred Little Friends of Boy Who Was Killed There Make Public Protest.

OTHER PARADE TO FOLLOW

Printed Signs and Placards to be Used in the Crusade Against the Central's Tracks.

CONDEMNS POLITICS IN GRADE CROSSINGS

Transit Commission Suggests a General Law to Remove 'Death Avenue' Peril.

Legislative Committee to Hold Further Hearings on Expenditure of $300,000,000.

A political moratorium is an essential preliminary to the removal of the New York Central tracks along Eleventh or "Death" Avenue, declared Transit Commissioner LeRoy T. Harkness, who testified yesterday at the first hearing of the Joint Legislative Committee on Grade Crossings. The committee, which is to devise legislative authority for the expenditure of the $300,000,000 bond issue ratified at the last election for grade crossing removal, met in the

THE NEW YORK

CHURCHES TAKE UP "DEATH AV." FIGHT

Pastors All Over the City Unite in Demanding That Central Tracks Be Torn Up.

A MENACE TO HUMAN LIFE

League Backing the Movement Hopes City Officials Will Now Push Injunction Suit Before Court of Appeals.

The officers of the league organized to do away with the tracks of the New York Central Railroad in Eleventh Avenue, which, owing to the number of deaths

CALLS 'DEATH AVE.' MUNICIPAL CRIME

"The Nuisance Stage Is Past," ex-Alderman Doull Says at Great Mass Meeting.

SPEAKERS ATTACK N.Y.C.R.R.

4–9
Newspaper clippings reporting the unsafe conditions of the street-level railway, 1895–1925

10
West Side Cowboy escorting train along Tenth Avenue, 1932

559 West 52 St
July 29, 1927

My Dear Mr. Mayor:
Thursday the 28inst. you finish the job giving Brooklyn the independant Subway and awarded the bus rights to the various boroughs.
Now why did you not finish the west side improvement for elimination of the N.Y.C. Railway tracks along Eleventh ave. at the same time, why pospone this improvement another 2 months, why not help us once too, do you think it right to keep putting us off any longer: Why must we people along this ave. suffer and put up with this nuisance any longer.
If you lived and slept along this ave. you would not stand for it.
These long heavy trains of cars & heavy locomotives and the noise they make during the night is something fearful they shake the whole building, they ought to be compelled not to run between 11PM & 6 AM and they should be made to have a push engine in the rear of the train as they had 40 & 50 yrs ago there is a hill up to 52 St.
Now Mayor Walker we have tried to get rid of the nuisance the last 45 yrs, and the railroad has been willing to make the change during Mayor Mitchel term. And during Mayor Hyland & his Controller Craig's administration they could do nothing for they were fighting the company in the courts where the city lost the case.
Now the legislator has passed a law and the governor has signed it, giving the city the right to go ahead and have this improvement made and why pospone it any longer now, why put it off another two months.

11
Letter from concerned citizen to Mayor James Walker, 1927

August, 1925 POPULAR SCIENCE MONTHLY 41

May Live to See

May Solve Congestion Problems

How You May Live and Travel in the City of 1950

Future city streets, says Mr. Corbett, will be in four levels: The top level for pedestrians; the next lower level for slow motor traffic; the next for fast motor traffic, and the lowest for electric trains. Great blocks of terraced skyscrapers half a mile high will house offices, schools, homes, and playgrounds in successive levels, while the roofs will be aircraft landing-fields, according to the architect's plan

12–16
Designs, cartoons, and speculative proposals addressing urban transportation issues, 1879–1925

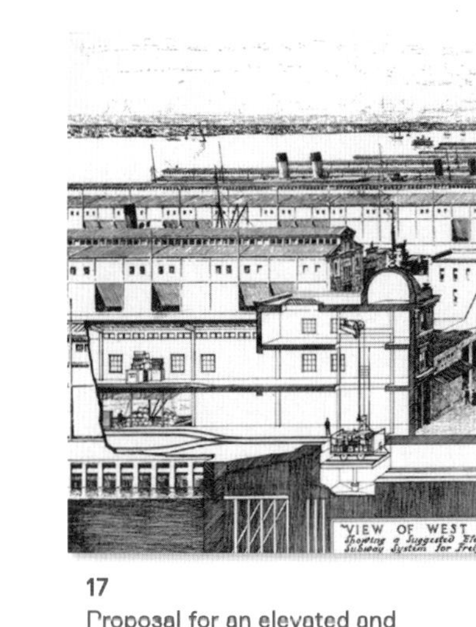

17
Proposal for an elevated and subterranean freight railway on the West Side of Manhattan, 1908

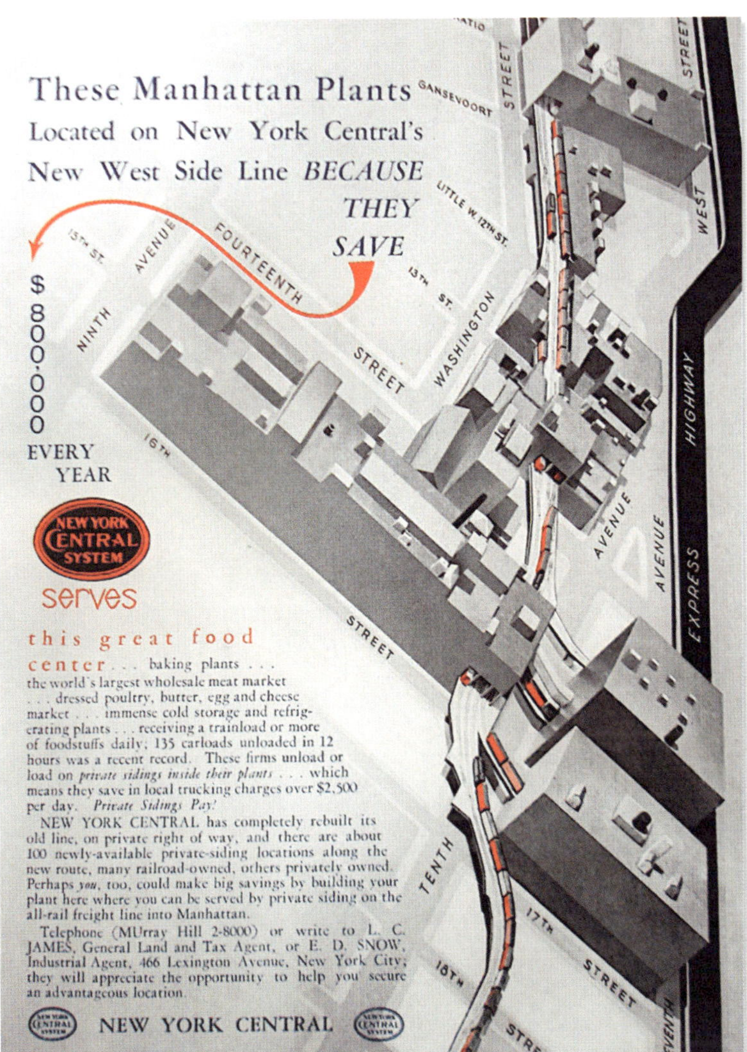

18–19
Advertisements for New York Central's elevated freight railway, 1937–1938

HUGE FREIGHT DEPOT TO BE STARTED SOON

Foundation Piers Being Laid for City's Largest Shipping Terminal on the West Side.

WILL OCCUPY FOUR BLOCKS

New York Central Project Will Contain 3,800,000 Square Feet of Floor Space and Cost $12,000,000.

CENTRAL'S NEW FREIGHT TERMINAL TO COVER FOUR WEST SIDE BLOCKS.

RIP UP FIRST RAILS IN DEATH AVENUE

Walker and Crowley, Head of New York Central, Wielding Crowbars, Loosen Spikes.

CALL THE EVENT HISTORIC

Mayor, Speaking in Shadow of Last Engine to Use Track, Voices Pride in Project.

CHEERS MARK CEREMONY

Railroad President Says Time for Talk of West Side Plan Is Past and "Time for Work Is Here."

20–21
Press clippings celebrating the demolition of the street-level tracks and plans for the elevated freight viaduct, 1930–1931

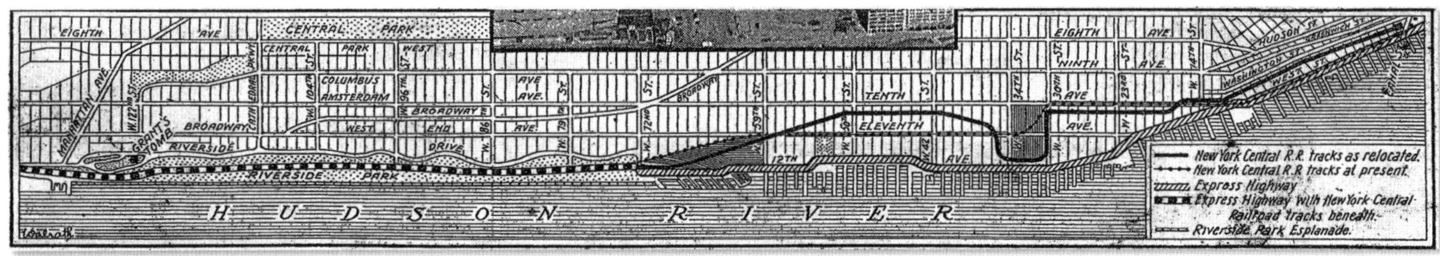

22
Illustration comparing the route of the new elevated railway to that of the street-level tracks being replaced, 1934

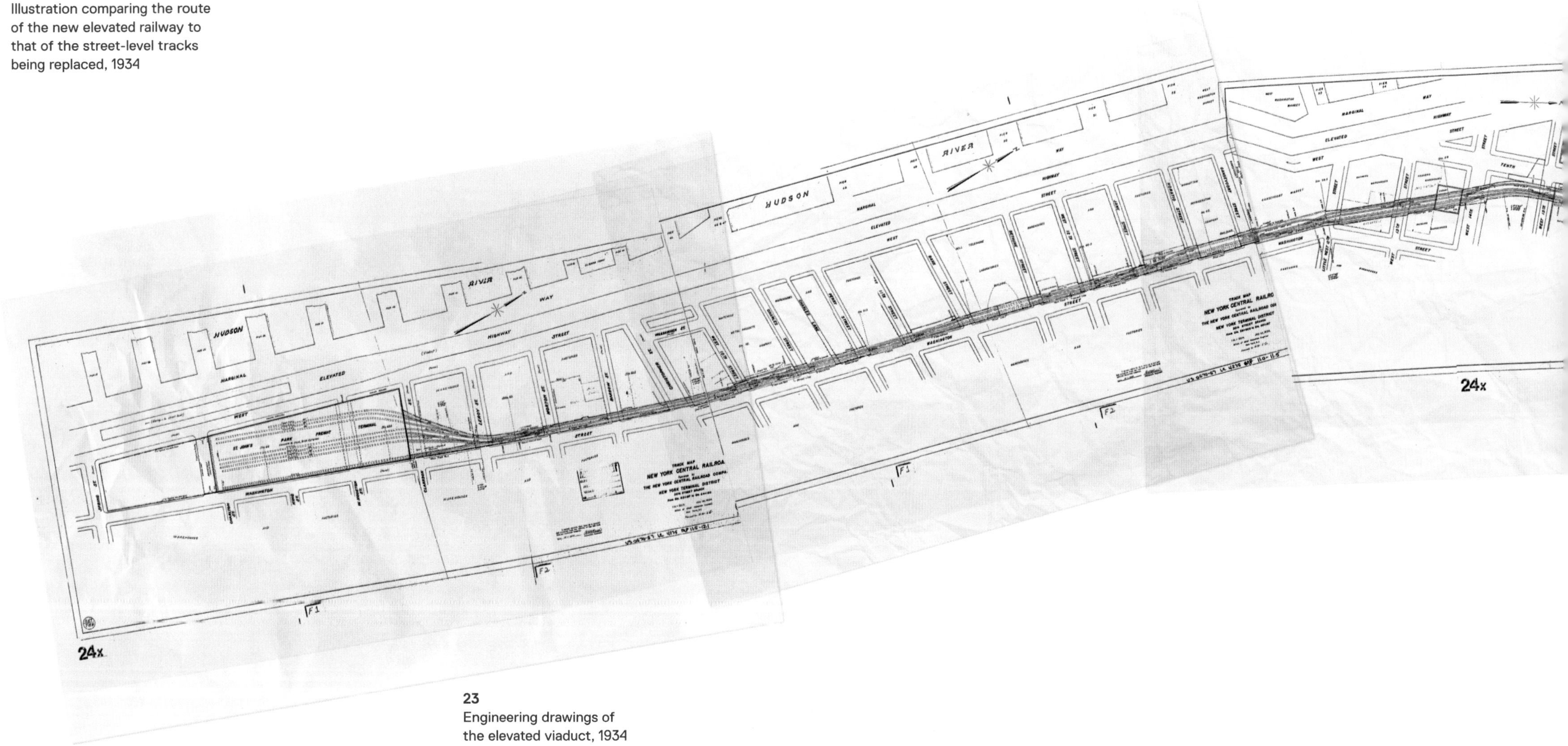

23
Engineering drawings of the elevated viaduct, 1934

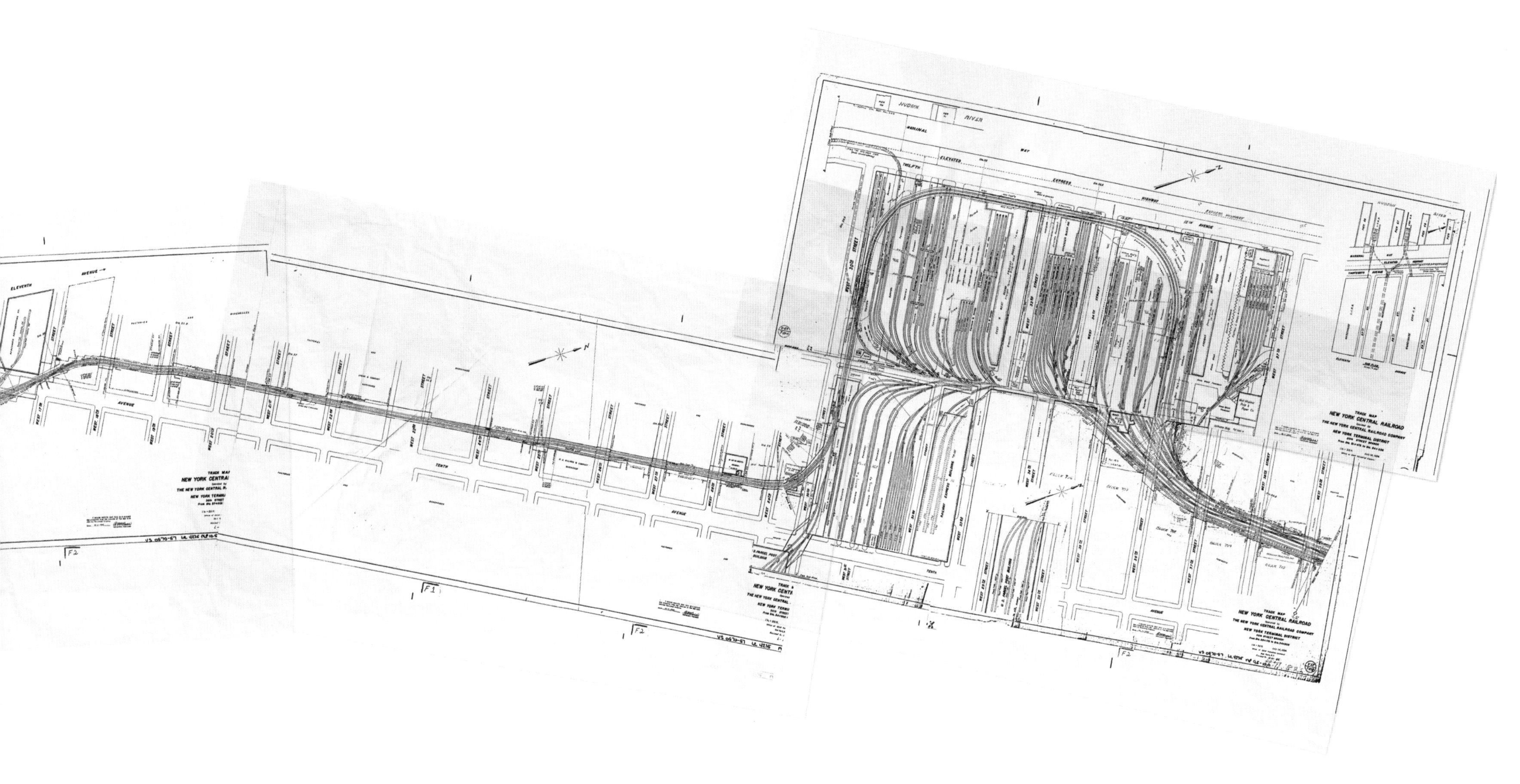

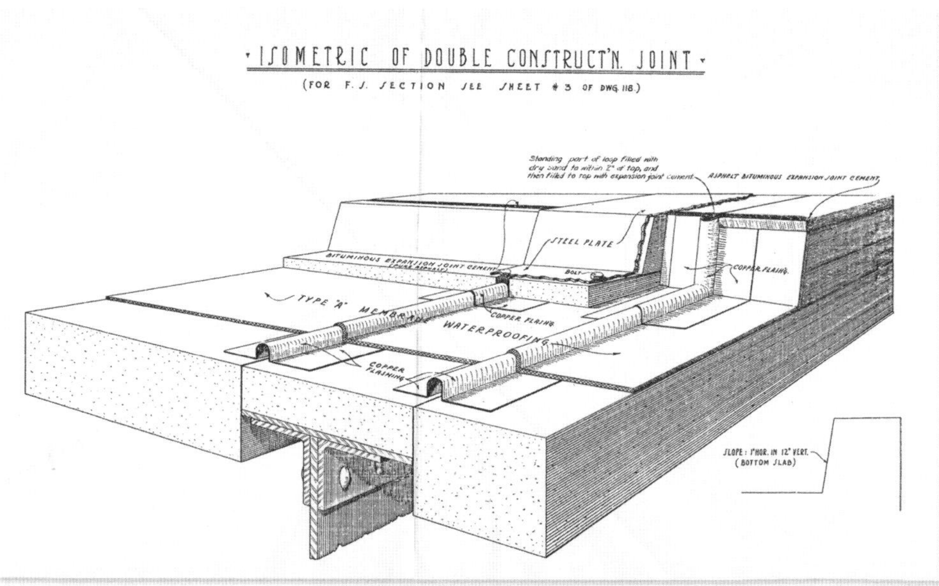

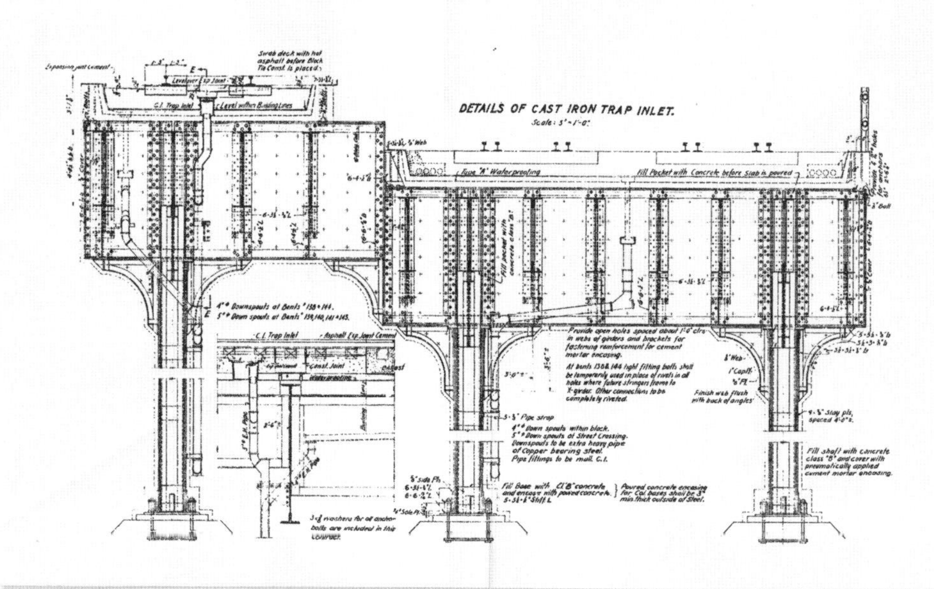

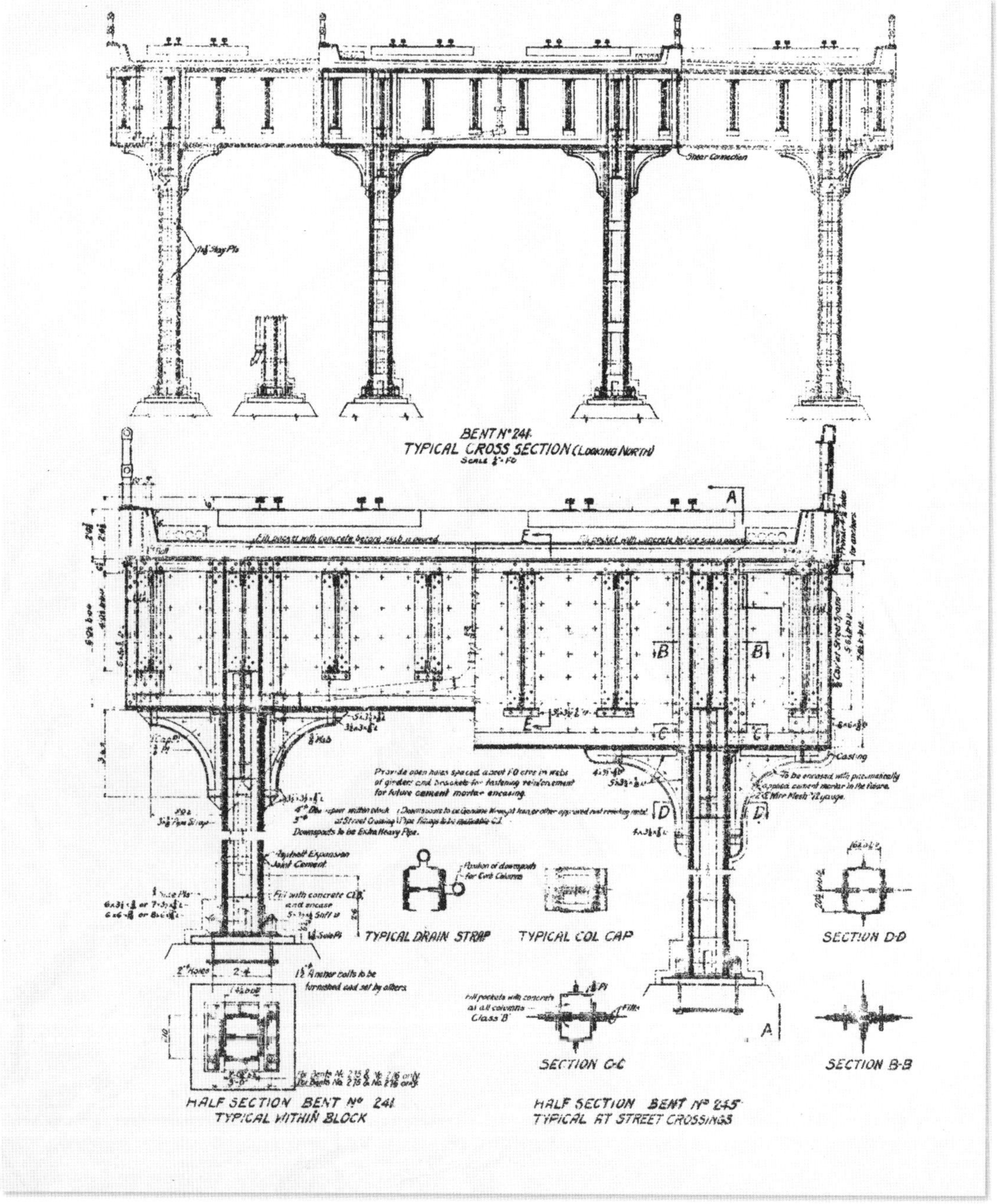

24–27
Construction drawings of New York City Railroad viaduct, 1931–1932

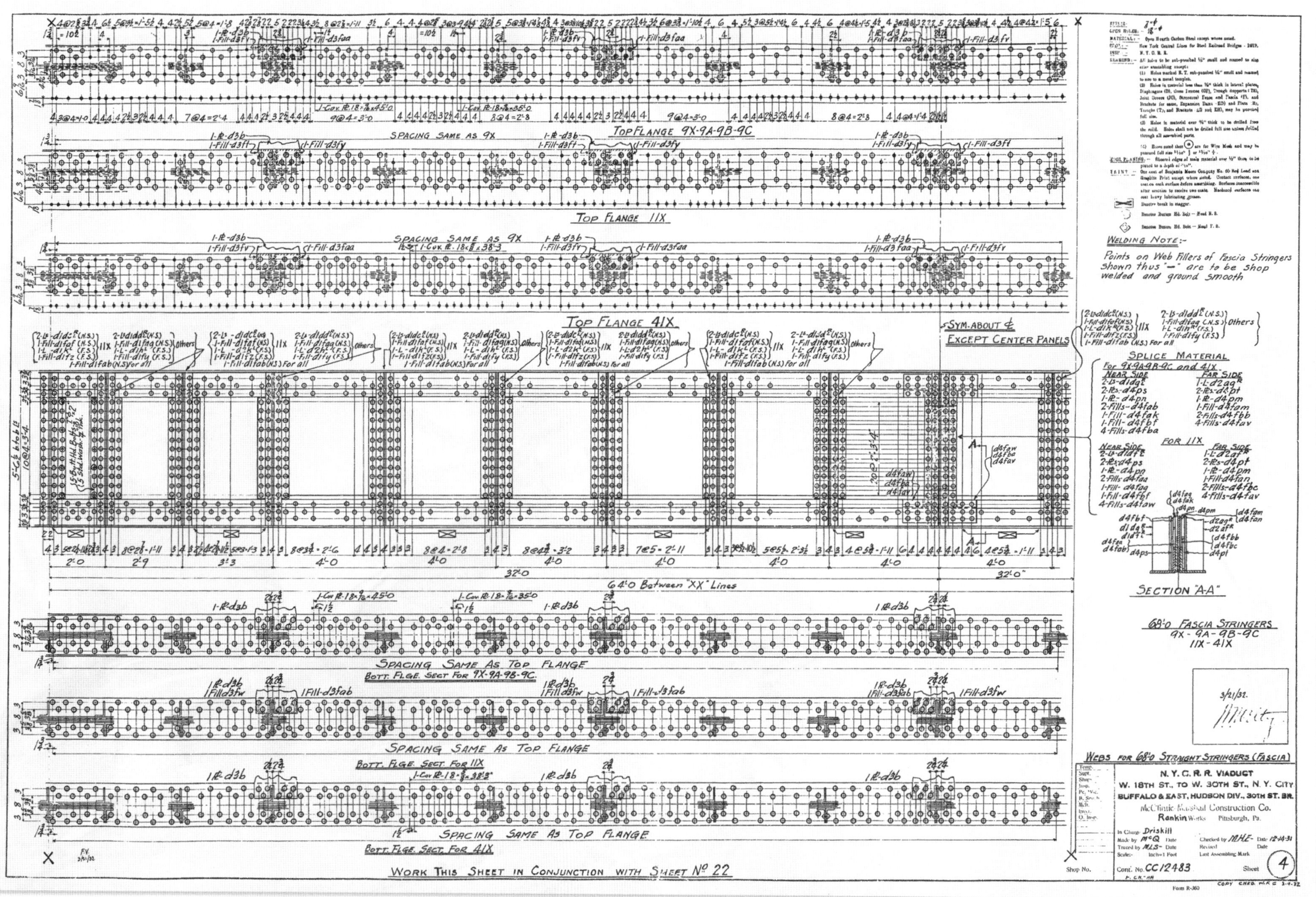
TOP FLANGE 9X-9A-9B-9C
SPACING SAME AS 9X
TOP FLANGE 11X
TOP FLANGE 41X
SYM. ABOUT ℄ EXCEPT CENTER PANELS
SPLICE MATERIAL
WELDING NOTE:-
Points on Web Fillers of Fascia Stringers shown thus "—" are to be shop welded and ground smooth
64'-0 Between "XX" Lines
SECTION "A-A"
68'-0 FASCIA STRINGERS
9X-9A-9B-9C
11X-41X
SPACING SAME AS TOP FLANGE
BOTT. FLGE. SECT. FOR 9X-9A-9B-9C.
BOTT. FLGE. SECT. FOR 11X
BOTT. FLGE. SECT. FOR 41X
WORK THIS SHEET IN CONJUNCTION WITH SHEET Nº 22
WEBS FOR 68'-0 STRAIGHT STRINGERS (FASCIA)
N. Y. C. R. R. VIADUCT
W. 18TH ST., TO W. 30TH ST., N. Y. CITY
BUFFALO & EAST, HUDSON DIV., 30TH ST. BR.
McClintic-Marshall Construction Co.
Rankin Works Pittsburgh, Pa.
In Charge Driskill
Made by McQ
Traced by MLS-
Checked by MHE- Date 12-14-31
Cont. No. CC12483
Sheet 4
Form R-360
COPY CHKD. W.K.C 3-4-32

28
Construction of the elevated West Side railway, 1932–1933

UNITED STATES
TRUCKING CORP
8294
6 NOV 4 32
N.Y.C. VIADUCT
NEW YORK
N.Y. CENTRAL
GEORGE A. FULLER COMPANY

28
(continued)

MOBO
STANLEY
FINE SOAPS
No 33 Taken MAR 13 33
N.Y. CEN VIADUCT Building
NEW YORK City
NEW YORK CEN Architect
GEORGE A. FULLER COMPANY
8359

29
Cover art about development on the West Side, 1933

MAYOR DEDICATES WEST SIDE PROJECT

'Death to Death Av.' Is Toast to Terminal and Vast System of Tracks on West Side.

SPUR TO MANY BUILDINGS

Shift of Business to Area Is Foreseen as Long Fight for Development Nears End.

30–31
City-sponsored pamphlet and newspaper clipping about the opening of the elevated railway, 1934

32
Train passing through Bell Telephone Laboratories building, 1936

33
Train running along 30th Street, 1957

34
Elevated railway at Bank Street and Washington Street, truncated in 1963

Vic DeLucia/The New York Times

A demolition crew at the railroad tracks that run through the West Coast apartment building at Washington and Gansevoort Streets. The Rockrose Development Corporation, owners of the building, plan to add apartments once the tracks are demolished.

Elevated Freight Line Being Razed Amid Protests

35–36
Elevated railway at Gansevoort Street and Washington Street, truncated in 1991

37–39
Meatpacking District, 1985–1986

40
Meatpacking District, 2008

41–42
Meatpacking District, 1985–1989

YOUR NEIGHBORS ARE ORGANIZING TO FIND SOLUTIONS TO VIOLENCE AND CRIME IN CHELSEA

FORUM ON

CRIME IN CHELSEA

FRIDAY, MAY 9, 1980

CHURCH OF THE HOLY APOSTLES,
9TH AVENUE AT 28TH STREET

8:30 PM

CO-SPONSORS

CHELSEA ACTION CENTER
CHELSEA CRIME WATCHDOG COORDINATING COMMITTEE
CHELSEA-ELLIOTT TENANTS ASSOCIATION
CHELSEA GAY ASSOCIATION
CHELSEA WEST 200 BLOCK ASSOCIATION
CHURCH OF THE BELOVED DISCIPLE
CHURCH OF THE HOLY APOSTLES
COMMITTEE FOR THE 19TH STREET YOUTH CENTER
THE HUDSON GUILD
"300 BLOCK ASSOCIATION OF 16TH & 17TH STREETS"
"200 WEST 25TH STREET BLOCK ASSOCIATION"
PENN SOUTH CO-OP
WOMEN MAKE MOVIES

JOIN US

Dress it up for the fall opening/Les Mouches/Thursday, September 14

LESBIANS AND GAY MEN

Meet Your Neighbors

Chelsea GAY Association

MEET

AT FLORENT
24 HOURS
989-5779 69 GANSEVOORT

STEVEN COHN SEZ "MOVE OVER, JOHNNY—" ITS AWESOME

MUSCLES AU GO-GO

SUNDAY, JANUARY 11, 1987
FROM 10 PM

A FINGER-LICKING FUNTAZY
WITH CHEAP DRINKS AND RAW MEAT!
ON THE BAR:
TRASHY GO-GO STUDS! NEARLY NAKED!
COMPLIMENTARY CREME DE BANANA
EIGHT DOLLARS PER PERSON
REGULAR ADMISSION TWELVE DOLLARS

TWELFTH AVENUE
AT TWENTY-SEVEN STREET
244•6444

CHECK OUT THOSE BULGING BONGOS!

43–47
Flyers, pamphlets, and posters distributed throughout Chelsea and the Meatpacking District, 1978–1987

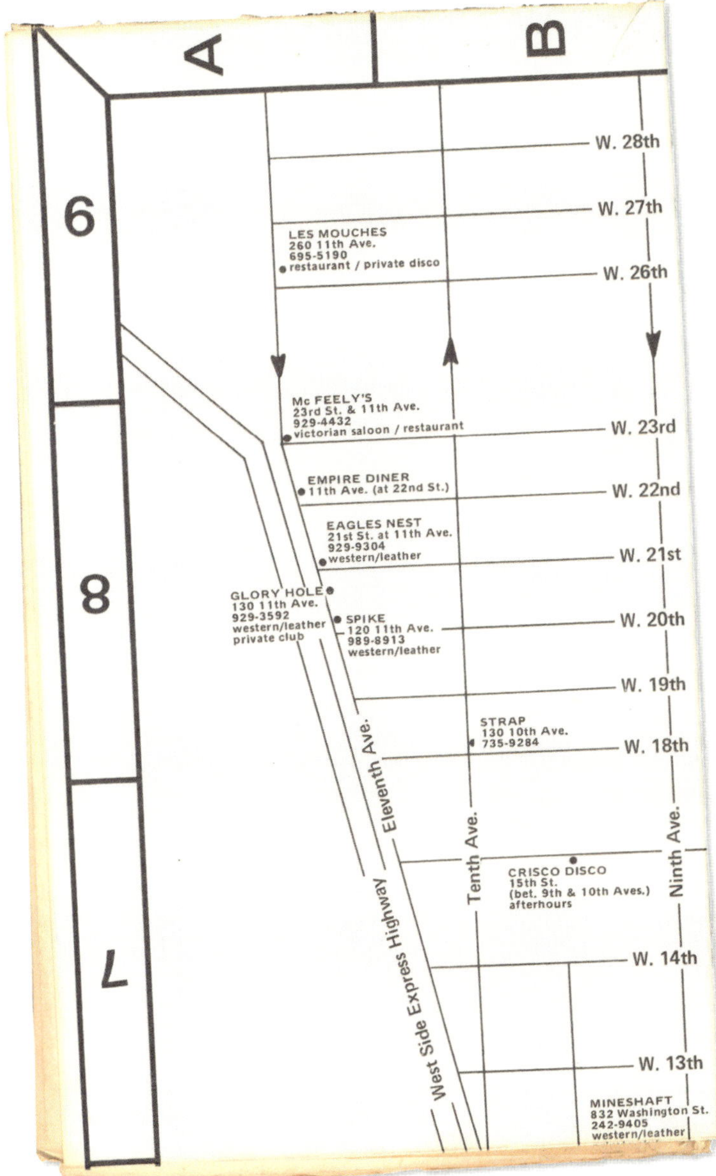

48
Gay city guide, 1980

Dia Foundation, Back From Brink, Opens New Center

"Brazilian Fond," by Joseph Beuys, at the Dia Art Foundation's new center for contemporary art.

By GRACE GLUECK

Two years ago, it looked as if the far-flung Dia Foundation, a major private financing source for certain contemporary artists, did not have much of a future. Backed by millions of dollars from a single patron, Philippa de Menil Friedrich, it was overextended in its commitments to venturesome projects. To make ends meet, it reduced expenditures and sold several Manhattan buildings that housed artists' work, along with a part of its extensive art collection. A new director was brought in, and the board of trustees was reorganized.

But now — leaner, trimmer and refocused in its aims — Dia will open a new center for contemporary art Friday at 548 West 22d Street. The handsomely refurbished four-story factory building will be the foundation's "primary New York space," according to the new director, Charles Wright. "We're trying to make a transition to a more public organization," said Mr. Wright, a former lawyer from Seattle. "The high visibility of this building and its programs are an important basis for our new fund-raising efforts."

With an exhibition area approximately equal to that of the Whitney Museum's main building, the center, according to Mr. Wright, will continue Dia's intention "to encourage major new work by artists in mid-career on a scale and of a nature that might not find accommodation elsewhere, and to facilitate the creation of art without imposing our own ideas."

The center, between 10th and 11th Avenues, stands in a Chelsea factory-and-warehouse neighborhood that is beginning to attract visual and performing arts facilities. Nearby are the Kitchen, the avant-garde multimedia center, and the Joyce Theater, devoted to dance performances. Several art galleries have also made an appearance in the area.

A Downtown Loft, Uptown

The building's renovation was accomplished with the help of Richard Gluckman Architects at a cost of about $500,000. With the second, third and fourth floor each providing a generous expanse — some 9,000 square feet — of exhibition space, punctuated by load-bearing columns, the effect is that of a SoHo loft building moved uptown. A second phase of renovation, to be completed in a year, will refit the ground floor for exhibitions and other projects.

For its opening program, Dia has installed the Minimal and Conceptually oriented work of three German artists in the foundation's collection: Imi Knoebel, Joseph Beuys and Blinky Palermo. Each display has been given an entire floor, and each

49
Newspaper clipping about the opening of new gallery space in West Chelsea, 1987

50
Guidebooks about fashion, art, and nightlife in the Meatpacking District, 2002–2004

51
Amateur photo shoot in front of meatpacking facility, 2006

52
Steven Holl's architectural proposal for reuse of elevated railway, 1981

TODAY
Cloudy, windy, mid 40s
TONIGHT
Mostly clear, breezy, 30-35
TOMORROW
Sunny, 50-55
Details, Page 2

NEW YORK POST

TUESDAY NOVEMBER 13 1984 35 CENTS ★ © 1984 News Group Publications Inc. Vol. 183, No. 312
40 cents beyond 50-mile zone, except L.I. AMERICA'S FASTEST-GROWING NEWSPAPER ABC AVERAGE SALES EXCEED 930,000

$10 railroad sale sidetracked by intrigue

By RICH FRIEDMAN

TEN bucks hasn't bought much in the way of Manhattan real estate since the Dutch got out of Indian trading — until now, that is.

Railroad buff Peter Obletz has closed a deal to buy a one-and-a-half mile stretch between 30 and 100 ft. wide on the island's West Side for $10.

It is an abandoned Conrail elevated freight spur, running south from Penn Central Yards to Bank St. It carried its last carload in 1980.

And the catch is that if Obletz, a real estate consultant to the MTA, takes it over he must operate a freight service on the track for at least two years.

Not surprisingly, perhaps, the city, the state, the Port Authority and the MTA all have passed on the privilege. The only interested party has been Obletz's West Side Rail Line Development Foundation.

Conrail is eager to give the thing away. The federal Interstate Commerce Commission has given 39-year-old Obletz its blessing. The city, though officially neutral, is unofficially ecstatic.

Only the State Dept. of Transportation has balked.

"We don't think his foundation has the ability to renovate the line," says DOT spokesman, Jack Bryan.

"The Department does not think there are any prospects at all for returning self-sufficient rail service to this line.

"We don't feel it is a legitimate application of the [abandonment provisions of the 1981 Northeast Rail Service Act (NERSA)]. There is no freight business to be had."

DOT has been throwing legal roadblocks on Buffalo-born Obletz's tracks ever since Conrail first moved to officially abandon the line last spring.

"Our feels have been dogged by the DOT since the minute we put in the application to buy the line," says Obletz, whose lawyers include New York heavyweights Paul, Weiss, Rifkind, Wharton & Garrison.

Obletz says that it will cost only about $77,000 to put the line back in shape because 98 percent of it is sound — a claim that DOT challenges.

"It doesn't sound like we're talking about the same property," says DOT's Bryan.

Obletz admits the line will not generate much freight traffic from the businesses around the line, which include Con Edison, building-suppliers, metal-wreckers and the 14th St. meat market.

He is figuring on about 300 carloads a year, or about one train a week, to be operated under a working agreement with the upstate Genessee and Wyoming Railroad.

There is also potential for a passenger service up and down the West Side, especially when the new Convention Center opens for business, says Obletz.

"Our long-term goal is to find something useful to do with this line until the city grows up around it," he says.

For Obletz's plan to work the line must be linked to Conrail's 9.75 miles of track running north of the Penn Central yards up the West Side to Spuyten Duyvil in the Bronx.

This route is part of Amtrak's planned renovation of its northeast corridor service. It also figures in distant plans to provide mass-transit links between the Bronx and lower-Manhattan.

Obletz's grand design also envisages community use of the century-old elevated structure, including parks and jogging and bicycle paths.

He claims he has the expertise for this because he has worked as fundraiser and administrator for community development and arts organizations.

Space is no problem because Conrail tore up one of the two tracks in 1981, he adds.

Anthony Riccio, director of the Mayor's Office on Rail Freight Development, has given Obletz his unofficial backing. His office is not interested in the track as it has enough on its plate already.

"If there's a private-sector railroad willing to take a stab at it, why stand in his way?" Riccio says.

"What you have is an entrepeneur taking a stand. Whether he succeeds or not is a question only he can answer. He has the right to try.

"I hope he succeeds. Anything that succeeds in rail freight augments the entire system."

Obletz has gleaned substantial support from local politicians in his battles with the DOT.

"Our position is that you should give it a shot," says Stephanie Pinto, aide to Assemblyman Nadler, chairman of the Assembly Subcommittee on Mass Transit and Rail Freight Operations.

Pinto is director of Nadler's subcommittee which virtually guarantees Obletz a warm reception for his scheduled testimony before it on the freight line saga on Thursday and Friday.

Nadler is a long time opponent of Manhattan's controversial Westway project and the rail-line stands smack in the way of planned Westway exit ramps.

Pinto hints darkly that the DOT's objections have more to do with Westway than Obletz's ability to make a success of the project.

"We're very distressed with DOT," she says.

"Their stated objection is that there's no shot at all, but somewhere they are convinced this will harm Westway."

Others, such as Bob Flahive, Manhattan program director of the Office of City Planning, say potential demolition costs could be the DOT's real concern.

At present, Conrail stands to pick up the $3 million tab if Westway plans demand demolition of line. If Obletz's group — funded by grants from private foundations — went belly up the state could be landed with the bill.

Air rights are another issue. The rail line runs through the second floors of four industrial buildings.

Obletz's $10 buys only the structure, the pillars on which it stands and air rights to a height of 18 feet above the tracks.

The air-rights, however, could affect anyone renovating nearby buildings, particularly those through which the line passes. This has generated opposition from Edison Parking Corp., developer Abraham Hirschfeld and the Rockrose Development Corp.

Obletz rejects claims that his real motive is real estate speculation.

"It has never been our intention to flip this thing," he says. "We see ourselves as an interim landlord."

The line, he adds, may eventually go to the MTA, for whom his firm supervises advertising contracts and concessions.

Could it be that in this, the most cynical of cities, there lives an honest-to-goodness railroad buff with a yen to translate his dreams into reality?

Well, until recently he lived in two elegantly renovated Amtrak dining cars in Penn Central Yard, virtually under the line he now hopes to own.

"I was bitten by the railroad bug in 1976," he says, "and I have never discovered any antibodies for it."

Map shows route of track, which cuts through four factories.

Peter Obletz says it will cost only $77,000 to restore the track.

Elevated track passes the new Convention Center under construction. View is from 33rd St. and 12th Av.

It cuts north through Chelsea (view from 17th St. and 10th Av.).

Rich Friedman is a freelance writer based in New York who specializes in financial topics.

53
Newspaper clipping about Peter Obletz's crusade to preserve the High Line as an operational railway, 1984

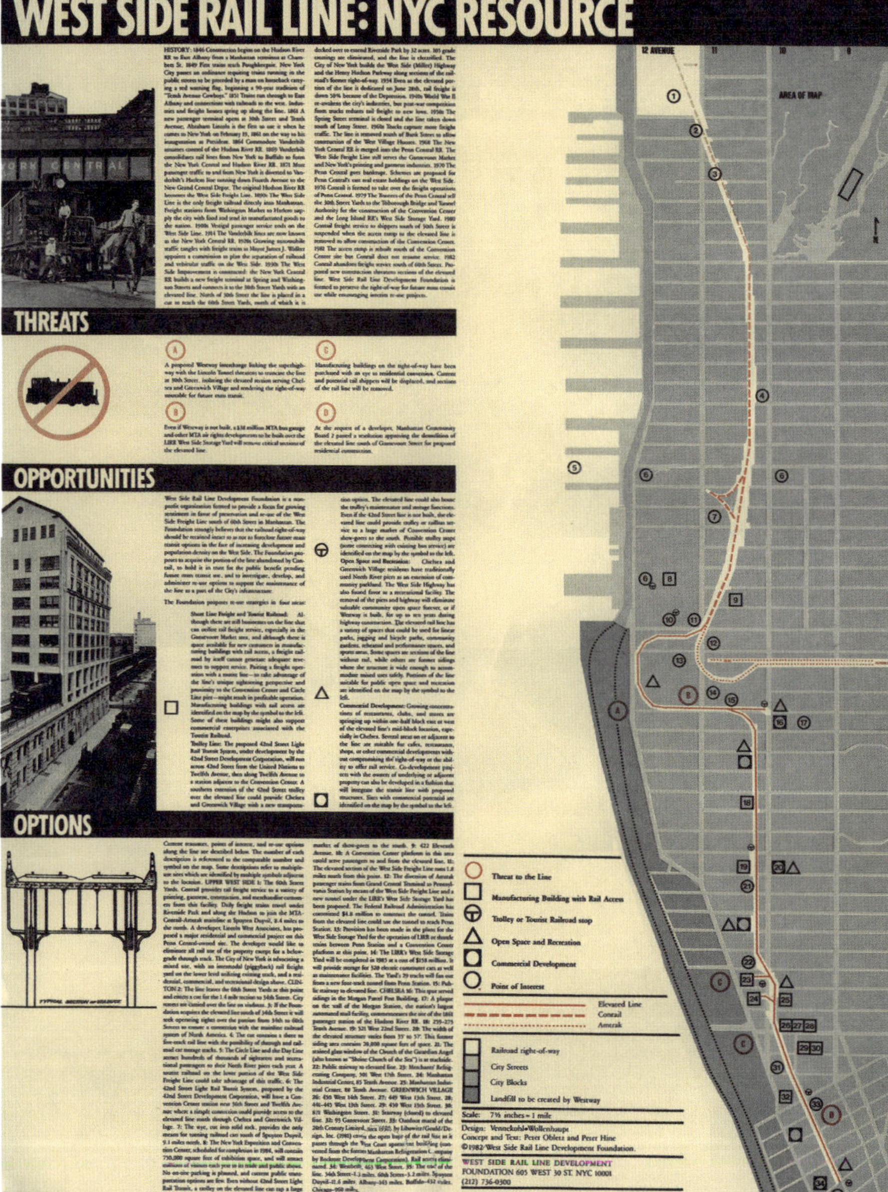

54
Educational poster distributed by Obletz's West Side Rail Line Development Foundation, 1982

55
Joshua David and Robert Hammond, 2001

56
Letterhead and business cards using Pentagram-designed High Line logo, 2000

NEW YORK JOURNAL

A WALK ON THE HIGH LINE

The allure of a derelict railroad track in spring.

BY ADAM GOPNIK

High is to New York what wet is to Venice—the necessary condition that has become the romantic condition. To be up, and above, though still felt as imprisonment in too many office-closeted lives, can, with the addition of a breeze or an eccentricity, become an escape, a source of renewal, and even provide a feeling of belonging. In Manhattan, to look down is not always to look down on. It is a communal experience, with something of the feeling of sailors in crow's nests looking at other sailors, a fellowship of the air—not avoiding the storm, exactly, but at least sharing news of it early. Moguls in the spires of skyscrapers stare at other moguls, and millionaire actors wave across the Park at other millionaire actors, and tourists go to the top of the World Trade Center to gaze with binoculars at tourists in the crown of the Statue of Liberty, and, if people crowd the Brooklyn Bridge, it is not to jump but to admire the falcons' scrape on one of the towers, an enviable home up high. When Superman is spotted in the sky above the city, people think mildly that he might be something else, a bird or a plane . . . The archeology of Manhattan is reversed: the past is not buried in the ground but held up in the air, on the upper floors. You see old things clearly: ghostly unlit Longchamps signs and forgotten Deco-Aztec metal detailing and abandoned penthouse night clubs. In New York, the overhead viewpoint is curiously peaceful and nostalgic—the beautiful vista, rather than the sublime. (The sublime vista is subterranean—the No. 6 train approaching the Fourteenth Street station through the gloom, eyes on fire.)

The most peaceful high place in New York right now is a stretch of viaduct called the High Line. The High Line is a derelict elevated railroad track, about two stories high, running a mile and a third along the western edge of the city, from Thirty-fourth Street to Gansevoort Street. It encloses about eight acres, or half a million square feet, of taffy-pulled, thirty-to-fifty-foot-wide horizontal space. Many people who pass under it think that it is an old El track. In fact, it is, or was, a New York Central Railroad track, used for fifty years to convey goods from all over America to little shuntings among the West Side warehouses. For more than two decades—ever since the last three carloads of frozen turkeys made their transit to Gansevoort Street—it has been under a provisional death sentence, condemned by the property owners caught in its shadow. But one thing or another has kept it from being torn down, and, just recently, it has become a gleam in the eye of some West Side do-gooders, who call themselves the Friends of the High Line and who see it as a potential midair park. The Giuliani administration has been hostile to the project—the Mayor's men apparently viewing it as exactly the kind of touchy-feely, hey, kids, let's make that broken-down railroad into a park!, Upper West Side quixotism that would leave the whole city carpeted with moss if left unchecked—but a lot of other local pols, topped off by Senator Clinton, are all for it.

For the moment, the High Line has gone not to wrack and ruin but to seed: weeds and grasses and even small trees sprout from the track bed. There are irises and lamb's ears and thistle-tufted onion grass, white-flowering bushes and pink-budded trees and grape hyacinths, and strange New York weeds that shoot straight up with horizontal arms, as though electrified. A single, improbable Christmas tree can be found there, and a flock of warblers have made themselves a home, too. In one sheltered stretch between two tall buildings is a stand of hardwood trees. The High Line combines the appeal of those fantasies in which New York has returned to the wild with an almost Zen quality of measured, peaceful distance.

The poet-keeper of the High Line is the photographer Joel Sternfeld. He has

57
Excerpt from Adam Gopnik's *The New Yorker* article about the High Line, 2001

58
Photographs from Joel Sternfeld's yearlong High Line project, 2000–2001

Regional Plan Association

WHAT TO DO WITH THE HIGH LINE?

Final Draft Report

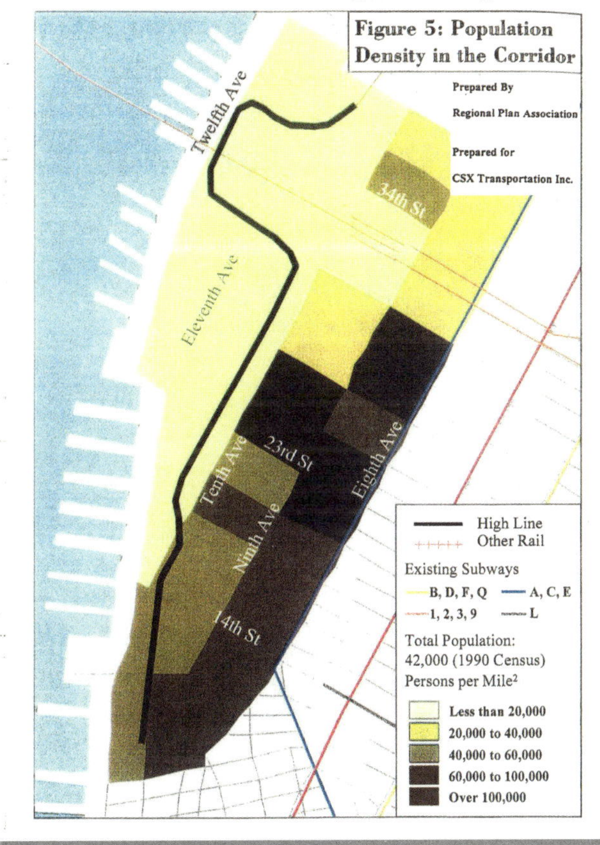

59
Regional Plan Association report assessing reuse scenarios for the High Line, 1999

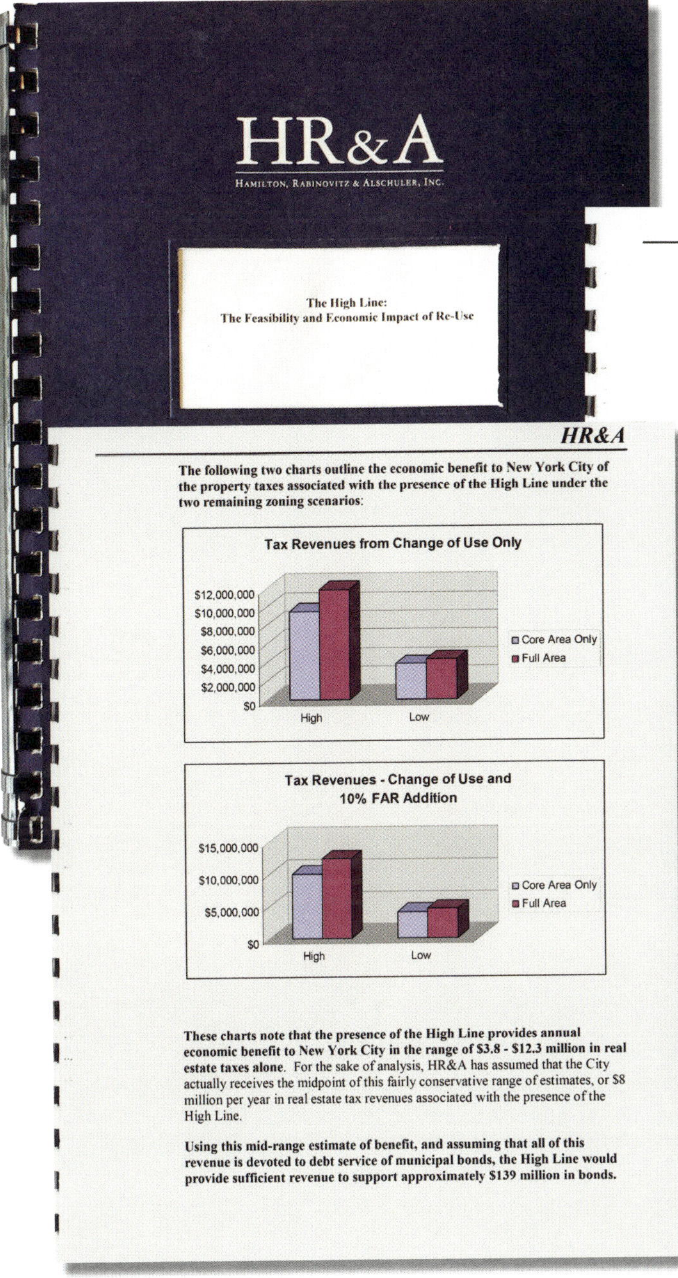

HR&A

The following two charts outline the economic benefit to New York City of the property taxes associated with the presence of the High Line under the two remaining zoning scenarios:

These charts note that the presence of the High Line provides annual economic benefit to New York City in the range of $3.8 - $12.3 million in real estate taxes alone. For the sake of analysis, HR&A has assumed that the City actually receives the midpoint of this fairly conservative range of estimates, or $8 million per year in real estate tax revenues associated with the presence of the High Line.

Using this mid-range estimate of benefit, and assuming that all of this revenue is devoted to debt service of municipal bonds, the High Line would provide sufficient revenue to support approximately $139 million in bonds.

HR&A

The Study Area

© HR&A not to be reproduced in any form without permission of HR&A

60
HR&A report analyzing the economic feasibility of the High Line, 2002

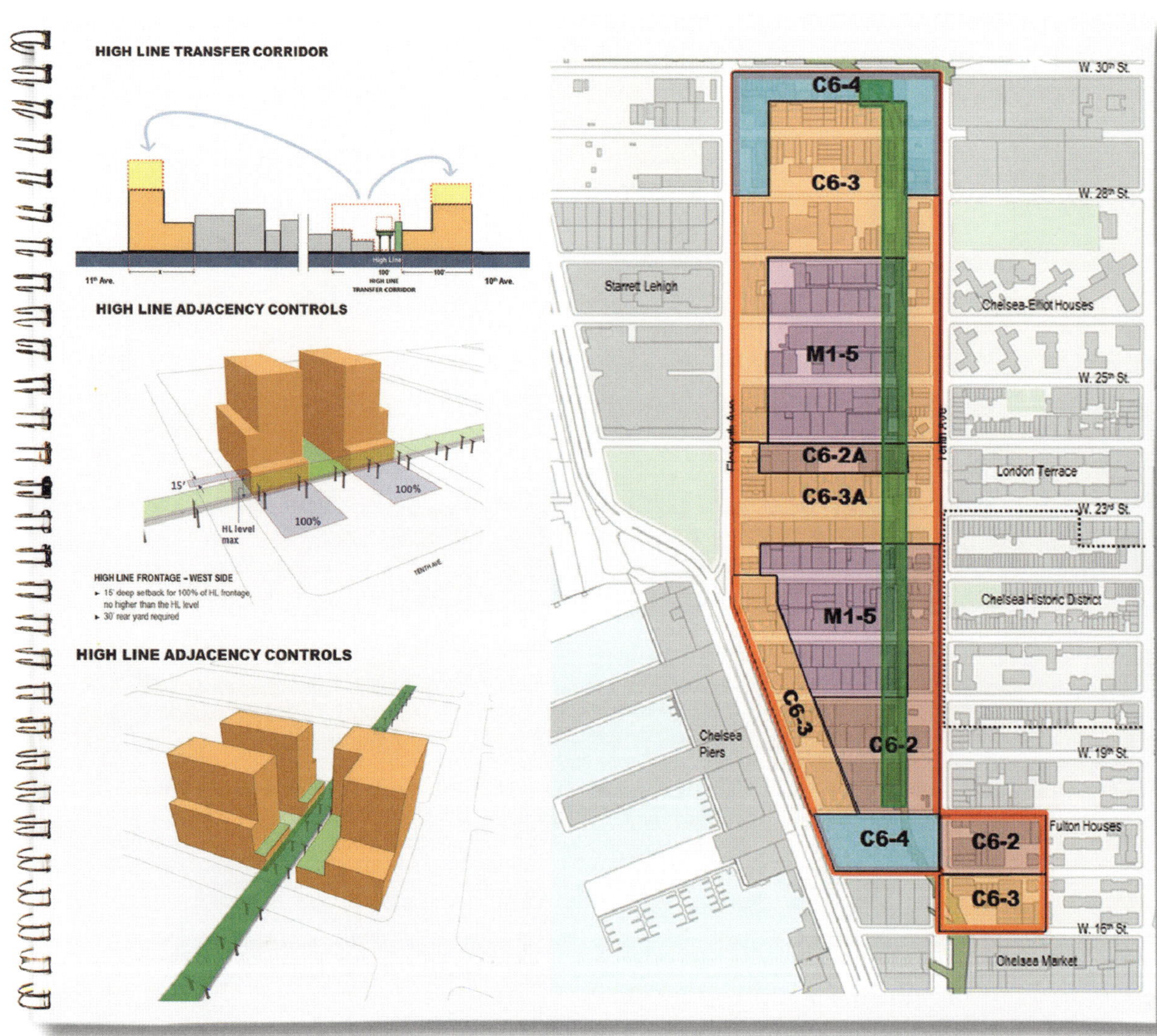
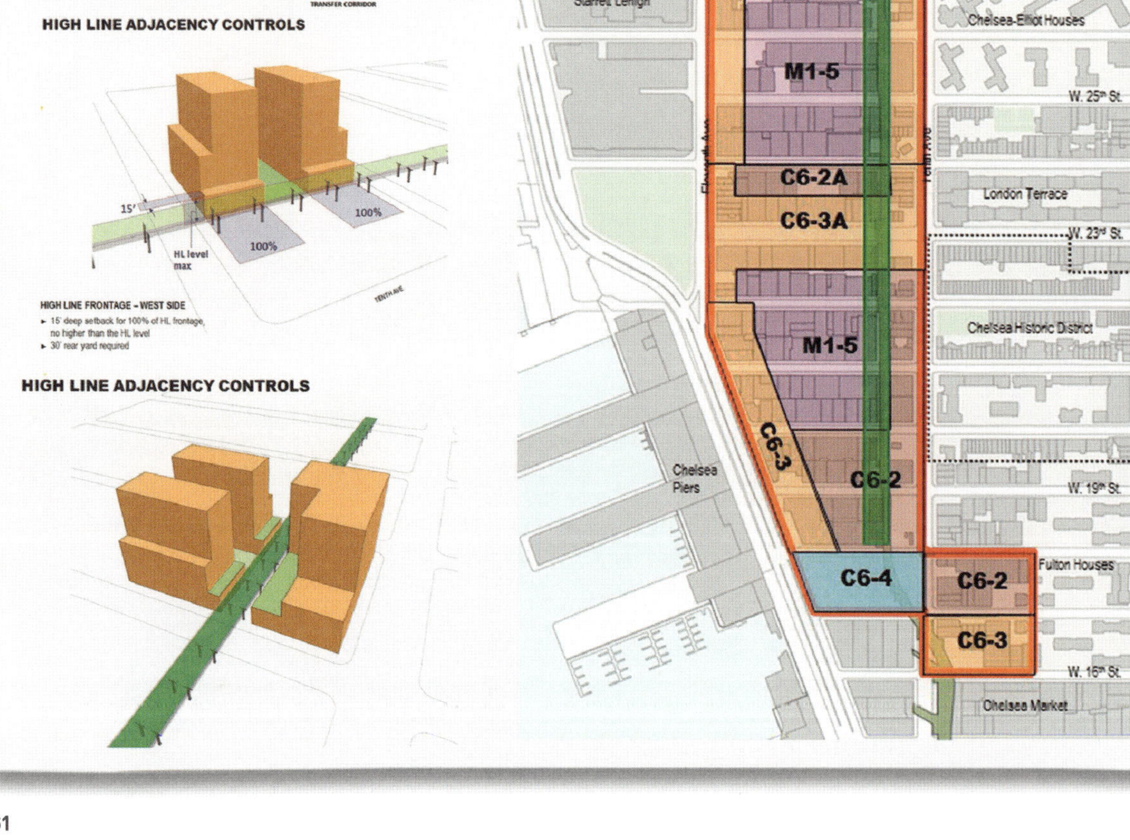

61
Department of City Planning proposal to introduce development incentives in West Chelsea, 2004

62
Design Trust for Public Space report documenting yearlong research study on the High Line, 2002

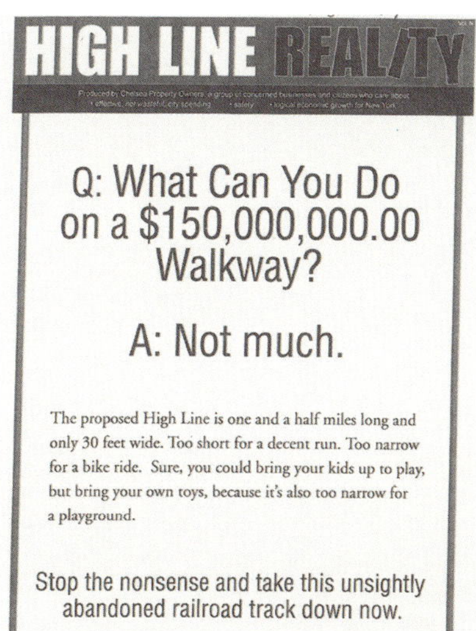

HIGH LINE REALITY

Q: What Can You Do on a $150,000,000.00 Walkway?

A: Not much.

The proposed High Line is one and a half miles long and only 30 feet wide. Too short for a decent run. Too narrow for a bike ride. Sure, you could bring your kids up to play, but bring your own toys, because it's also too narrow for a playground.

Stop the nonsense and take this unsightly abandoned railroad track down now.

HIGH LINE REALITY

THE HUDSON RIVER PARK WILL HAVE EVERYTHING THE HIGH LINE DOESN'T.

The Hudson River Park will be a wide-open space with spectacular unhindered views of the water, and room to run. And it's located literally a stone's throw from the High Line. The only thing that the Hudson River Park has in common with the High Line is that there is not enough money to finish it. **It still needs $180,000,000 to be completed. How can we even consider spending money on the High Line, which will be substandard on almost all accounts, when we don't even have the money to finish a project that has already been started?**

RECEIVED
AUG 2 9 2002
MANHATTAN COMMUNITY BOARD NO. 4

Our city needs money for important things–stop wasting money on the High Line.

63
Flyers distributed by the Chelsea Business and Property Owners Association, 2002

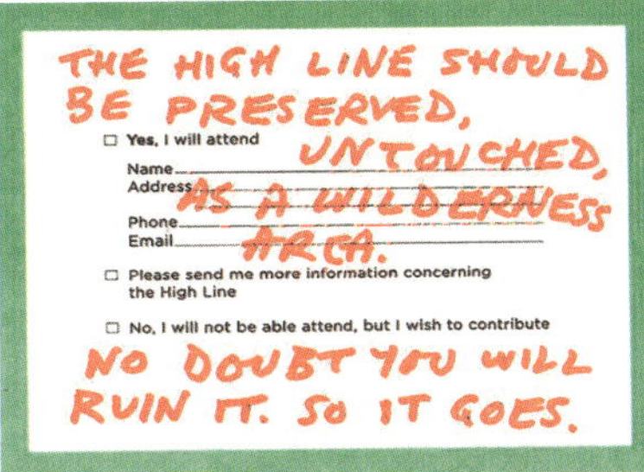

THE HIGH LINE SHOULD BE PRESERVED,

☐ Yes, I will attend

Name UNTOUCHED,
Address AS A WILDERNESS
Phone AREA.
Email

☐ Please send me more information concerning the High Line

☐ No, I will not be able attend, but I wish to contribute

NO DOUBT YOU WILL RUIN IT. SO IT GOES.

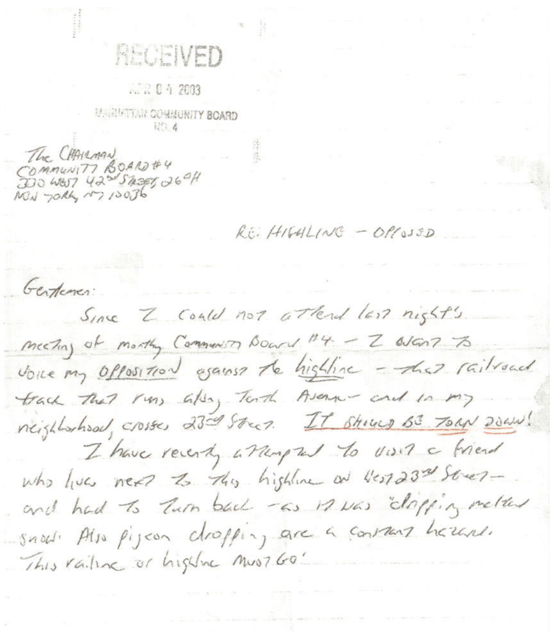

RECEIVED
APR 0 4 2003
MANHATTAN COMMUNITY BOARD NO. 4

The Chairman
Community Board #4
330 West 42nd Street, 26th
New York, NY 10036

RE: HIGHLINE – OPPOSED

Gentlemen:

Since I could not attend last night's meeting of monthly Community Board #4 – I want to voice my <u>OPPOSITION</u> against the <u>highline</u> – that railroad track that runs along Tenth Avenue – and in my neighborhood, crosses 23rd Street. <u>IT SHOULD BE TORN DOWN!</u>

I have recently attempted to visit a friend who lives next to this highline on West 23rd Street – and had to turn back – as it was "dripping melted snow." Also pigeon droppings are a constant hazard. This railine or highline must go!

64–65
Selected community input materials, 2003

66
High Line ideas competition exhibition at Grand Central Terminal, 2003

67
Renderings from the ideas competition winning proposal, 2003

HILLARY RODHAM CLINTON
NEW YORK
SENATOR

DIRKSEN SENATE OFFICE BLDG.
WASHINGTON, DC 20510-3204
202-224-4451

United States Senate

WASHINGTON, DC 20510-3204

April 17, 2001

The Honorable Peter F. Vallone
Speaker
New York City Council
City Hall
New York, NY 10007

Dear Speaker Vallone:

The High Line, an unused railroad viaduct between West 34th Street and Gansevoort Street in Manhattan, has been abandoned since 1980 and is now the subject of local debate about its future.

Built in the 1930's the High Line, as the elevated rail is commonly known, was used as a freight rail link in lower Manhattan. A not-for-profit organization called Friends of the High Line, along with other concerned community and political leaders, have joined together to look seriously at alternatives to demolition. One such proposal being considered is conversion of the rail structure to a pedestrian walkway.

In New York State, a nationally known organization called Rails-to-Trails Inc. has been assisting Friends of the High Line with determining alternatives to razing the viaduct. They have a significant track record of converting portions of unused railroads for community use while leaving the structure intact.

In 1983, an amendment to the National Trails System Act created the *railbanking* program such that rail lines proposed for abandonment can be preserved through provisional conversion to trail use. Should proposals be considered for re-use of the High Line commercially, there is some recourse through *railbanking*.

Friends of the High Line have garnered an impressive list of support from local, political and business leaders. That is a testament to how important this matter is to the residents of the area. The High Line's value to the future of Chelsea and the surrounding neighborhoods is important. The interesting proposal put forth by Friends of the High Line seems to have merit. I urge you to look at it closely and study its feasibility.

Sincerely yours,

Hillary Rodham Clinton

Hillary Rodham Clinton

THE CITY OF NEW YORK
OFFICE OF THE MAYOR
NEW YORK, N.Y. 10007

JOSHUA D FILLER
DIRECTOR OF CITY LEGISLATIVE AFFAIRS &
CHIEF OF STAFF TO THE DEPUTY MAYOR FOR OPERATIONS

City Hall, Room 1
(212) 788-3108
FAX: (212) 788-3127

May 31, 2001

Congressman Jerrold Nadler
2334 Rayburn Building
Washington, DC 20515

Dear Congressman Nadler:

On behalf of Mayor Giuliani, I am pleased to respond to your letter regarding City Council Resolution Number 1747. While the Giuliani Administration shares your interest in the further development of Manhattan's far West Side, we do not support Resolution 1747.

As you know, the Highline is an antiquated structure that has not been in use for over twenty years. In the years to come, we do not believe that the structure will be of any use to the community, and the Resolution's call for the creation of an elevated park on the old rail bed appears unrealistic. Therefore, the Administration concurs with the many local business people who believe that the Highline should be torn down. We believe that by removing this rusting eyesore, the City will take an important step toward opening the far West Side for greater economic development.

As you know, the development of the far West Side has been a key piece of Mayor Giuliani's agenda. We hope to work in concert with you and other elected officials to bring new projects and economic opportunities to the area. On the fate of the Highline, however, we respectfully disagree.

Sincerely,

Joshua Filler

Joshua D. Filler

cc: Deputy Mayor Robert M. Harding

68–69
Letter of support from Senator Hillary Clinton and letter of opposition from the office of Mayor Giuliani, 2001

The New York Times

Sunday, December 3

Real Estate

Section 11

Which Track for the High Line?

The Villager

West Village, East Village, Chelsea, Soho, Tribeca and Lower East Side

Editorial

Put the brakes on rush to raze the High Line

DAILY NEWS

www.nydailynews.com NEW YORK'S HOMETOWN NEWSPAPER Saturday, December 30, 200

High noon for High Line

Give High Line a chance

Built in the 1930s and used until 1980, the High Line freight railroad once moved goods up and down Manhattan's West Side. Today, the elevated line sits forlorn, awaiting its fate. Will it be torn down or transformed? The case for the latter seems persuasive.

A public hearing on the matter will be held at City Hall at 1 p.m. today. A Council committee will consider a resolution sponsored by Manhattan members Gifford Miller and Christine Quinn urging the city and state to save the High Line and turn it into a trailway park. This could be done under the federal government's successful rails-to-trails program, designed for projects exactly like this.

Such conversions are being done around the world. In Paris, for example, an unused elevated rail line was transformed into an aerial linear park 1½ miles long — the same length as the High Line.

Stretching from Gansevoort St. to the Javits Center at 34th St., the High Line was once part of a freight line that ran to the northern tip of Manhattan. Some local property owners, led by a parking lot concern, want it torn down. But many West Side officials back the trailway concept, as do civic and environmental groups.

Built to last and to carry fully loaded trains, the High Line is at no apparent risk of collapse, so it would be silly to rush to demolition without exploring the options. A planning study will be completed in August. If there's a chance the High Line can be turned into a viable park or other useful public purpose — which appears quite possible — it should not be dismissed.

If you're interested in the High Line and its potential, go to City Hall today to listen. And speak out.

70–73
Press clippings concerning demolition threat to the High Line, 2000–2001

THE ASSEMBLY
STATE OF NEW YORK
ALBANY

RICHARD N. GOTTFRIED
64th Assembly District

Room 822
Legislative Office Building
Albany, New York 12248
(518) 455-4941

242 West 27th Street
New York, New York 10001
(212) 807-7900

CHAIRMAN
Committee on Health

COMMITTEES
Rules
Higher Education
Codes
Insurance
Social Services
Majority Steering Committee

High Hopes for the High Line

Statement before the Community Board 4 Public Forum on the High Line
by Assembly Member Richard N. Gottfried, U.S. Representative Jerrold Nadler,
State Senator Thomas K. Duane, Assembly Member Deborah Glick
and Councilmember Christine Quinn
February 24, 2003

As the elected officials representing the areas affected by the High Line, we strongly urge the Chelsea Preservation and Planning Committee of Community Board 4 and the full board of Community Board 4 to support the reuse of the High Line as public park space.

More than 70 years ago, the High Line elevated rail structure was built through public funds as part of the West Side Improvement Project. It served western Manhattan as a rail freight line, bringing food and merchandise into the area. In recent years it has sat dormant, but while its utility as a transportation structure may have faded, its future as urban park space has just begun.

The vistas from the High Line are breathtaking. Preserving and reusing the High Line would create a world-renowned urban amenity that would also provide a special pedestrian link between the communities of Chelsea, Hell's Kitchen, Greenwich Village and the Meat Packing District on the West Side. The High Line would also complement the Hudson River Park. Like the Hudson River Park, it offers the opportunity to convert abandoned facilities into recreational public space that would attract the local community and visitors. The High Line would add value to surrounding properties and contribute to the long-term economic health of the City.

We applaud the Friends of the High Line, a not-for-profit organization, which has done extensive work organizing support for a "Rails To Trails" program for the High Line.

We are grateful to have the City Administration's support for this project. If the City is successful, the seven acres of the High Line will be converted into a public park through the federal "rail-banking" program. The project will be funded with minimal City investment by using funds from private foundations, individual donors, the federal government and other sources. Studies by Friends of the High Line, reviewed by the City of New York, have demonstrated that the High Line would be a safe and secure environment for the public to enjoy.

74
Statement of support from local, state, and federal officials, 2003

Copyright © 2005 The New York Times NEW YORK, WEDNESDAY, JUNE 15, 2005

James Estrin/The New York Times

A Frog of a Rail Line Is Set to Become a Prince of a Park

A federal agency has given New York City approval to turn the abandoned High Line railroad viaduct on the West Side of Manhattan into an elongated, elevated park. Only Paris has anything like it. Page B1.

Rusty Railroad On Its Way To Pristine Park

City Gets U.S. Approval To Transform Old Line

By PAUL VITELLO

Plans for the city's first elevated park — a singular ribbon of green space stretching a mile and a half along an abandoned railroad viaduct 30 feet above the streets of Chelsea — have taken a major step forward with a favorable ruling by a federal transportation board.

The ruling, on Monday, essentially cleared the way for the city to begin negotiating use and development of the High Line, a weed-overgrown railroad bed that has not been used since the late 1960's and that, seen from above, looks like a painter's thick stroke of brilliant green along the gritty Lower West Side of Manhattan, between 34th Street and Gansevoort Street, in the meatpacking district.

If the plans materialize, the project would become one of only two elevated parks in the world; the other, also carved out of an abandoned railroad viaduct, is the Promenade Plantée in Paris.

"This is one of the most unique open spaces in the world," said Amanda M. Burden, chairwoman of the New York City Planning Commission and an outspoken advocate of the High Line project. "You will be able to walk 22 blocks in the city of New York without ever coming in contact with a vehicle."

The project has had a long gestation, beginning in 1999, when some neighborhood residents, organized as Friends of the High Line, first intervened to block plans for demolishing the viaduct.

Property owners along the right of way, just east of the Hudson River, sought to develop their land beneath the elevated tracks.

The administration of former Mayor Rudolph W. Giuliani supported those efforts. But Michael R. Bloomberg, a year after taking office as mayor, reversed the city's position to support preservation.

In 2004, with the enticement of a promised $50 million city investment in the park and other incentives to satisfy local businesses, the property owners withdrew their opposition to the city's plans to develop its first midair park.

On Monday, the federal Surface Transportation Board issued the city what is called a "certificate of interim trail use." That, in effect, permits the city to remove the segment of unused rail line from the national railway grid.

Under the terms of a federal rail-preservation law, such an "interim" use could be revoked in the future should the Surface Transportation Board decide the rail line is again needed, though such revocations are

Continued on Page B7

75
Press clipping announcing federal approval to convert the High Line into a public park, 2005

EXTENDED CAPTIONS

1

City of New York Department of Docks and Ferries, "Map Showing Location of Markets on the North River," May 7, 1912.
After the Hudson River Railroad started construction on the freight tracks along the West Side of Manhattan in 1847, the surrounding area grew to be the city's central hub for food and freight. The street-level railway, later acquired by the New York Central Railroad, originally ended just south of Canal Street, and served the specialized meat, milk, and produce markets that stretched along the river.

2

"Famous old chicken yard looking north from 60th Street," c. 1925.
In Hell's Kitchen, Chelsea, and the Meatpacking District, merchants, manufacturers, and food suppliers received freight from both the port and the railway. Trains ran day and night from Albany to deliver shipments to a rapidly growing New York City. Between 1860 and 1890, the combined population of Brooklyn and Manhattan grew from one million to over 2.3 million as immigrants poured in. With Greenwich Village to the south and the Upper West Side to the north, the area between the New York Central tracks and the Hudson River was a neighborhood of industry and ambition, home to factories, warehouses, and crowded tenement buildings full of working-class immigrants.

3

"Old crossings of 11th Avenue through 33rd Street Yard," c. 1925.
As the neighborhoods of the far West Side grew dense with development, traffic congestion grew worse. Pedestrians, carriages, trucks, and trains intersected on the street, causing frequent accidents. As early as 1892, local press dubbed the freight route along Tenth and Eleventh Avenues "Death Avenue." In 1908, the Bureau of Municipal Research published a report stating that 436 people had been killed and 1,500 had been maimed by railroad accidents over the course of the line's history.

4–9

Clockwise from top left:
4 "West Side Citizens Ask for Help," ***New York World*****, August 30, 1895.**
5 "Death Avenue Claims Another," ***New York World*****, October 21, 1895.**
6 "Children Parade Against Death Ave.," ***New York Times*****, October 25, 1908.**
7 "Calls 'Death Ave.' Municipal Crime," ***New York Times*****, April 8, 1910.**
8 "Churches Take Up 'Death Av.' Fight," ***New York Times*****, May 9, 1910.**
9 "Condemns Politics in Grade Crossings," ***New York Times*****, November 21, 1925.**
For decades, people living and working in the neighborhood complained about the dangers of "Death Avenue." In 1908, a collision killed a young boy and provoked a protest that consisted of five hundred marching children. The League to End Death Avenue, a local citizen's group, rallied around the boy's death and pressured the city to remove the tracks.

10

"Train Wrangler," 1932.
To address the danger of at-grade collisions, the city employed a troop of horseback riders—the famous "West Side Cowboys"—to warn pedestrian, car, and carriage traffic of oncoming trains. During the day, the men waved bright red flags; at night, they flashed ghostly red lanterns. The cowboys first rode in the 1850s after the city issued an ordinance requiring that freight trains entering the city be led by a man on horseback at a maximum of six miles per hour. The troop remained a mainstay of the neighborhood for another ninety years.

11

Letter from concerned citizen to Mayor James Walker, July 29, 1927.
Jimmy Walker, best remembered as a fabulously corrupt mayor backed by the Tammany Hall political machine, targeted the revitalization of the West Side—and the "Death of Death Ave."—as a major goal. Walker's administration established the West Side Engineering Committee to negotiate a plan with the railroad. Along with the proposal for the West Side Highway, this became the first major project of the city's West Side Improvement plan, a program that would continue under Mayor La Guardia after Walker resigned amid scandal in 1932.

12–16

Clockwise from top left:
12 "The Wonder City You May Live to See," ***Popular Science Monthly*****, August 1925.**
13 William Allen Rogers, "Grand Completion of the Broadway Elevated Railroad System," ***Harper's Weekly*****, May 28, 1887.**
14 Louis Biedermann, "New York City As It Will Be in 1999," ***New York World*****, December 30, 1900.**
15 "The Elevated Railway at 110th Street and Eighth Avenue," ***Scientific American*** **magazine, October 25, 1879.**
16 "Meigs Elevated Railway," ***Scientific American*** **magazine, July 10, 1886.**
Early renderings by various engineers and inventors projected that elevated railways would allow for efficient urban transportation and promote peaceful street life below. In reality, these looming structures were often dark, heavy, and noisy: the elevated passenger train tracks built throughout Manhattan as early as the 1870s were often derided as a blight on the downtown streetscape. The worsening urban congestion became a central issue in architecture, engineering, and urban planning circles. Along with architect Raymond Hood—the "brilliant bad boy" of his discipline, according to *The New Yorker*—architect Harvey Wiley Corbett and delineator Hugh Ferriss leveraged transportation issues to rationalize their high-density visions. Their design and engineering work would form the basis of the modern paradigm of city planning, which influenced U.S. policy for decades.
As evidenced in the 1925 feature in *Popular Science Monthly*, Corbett envisioned a future New York in which car, train, and foot traffic would be distributed across different levels of multitiered streets. He believed this plan a solution to the city's traffic and safety problems in the face of rapid population growth. Corbett opposed above-ground rail solutions, seeking instead to bury these services below ground.

17
W. J. Wilgus, "Freight Subway Proposal: View of West Street," September 16, 1908.
Proposals to eliminate the New York Central tracks and other at-grade railroad crossings in the city gained political traction in the 1900s as public outrage over track danger mounted. W. J. Wilgus, the engineer behind the design and construction of Grand Central Terminal, presented a report that envisioned elevating freight tracks and creating subterranean tunnels that connected loading docks to individual buildings along the route.

18–19
From left:
18 Advertisement for New York Central West Side Line, *The Westsider*, 1937.
19 Advertisement for New York Central West Side Line, *The Westsider*, 1938.
Under Mayor Walker, engineers developed plans for an elevated railway that carved through buildings, freeing up the street for cars and pedestrians. According to the proposal, manufacturing buildings adjacent to the line would have second-story loading docks, allowing workers to accept freight and ship out finished products without having to leave the building. City officials and the New York Central Railroad promoted the public-private elevated tracks project as an efficient plan to improve industry locally and nationally, and projected quick returns on the massive initial investment of over $100 million. New York Central's advertising campaigns during the 1930s emphasized the railway's safety, centrality, and decreased operating costs.

20–21
From top:
20 "Huge Freight Depot to Be Started Soon," *New York Times*, November 27, 1931.
21 "Rip Up First Rails in Death Avenue," *New York Times*, January 1, 1930.
With the demolition of the dangerous street-level tracks along Tenth and Eleventh Avenues, the city celebrated the railway project as the beginning of a new era of business and neighborhood improvement. Officials hailed the public-private partnership that funded the enterprise—the largest of its kind in the history of the city—as a milestone in the development of Manhattan.

22
Illustration from "Transforming the West Side: A Huge Project Marches On," *New York Times*, June 3, 1934.
The elevated viaduct loosely followed the path of the old street-level line. Instead of following the avenues, engineers ran the tracks midblock, cutting through buildings to directly access warehouse loading docks above street level. North of the 30th Street rail yard, the city planned for the trains to run on a depressed track to 72nd Street, which led to a covered tunnel farther north.

23
New York Central Railroad Company, "Track Map," July 1, 1934.
With agile attention to New York's urban fabric, engineers drew a careful line among buildings, streets, and other preexisting infrastructure. To provide enough distance for the elevation change, the structure looped around the 30th Street rail yards before connecting with the below-grade tracks that ran north from 35th Street. On West 30th Street, a spur connected the tracks to a large platform serving the Post Office Building across Tenth Avenue.

24–27
Counterclockwise from top left:
24 J. J. Fisher Co., Inc., "Construction Joint Details for New York City Railroad Viaducts, Drawing #118," August 31, 1932.
25 New York City Railroad Engineering Department, "Superstructure for Viaduct, W. 18th St. to W. 30th St.," April 1, 1931.
26 New York City Railroad Engineering Department, "Superstructure for Viaduct, Horatio St. to Gansevoort St.," October 5, 1931.
27 McClintic-Marshall Construction Company, "Webs for 68'-0 Straight Stringers (Fascia), W. 18th St. to W. 30th St.," December 14, 1931.
The two-track viaduct, constructed from hand-riveted steel with a concrete floor and stone ballast, was built to carry hefty freight loads at least fourteen feet (just over four meters) above street level. Engineers designed a system of modular components that enabled the design to accommodate changes in grade and direction for building connections.

28
George A. Fuller Company, construction photographs, November 1932–July 1933.
Construction along the West Side began just as the Great Depression hit. By the time it was completed, the project had nearly bankrupted the railroad company.

29
Harry Brown, cover art, *The New Yorker*, September 16, 1933.
As the elevated tracks neared completion, the administration under Mayor La Guardia pushed for the continuation of the West Side Improvement plan and other large-scale infrastructure projects. This ambitious building program included the West Side Highway, a project spearheaded and eventually realized by the powerful and polarizing urban planner Robert Moses.

30–31
From top:
30 West Side Improvement pamphlet, June 28, 1934.
31 "Mayor Dedicates West Side Project," *New York Times*, June 29, 1934.
In 1934, high-ranking officials from the city administration, New York State, and the New York Central Railroad gathered at the new St. John's Park Freight Terminal—the southern terminus of the freight route—to celebrate the official opening of the freight line that ran from Spring Street to the rail yards between 30th Street and 34th Street.

32
Photo, *National Geographic Magazine*, 1936.
The elevated railway was fully operational from Spring Street to 30th Street until 1960. The route served a wide range of buildings, from meatpacking warehouses to technology manufacturers. The Bell Telephone Laboratories building had advanced construction technologies that allowed trains to pass through its tunnel without disturbing sensitive telecommunications equipment.

33
Jim Shaughnessy, "11th Avenue and West 30th Street," April 13, 1957.
For the first two decades of its operation, the elevated railway was a primary means of delivering freight to the island. In the 1950s, however, postwar planners and developers pushed for major automobile infrastructure projects in New York and throughout the country. As this network of highways and bridges grew, the New York Central Railroad faced stiff competition from the booming interstate trucking business, and freight traffic along its Manhattan railway declined considerably. In 1960, the railroad sold St. John's Park Terminal on Spring Street and terminated service south of Bank Street.

34
Michael Syracuse, "Bank Street," 1999.
In 1963, the city demolished the elevated track south of Bank Street and, after much debate, allocated the lot to a low-rise housing project. This was, in part, the result of a campaign by the Committee to Save the West Village, headed by community activist and urban planning critic Jane Jacobs.

35–36
From top:
35 Michael Syracuse, "Gansevoort Street," 1999.
36 David W. Dunlap, "Elevated Freight Line Being Razed Amid Protests," *New York Times*, January 15, 1991.
As the railroad business rapidly declined, ownership of the elevated railway changed hands: first from New York Central to Penn Central in 1968, and then to the federal government's Consolidated Rail Corporation (Conrail) in 1976. The line closed permanently in 1980; *The Villager* reported that its last train carried three boxcars of frozen turkeys. Ownership of the structure later passed to CSX, which demolished most of the railway south of Gansevoort Street in 1991. Only a small portion—underneath Westbeth Artists Housing, between Bank Street and Bethune Street, housed in the former Bell Laboratories Building—remained intact. Estimated costs for further demolition work were so high that the railroad chose to leave the structure as it was, against the wishes of property owners with adjacent lots.

37–40
Clockwise from left:
37 Efrain John Gonzalez, "West Street, 2 a.m." 1986.
38 Efrain John Gonzalez, "Little West 12th Street around Midnight," 1985.
39 Efrain John Gonzalez, "Young Transgirl Talking to Cab Driver," 1986.
40 Pamela Greene, "Presentation," 2008.
After the railroad discontinued freight service, the structure languished, a rusting symbol of the bygone industrial era. While the meatpacking industry remained concentrated around 14th Street, most manufacturers, once reliant on the elevated track, fled Manhattan during the economic decline of the 1970s. As industry fled, empty warehouses proliferated. A diverse community moved in, much of it low-income and marginalized. Meat handlers, tenement dwellers, sex workers, and gay clubbers shared the streets night and day.

41–42
From top:
41 Brian Rose, "West 14th Street," 1985.
42 "Florent Morellet as Marie Antoinette on Bastille Day," 1989.
In the 1980s, downtown culture rushed to fill the voided postindustrial landscape of the far West Side; former warehouses were converted into alternative clubs and social spaces. The original Restaurant Florent, a 24-hour French diner owned and operated by the cross-dressing social icon Florent Morellet, opened in 1985 and quickly became a fixture of the downtown scene.

43–47
Clockwise from top left:
43 Flyer for anti-crime forum, 1980.
44 Poster for party at Les Mouches, 1978.
45 Chelsea Gay Association pamphlet, 1979.
46 Flyer for party at Tunnel, 1987.
47 Tibor Kalman, advertisement for Restaurant Florent, c. 1985.
Throughout the '70s and '80s, gay culture, once concentrated in the West Village, began to extend northward into Chelsea. As this new subculture met neighborhood resistance, organizations assembled muscle groups to respond to rampant anti-gay violence; others, like the Chelsea Gay Association, sought to involve city officials in restoring peace. When the AIDS epidemic hit New York in the 1980s, the neighborhood became a center for activist efforts, providing a safe space for the Gay Men's Health Crisis and other groups to organize protests against political inaction and widespread discriminatory health practices.

48
"Christopher Street Book Shop City Guide to Bars, Discos, Hotels, Theaters, Baths, Restaurants, and Clubs," 1980.
Neighborhood organizations distributed discreet pamphlets delineating local gay bars and gay-friendly establishments.

49
Grace Glueck, "Dia Foundation, Back from Brink, Opens New Center," *New York Times*, October 7, 1987.
With the opening of the Dia Center for the Arts in 1987, the art scene began to flourish in Chelsea. Rising rents in SoHo sent galleries looking for cheaper spaces farther uptown. The crumbling warehouses and empty lofts of the far West Side provided suitable spaces, accelerating the neighborhood's transformation from an industrial zone to an enclave of cultural production. As in SoHo and TriBeCa, the arrival of artists heralded a new era of neighborhood transformation in which old commercial buildings were converted to galleries and residential lofts.

50
***Meat Market* guidebooks, 2002–2004.**
In 1999, Rei Kawakubo, the celebrated antifashion icon of Comme des Garçons, opened her West 26th Street boutique, the first high-end shopping outpost in West Chelsea. That same year, the luxury boutique Jeffrey opened on 14th Street, luring affluent customers to a neighborhood still dense with meat processing plants. By 2003—the year that local activists convinced the city to officially designate Gansevoort Market as a historic zone—the Meatpacking District had become one of the most fashionable mixed-use neighborhoods in Manhattan.

51
Photo shoot outside Friends of the High Line office in Meatpacking District, 2006.
Despite the rank smells of the area and the meat-littered, high-heel-snagging cobblestone streets, the crowds piled in. Within a few years, the Meatpacking District had become a destination for bustling nightlife and highbrow luxury fashion brands like Diane von Furstenberg.

52
Steven Holl, Bridge of Houses, *Pamphlet Architecture*, 1981.
Steven Holl's speculative project featured a collection of seven urban villas bridging the High Line with a public promenade beneath.

53
Rich Friedman, "$10 Railroad Sale Sidetracked by Intrigue," *New York Post*, November 13, 1984.
In 1984, Peter Obletz, a railroad fanatic who lived in two abandoned railcars parked behind Penn Station, incorporated the West Side Rail Line Development Foundation to save the elevated tracks from demolition and preserve them for future reuse as an active railroad. His name for the structure—the High Line—remains. With support from a few local and state politicians, the Interstate Commerce Commission (ICC) granted Obletz the right to purchase the railroad from Conrail for the price of $10.

54
West Side Rail Development Foundation poster, 1982.
While happy to be relieved of the decision regarding the rail's future, Conrail faced serious opposition from local property owners, development groups, and New York City and State government officials who wanted to see the line torn down. In 1987, the ICC reversed its decision, nullifying the sale of the line to Obletz. In 1991, Rockrose Development Corporation succeeded in negotiating with Conrail for the demolition of the southernmost five blocks of the High Line (extending to Gansevoort Street). However, the ICC declared in 1992 that they would only allow the line to be taken down if the Chelsea Business and Property Owners Association committed to the majority of the financing and insurance for the demolition. With the CBPOA unwilling to commit the necessary funds, the line continued to lie vacant throughout the 1990s.

55
Joel Sternfeld, photo, 2001.
In 1999, Chelsea residents Joshua David and Robert Hammond met at a community board meeting about the future of the High Line. They decided to join forces to fight for the High Line's preservation.

56
Pentagram, Friends of the High Line visual identity, 2000.
Without any funding, political experience, or even a clear vision for what the structure would eventually be, Hammond and David's first step was to give their organization a name and an identity: Friends of the High Line. The organization's logo and stationery were conceived by Paula Scher of Pentagram.

57
Adam Gopnik, "A Walk on the High Line," *The New Yorker*, May 21, 2001.
Published in the *The New Yorker* alongside reproductions of Joel Sternfeld's large-format photographs, Adam Gopnik's 2001 essay highlighted the activist efforts of Friends of the High Line and described the otherworldly experience of visiting the site, "a place where the discordant encounters of its city are briefly resolved."

58
Joel Sternfeld, *Walking the High Line*, 2001.
From 2000 to 2001, photographer Joel Sternfeld documented the wild, overgrown beauty of the High Line in different seasons. Paired with Adam Gopnik's essay, the project brought widespread public recognition and support for the preservation of the High Line.

59
Regional Plan Association, "What to Do with the High Line?" 1999.
CSX Transportation, the private railroad company that owned the High Line, contracted the Regional Plan Association for an assessment of the structure and a proposal for its revitalization. CSX hoped to avoid the tremendous cost of removing the structure—upwards of $30 million. Informed by recommendations from experts in urban planning and policy, the RPA's report advocated for the reuse of the High Line as a greenway. The Giuliani administration dismissed the report, arguing that, short of an active railway system, the structure was without sufficient use and should be torn down.

60
HR&A Advisors, "The High Line: The Feasibility and Economic Impact of Re-Use," 2002.
In an effort of appeal to the city, the Friends of the High Line asked HR&A, a development consulting firm, to prepare an assessment of the economic feasibility of a revitalization effort. The document outlined development scenarios, construction cost estimates, and projected outcomes for real-estate development and business relocation. The proposal hinged on strategic use of transferable development rights, particularly air rights. This urban planning concept, manipulated for decades to protect overdevelopment above landmarks like Grand Central Terminal, stipulated that property owners of lots below and adjacent to the High Line could sell their development air rights. Developers building elsewhere could purchase these air rights and use them to obtain zoning allowances for taller structures on their property, essentially trading air space from one block to another. Ideally, the buildings to which the air rights were being transferred would be located in a part of the neighborhood better suited to high-density structures. In this way, the High Line project could avert two dangers—opposition from the Chelsea Business and Property Owners Association, and overdevelopment of immediately adjacent properties. It could also generate enough tax revenue for the city to repay its initial investment in project costs.

61
New York City Department of City Planning, "West Chelsea Rezoning Proposal," 2004.
The High Line played a central role in the city's revitalization of the West Side. In 2003, a grassroots preservation campaign succeeded in securing landmark designation for most of the Meatpacking District, including the southernmost section of the High Line, from Gansevoort Street to West 16th Street. After creating the Gansevoort Market Historic District, the Department of City Planning

focused its efforts on West Chelsea, stretching from West 16th Street to 30th Street between Tenth and Eleventh Avenues. At that point, most of the neighborhood was still zoned for manufacturing. A rezoning plan proposed by the city in 2004 introduced mixed-use residential and commercial development while protecting existing businesses from eviction, including art galleries and the remnants of the manufacturing sector. After negotiating with public housing advocates, the Department of City Planning guaranteed that over a quarter of the area's new housing would be affordable. The rezoning plan also replicated the transferable air rights strategy outlined in HR&A's feasibility report two years earlier, a clear endorsement of the High Line preservation effort. With this plan, the city hoped to balance a number of competing demands: protecting the High Line while placating its opponents, and catalyzing development in the area to generate tax revenue. After undergoing an intense approvals and community input process, the rezoning proposal passed in June 2005, allowing the city to throw its full support behind the High Line project.

62
Friends of the High Line and the Design Trust for Public Space, *Reclaiming the High Line*, 2002.
The Design Trust for Public Space commissioned a broad feasibility study on the High Line in 2001. Over the next year, two Design Trust fellows, Casey Jones and Keller Easterling, conducted research that explored the past, present, and possible futures of the structure. The team examined the High Line's potential to improve the surrounding neighborhoods, generate economic activity, and prompt innovative designs for reuse. The results were published in a 2002 study.

63
Chelsea Business and Property Owners Association flyer, 2002.
Convinced that the High Line lowered the value of their real estate, a group called the Chelsea Business and Property Owners Association distributed flyers throughout the neighborhood, framing the Friends of the High Line's mission as a plan to make permanent a structure they believed to be a blight on their neighborhood.

64–65
From top:
64 Mail-in community input card, 2003.
65 Letter of opposition, April 3, 2003.
While community support for Friends of the High Line gained traction early, some neighbors remained skeptical.

66
Ideas competition exhibition, Grand Central Terminal, July 2003.
In 2003, Friends of the High Line organized an international ideas competition, hoping to generate awareness and garner support for the preservation of the High Line. The jury received 720 submissions from 38 countries.

67
Nathalie Rinne, "Mile-Long Swimming Pool," July 2003.
Publicly exhibited at Grand Central Terminal, submissions presented a diverse range of fantasy proposals, from a cow pasture to a one-track roller coaster. One of the winning entries imagined reusing the High Line as a mile-long lap pool.

68–69
From left:
68 Letter from Senator Hillary Rodham Clinton to the New York City Council, April 17, 2001.
69 Letter from the office of Mayor Giuliani to Congressman Jerrold Nadler, May 31, 2001.
Although the High Line had powerful political allies at the state capitol, the office of the mayor continued to reject proposals for the adaptive reuse of the High Line. Mayor Giuliani's administration echoed the arguments of lobbyists from the Chelsea Business and Property Owners Association, who claimed that demolition of the railway would increase property values and kick-start the mayor's own West Side revitalization project. In his final days in office, Mayor Giuliani signed an executive order stating that the structure be razed.

70–73
Clockwise from top left:
70 David W. Dunlap, "Which Track for the High Line?" *New York Times*, December 31, 2000.
71 "Put the brakes on rush to raze the High Line," *The Villager*, April 11, 2001.
72 "Give High Line a chance," *Daily News*, April 18, 2001.
73 "High Noon for High Line," *Daily News*, December 30, 2001.
As news of Giuliani's decision reached the press, a community of High Line supporters at the local, regional, and national level rallied around the preservation effort.

74
Assembly Member Richard N. Gottfried, U.S. Representative Jerrold Nadler, State Senator Thomas K. Duane, Assembly Member Deborah Glick, and Councilmember Christine Quinn, "High Hopes for the High Line," February 24, 2003.
Mayor Bloomberg had endorsed the High Line project during his election campaign, and many of his senior staff—including Amanda Burden, Andrew Alper, and Dan Doctoroff—had worked to promote the grassroots advocacy efforts led by Friends of the High Line. In January 2001, his first month in office, Bloomberg reversed Giuliani's demolition order. This mayoral support, coupled with the favorable majority opinion of City Hall, gave the project the necessary allies and endowed the plan with a newfound sense of possibility.

75
Paul Vitello, "Rusty Railroad on Its Way to Pristine Park," *New York Times*, June 15, 2005.
On June 13, 2005, after four more years of fundraising, negotiation, and litigation, the High Line finally secured the legal status necessary for its owner, CSX Transportation, to transfer the structure to the city and Friends of the High Line so that it could be transformed into a park. Overcoming tremendous odds, the project had become a site for imagination and invention, making the transition from a campaign for preservation to an architectural reality—the challenge of making a park in the sky.

03_CONCEPT

Over the course of a four-month design competition, our team developed a vision for the park, mapping out its qualitative underpinnings and conceptual framework. These initial steps would define the work of the next decade. After winning the competition, we drafted the Framework Plan, which outlined design principles and created the guiding strategies for the paving, planting, lighting, and vertical-access systems. At the beginning of this process, we were skeptical as to whether the project would ever materialize: the project still faced considerable legal, political, and financial hurdles. In the face of these challenges, we remained intensely focused on executing our vision for the park. We were committed to the preservation of the High Line and our core intent: to keep the High Line simple, wild, quiet, and slow.

APRIL – MAY 2004: COMPETITION PROPOSAL, STAGE I

Following an open call for qualification submissions, seven short-listed design teams were selected to participate in the first stage of the competition, which involved developing a programmatic and design approach for the High Line. Representatives from Friends of the High Line and the City of New York served on the competition jury.

PROGRAMS

HABITATS

ATMOSPHERES

MICRO-CLIMATES

CONNECTIONS

ECOSYSTEMS WILL GROW HERE.

NOCTURNAL LIFE

ECONOMIES

COMMUNITIES

PRESERVATION

NEW ECOSYSTEMS:

More than half of this project is already in place. We propose to capitalize on existing potential to "grow" something new out of something old.

As a singular, autonomous entity, the High Line has grown its own ecology, its own ecosystem. The surrounding city fabric too has evolved its own ecology of use, economy, cultures and identity. The two are separate.

What will happen when they are linked?

What new ecologies will grow here?

The two systems must continue to function independently, to retain their differences, but they must also enter into a new exchange, a feedback loop, a new ecology of interaction.

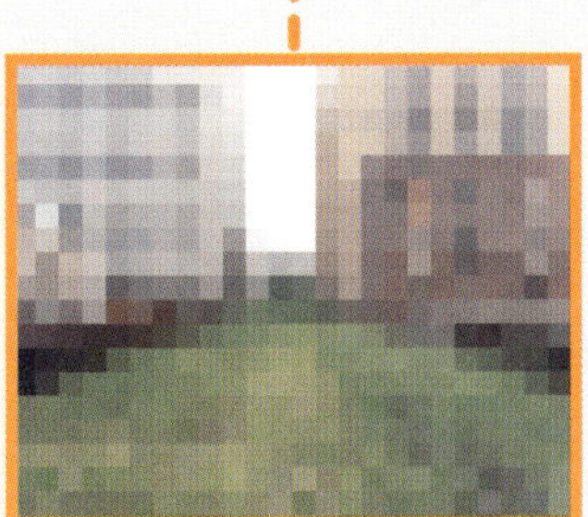

EXTREME RECONSTRUCTION

PROGRAMS WILL GROW HERE.

HABITATS

ATMOSPHERES

MICRO-CLIMATES

CONNECTIONS

ECOSYSTEM

NOCTURNAL LIFE

ECONOMIES

COMMUNITIES

Hudson River Park, a linear park west of the High Line, is currently being developed along the waterfront. It sustains typical park programs in the city including biking, running, sports, arts and play. The High Line should not duplicate these programs. It should be distinctive and offer uses and experiences that are unique to it.

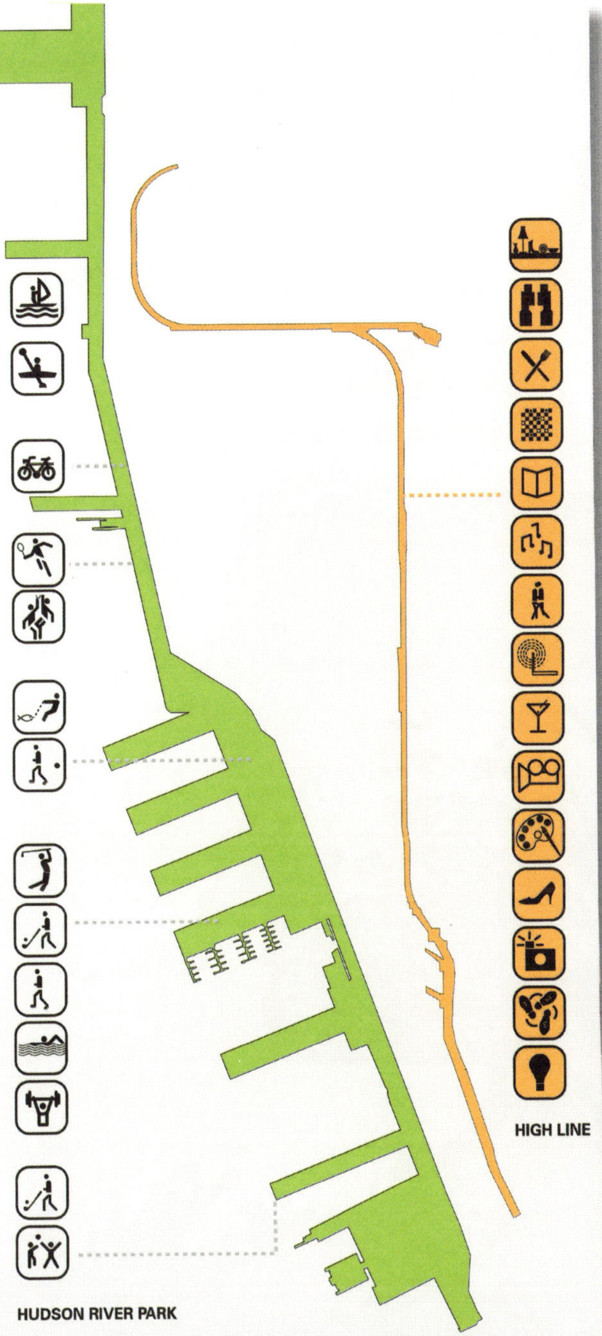

HUDSON RIVER PARK

HIGH LINE

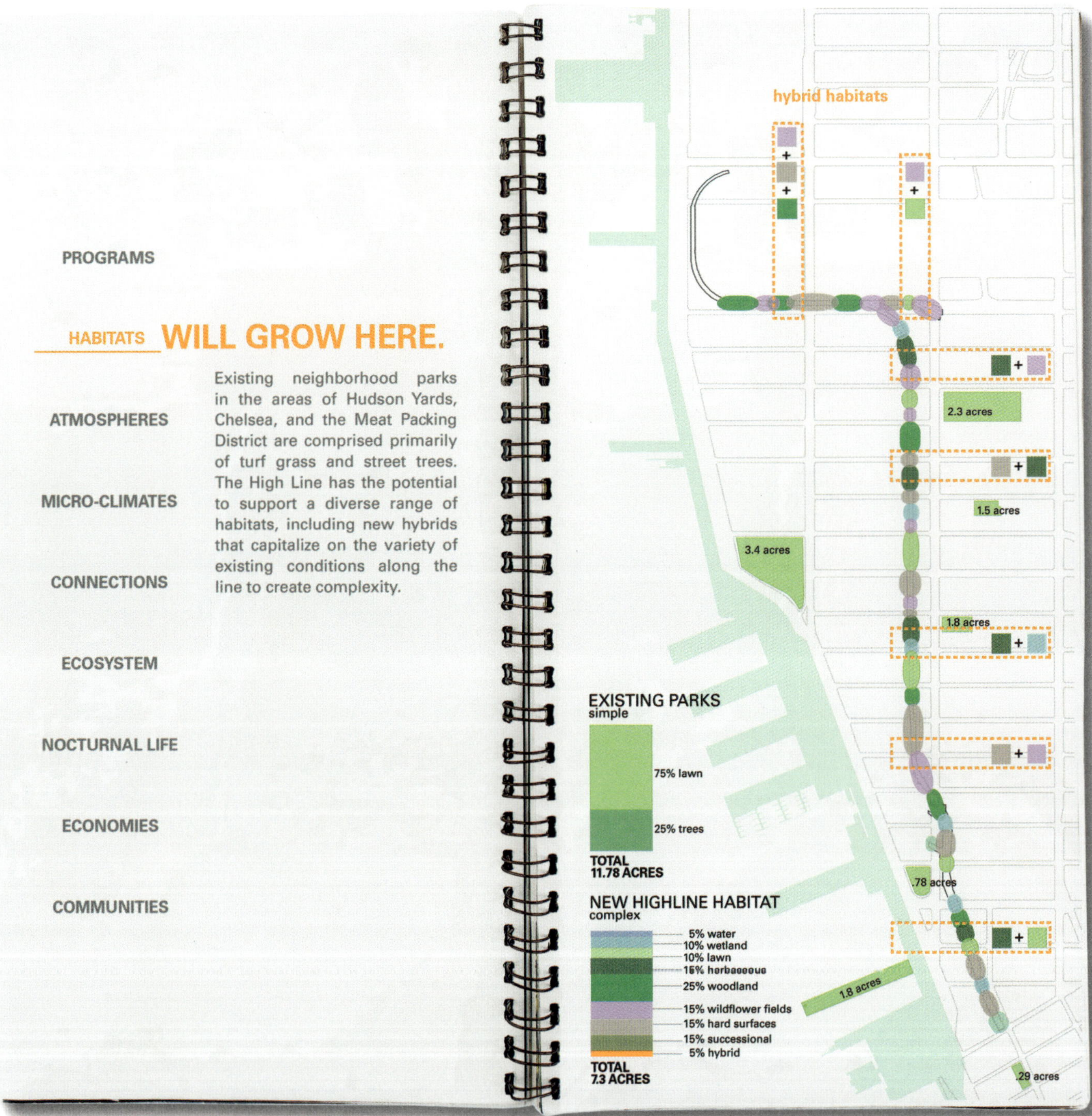

PROGRAMS

HABITATS

ATMOSPHERES WILL GROW HERE.

MICRO-CLIMATES

CONNECTIONS

ECOSYSTEM

NOCTURNAL LIFE

ECONOMIES

COMMUNITIES

The High Line cuts through diverse neighborhoods, revealing the backsides, topsides and undersides of the city. It shelters and absorbs sound, collects and releases water, and shields and attracts sun in myriad ways. The unique perspective from the air allows for intimate contact with the unusual material and urban conditions that characterize the High Line and its surroundings – an ambient space of experience, not an object or form.

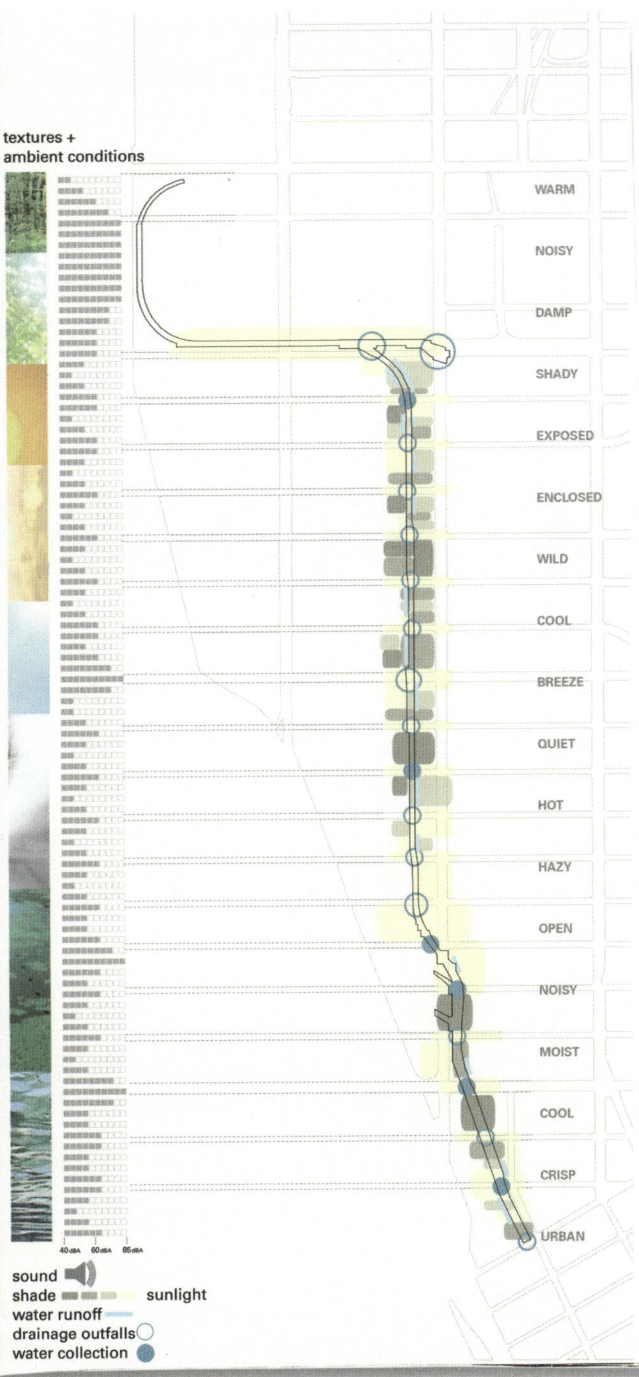

PROGRAMS

HABITATS

ATMOSPHERES

MICRO-CLIMATES **WILL GROW HERE.**

The existing vegetation on the site is opportunistic, comprised of short grasses where it is open, exposed and dry; whips and trees where it is enclosed, shady and wet. Hardy native and alien species common to abandoned landscapes have colonized the site and are gradually thickening the living mat.

CONNECTIONS

ECOSYSTEM

NOCTURNAL LIFE

ECONOMIES

COMMUNITIES

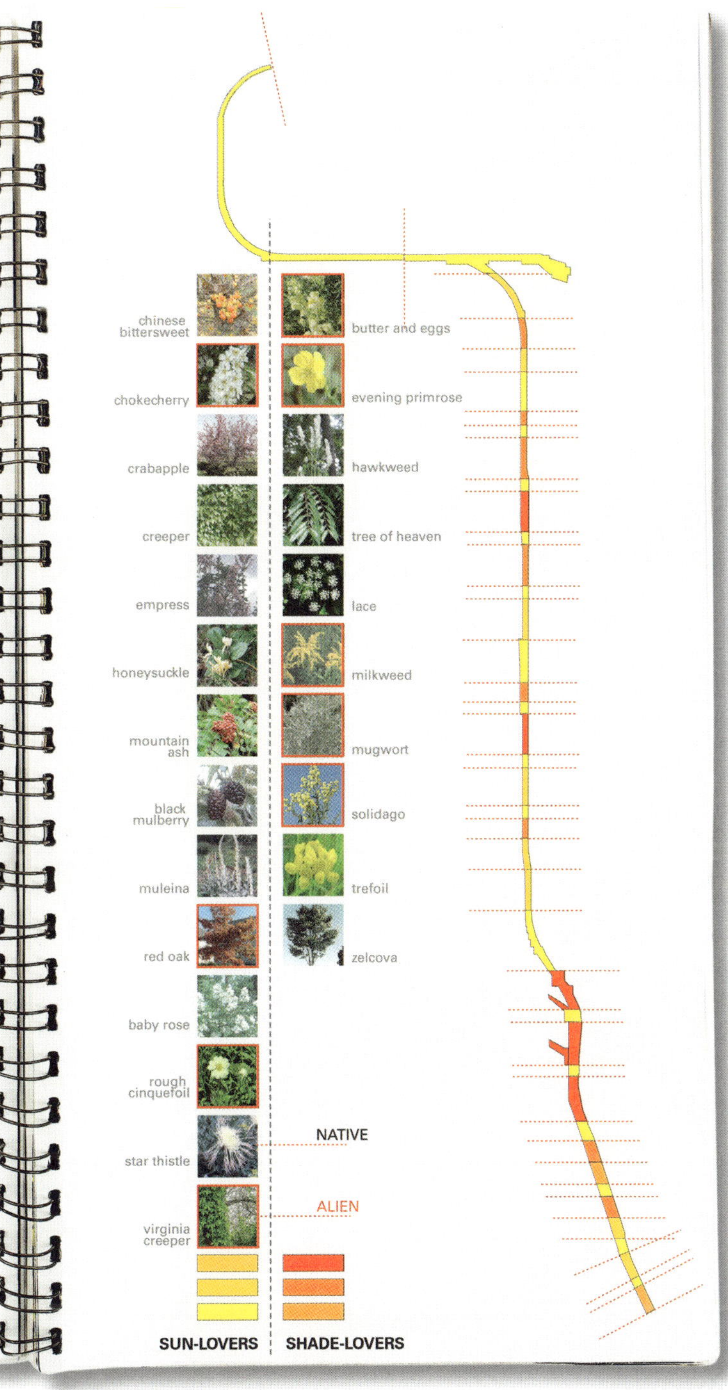

PROGRAMS

HABITATS

ATMOSPHERES

MICRO-CLIMATES

CONNECTIONS

ECOSYSTEM

NOCTURNAL LIFE **WILL GROW HERE.**

ECONOMIES

COMMUNITIES

An art, nightclub and fashion scene has been rapidly developing in Chelsea and the Meat Packing District. Returning home from work, most of the time residents spend in the neighborhood is lived in the evening. While Hudson River Park will close at dusk, the High Line has the potential to create its own distinct kind of night life.

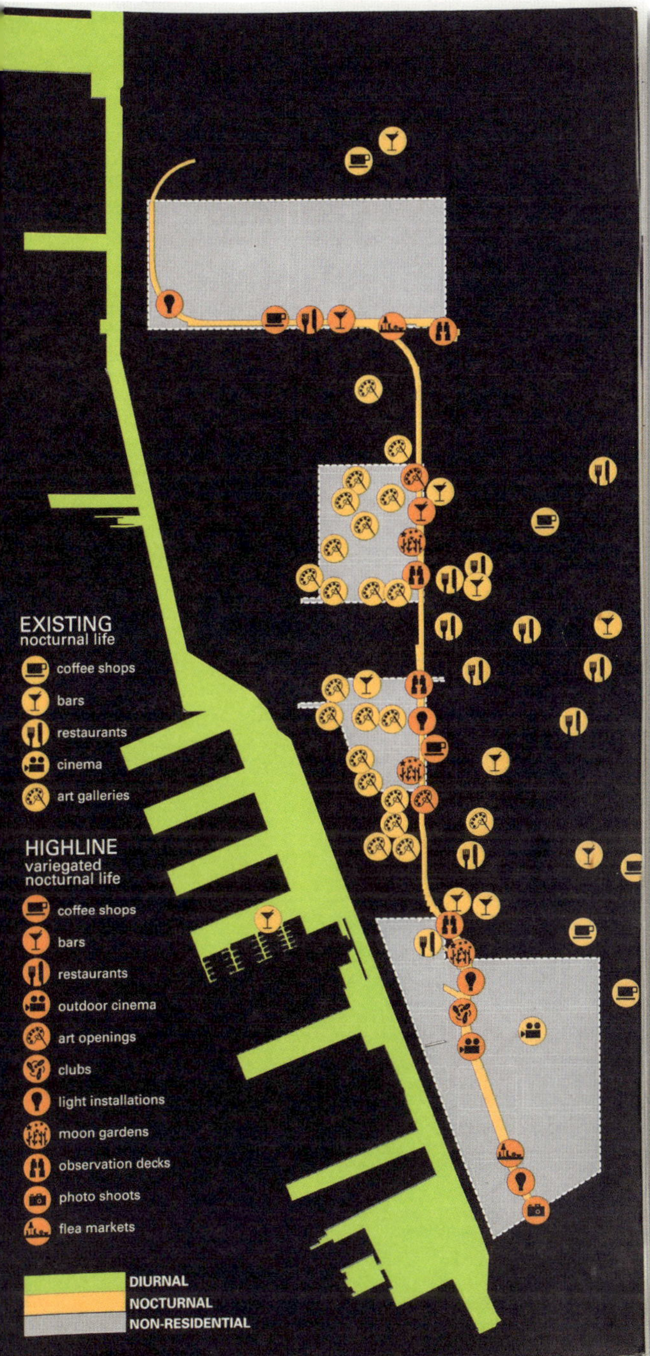

PROGRAMS

HABITATS

ATMOSPHERES

MICRO-CLIMATES

CONNECTIONS

ECOSYSTEM

NOCTURNAL LIFE

ECONOMIES **WILL GROW HERE.**

COMMUNITIES

As the High Line becomes a public space, it will significantly influence development of the surrounding areas. It will integrate adjacent neighborhoods and become a destination point for visitors. It will support existing local economies and generate new ones, as it did when it was first erected.

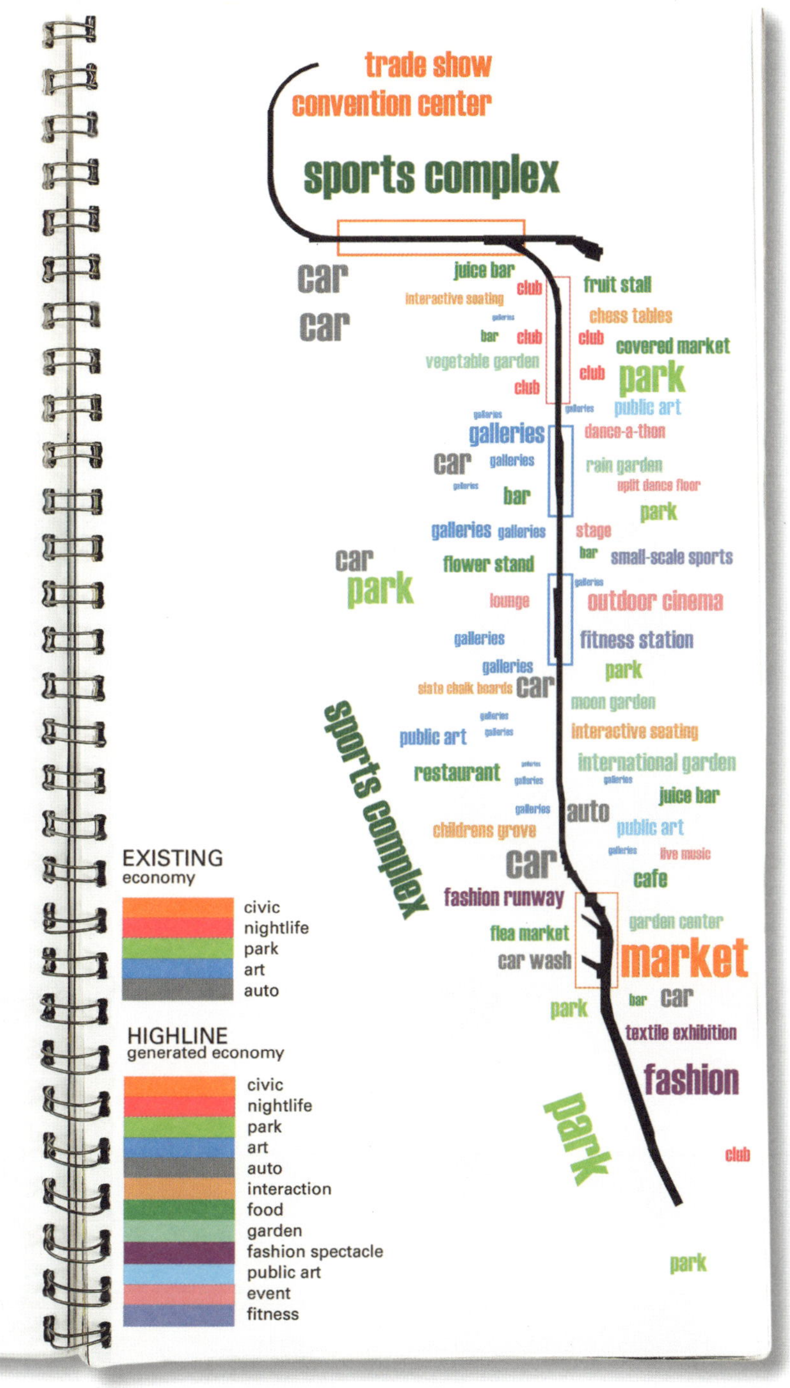

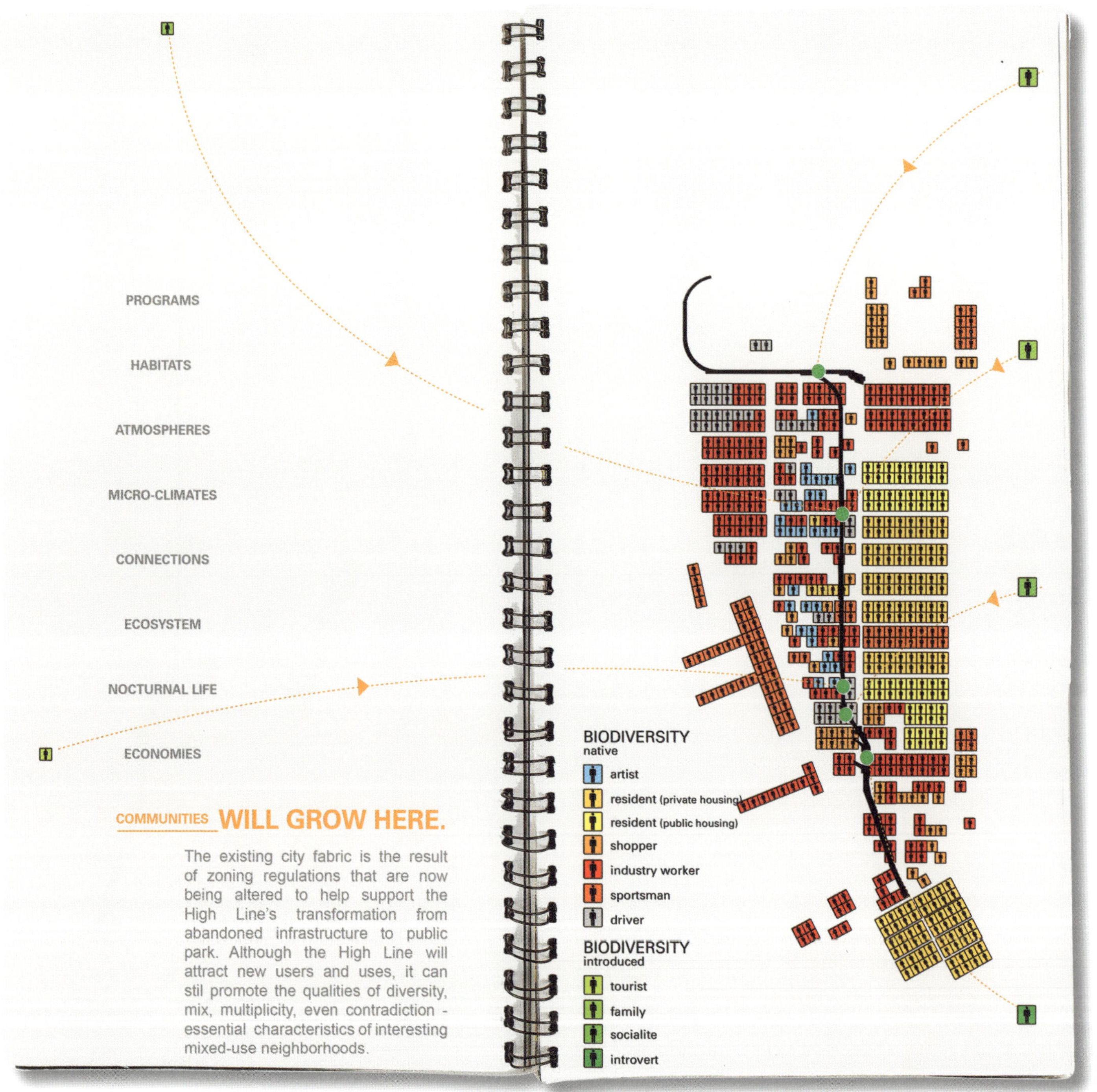

NO / people and plants separated

YES / people and plants intertwined

MAY 2004: FINALISTS ANNOUNCED

The jury named the team led by James Corner Field Operations and Diller Scofidio + Renfro as one of four finalists. Competitors included Steven Holl with Hargreaves Associates, Zaha Hadid with Balmori Associates, and Michael Van Valkenburgh with D.I.R.T. Studio.

THE NEW YORK TIMES, SUNDAY, JULY 11, 2004 AR 29

ARCHITECTURE

Elevated Visions

Four High-Powered Firms Offer Designs for the High Line

1. FIELD OPERATIONS WITH DILLER, SCOFIDIO & RENFRO

The Villager July 21 - 27, 2004 3

High Line forum packed tighter than a subway car

BY ALBERT AMATEAU

If the overflow crowd at the Center for Architecture's forum on the High Line last week is any indication, future visitors to the elevated park between the Gansevoort Market and the Javits Convention Center will barely fit on the 30-ft. width of the old rail viaduct.

"Since we opened last fall, this is the largest crowd we've had here," said Rick Bell, executive director of the New York Chapter of the American Institute of Architects, referring to the 500 people who crammed into the Center at 536 LaGuardia Pl. for the July 15 presentation on the future of the High Line. Others who tried to get in could not, and were left standing outside on the sidewalk.

The focus of all that attention was the four teams that submitted scenarios to convert the disused 1.5-mile railroad viaduct into an elevated park that traverses Chelsea along the west side of 10th Ave. — where more than 200 art galleries occupy old warehouse space — and the Meat Market in Greenwich Village.

Team leaders used words like "magical," "unruly" and "wild," to describe aspects of the elevated railroad that they intend to honor and enhance but inevitably change by transforming it into a public park. And to one degree or another, all four teams are committed to providing public access to the High Line as soon as possible, even if that access is only temporary at first.

Steven Holl, an architect and leader of one of the teams whose office overlooks the High Line at 31st St., recalled seeing a blue butterfly on the viaduct during a recent visit. Looking ahead to 2050 to "a suspended valley" among the tall buildings

Villager photo by Elisabeth Robert

Over 500 people attended a forum on the future of the High Line elevated railroad at the Center for Architecture on LaGuardia Pl. last week.

4 Teams 4 Visions

Design Approaches to the High Line Master Plan

Field Operations with Diller Scofidio + Renfro, Olafur Eliasson, Piet Oudolf, and Buro Happold

Zaha Hadid Architects with Balmori Associates, Skidmore, Owings & Merrill LLP, and studio MDA

Steven Holl Architects with Hargreaves Associates and HNTB

TerraGRAM: Michael Van Valkenburgh Associates with D.I.R.T. Studio and Beyer Blinder Belle

These four teams have been selected as finalists to create a master plan for the High Line. One will be selected by the end of this summer to begin designing New York City's most exciting new public open space. These aren't final plans; they're illustrations of each team's proposed approach. The master plan itself will be developed by the selected team starting this fall, with many opportunities for you and the community to play a role. Please register for e-mail updates at www.thehighline.org.

MAY 28 – JULY 15, 2004: COMPETITION SUBMISSION, STAGE II

The final stage of the competition required that each team articulate a full conceptual vision for the High Line, including strategies for landscape, paving, programming, and access. An exhibition at the Center for Architecture showcased the presentation boards for each of the four finalist proposals.

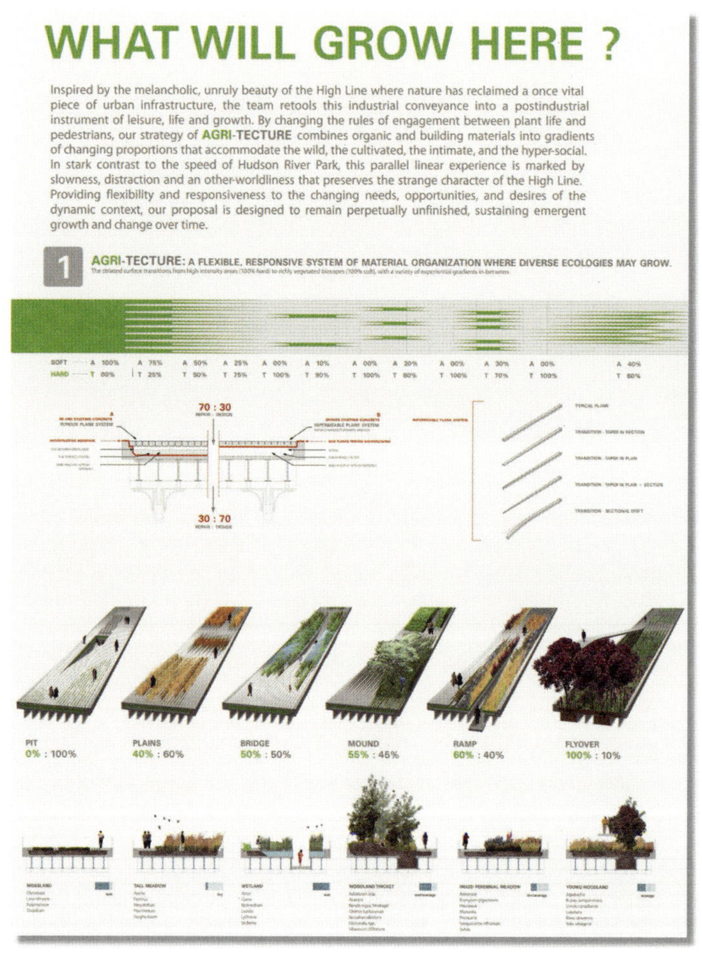

Board 1

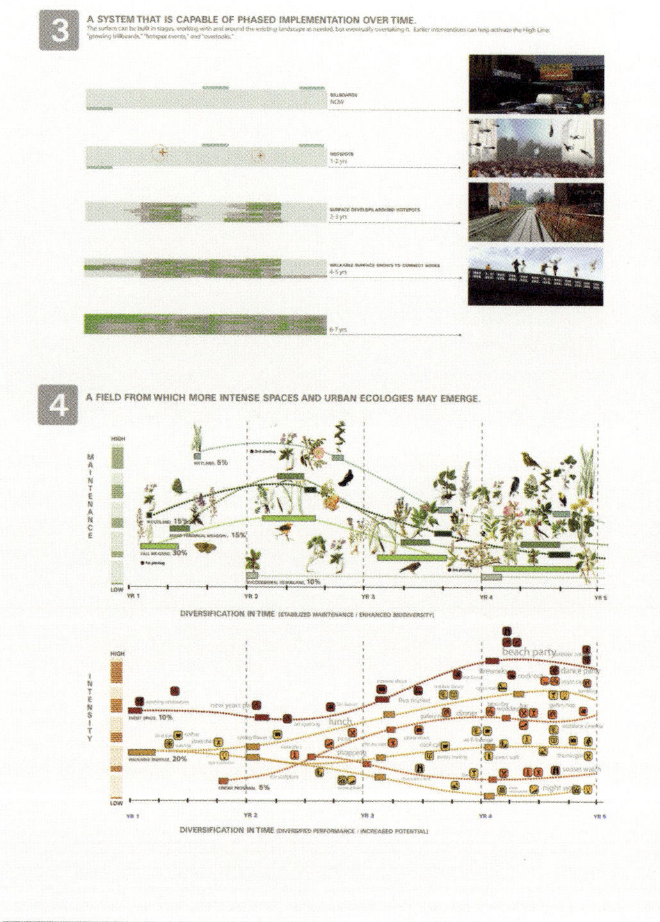

Board 2

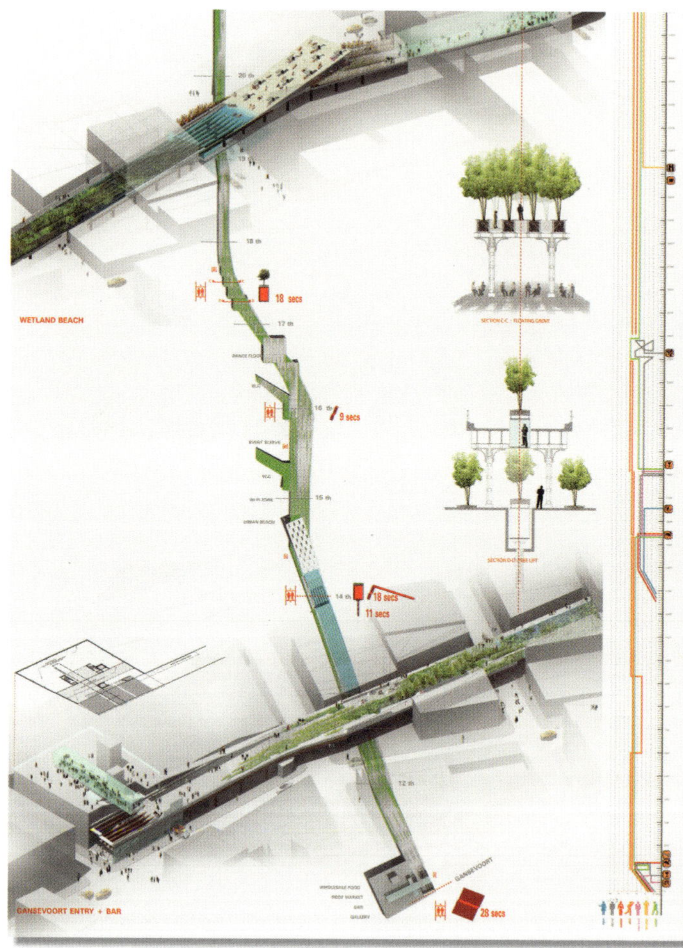

Board 3

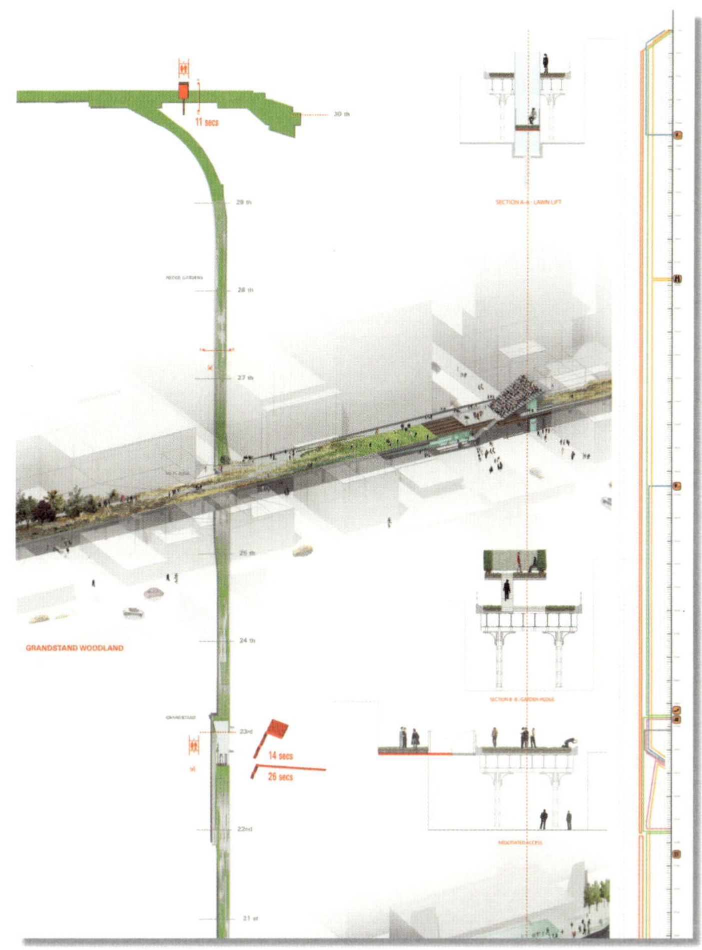

Board 4

Board 5

Board 6

WHAT WILL GROW HERE ?

Inspired by the melancholic, unruly beauty of the High Line where nature has reclaimed a once vital piece of urban infrastructure, the team retools this industrial conveyance into a postindustrial instrument of leisure, life and growth. By changing the rules of engagement between plant life and pedestrians, our strategy of **AGRI-TECTURE** combines organic and building materials into gradients of changing proportions that accommodate the wild, the cultivated, the intimate, and the hyper-social. In stark contrast to the speed of Hudson River Park, this parallel linear experience is marked by slowness, distraction and an other-worldliness that preserves the strange character of the High Line. Providing flexibility and responsiveness to the changing needs, opportunities, and desires of the dynamic context, our proposal is designed to remain perpetually unfinished, sustaining emergent growth and change over time.

AGRI-TECTURE: A FLEXIBLE, RESPONSIVE SYSTEM OF MATERIAL ORGANIZATION WHERE DIVERSE ECOLOGIES MAY GROW.

The striated surface transitions from high intensity areas (100% hard) to richly vegetated biotopes (100% soft), with a variety of experiential gradients in-between.

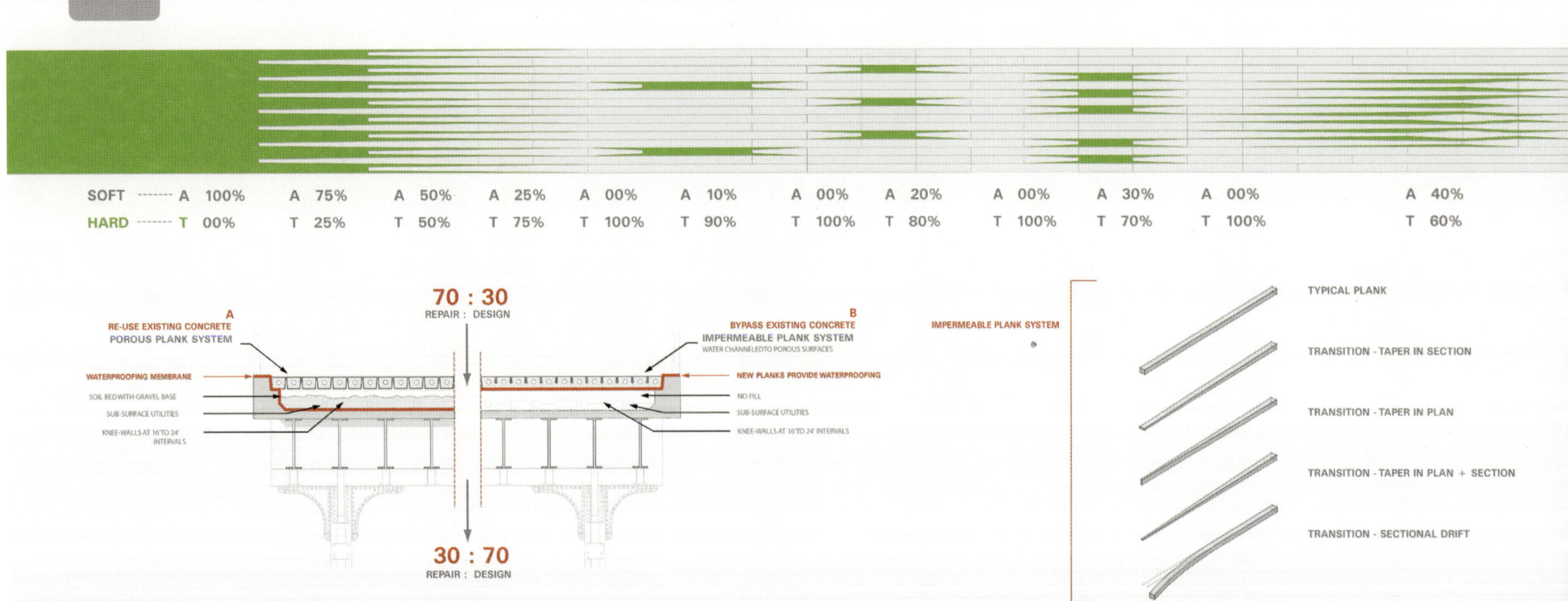

2 A METHODOLOGY FOR CONSTRUCTING HARD SURFACES AND STRUCTURES AS MEANS OF PRODUCING DIVERSE SOCIAL AND NATURAL HABITATS.

Designed as a continuous, single-surface, yet built from individual pre-cast units that may fold down to permit travel through the thick structural section of the High Line or fold up to pass over it without disturbing the natural "preserves."

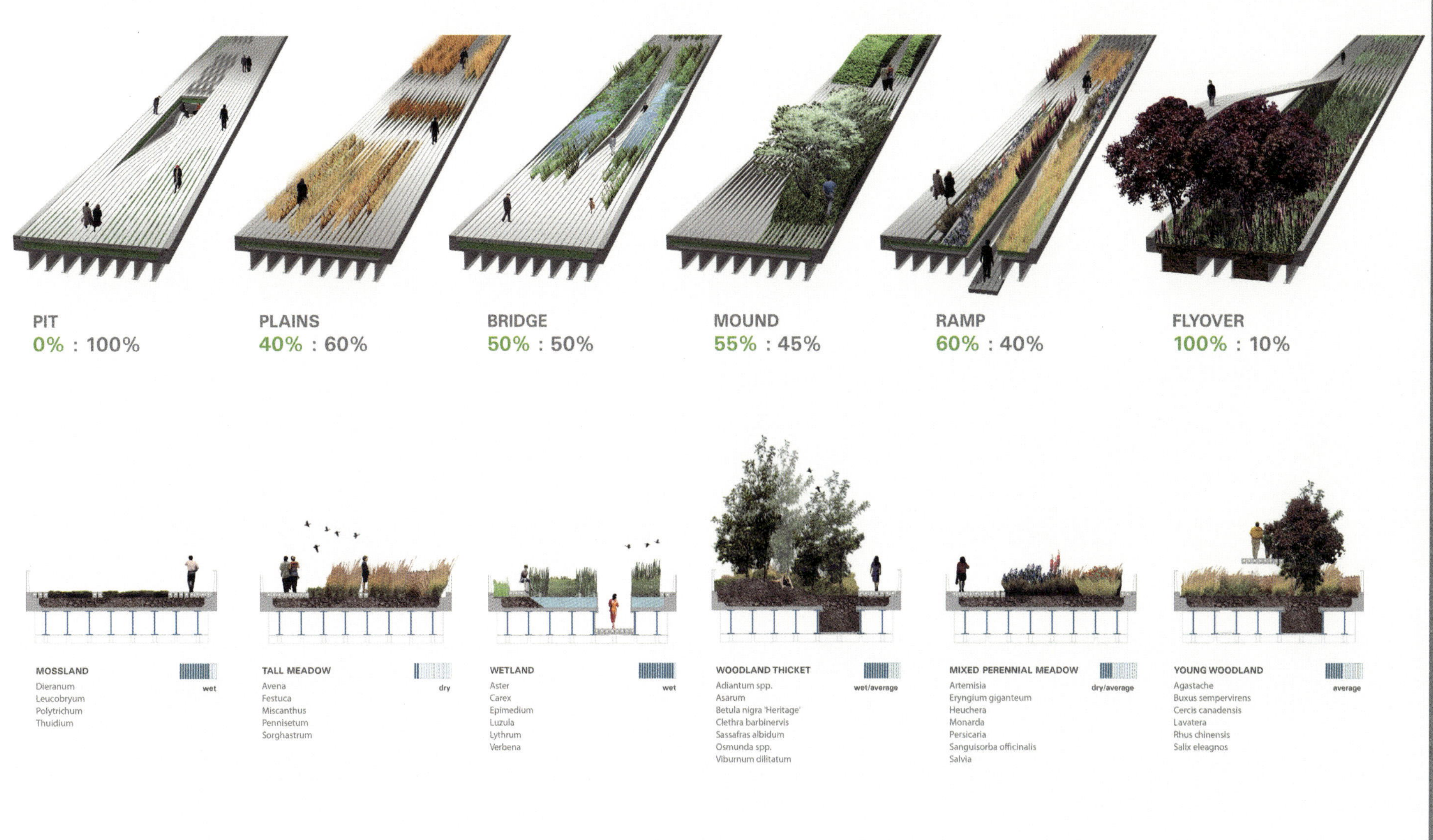

<< Board 1

A SYSTEM THAT IS CAPABLE OF PHASED IMPLEMENTATION OVER TIME.

The surface can be built in stages, working with and around the existing landscape as needed, but eventually overtaking it. Earlier interventions can help activate the High Line: "growing billboards," "hotspot events," and "overlooks."

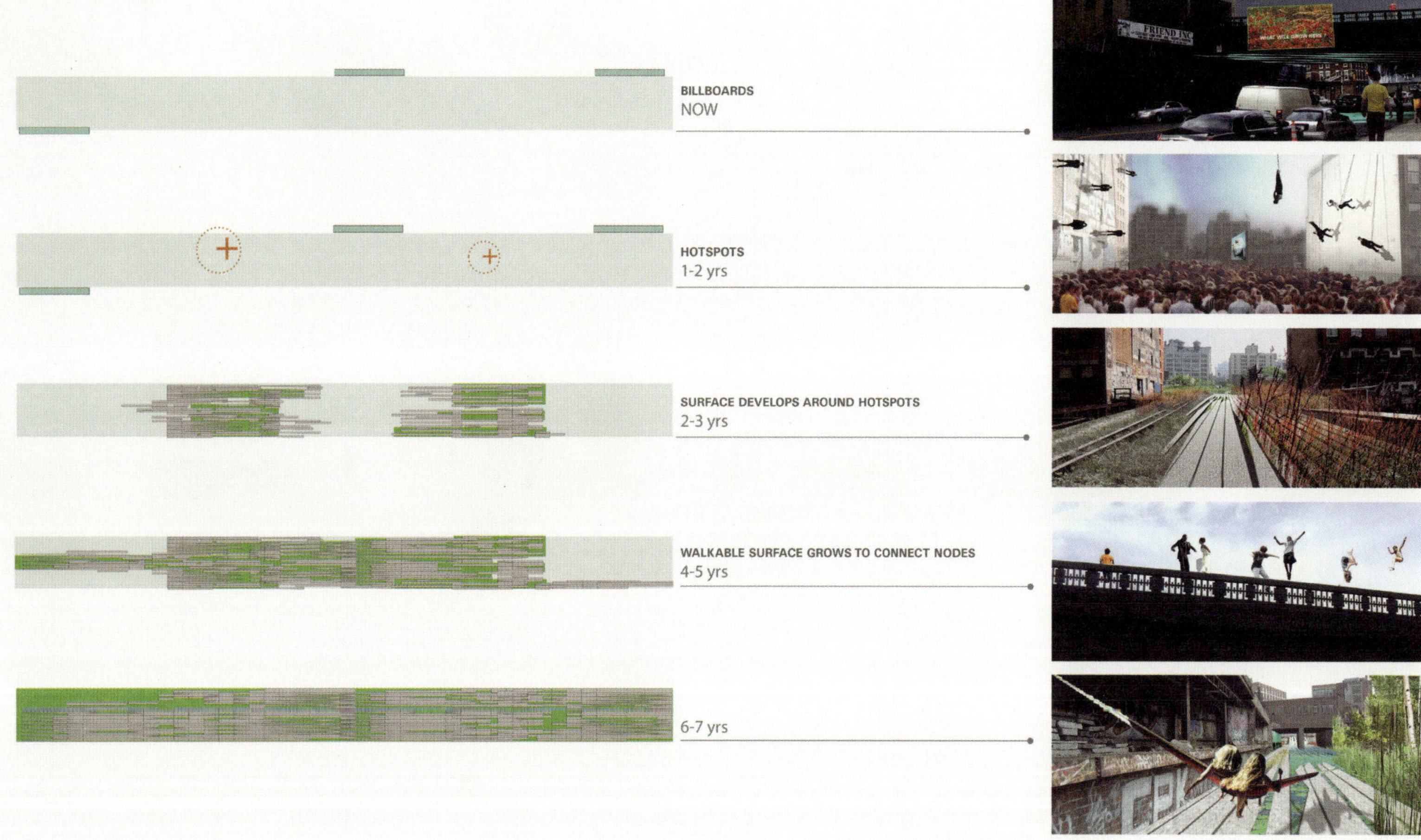

A FIELD FROM WHICH MORE INTENSE SPACES AND URBAN ECOLOGIES MAY EMERGE.

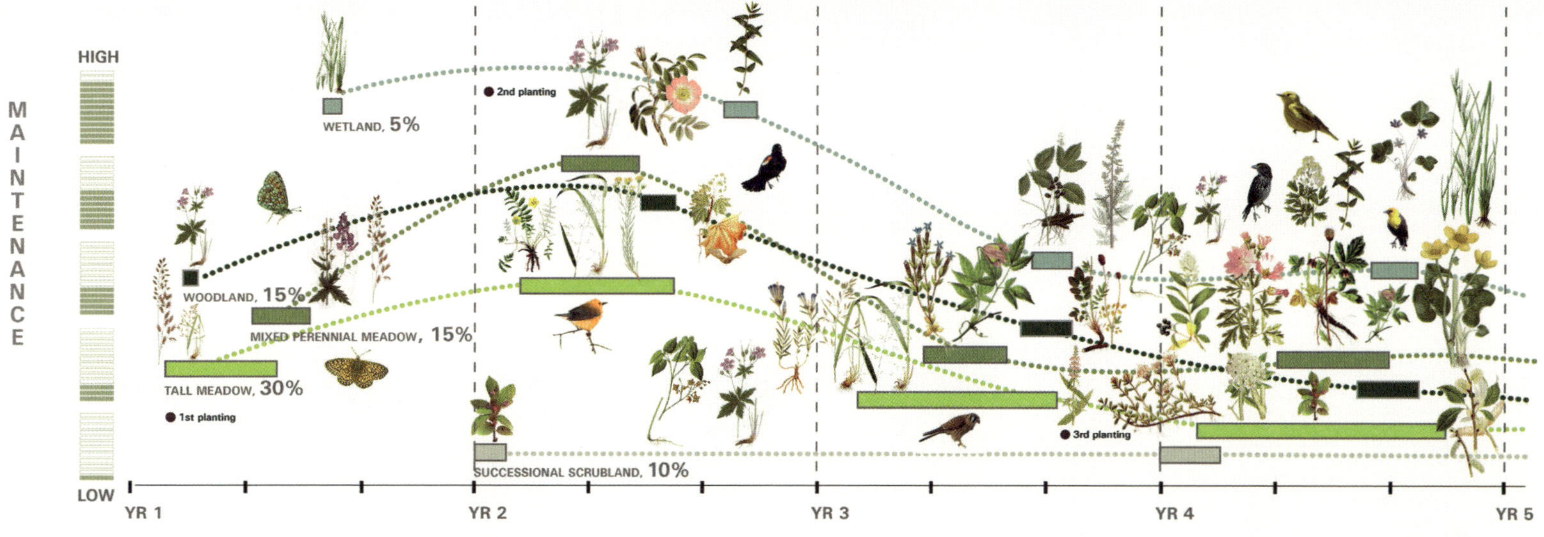

DIVERSIFICATION IN TIME [STABILIZED MAINTENANCE / ENHANCED BIODIVERSITY]

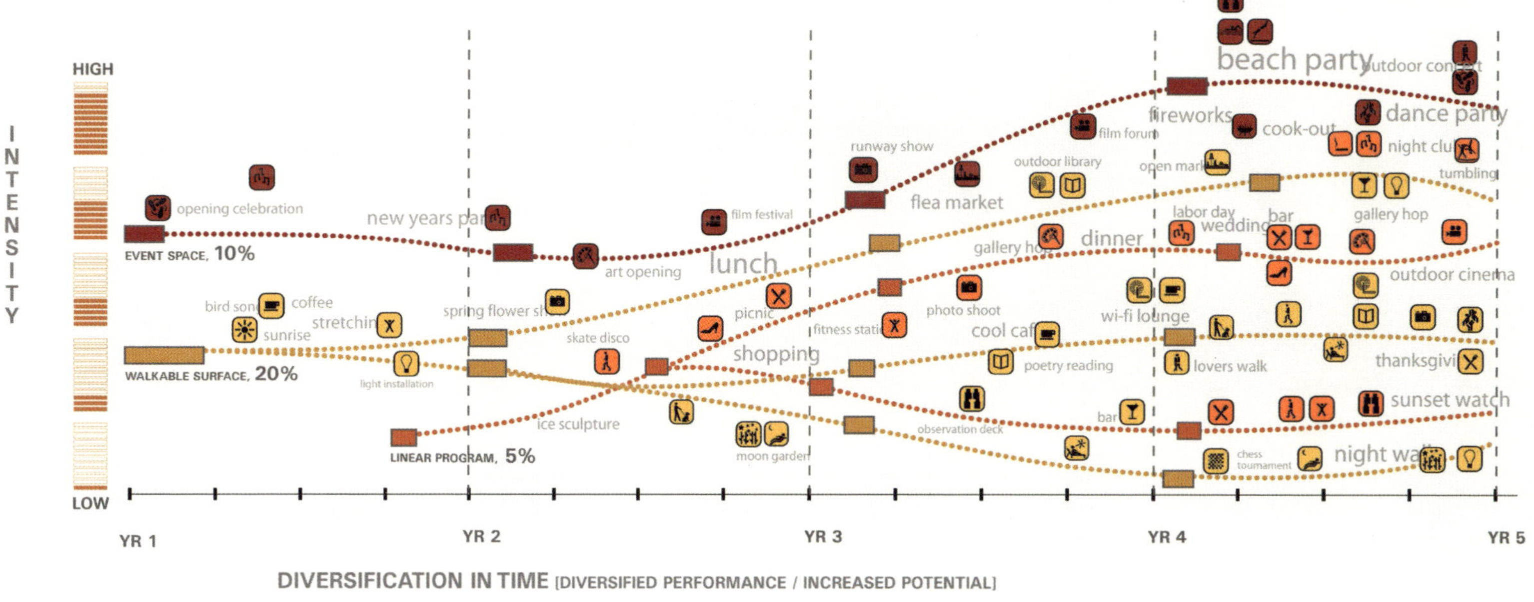

DIVERSIFICATION IN TIME [DIVERSIFIED PERFORMANCE / INCREASED POTENTIAL]

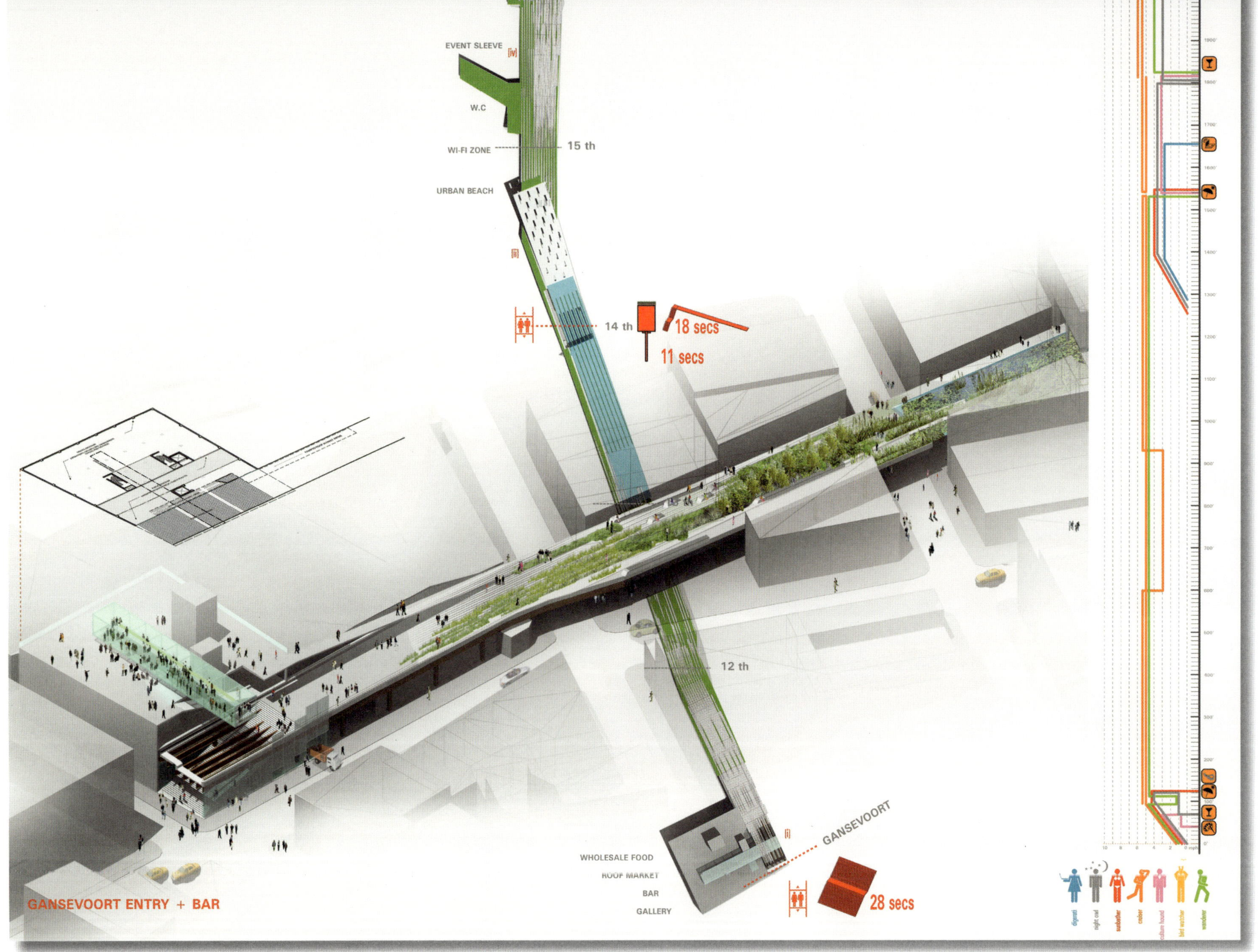

Board 3

Rendering from Board 6 >>

Board 3 ⌄⌄

Rendering from Board 6 ››

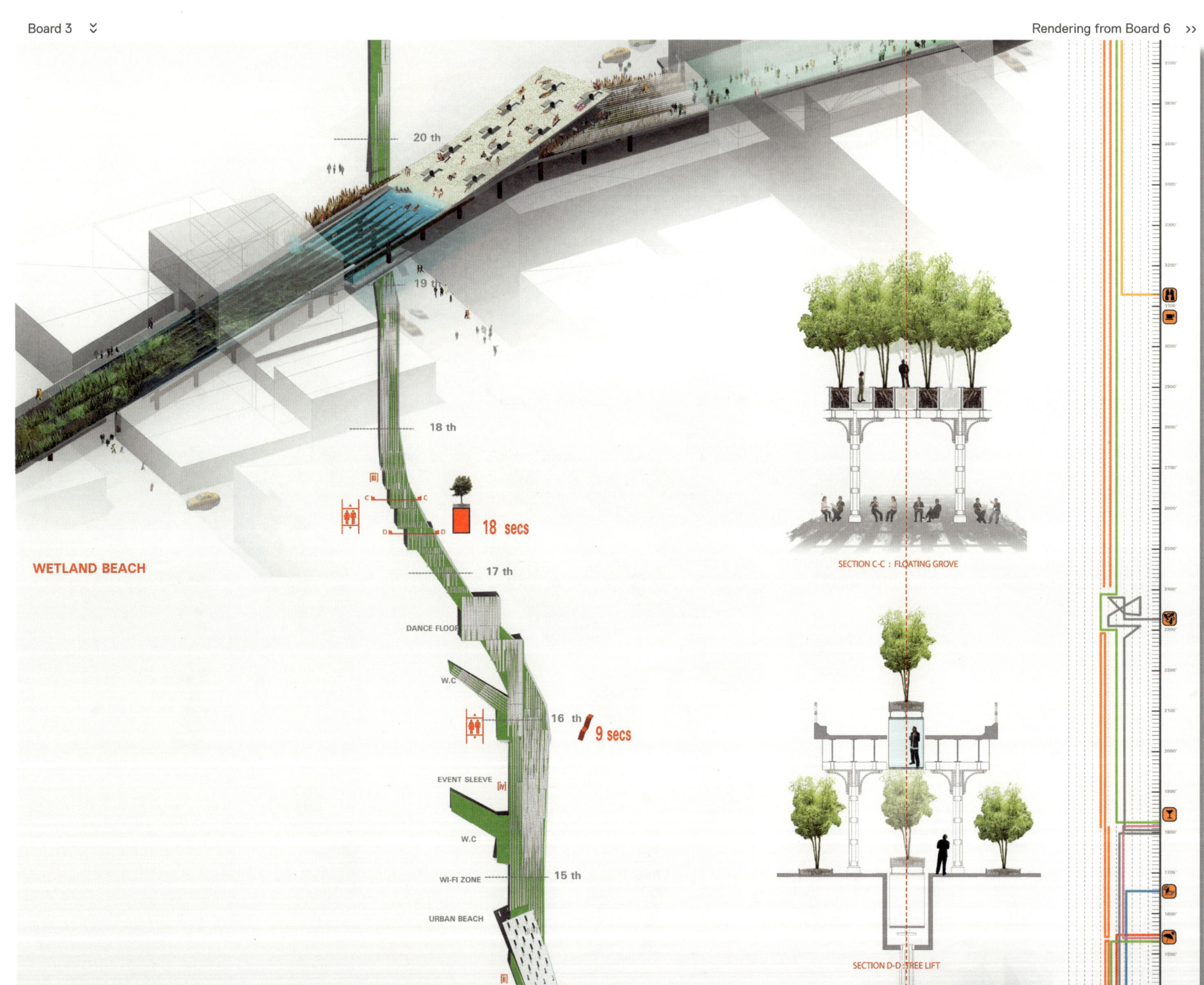

FLAVOR YOUR NIGHT

FLAVOR YOUR NIGHT

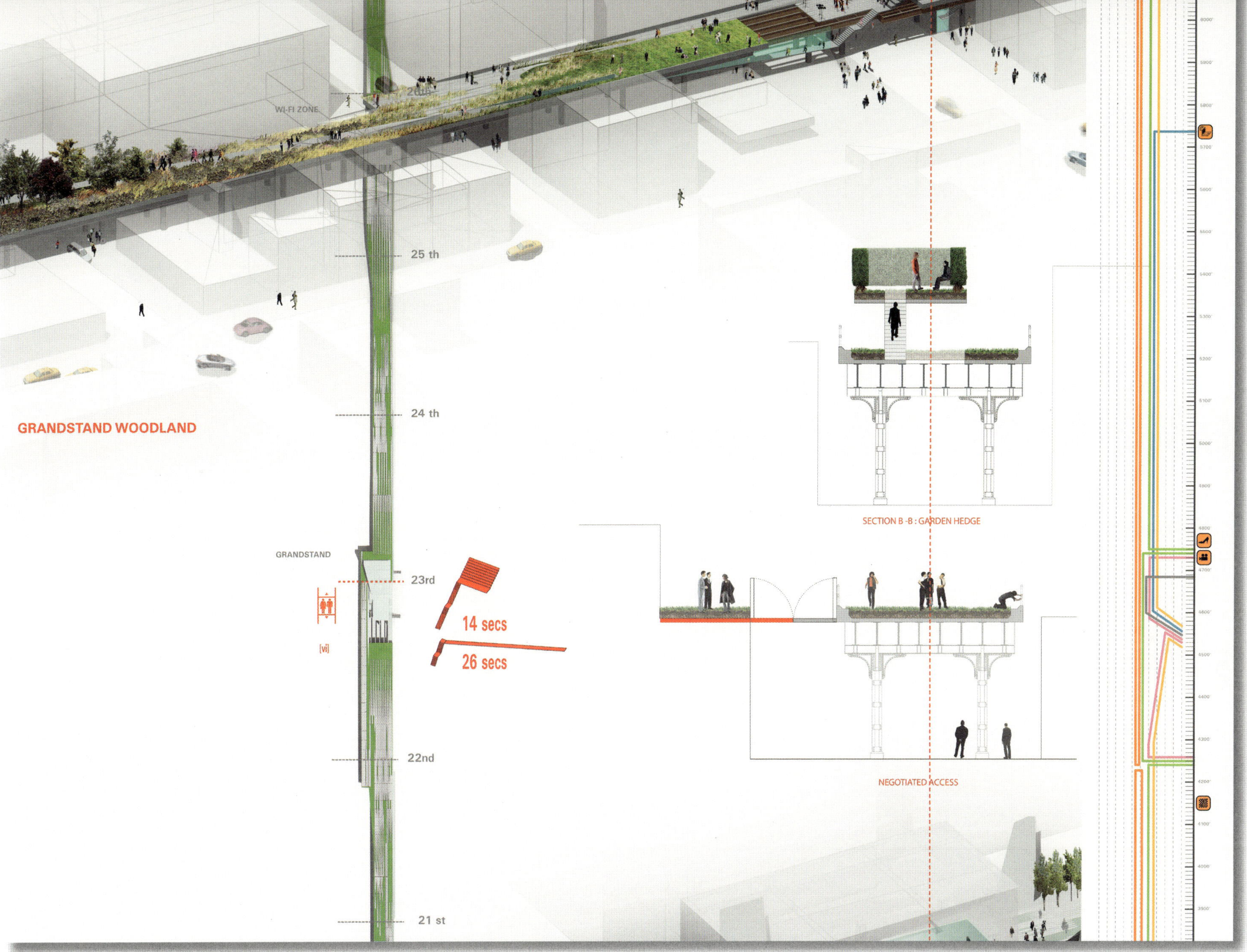

<< Rendering for New York Times Press Release Board 4 ^ Renderings from Boards 5 & 6 >>

what will grow here?

Board 4

Board 5

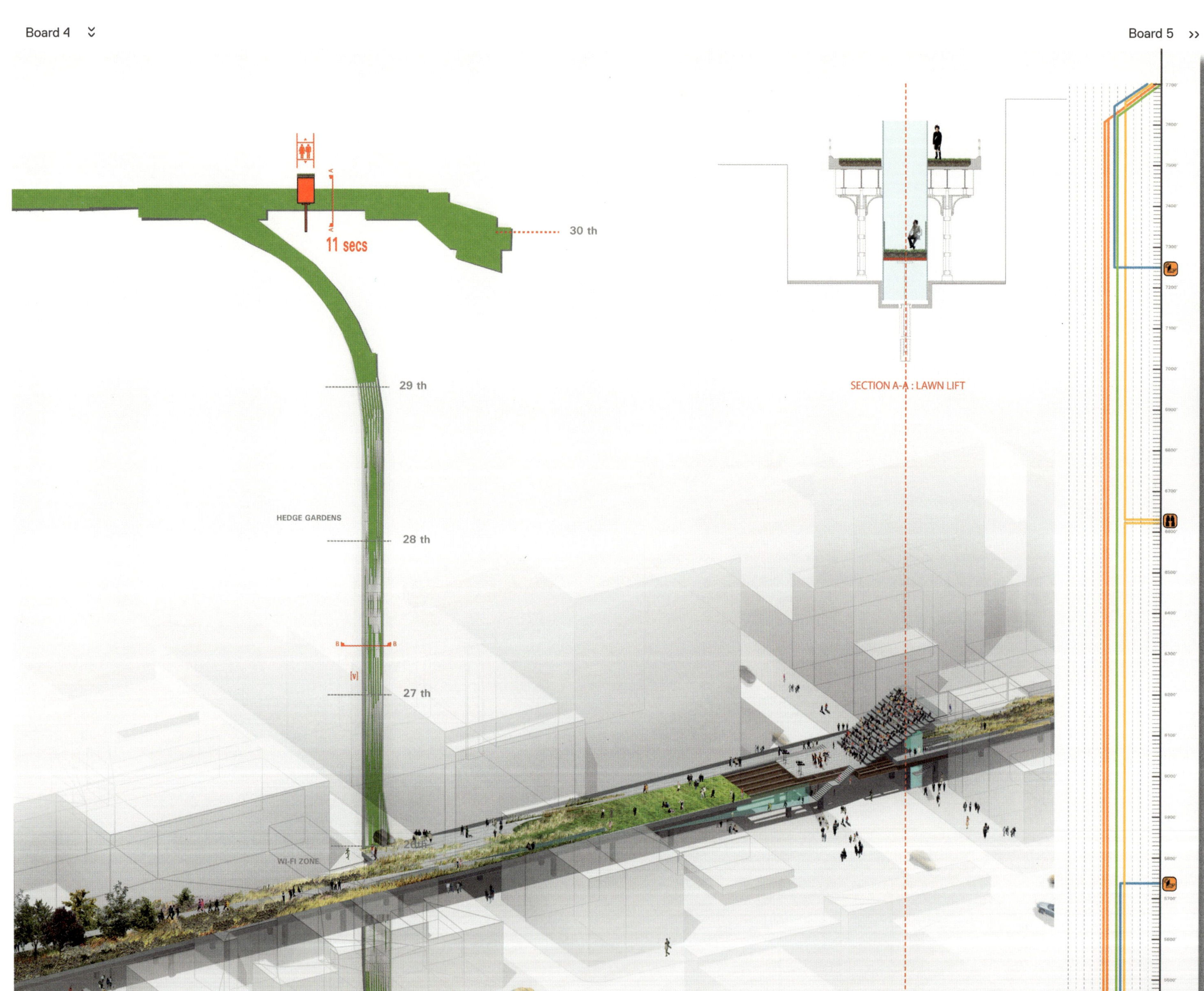

Ryder

AUGUST 14, 2004: WINNERS SELECTED

After a final vote in City Hall, James Corner Field Operations and Diller Scofidio + Renfro were announced as the winners. In a press release, the Friends of the High Line explained that the vision of the team—translating the High Line from a ruin to a park without losing all of its wildness—aligned with the founding mission of the organization and resonated most strongly with the jury.

The Arts

The New York Times

N E1

THURSDAY, AUGUST 12, 2004

Gardens in the Air Where the Rail Once Ran

Architects Selected to Make Over the High Line

SEPTEMBER 2004 – FEBRUARY 2005: ›› PHASE I REPORT

Limited resources required that the High Line be constructed in phases. The Phase I Report, completed six months after the end of the competition, included two major components: a Framework Plan for the overall structure, and a preliminary design of four blocks, from Gansevoort Street to 15th Street. The document laid out the essential design principles that would guide the realization of the one-and-a-half-mile (2.4 km) park over the course of the next decade.

02.18.05
THE HIGH LINE
PHASE I REPORT
FRAMEWORK PLAN
PRELIMINARY DESIGN OF SECTION 1A
EXISTING CONDITIONS REPORTS
FIELD OPERATIONS
DILLER SCOFIDIO + RENFRO

DESIGN PRINCIPLES

- Autonomy and Consistency: Keep the High Line separate from but responsive to its surroundings with a design that is continuous and consistent rather than segmented.
- Slowness: Develop a varied and intimate choreography to encourage visitors to keep a slow pace and allow themselves to be distracted.
- The Otherwordly: Build upon and enhance unusual, wild, and found conditions.
- Reveal Structure: Expose and dramatize the physical characteristics of the railway trestle.
- Sightlines and Overlooks: Support north-south sightlines and east-west views.
- Topside and Underside: Explore connections between the top and bottom of the structure.
- Program Mix: Cultivate a diverse range of activities at all times of day and year that promote exchange and chance encounters.
- Limit Consumption: Limit commercial activity and manage connections to adjacent developments.

DESIGN GOALS

- Create an innovative public space.
- Create a distinct identity that draws on the unusual found conditions of the site.
- Provide access points that respect the character of the structure.
- Encourage meaningful relationships between neighborhoods and buildings.
- Preserve the industrial presence, character, and spirit of the High Line.
- Promote public art projects that engage with the site.
- Create a safe, secure park that meets all code requirements.
- Create a dynamic public landscape that reflects seasonal change.
- Create an environmentally sustainably and cost-effective project.
- Create a flexible and responsive framework design capable of phased implementation over time.

KEEP IT SIMPLE

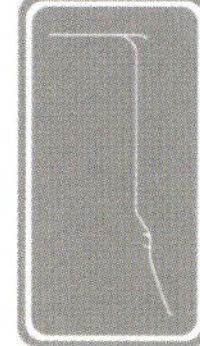

KEEP IT WILD

KEEP IT QUIET

KEEP IT SLOW

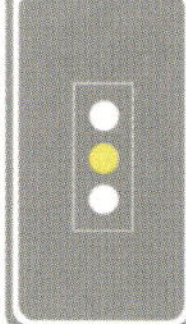

KEEP IT

PRESERVE NORTH-SOUTH SIGHTLINES AND LINEAR CONSISTENCY OF THE HIGH LINE

PRESERVE SLOW MEANDERING EXPERIENCE THROUGH VARIED CONDITIONS

PRESERVE UNUSUAL AND FOUND CONDITIONS ON THE HIGH LINE

PRESERVE WILD, OPPORTUNISTIC LANDSCAPE BY ENHANCING EXISTING PLANT SPECIES

PRESERVE INDUSTRIAL PRESENCE OF THE HIGH LINE AT THE STREET LEVEL

PRESERVE AND REVEAL THE STRUCTURE PROVIDING OPPORTUNITIES TO INHABIT AND APPRECIATE DETAILS

PRESERVE TYPICAL RAILINGS AND UPGRADE TO FULFILL CODE AND ENSURE SAFETY

Physiognomic Vegetation Zones

RW **RANK WEED:**
early successional weed species

LG **LOW GRASSLAND:**
predominantly native grasses

LGE **LOW GRASSLAND WITH ENCROACHMENT:**
intermediate zone between rank weed and low grassland communities

SW **SUMAC WOODS:**
shady zone with woody vegetation as the dominant species

WET POCKETS:
wet areas in shallow depressions

OT **OTHER:**
gravel, moss, debris, or covered tunnel areas

SUN EXPOSURE:
Shady to full shade
WIND EXPOSURE:
Partially exposed
SPECIES IDENTIFIED:
Celastrus orbiculatus (Chinese bittersweet)
Parthenocissus quinquefolia (Virginia creeper)

NOTES:
Largest rank weed zone, located at the southern end; dominated by invasive vines that commonly occur in disturbed landscapes.

SUN EXPOSURE:
Partial to full sun
WIND EXPOSURE:
Exposed

NOTES:
Moss, gravel, rocks, glass

SUN EXPOSURE:
Full sun
WIND EXPOSURE:
Exposed

NOTES:
Decked over, no eco:
exposed rail ties (no rail), with mosses; wood pile

SUN EXPOSURE:
Full shade
WIND EXPOSURE:
Full shelter (tunnel)

SPECIES IDENTIFIED:
No eco

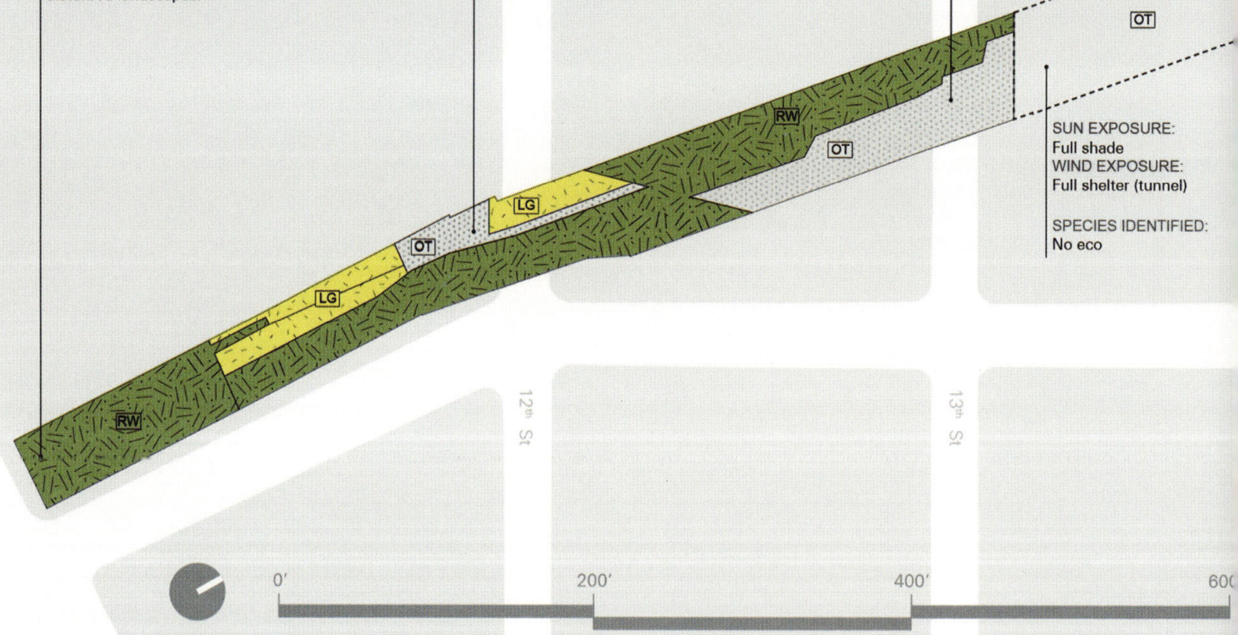

MICROCLIMATES

In the fall of 2004, the design team worked with Applied Ecological Services to conduct an ecological assessment of existing conditions along the High Line, from Gansevoort Street to 30th Street. The portion north of 30th Street at the Rail Yards was not assessed, as this section had yet to be acquired as part of the park. This drawing maps the observed conditions, inventories existing plant species, and provides general notes and initial conclusions on the ecological character of the site.

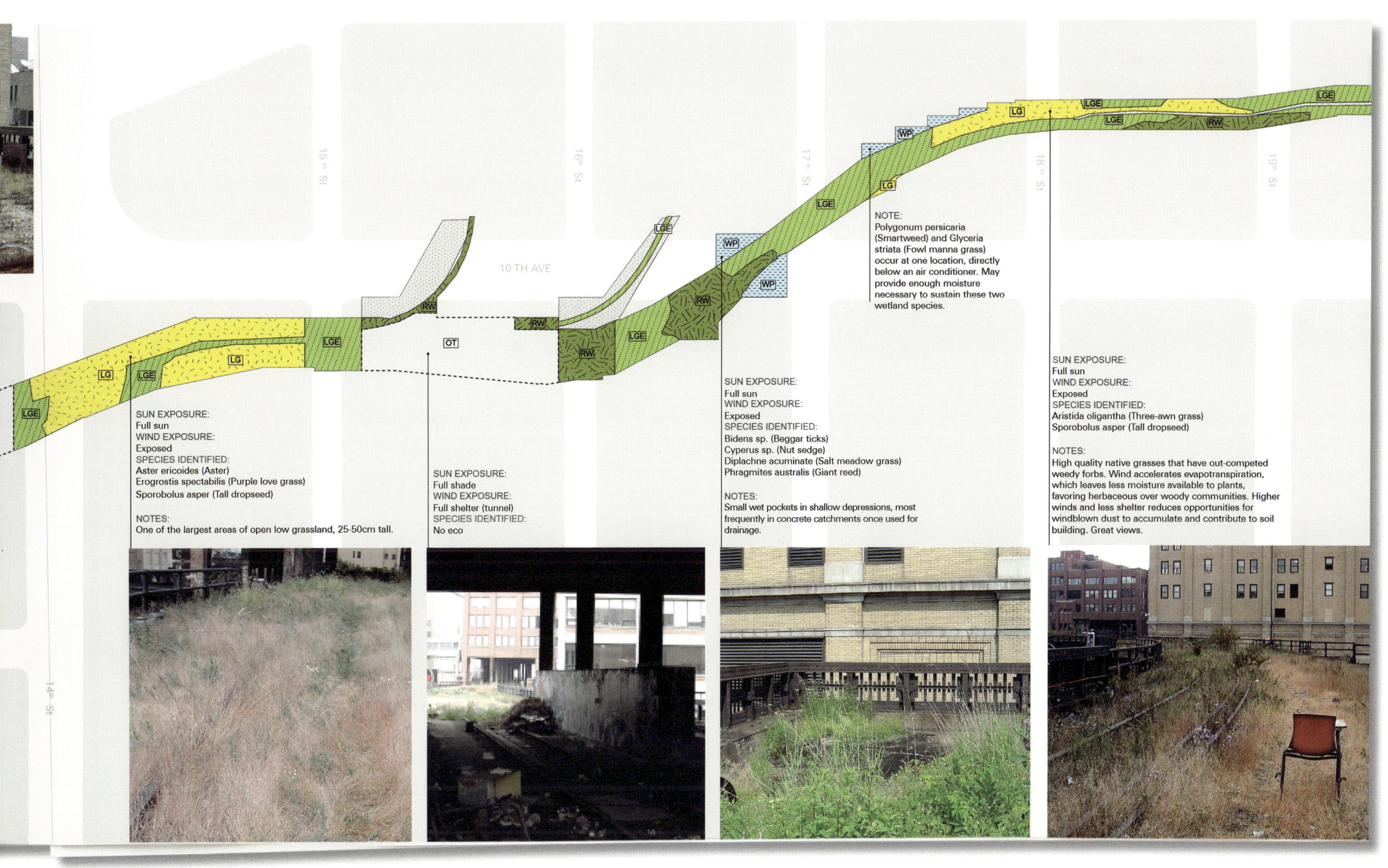

15th St
16th St
17th St
18th St
19th St
14th St
10 TH AVE
LGE
LG
RW
OT
WP
SUN EXPOSURE:
Full sun
WIND EXPOSURE:
Exposed
SPECIES IDENTIFIED:
Aster ericoides (Aster)
Erogrostis spectabilis (Purple love grass)
Sporobolus asper (Tall dropseed)
NOTES:
One of the largest areas of open low grassland, 25-50cm tall.
SUN EXPOSURE:
Full shade
WIND EXPOSURE:
Full shelter (tunnel)
SPECIES IDENTIFIED:
No eco
SUN EXPOSURE:
Full sun
WIND EXPOSURE:
Exposed
SPECIES IDENTIFIED:
Bidens sp. (Beggar ticks)
Cyperus sp. (Nut sedge)
Diplachne acuminate (Salt meadow grass)
Phragmites australis (Giant reed)
NOTES:
Small wet pockets in shallow depressions, most frequently in concrete catchments once used for drainage.
NOTE:
Polygonum persicaria (Smartweed) and Glyceria striata (Fowl manna grass) occur at one location, directly below an air conditioner. May provide enough moisture necessary to sustain these two wetland species.
SUN EXPOSURE:
Full sun
WIND EXPOSURE:
Exposed
SPECIES IDENTIFIED:
Aristida oligantha (Three-awn grass)
Sporobolus asper (Tall dropseed)
NOTES:
High quality native grasses that have out-competed weedy forbs. Wind accelerates evapotranspiration, which leaves less moisture available to plants, favoring herbaceous over woody communities. Higher winds and less shelter reduces opportunities for windblown dust to accumulate and contribute to soil building. Great views.

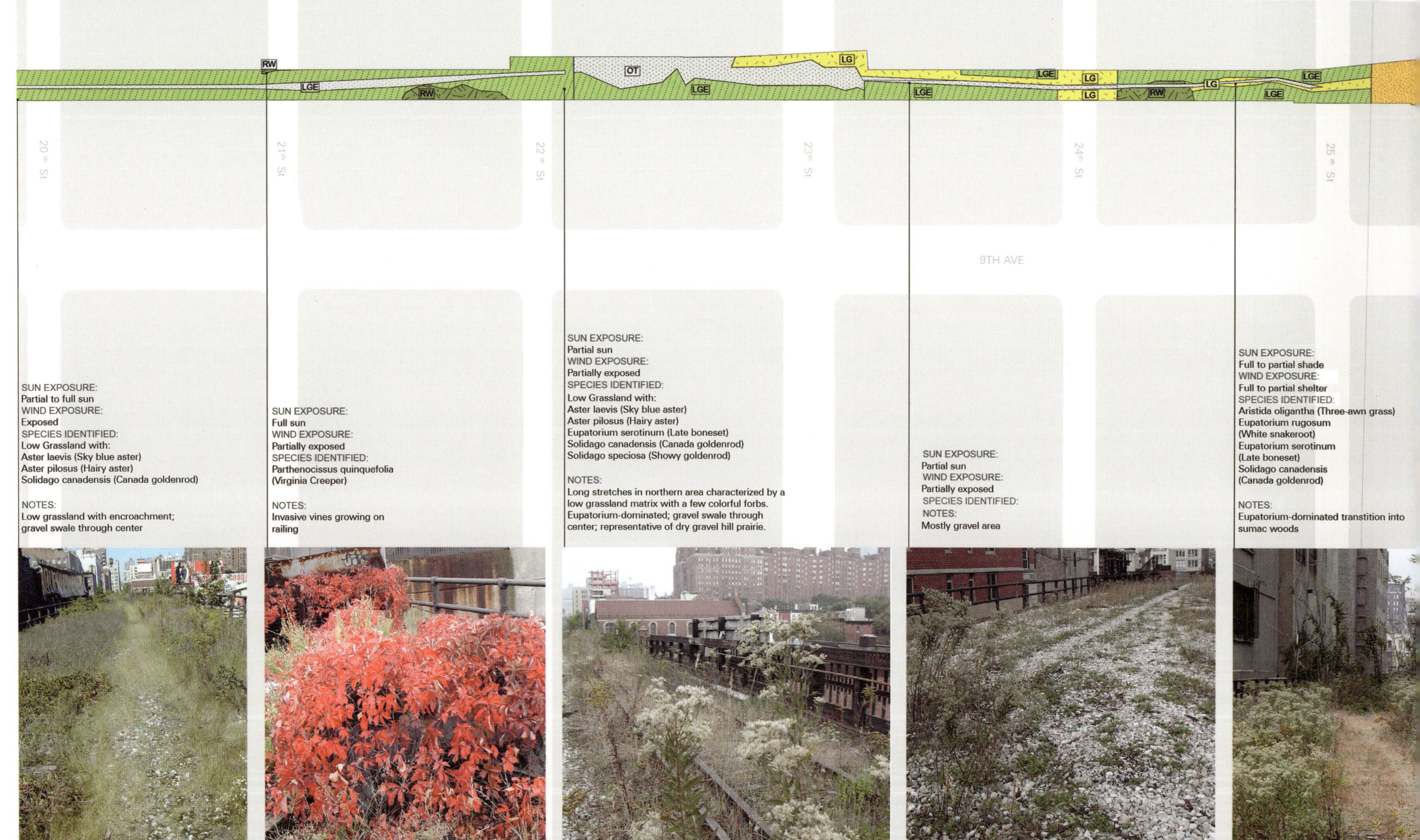

SUN EXPOSURE:
Partial to full sun
WIND EXPOSURE:
Exposed
SPECIES IDENTIFIED:
Low Grassland with:
Aster laevis (Sky blue aster)
Aster pilosus (Hairy aster)
Solidago canadensis (Canada goldenrod)

NOTES:
Low grassland with encroachment; gravel swale through center

SUN EXPOSURE:
Full sun
WIND EXPOSURE:
Partially exposed
SPECIES IDENTIFIED:
Parthenocissus quinquefolia
(Virginia Creeper)

NOTES:
Invasive vines growing on railing

SUN EXPOSURE:
Partial sun
WIND EXPOSURE:
Partially exposed
SPECIES IDENTIFIED:
Low Grassland with:
Aster laevis (Sky blue aster)
Aster pilosus (Hairy aster)
Eupatorium serotinum (Late boneset)
Solidago canadensis (Canada goldenrod)
Solidago speciosa (Showy goldenrod)

NOTES:
Long stretches in northern area characterized by a low grassland matrix with a few colorful forbs. Eupatorium-dominated; gravel swale through center; representative of dry gravel hill prairie.

SUN EXPOSURE:
Partial sun
WIND EXPOSURE:
Partially exposed
SPECIES IDENTIFIED:
NOTES:
Mostly gravel area

SUN EXPOSURE:
Full to partial shade
WIND EXPOSURE:
Full to partial shelter
SPECIES IDENTIFIED:
Aristida oligantha (Three-awn grass)
Eupatorium rugosum
(White snakeroot)
Eupatorium serotinum
(Late boneset)
Solidago canadensis
(Canada goldenrod)

NOTES:
Eupatorium-dominated transtition into sumac woods

RW
LGE
RW
LG
26th St
28th St
29th St
30th St
10 TH AVE
SUN EXPOSURE:
Shade
WIND EXPOSURE:
Sheltered
SPECIES IDENTIFIED:
Rhus typhina (Staghorn sumac)
Eupatorium rugosum (White snakeroot)
Eupatorium serotinum (Late boneset)
Euphorbia sp. (Spurge)
Aster laevis (Smooth aster)
NOTES:
Very special and discrete area flanked by tall buildings, creating a canyon-like effect. Among the shadiest and smallest zones, and the only zone where woody vegetation is dominant. A similar condition can be expected to develop more quickly in areas of the site where simliar canyon-like effects may exist in the future.
SUN EXPOSURE:
Full sun
WIND EXPOSURE:
Partially exposed
SPECIES IDENTIFIED:
Rhus typhina (Staghorn sumac)
NOTES:
Gravel, garden
SUN EXPOSURE:
Full sun
WIND EXPOSURE:
Partially exposed
SPECIES IDENTIFIED:
Rhus typhina (Staghorn sumac)
NOTES:
Gravel, garden
SUN EXPOSURE:
Full sun
WIND EXPOSURE:
Exposed
SPECIES IDENTIFIED:
Sporobolus asper
(Tall dropseed)
NOTES:
Special low grassland

ACCESS POINTS

Access points are conceived as durational experiences, from fast elevators that pop up directly into the surreal urban meadow, to leisurely ramps that allow visitors to gradually emerge across the new horizon of the park. 'Slow stairs' throughout the park prolong the experience of transitioning from the frenetic pace of the city street to the slower pace of the park above. Each entrance is strategically positioned under, within, or above the High Line to provide close-up contact with the historic structure.

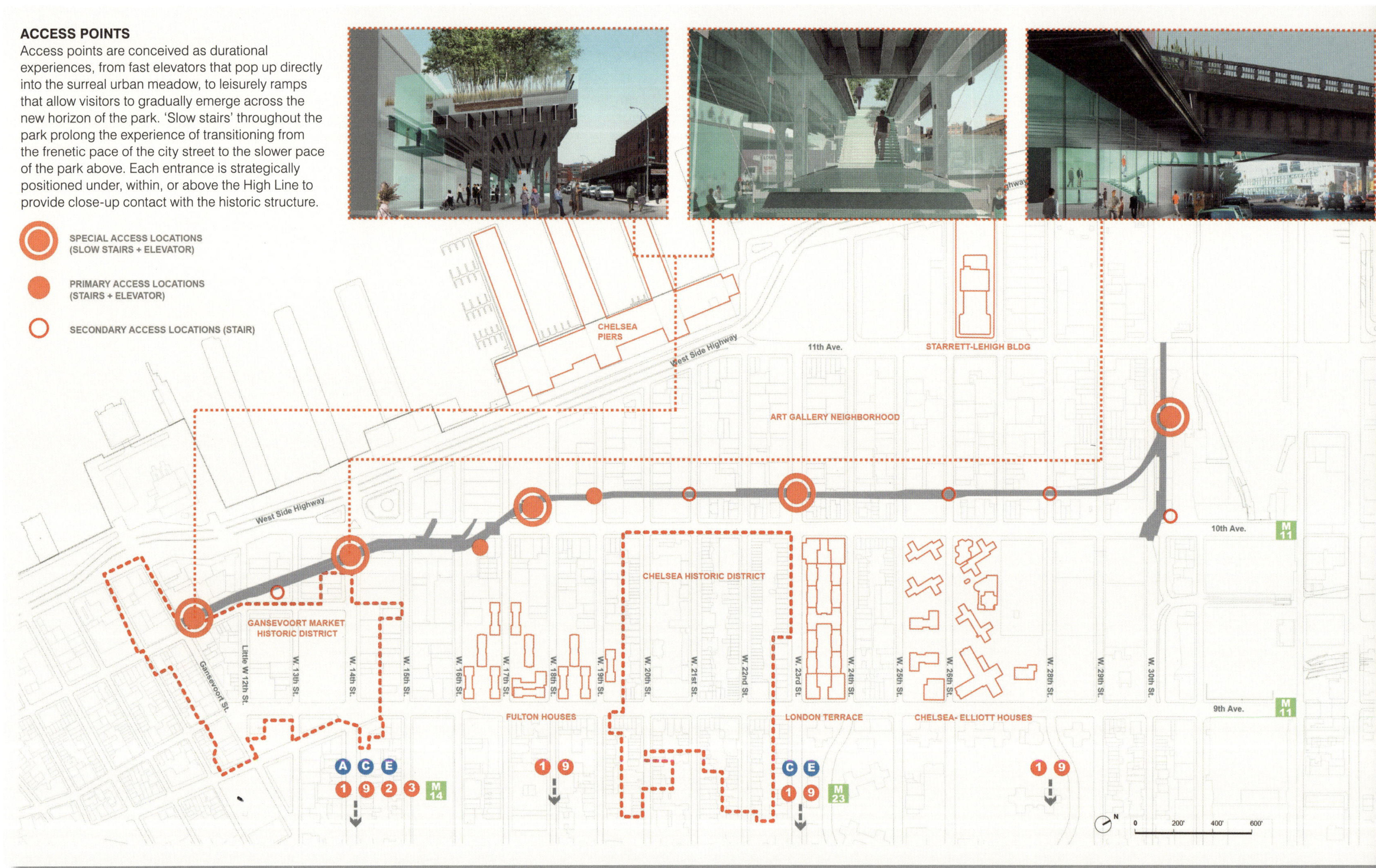

PLANKING STRATEGY

Rather than separating pathways from plantings, the park's striated system of modular planking blurs the boundary between hard and soft surfaces. Tapered concrete planks comb into planting beds of thick vegetation, creating indeterminate areas of paving that encourage the public to meander. This system allows for varying ratios of hard and soft surfaces throughout the park as it transitions from high-use gathering spaces (100 percent hard) to densely planted gardens (100 percent soft), and every gradient in between. Seamlessly adapting to the demands of different areas, the park's surface is both continuous and variable, allowing for diverse social and sensory atmospheres to emerge along its length.

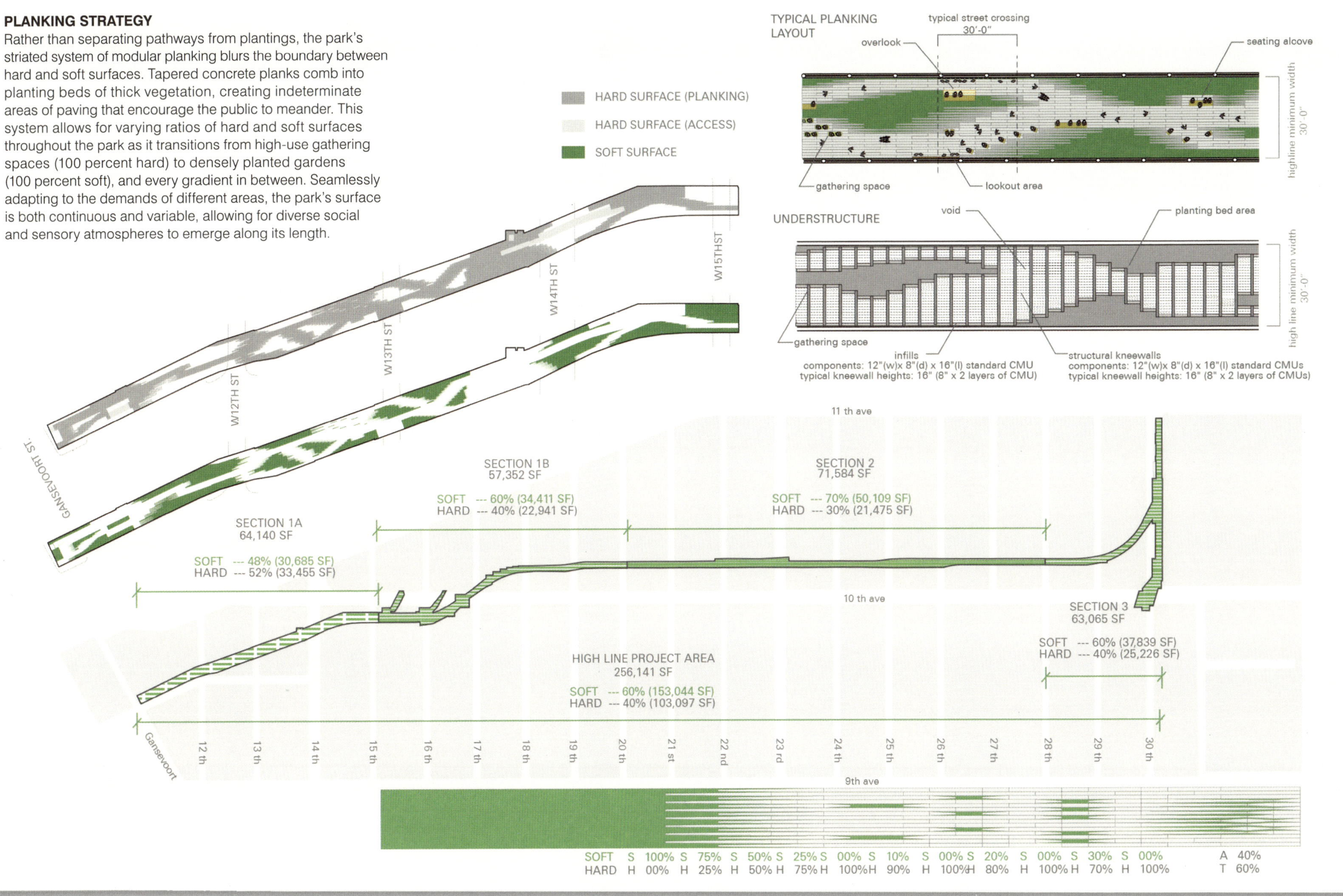

grama grass
Bouteloua curtipendula
1-3′ tall

blue grama
Bouteloua gracilis
1-2′ tall

purple lovegrass
Eragrostis spectabilis
1-2′ tall

prairie junegrass
Koeleria macrantha
3′ tall

flowering spurge
Euphorbia corollata
2-4″ tall

prairie dropseed
Sporobolus heterolepsis
2-4′ tall

NATIVE GRASS MATRIX

butterfly milkweed
Asciepias tuberosa
1-2.5′ tall

purple prairie clover
Dalea purpurea
2 tall

shooting star
Dodecatheon meadia
5-1.5′ tall

flowering spurge
Euphorbia corollata
2-4″ tall

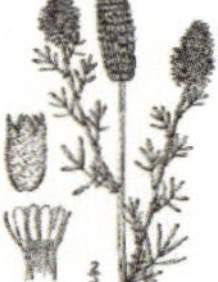

WOODLAND THICKET

PLANTING APPROACH

The planting strategy builds upon the wild character of the High Line and works with the environmental conditions and microclimates associated with the site: sunny, shady, wet, dry, windy, noisy, open, and sheltered. The resulting landscape is primarily native, resilient, and low-maintenance. Variety in height, color, form, and density creates a vibrant collage of textures and atmospheres. Species were carefully selected to maintain year-round change and surprise.

Grassland mixes rise one to three feet (0.3 – 0.9 m) above the surface of the High Line, creating a sense of enclosure that reinforces the intimate character of the site. Wetland and dry woodland species add variation to the horticultural mix. While most of the recommended grassland species are typical of native dry-gravel prairies, some non-invasive, non-native species were incorporated into the planting scheme to create punctuated, theatrical spaces for plants with special tactile properties, fragrances, and color palettes.

SEASONAL CHANGES ▶

SPRING

bottle gentian
Gentiana andrewsii
1-2' tall

prairie smoke
Geum triflorum
8"-1.5' tall

wild petunia
Ruellia humilis
8"-2' tall

allegheny serviceberry
Amalanchier laevis
12-25' tall

american hazelnut
Corylus americana
8-15' tall

eastern wahoo
Euonymus atropurpureus
12-20' tall

fragant sumac
Rhus aromatica
2'-6' tall

winged sumac
Rhus copallina
7-15' tall

hillside blueberry
Vaccinium pallidum
2' tall

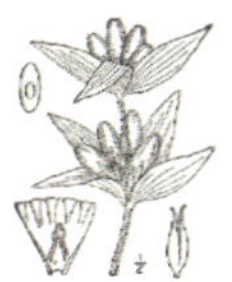

FLOWERING PERENNIALS

SUMMER

FALL

WINTER

SEATING

The custom designed 'peel-up' benches appear to grow out of the planking to form a cantilevered seating surface, oriented toward particular views and aggregated for increased sociability. Benches cluster at key intersections and are less present along narrow walkways or denser planting areas. The benches are variations on a standard unit—they differ in length and are designed both with and without back supports. Unique variations include a two-part double bench, a seesaw bench on a pivot, and intersecting benches at a crossroad of foot traffic.

Lounge chairs populate the sundeck. Some of these chairs are on wheels that can roll across the original train tracks and converge to form communal seating areas. Throughout, lighting is integrated beneath the benches to illuminate adjacent paths.

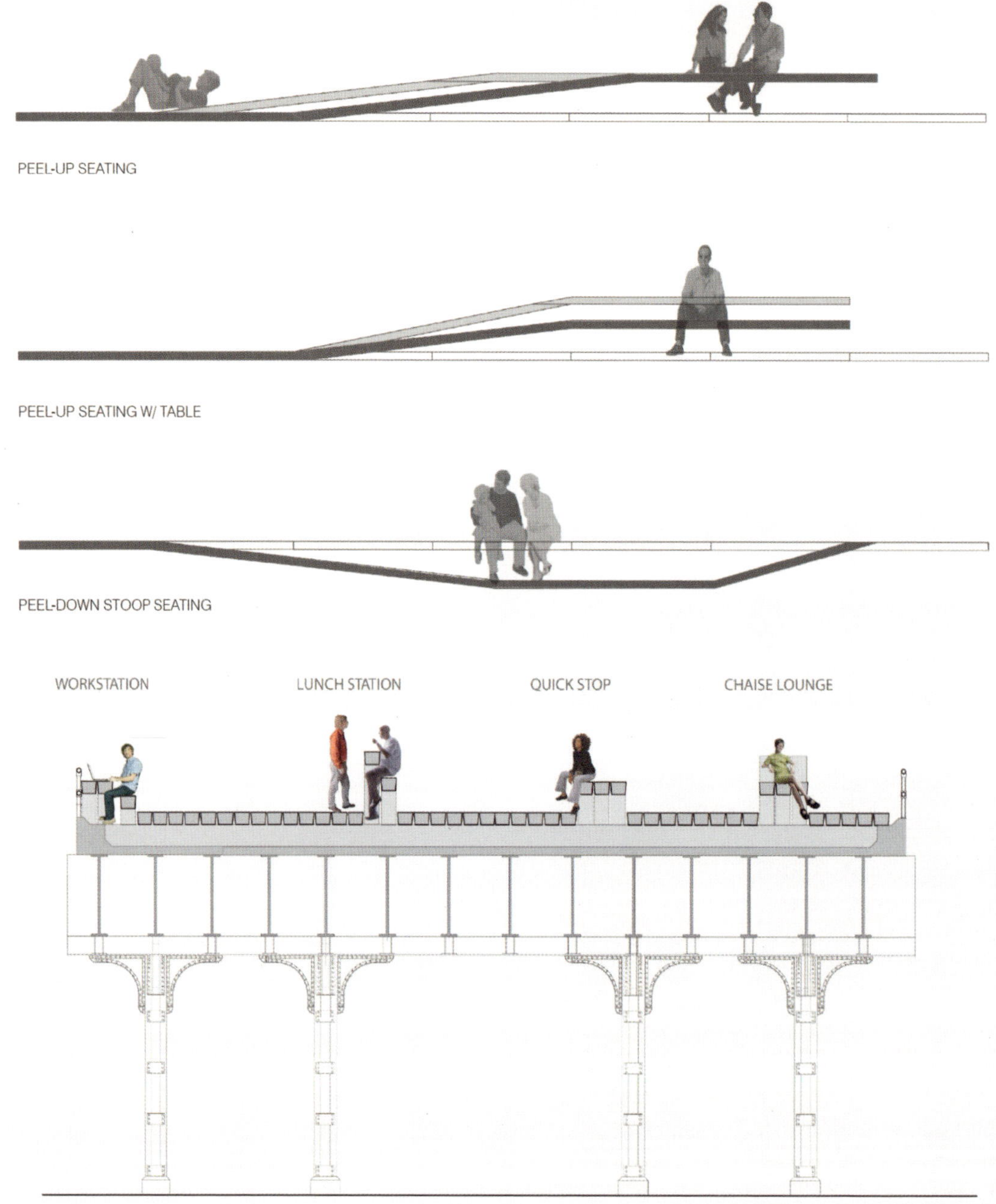

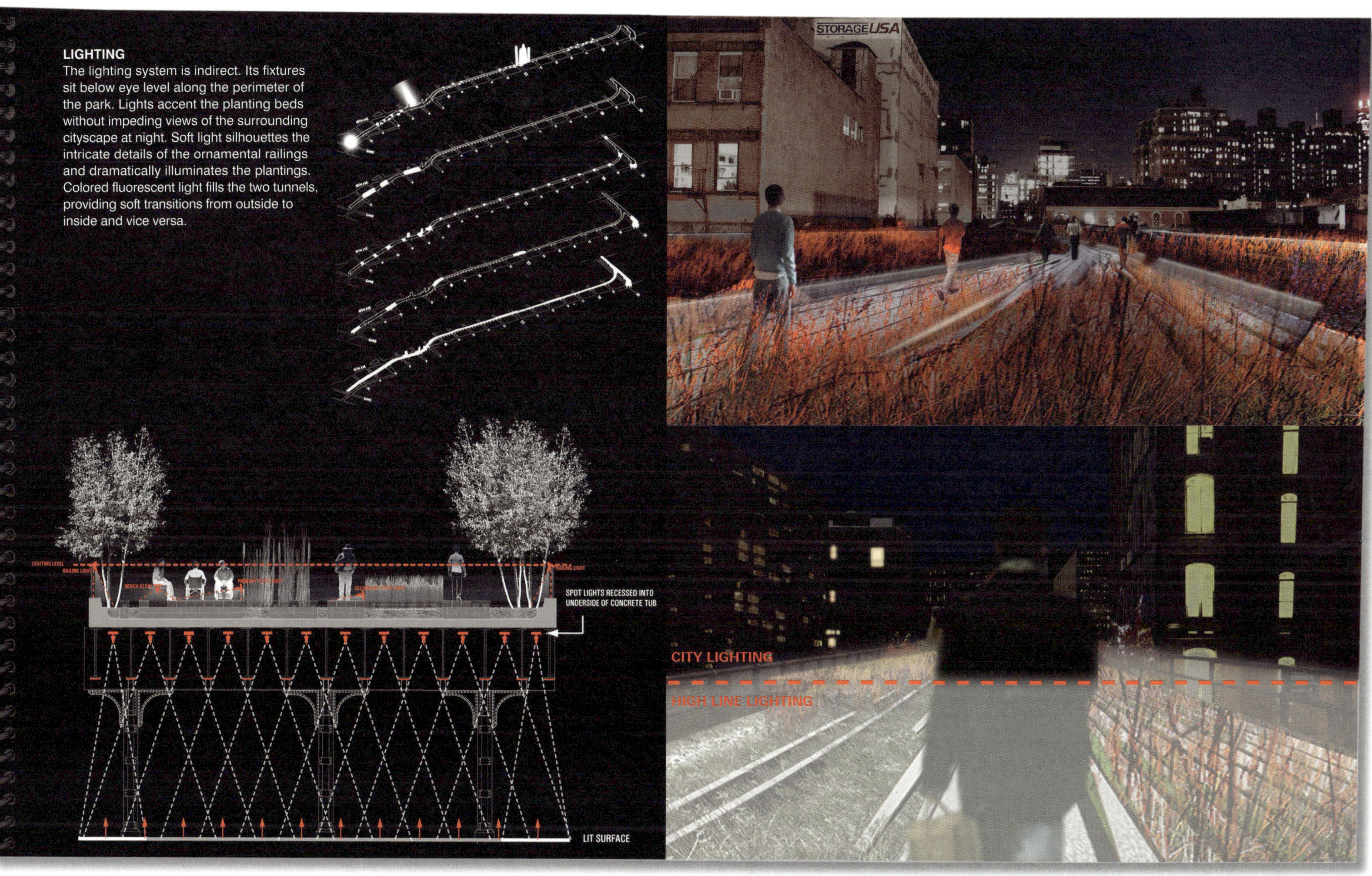
LIGHTING

The lighting system is indirect. Its fixtures sit below eye level along the perimeter of the park. Lights accent the planting beds without impeding views of the surrounding cityscape at night. Soft light silhouettes the intricate details of the ornamental railings and dramatically illuminates the plantings. Colored fluorescent light fills the two tunnels, providing soft transitions from outside to inside and vice versa.

APRIL - OCTOBER 2005: MOMA SHOW

The Museum of Modern Art's Department of Architecture & Design exhibited the preliminary design of the High Line to inaugurate the reopening of the museum after a long period of renovation. The show was an unexpected hit, and the museum extended its scheduled run from three to six months. The exhibition included Joel Sternfeld's 2001 photographs of the site and Steven Holl's Bridge of Houses proposal, conceived for the High Line in 1980. New materials by the design team filled the gallery walls. A model of a section of the future park hung suspended at the center.

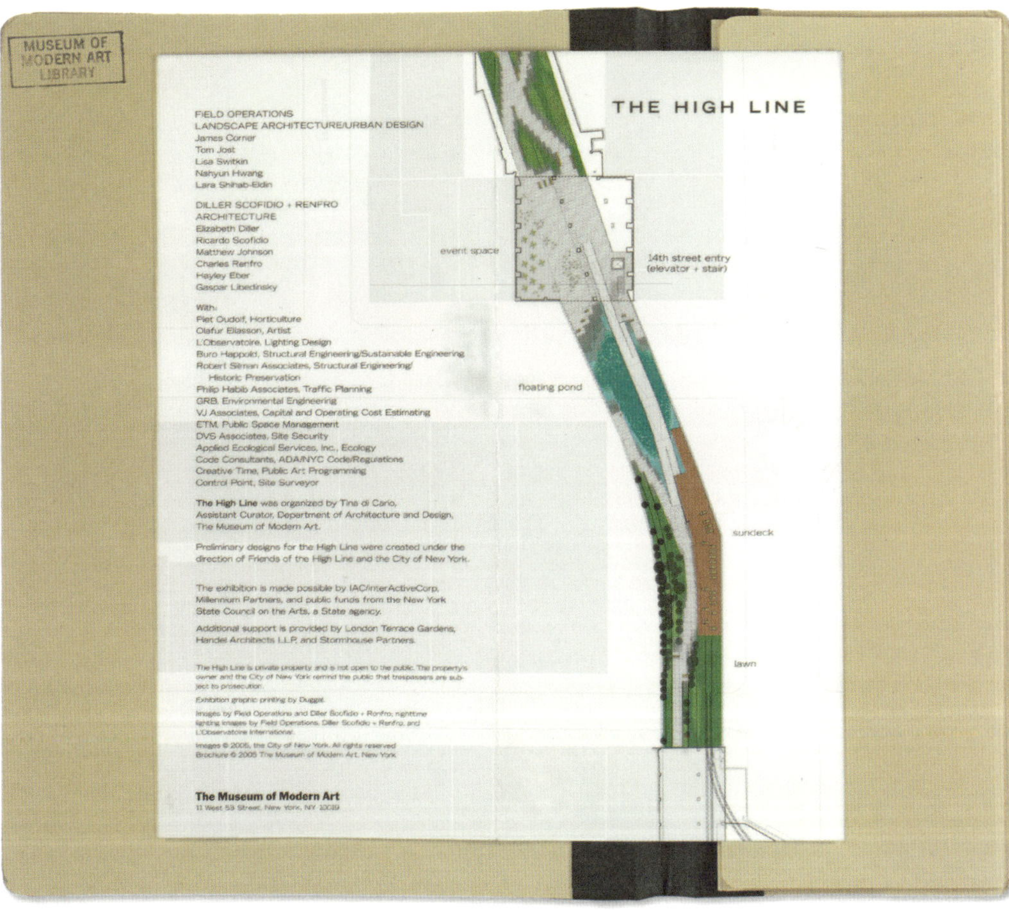
MUSEUM OF MODERN ART LIBRARY

THE HIGH LINE

FIELD OPERATIONS
LANDSCAPE ARCHITECTURE/URBAN DESIGN
James Corner
Tom Jost
Lisa Switkin
Nahyun Hwang
Lara Shihab-Eldin

DILLER SCOFIDIO + RENFRO
ARCHITECTURE
Elizabeth Diller
Ricardo Scofidio
Matthew Johnson
Charles Renfro
Hayley Eber
Gaspar Libedinsky

With:
Piet Oudolf, Horticulture
Olafur Eliasson, Artist
L'Observatoire, Lighting Design
Buro Happold, Structural Engineering/Sustainable Engineering
Robert Silman Associates, Structural Engineering/ Historic Preservation
Philip Habib Associates, Traffic Planning
GRB. Environmental Engineering
VJ Associates, Capital and Operating Cost Estimating
ETM, Public Space Management
DVS Associates, Site Security
Applied Ecological Services, Inc., Ecology
Code Consultants, ADA/NYC Code/Regulations
Creative Time, Public Art Programming
Control Point, Site Surveyor

The High Line was organized by Tina di Carlo, Assistant Curator, Department of Architecture and Design, The Museum of Modern Art.

Preliminary designs for the High Line were created under the direction of Friends of the High Line and the City of New York.

The exhibition is made possible by IAC/InterActiveCorp, Millennium Partners, and public funds from the New York State Council on the Arts, a State agency.

Additional support is provided by London Terrace Gardens, Handel Architects LLP, and Stormhouse Partners.

The High Line is private property and is not open to the public. The property's owner and the City of New York remind the public that trespassers are subject to prosecution.

Exhibition graphic printing by Duggal.

Images by Field Operations and Diller Scofidio + Renfro; nighttime lighting images by Field Operations, Diller Scofidio + Renfro, and L'Observatoire International.

Images © 2005, the City of New York. All rights reserved
Brochure © 2005 The Museum of Modern Art, New York

The Museum of Modern Art
11 West 53 Street, New York, NY 10019

The Paul J. Sachs
Drawings Galleries
WEST 14TH STREET

FUNDRAISING

The team collaborated closely with the Friends of the High Line in their fundraising and community awareness efforts, assisting the organization with neighborhood forums, benefit dinners, and site tours. From left: "Meat Dress," 2005; Florent Bi-Decade(nt) Ball and Miss Meat Market Gown Contest, October 2005; Bastille Day at Florent, July 2004.

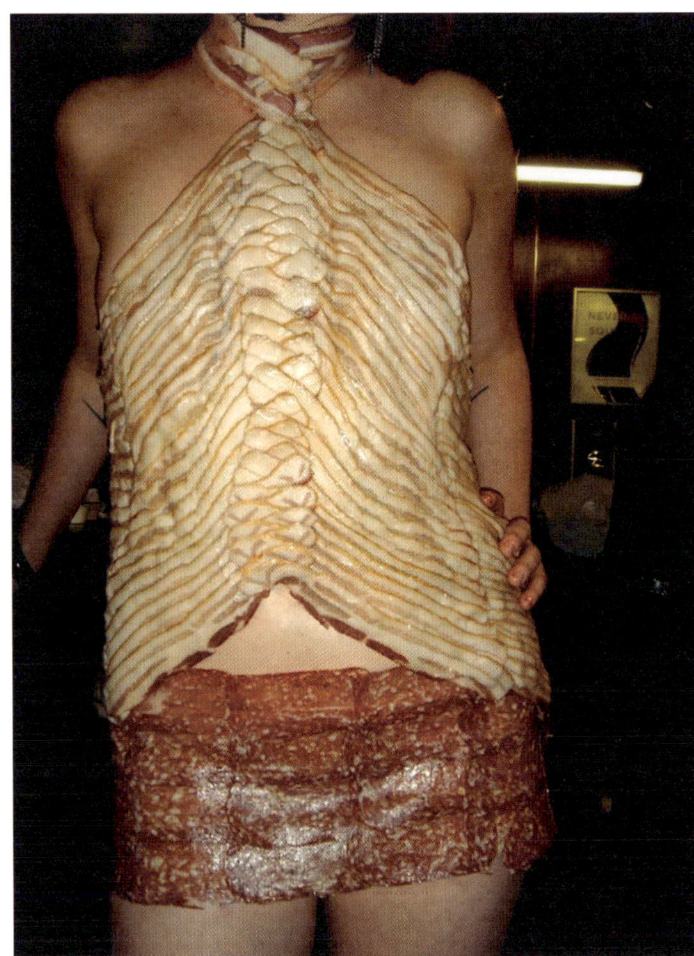

Fundraising events ranged considerably, from an adults-only Miss Meat Market competition at the Roxy (DS+R took home the first prize with their lunch-meat dress) to kid-friendly block parties. Clockwise from top left: 4th Annual Summer Benefit & Design Competition Preview, July 2004; 5th Annual Summer Benefit, July 2005; The Kitchen/ High Line Block Party on West 19th Street, September 2005; 6th Annual Summer Benefit, June 2006; "Chalk Shoes to the High Line" performance led by Julia Mandle, April 2008.

CORE DESIGN TEAM

Elizabeth Diller	Matthew Johnson	James Corner	Ricardo Scofidio	Lisa Switkin
Diller Scofidio + Renfro	Diller Scofidio + Renfro	James Corner Field Operations	Diller Scofidio + Renfro	James Corner Field Operations

CONVERSATION PART TWO: PROCESS

MODERATOR: How did the collaboration come about? What was your disposition entering the collaboration, and how did it play out in the working dynamic?

LISA SWITKIN (LS): After the Friends of the High Line and the City of New York made a request for qualifications, our first move was to assemble a team. The novelty of the project demanded a fresh approach and collaborators who were challenging their disciplines — working both within the boundaries of their respective professions and at their margins. We were inspired by the theatricality of DS+R's work, especially because our own office was trying to rethink landscape architecture. We called Piet Oudolf right away because of his expertise in perennial and meadow plantings, which seemed right for the project.

ELIZABETH DILLER (ED): When James and Lisa approached us about working together, we thought it would be a perfect match because we were all misfits in our respective fields. Our various outsider approaches uniquely qualified us to breathe new life into this industrial relic. We started without roles or rules. The early work was a seamless collaboration across disciplines. As the project progressed, we each had to delve deeply into our particular expertise.

JAMES CORNER (JC): No single firm could have had the right experience for this project. It was outside of everyone's particular expertise. It demanded new thinking, especially as the design evolved. It became technically challenging to meet codes and regulations, to bring the structure up to environmental and public-safety standards. The High Line's narrow dimensions and shallow depth created accessibility issues and made planting difficult. The historical railings weren't high enough to be code-compliant, and we struggled to keep the lighting low while still meeting regulations. Given these hurdles, the multidisciplinary, collaborative character of the team was essential. Field Operations was the project lead with DS+R as our partners.

What happened after you won the competition and you had to deal with actual stakeholders?

LS: We had a multiheaded client: Friends of the High Line, of course, and also four city agencies — the New York Economic Development Corporation held our first contract, and we worked with the Parks Department, the office of the mayor, and the Department of City Planning. Representatives from each of these entities formed the development team that we met with every two weeks. Everyone was passionate about the project and wanted to be involved in every decision.

MATTHEW JOHNSON (MJ): We brought the community along with us. Friends of the High Line organized several community engagements that started immediately after we won the competition and continued throughout the design process. We were able to share our ideas with the neighbors and get their direct feedback. The turnouts were substantial, and it was clear that the community was deeply invested in the High Line's success.

JC: We put forward a very strong poetic vision for the High Line in the competition phase, derived from the found conditions of the site. Of course, once we began working with all the stakeholders and dealing with the regulations and technical challenges of building a park in the air, it was a challenge to maintain this sense of vision while at the same time resolving so many day-to-day issues.

ED: Technical decisions were inseparable from our aesthetic and experiential goals and were guided by our design ethos of simplicity. Every decision was processed through multiple filters. For example, how do you get thirty feet (9 m) up from the street to the High Line? How many access points would there be along the one-and-a-half-mile (2.4 km) stretch? We could have stairs and elevators at every block, but why would we replicate the logic of the city grid? Alternatively, we could practice a rigid sparseness, placing access points every ten blocks, but perhaps too few egress points would leave visitors feeling trapped. What if you sensed someone following you and wanted to escape, but the next exit was a quarter mile (400 m) away? This led to the question: how would security actually be managed — personnel on foot, electric car, horseback, security cameras? In these discussions, qualitative, quantitative, and regulatory issues were inextricably bound together.

RICARDO SCOFIDIO (RS): There was no reference book on how to make a park thirty feet (9 m) in the air. Every convention of park design had to be reconsidered.

MJ: Safety was a recurring theme. How do we make people feel safe within these long stretches? How do we actually protect their safety? When the Department of Buildings asked us to work with the Department of Parks and Recreation on safety issues, they didn't have established guidelines for the hundreds of decisions we would have to make, so we had to build the rules along with the park. We developed custom security standards, culling from various sources of governance in order to provide guidance for our designs.

JC: Designing public space is extraordinarily challenging due to the stringency of regulations, which are notoriously conservative and risk-averse; consequently, it is very difficult to design public space in ways that are novel and fresh. However, because the High Line escaped all precedent, we were encouraged to propose unconventional solutions for social space: the paving, furnishings, planting, lighting, and signage were all designed for this particular project.

LS: In some ways, not having a default mode — the burden of the precedent — opened up our minds to think differently.

MJ: Yes, but having limited precedent also meant that we were sometimes subject to the most conservative regulations. For example, spanning the park over streets and sidewalks meant the structure would, by strict definition, qualify as a bridge. This meant it would need to be lined with oppressively high fences.

LS: Originally, the Department of Transportation mandated eight-foot (2.4 m) railings with a bear claw at every street crossing along the length of the High Line. Eventually, with the help of parks commissioner Adrian Benepe, we convinced them that three feet six inches (1 m) was sufficient.

RS: We researched bridges in New York built before the fencing restrictions were enacted. These regulations were ostensibly put in place to keep kids from throwing things — or each other — onto moving traffic.

Let's discuss the design features.

JC: We felt very strongly that the material vocabulary of the High Line should be simple and consistent across the entire mile-and-a-half (2.4 km). This required the design of a rational system that was flexible enough to provide variation. We drew inspiration from railroad design, marked by a systematic approach toward the constituent parts and the whole. The paving design in particular reflected a systematic approach that at the same time created a lot of variation and interest, especially in terms of how it interfaced with the planting.

ED: This lack of delineation was precisely what made the design distinctive. In a space as narrow as the High Line, the knee-jerk approach would have been to subdivide the available surface into two parallel lanes, one paved for walking, the other for planting — every species would stay in its distinct lane with no trespassing. This would have been efficient but aesthetically fatal for the project. Our strategy combined the vegetal and the mineral into a shared meandering surface made up of units of planting and paving to be combined in different proportions. People and plants could fluidly commingle.

JC: At first, the planking system met a lot of resistance because of the perceived need for curbs and clear separations in order to protect planting beds. It took considerable effort to design the details that resolved these issues to everyone's satisfaction: the small, beveled curb rim, the curvature and bump-up of the tapering planks, the dimensioning, spacing, and metrics of the planking layout, even the tactile finish of the surface.

ED: This new hybrid surface needed a design vocabulary of edge conditions that included the "tapered paver": a condition in which plants were encouraged to grow between joints, like shoots of grass pushing their way through cracks in a concrete sidewalk. We were all interested in how the site's found state of dereliction might inspire a design language and in how the metaphor of the ruin and its association with nostalgia and dystopia might be addressed. The site we inherited was evidence of the conquest of nature over culture. Now it was time for culture to step back in, but this time the two entities would coexist.

RS: We didn't want the plants to be imprisoned by hard-edged curbs; we wanted to blur the line between plants and hardscape. We were uninterested in the question of who contains whom, so we encouraged the plants to overtake the structure, to grow through the cracks.

JC: From railing to railing, the ground surface becomes a combed, integrated system. It transitions from thickets to meadows and from walkways to gathering areas. This "pathway-garden" was informed as much by agricultural and manufactured landscapes as by engineering and construction.

LS: Everything — plants, concrete, and the steel rail tracks — would occupy and share this single surface. Each of the tapers was sized so that you could fit a rail track or four-inch (100 mm) pot into it. In the early days of the project, I remember Jim playing with a piece of clay, combing through it to get a surface of ridges, furrows, and striated lines that we later used as a model for the surface concept.

RS: In the end, we all came to the conclusion that the paving and planting were to be two parts of one system; an indeterminate surface with soft and hard attributes.

MJ: That led to the irreducible industrial unit — a concrete plank supported on sleepers that allowed water to drain freely into the adjacent planting beds while also allowing space and access for conduits below.

Let's talk about the planting.

JC: One of the most powerful impressions when we first stepped onto the High Line was the effect of nature taking over the ruin. The High Line is a massive steel-and-concrete structure, and so the sheer abundance of plants and even birdsong was a real surprise. The ingenuity, variation, and opportunism of nature! The inspiration for the new design was right in front of us: this wild, self-seeded, multitextural, highly diverse meadow that was continually evolving, each year creating new conditions for more plants to grow.

ED: We discovered that dozens of native and immigrant species had found their way onto the High Line and taken root in the gravel ballast. This unruly found condition was the starting point.

RS: A lot of the planting species that we selected are what most people call weeds.

LS: Piet admitted to us that we pushed him out of his comfort zone. We kept pushing him to go wilder. We used a lot of plantings that would not normally be considered horticultural. But we wanted to evoke the spirit of the wild, to bring the weeds and common species together to create a rough, informal aura.

RS: I took an old friend — an amateur gardener — up for the first time. He kept stopping, wandering into the plant beds, looking around, and then he started to pull a few plants out. I was horrified and said, "What are you doing?" and he explained, "I'm pulling out the weeds! They shouldn't be in the garden!" I guess one man's weed is another's horticulture.

JC: Piet's choice of plantings helped amplify the found conditions — the range of textures, the dynamic succession from section to section, the seasonal variation in which every month there was something different in bloom. Even through the winter, the plantings hold a textural feel. We wanted mostly perennial and herbaceous plantings: wild, textural, intermixed, varied, more biodiverse than they would be even in nature. We chose plants that are highly robust, that can tolerate hot, dry summers as well as cold, windy winters. This was a radically new direction in terms of planting for public spaces.

LS: We scripted the experiences we wanted along the line — areas of transition, places to pause and gather, or intimate alcoves. First, we defined the sequence of experience that we wanted to create along the mile-and-a-half (2.4 km) and created a corresponding drawing for each new piece: "We want this to feel enclosed; we want this to feel open and light; we want this to be about textures; smell is important here; this should feel like a transition; this should feel intimate." Piet would then figure out a way to make those various atmospheres link together cohesively with natural gradients so there weren't any jarring transitions. We considered everything — blooms, foliage, texture, life cycles of plants, how they both fit into the established atmospheres and responded to the new features. The intent was to compose a dynamic landscape that changed constantly as the seasons shifted.

JC: The High Line might look natural, but it has required an incredible effort of design and maintenance to achieve that sense of effortlessness.

ED: Piet's approach to the seasonal cycle is unique. We're used to plants budding in spring, being lush and colorful in summer, and then waning in fall. Winter is usually the unnoticed season, when plants go dormant. For Piet, it's the most exciting time of year, because it's when you can see the structure of the plants. He has a beautifully morbid sensibility, designing for dormancy, when plants appear dead, but they are more powerful in this state than when they're in bloom.

LS: He carefully considered the seed head of each plant. Once one species starts growing, the seed head on another dies, becoming a skeletal form against a blooming backdrop.

JC: The planting has such a sense of life — a buzz, a scent, a tactility — alongside decay.

RS: Piet's hand drawings evoke his rich horticultural imagination — a great patchwork of color, symbols, and notations that abstractly capture the qualities, durations, and scents.

MJ: The consistent, systematic nature of the planking is the perfect foil for the lyricism of the plants.

JC: Yes, this dialogue between the paving and the planting forms the primary vocabulary of the High Line, but there are also many other components. We would organize our biweekly meetings with the client to review each of the layered systems that went into the design: the drainage layer, the soils layer, the planting layer, the paving, furniture, railings, edges, lighting, signage, access points, and special features.

Let's discuss some of those other systems. What about access? How do you get up to the High Line? How do you light it?

RS: Rather than thinking of stairs and elevators pragmatically as conveyances, we designed vertical access points as durations. How long should it take to travel between the chaos of the street and the serenity of the High Line? Thirty seconds? Three minutes? We imagined that, occasionally, you could pop instantly from one atmosphere to another in a clear elevator cab; other times, the experience could be prolonged. The "slow stair" at Gansevoort Street stretches the entrance through a deep slice in the structure that exposes the mass of steel and rivets that once carried moving freight trains.

MJ: It was important that visitors could be uniquely exposed to the historical structure as a kind of introduction to the High Line, positioning them directly under and then within the depth of its massive beams. We wanted to slightly delay visitors and build anticipation for the moment when they would cross the threshold of the High Line surface, when the horizon drastically changes from everyday streetscape to the unfamiliar.

RS: Lighting was built into the primary language of the High Line, the benches and the tunnels, and it also helped the design team solve a separate problem. The existing railing at the edge of the High Line was obviously strong enough to stop a runaway locomotive from crashing into the streets of the city, but it was not high enough to meet the buildings department standard for a railing height. We designed a continuous light strip that was mounted on the railing at the height required by code regulations. This linear element emphasized the length and continuity of the High Line and at night cast a soft glow on the planking and plants. Because the lighting was mounted at waist height, the light didn't interfere with night views of the city.

ED: In essence, the architecture of the High Line was already there. As the architects, our self-defined mission was to defend the High Line from architecture.

Let's turn to programming. What opportunities did the High Line present?

JC: There was a lot of pressure from the clients to embed programming into the design. We would often be asked, "Are you doing enough? Where are the attractions?" It was hard for us to communicate the power of this simple walk. But as time went by, excitement and optimism built around the simplicity of the design approach. The idea was that the design would not be subservient to prior programming, but that programming would follow the design. The design provided "settings" that would both inspire and support a variety of programs. The Friends of the High Line have since responded to this approach brilliantly. They have very creative arts and education programming. These are all things that we only implicitly created space for — we never prescribed specific uses for any spaces in the park.

ED: The narrow width of the High Line limits activity in the park. We established a set of rules to keep things simple: you can't throw a ball, you can't skateboard or ride a bike, and you can't walk a dog. This is a blessing. On the High Line, one can walk or sit and watch the city or other people.

LS: The High Line helped people rediscover the art of promenading, a very popular activity in parks and along boulevards during the nineteenth century. People would get dressed up on a Sunday afternoon and go the park to stroll and be seen. The High Line introduces a new type of strolling; it's a way of seeing the city. Even though there are places where people linger and congregate, most people walk the entire line. It's different than just going to a place and parking yourself for the day.

RS: Historically, the rise of the promenade aligned with the development of cities and urban spaces. Eventually, cities lost these spaces, and people stopped strolling. In revitalizing the postindustrial Meatpacking District, we sought to revitalize a lost ritual.

ED: The promenade somehow feels contemporary in a transient, fast-paced city like New York. People pass each other, exchange glances, smile. On a warm night, there's a sexy feeling in the air.

MJ: One of my favorite places on the High Line is the seating area between 14th and 15th Streets. We intentionally compressed the path between the water feature and the wooden chaise lounges that are mounted to the rail tracks. These are some of the most coveted seats in the park during the summer, especially by those looking to show off a little while a continuous flow of people stroll just inches in front of them. Here, everyone pretty much has to be a voyeur. And if you happen to make a connection with your neighboring lounger, some of the chaise lounges are designed with moving rail wheels so they can roll closer together on the track.

JC: The potential of the strolling promenade required us to see the park's organization as a choreography. We scripted movement block by block, vista by vista. There's a tradition in landscape architecture called scenography — the orchestration of scenes as people move among topographical moments, up and down, around and through. By coordinating the way scenes unfold, we sought to dramatize the theatrical element of urban experience. One of the best theatrical moments is the Sunken Overlook across Tenth Avenue. It creates an amazing effect with the yellow taxicabs passing below. Taxis are everywhere, and seeing them is commonplace, but this vantage point puts each car into a rapid-fire, one-point perspective. It makes you see New York City taxis afresh, with new eyes.

ED: If visitors to the High Line are mobile viewers in a relatively static landscape, at the Sunken Overlook visitors can be stationary, suspended over a fast-moving cityscape. The repetitive motion — green light, red light, stop and go — has a mesmerizing effect, like an urban lava lamp. It compels us to stop even our highly limited activities on the High Line and do absolutely nothing. As contemporary urbanites, we are always being productive, either working at our jobs or burning calories in the gym. We don't often choose to do nothing, especially in public. Here, it's the attraction. The view of taillights is a huge contrast to the lush planting you've just detoured from. Both are equally beautiful. The view of cars disappearing into deep perspective is a new form of the picturesque, where the hyperbanal becomes sublime.

RS: It's a space for daydreaming. We live in a world that doesn't allow for unprogrammed time. The smartphone, the computer, and the TV keep us totally occupied. Much like the loss of the promenade, daydreaming may be a lost form to be rediscovered. Sitting in the Sunken Overlook looking at traffic requires little attention. You can just stare endlessly at the stream of traffic. Your brain is free to wander elsewhere. It's like staring into a fireplace — it's hypnotizing.

MJ: Like many of the design features, the Sunken Overlook took advantage of what was already there — a spur over Tenth Avenue. We cut out the steel beams to suspend a bank of cascading seating, and we replaced steel plates at the north-facing girder with glass. The remaining ornamental steel railing strategically crops the horizon so that all you see is a steady stream of traffic and the nearby intersection. It's a mini theater for a simple urban drama. And it is very startling from the street when you look up and suddenly realize you have an audience. However, in this case, the audience is also on stage.

LS: That dialogue with the city is unique to the High Line. It also happens at the 26th Street Viewing Spur and, to some extent, at every street crossing. This gives a certain cadence to the experience.

JC: The 14th Street stair is another important detail. The landing is dropped just a few inches below the beam, so that you can glimpse only moving feet from the street below.

LS: One of our core design objectives was to make the High Line unlike the street. The experience is designed to be slower. A literal change of pace from the streets below. The set of sensory stimulations experienced up there are so different from those found on the street, whether it's the smell of a certain kind of grass in October or the striking skeletal form of seed heads in the winter. Everything is so tactile and close, the buildings serving as a diverse background.

JC: The notion of the background is pervasive in landscape architecture. In his reflections on the city, Walter Benjamin observed that architecture differs from painting, sculpture, and music because we are always experiencing the city in a distracted state, and therefore it's always background. We're not paying attention to it. With the High Line, we tried to feature everyday situations that are at the same time a little unexpected, calling for renewed attention to derelict buildings, old fire stairs, taxicabs on the street, grasses and flowers in cracked pavement — everyday things that are easily overlooked. One of the things I enjoy most about walking on the High Line is that I'm usually on it in a distracted state, and yet it awakens me with a palpable sense of place and eventfulness.

ED: The High Line produces less a state of distraction or concentration than a state of limbo. We are freed from the everyday in order to see the everyday anew, a parenthesis in our day that is unaccounted for.

Can we come back to programming?

ED: The design was not driven by programming. It evolved from a close reading of site attributes and atmospheres. The Chelsea Market tunnel, for instance, was shady and long; the Venturi effect made it cool and breezy in the summer, while the sidewalls kept it sheltered in the winter. Sound resonated inside it, making it acoustically interesting. We thought, with lighting, it might be a great place for informal social events, but we didn't move to specify its use beyond that.

RS: We took our cues from what we found there: what grew in the shade, what grew where it was open and sunny — the microecologies created by the strange conditions of this postindustrial site. We didn't think: "Let's do a sundeck." Instead, we figured: this is an area open to the sun where certain plants thrive. Maybe people will, too. There was an area of leakage where water collected; it was fertile and rich — the plants told us that. So rather than specifying particular sites for particular activities, we counted on activities drifting to sites where they naturally fit.

MJ: In a way, it wasn't about creating space for programming, it was about leaving space for it. We left a lot untouched. In the tunnels, we simply added light fixtures that created a sleeve of tinted light and added utility services that could support changing events and potential programming.

JC: We just wanted to create the stage set for things to happen. The tunnel at Chelsea Market can be used for pop-up commerce, gala dinners, yoga classes, and lectures. At the Sunken Overlook, I've seen people proposing in the window; there are weddings, children's birthday parties, and quartets. We strived to create unusual, open, and generous spaces in which myriad things could simply happen.

MJ: There was one exception. Early on, we were challenged by the Friends of the High Line to find a place that could be dedicated for children to play. Our response was that the entire High Line was a place of discovery and imaginative play. We were all reassured when the first phase opened and we could witness kids reinterpreting everything we designed in ways we had never imagined. In the third phase, we made a dedicated place for kids. Here, the hard planking gives way to expose a grid of steel beams softly padded with a liner of recycled sneakers. There are openings within the maze of beams to crawl through, periscopes through which to observe the streets below, and a gopher hole that leads to a planting bed.

LS: But these special moments were very much a response to the context. It's not a coincidence that the flyover happens between what were the two tallest buildings and where the trees were growing up to catch the light — where one could actually walk through the canopy of trees. It's not a coincidence that we decided to peel up the lawn directly over 23rd Street — it's one of the major avenues, and at that vantage point you can see clear to both the Hudson and East Rivers. We created the Sundeck because, in the original zoning, there were no buildings planned to the west, only a park. We knew it was going to have a view of the sunset in perpetuity. All of these cases had to do with not only the local conditions, but with the future plan of the neighborhood.

ED: True. The planning was based on the microecologies that flourished after the rail delivery system collapsed. As a park, the High Line is now altering that found environment with new buildings, new shadows, new shafts of sunlight, and a new public prompted by the project's success. The new biodiversity on the High Line, flora and fauna aside, now includes cruisers, stargazers, naturalists, retirees, fitness buffs, migratory birds, boxers, toddlers, tango dancers, butterflies, socialites, buskers, and fashionistas.

INTERVIEW
PIET OUDOLF
PLANTING DESIGNER

What do you consider yourself — a botanist? A horticulturist? A gardener? How did you get your start?

PIET OUDOLF (PO): I'm a garden and landscape designer. A horticulturist's concern is plants and not design; I have a deep knowledge of plants, but my work is primarily about composition and materials. I came late to this field, at twenty-five years old. Before, I owned a restaurant, but I decided to escape that world. I was interested in art and design, and then I became interested in gardens. I became so fascinated by plants that I decided to go back to school. After five years, I became a landscape contractor and started my garden design firm. That was in the late '70s. My wife and I were living near Amsterdam and decided to move to a rural area in the Netherlands, where we started a nursery to grow plants that I could use in my work. The nursery became well known because of the range of plants we grew, and we were introduced to a new circle of colleagues — historians, botanists, horticulturists, philosophers, scientists, and others who shared an interest in gardens.

When you came to the High Line project in 2004, did you have any preconceptions? Had you seen Joel Sternfeld's photos?

PO: Lisa called me in 2004 to ask if I was interested in joining the team. At first I hesitated, but then I found a short movie on the Internet made by Friends of the High Line with people arguing to save the structure. Of course, Joel Sternfeld's photos were critical, but it was all of the individuals passionately advocating to save the High Line that persuaded me. It was also about the potential I saw to make a unique environment.

What were your initial impressions of the High Line when you first visited, and what were your first instincts about what to do there?

PO: I'm very practical. I thought: I love it, but there's no way it can be kept as it is. With nature, you can never freeze it in place. The choice was either to leave it unchanged, with the understanding that it would eventually be lost, or to interpret it and, in the process, save it, but accept that it would be different.

What opportunity did you see for the planting?

PO: The only way forward was creating an ambience that carried the essence of what was once there — that commemorated its attitude, its spirit. In this I was trying to discover a new planting strategy apart from a home garden or a corporate garden or any other sort of garden typology, for that matter. I traveled extensively to conduct research. Seeing different ecologies helped me understand what would work and what wouldn't. There was a narrative — a sort of experiential story, a script — that was conceived by the design team. The lead designers had walked the High Line so many times, and they knew exactly where they wanted particular experiences. Even though I had a very strong idea of what it might look like, I depended on the team's narratives to provide a creative translation. In the end, we created habitats — places where plants would feel happy together, where it would look and feel as if the plants were born there.

Can you elaborate on the idea of the controlled wild in the context of the New Perennial movement?

PO: It's important to realize that the New Perennial movement is still garden design, which is about control. Everything that is planted must be controlled as you account for the limitations of the site, the impacts of the environment, and the parameters set by the landscape architect. For the High Line, the plants have to grow on a bridge that is exposed above and below, which makes them vulnerable to freezing temperatures in the winter. As a result, my concern was not only about habitats and ecosystems, but also about survival. I also had to keep in mind that the plants would change over time. In ten years, everything could be different. If you create a garden that you control completely, it would be static and decorative. It would have no emotion. My work is about succession, about a freedom within limits. I check in regularly with the gardeners at the Friends of the High Line — a conversation that helps keep the design intent, if not the specific plants, permanent.

Regarding the design, have you felt the urge to change anything that was conceived a certain way but didn't work out?

PO: Well, there's always something that doesn't work. Sometimes you find out right away, like problems with watering or insects. Most things are out of your control. The first year you notice which plants don't do well; the second year you find more problems that you can adjust for; and after five years you find that because certain plants have grown well, others beneath them have suffered as a result. We have to assess the situation every year. If we were to suspend maintenance for ten years, then we'd probably have to start all over again, because the plants would have found a totally new logic.

How has the planting design on the High Line changed the way people think about ecological diversity and weeds?

PO: Even my own understanding of these ideas is constantly changing – that's why I have to come back all the time! I have to follow the project's progress myself. It's an entirely new way of gardening. I think it's the first project of its kind. For me, it's a very serious experiment.

The High Line has also become a model – it has inspired other cities to try to create similar projects.

PO: That's true. It's not easy, though. The challenge is not just about planting trees. It's about producing a complete environment – a dynamic landscape. The project has also made people aware that creating a successful landscape isn't just about picking plants; it's also about a great support system of people in the field who know their craft.

Are you still supervising the evolution of the High Line?

PO: Yes, but, while it's important that I educate people who will care for it in the future, my part in the evolution of this landscape is actually quite small. I meet with Tom Smarr, the park's director of horticulture, every year. We discuss what's going wrong and what's going right. Planting is a very slow process of incremental, daily change, just like the growth of humans. By the time you grow old, you almost don't realize you have lived so long. In the meantime, you have to maintain yourself. It's not just about manicuring; it's about living a healthy life. You have to nurture the garden in the same way.

Have you been asked to do many similar projects?

PO: Yes, of course. The High Line is an iconic project – everyone knows it. Today, people invite me to work on projects all over the world, from South America to the Middle East. But I only work in the climate zones I'm familiar with; I usually say that I can work from the south of France to Siberia. For me, the pleasure is not about doing more projects, but about who I'm working with, the quality of the project, and an assurance that it will be cared for in the future.

INTERVIEW
CRAIG SCHWITTER AND JOE TORTORELLA
ENGINEERS

The complexity of repurposing the historic structure of the High Line might not be immediately apparent given the final park design. This is an opportunity to shed some light on that process. How did the two engineering firms split the work? How did you phase the work?

JOE TORTORELLA (JT): My firm, Silman Associates, was charged with the preservation and restoration of what was already there: the steel-and-concrete structure of the High Line and its foundations.

CRAIG SCHWITTER (CS): My firm, BuroHappold, did the structural, mechanical, electrical, fire, and life safety engineering for the new design. Silman's work – site prep, remediation, structural stability – happened early. And the second phase involved just scraping it bare. We took off the wearing slabs and the primary slabs and then replaced them. That's one way we gained the requisite planting depth. Silman gave it a checkup, BuroHappold gave it a haircut, and everybody else gave it the makeup.

JT: The construction phase was a convoluted process because the project evolved in three successive phases, each with different contractors. The first phase went very smoothly. The contractor had it down to a science; he knew every column and every rivet. It was hard to start all over again with a second contractor and then again with a third.

Some historians believe that restoration should mimic original structures; others believe it should be clearly defined as new. Which strategy was used for the concrete-and-steel restoration of the High Line?

JT: Lots of people assume that preservation work should blend into historic structures. But actually, the guidelines from the Department of the Interior recommend that a preservation project distinguishes between new and old. The philosophy is to make apparent any changes to the original structure so that one day, if the next generation decides to restore the structure to its original historic state, it would be easier to reverse the process. For the most part, we were very deliberate about making the repairs clearly visible. Where the appearance was sensitive, we tried to have the changes look similar without replicating the old structure.

CS: It was important that the new design be sympathetic to the existing system but not the same.

What challenges did you face when evaluating the High Line structure? Were the historic shop drawings helpful?

JT: In preservation, it's not often that you're presented with such a robust structure. This railway was built to hold multiple freight trains. This meant that we could remove significant portions of it without concern about supporting the live loads of the park. Learning all of the details of the structure was a challenge due to the sheer relentlessness of its length. It was difficult to keep track of the columns along the mile-and-a-half (2.4 km) we had surveyed and to develop a system for recording each and every one. There were volumes and volumes of archival shop drawings to reference, but it was a major challenge to find the drawing you needed for a better understanding of a particular juncture.

How did you evaluate and assess the underside of the High Line structure when much of it was encased by private properties? What were the surprises you found when looking under the hood?

JT: Private property was a challenge. When we were given permission to enter a site, we often had to be escorted. Many of the adjacent buildings were abandoned. We had to find creative ways to enter them and climb around piles of debris with no lighting. The spaces smelled awful. There was a Drug Enforcement Agency next door, and its agents would interrogate us whenever we walked by.

What were some of the challenges that you faced incorporating the historic structure into the new landscape design, stairs, and special features?

CS: It's important to realize that the High Line is a freestanding bridge structure. It moves. It has dynamic joints at intervals so that the entire structure is able to expand and contract. We had to bridge over the expansion joints with all our new systems. The design of the High Line was very precise, with tight tolerances, and working with the original structural dynamics was an important part of the technical design. When I walk the High Line today, I notice slight changes in those movement joints, and I'm happy to see the structure is alive, that it actually moves back and forth. Another difficult task was cutting the steel to incorporate new stairs and other openings. We had to do this to several deep girders to provide a visual connection to the street. The steel removed had to be carefully analyzed to ensure that the remaining structure was strong enough to withstand the crowd loads.

Much of the engineering (utilities, substructure, drainage, and so on) on the High Line is meant to be out of view. What is the most interesting engineering feature that we can't see when we walk on the High Line today?

CS: From the beginning, it was a challenge to get everything to fit. Within a relatively narrow structural width and depth, we had to fit drainage, a walking surface, soil for plantings, area for conduit, and area for getting the trash out. It's very compact. When you walk the High Line, you don't sense any of that; it's all hidden. It's amazing to think that we could create this park "machine" within only eighteen inches (460 mm) of depth. On the other hand, the most visible engineered element on the

High Line is the planking. Developing a custom planking system had lots of stressful moments. The design was simple, but the approvals process involved many steps. I remember an Office of Management and Budget peer review of the planking in which we were told that the system was too complicated. There were only three pieces to the damn system! There's a plank, there's a cross tie, and there's an adjustment block. How much more simple could it get? The reason we designed a custom system in the first place was because there were no products available on the market that had the width-to-length aspect ratio we needed. Now I see striated planking patterns all over the world. These are definitely influenced by the High Line.

On that note, how do you feel about the park's role and influence since its opening?

CS: I love how often I hear the project referenced. I'll be flying into New York and overhear two people planning their trip to the High Line. Or you hear about a city halfway around the world that's developing a new park similar to the High Line. I enjoy that — knowing that I played a role in a project that's had so much influence around the world. It's an amazing story about how cities can reinvent themselves in rapid fashion.

JT: You only get an opportunity to be a part of a project like the High Line once in a lifetime. We were so fortunate to be part of a project that changed entire neighborhoods.

INTERVIEW
HERVÉ DESCOTTES
LIGHTING DESIGNER

What is your first memory of the High Line?

HERVÉ DESCOTTES (HD): My first visit to the High Line was illegal, actually. This was years before the competition. My friends and I decided to jump the fence one evening and have a picnic up there. It was late June and the weather was perfect. The sun had just set and the sky was turning a deep blue. We stayed there for hours. By the time we left, it was completely dark — a sort of darkness that heightened my senses to everything around me. It was a totally new experience of Manhattan. We could see the sky! My memories from that trip — of the mystery, the calm, and the darkness of the High Line — later became the conceptual foundation of the lighting design.

What atmospheres did you find there at night?

HD: There was so much grass, so much debris, and it was so dark that you could not tell where you were. There was little light carried from the street. The structure was mostly surrounded by industrial buildings that were shut down at night or abandoned. I find Manhattan to be overlit anyway — there's not enough mystery, sense of discovery, playfulness. When it's dark, your pupils grow, and you're more sensitive to light. Up on the High Line, I could see so much more than I could see at the level of the street. That experience led to the lighting concept. I wanted to keep the park free of bright overhead lights and proposed that the lighting always be below eye level. The essential principle of the lighting design was to avoid glare. I didn't want to see light fixtures, as I wanted no interference with the view of the city. The idea was to maintain the sensation of connection with everything above head height — of buildings glowing and growing around the park as nighttime fell.

Is this unusual in landscape lighting design?

HD: Yes. The lighting on the High Line was designed for the purpose of illuminating the walking surface with soft light. At the beginning, my hope was to keep some portion of the High Line completely dark, but this wasn't possible because of building code restrictions. But in general, we were extremely lucky: with every other park in the city — say, Central Park — the landscape is dark and the pathways are lit. The High Line, however, is so narrow that when we lit the walkways and railings, we also lit the planting. I thought this was so great: for once I didn't have to solely light paths. Moving through the High Line is like floating over the city on a flying carpet: you can see where you're walking, but the space isn't entirely polluted with light. And because there's no lighting overhead, you engage with the rest of the city.

Can you speak about how you used the existing architecture — the tunnels and the guardrails?

HD: I love working with limited resources, being creative with what's there. The High Line has two railings, so I used them. It has two tunnels, so I had to figure out how to light them in the daytime and at night. I didn't want them to feel too much like tunnels.
In the daytime, the lighting provides a soft transition from one side of the tunnel to the other — a bridge of light, essentially — and at night, it creates an even softer transition with a mix of colored and white light.
The idea of the mix came accidentally. It was supposed to be colored light at night and white light during the day, but we realized that the two worked very well together, so we kept both all the time.

Has the development of the sites around the High Line affected your original design intent?

HD: No — I love it! It's like you begin to work on a project and someone adds a new idea that you never thought of. Then a third idea is built on the first two. Suddenly, you have many more players in the game, which makes the project more complex, more interesting, and more organic.

INTERVIEW
PAULA SCHER
GRAPHIC DESIGNER

What was the concept behind the logo?

PAULA SCHER (PS): It took me about two seconds to make the logo. Railroads have tracks. The High Line has the letter "H." I made a track that's an "H." Getting me to design this logo was one of the first things that Robert Hammond and Joshua David did — it legitimized the organization way before they had an office or a single employee. The typography, including the signage, was a much more difficult process. Everybody had their idea of what the font should be. I chose Rockwell, a slab-serif typeface that comes from a period when the British were building the Suez Canal. Slab-serif typefaces were often used for the logos of railroads and became emblematic of the industrial age. I knew it was exactly the right choice.

How did you develop a signage strategy?

PS: We took a less-is-more approach. People are walking one way or they're walking the other way. They need to know where a bathroom is and where the stairs are — that's it. This was a very simple job that was fraught with a very long approvals process. Originally, we wanted to use the railings as a signature, like a measuring stick, to give people some sense of how far they had walked and where they were in relationship to the street. Eventually, most of the decision makers determined that this idea was superfluous.

Do you think that the evolution of the High Line's brand is a product of the visual identity you created for it?

PS: Designers don't control that. That's a myth. All I can do is make a mark that people remember. A mark is neutral. The architecture, landscape, restaurants, stores, museums, and hotels in the area give the identity its meaning. Otherwise it's just a railroad track that makes an "H." But the identity wouldn't have worked if we had used a little choo-choo train icon. That would have been a departure from the high-design style the project called for. The style of the logo is industrial rather than garden-like. That's a deliberate choice. The High Line challenged the conventions of park design, so we had to challenge the conventions of signage and identity in return.

Why do you think the High Line was so successful?

PS: It was about New York reclaiming this industrial territory and reinventing it in a completely modern and urban way. That's the true brand.

04_DESIGN

Schematic design began in mid-2005. Guided by the concepts established in the Framework Plan, the team created a complete proposal for the High Line's architectural, engineering, lighting, and planting systems, as well as its site-specific features. The guiding ethos of the design was simplicity and restraint. This disposition was meant to complement and amplify the existing conditions of the High Line as we found it: a self-seeded landscape that had formed over the course of decades of disuse and neglect. The plan included dozens of variations on the precast concrete paving plank and a selection of over four hundred plant species, including bulbs, grasses, perennials, shrubs, and trees. We developed the design with the close involvement of many stakeholders, including the Friends of the High Line, the New York City Department of Parks and Recreation, the New York City Department of City Planning, the New York City Economic Development Corporation, and the Office of the Mayor. Through an intense, cross-disciplinary collaborative process, concepts evolved into designs, designs developed into construction documents, and the specific formal details of the High Line emerged.

300 FT
(91 M)
500 FT
(152 M)
PHASE 1: 2006–2009
20TH STREET

PHASE 3: 2011–2014
PHASE 2: 2009–2011
30TH STREET

300 FT
(91 M)
500 FT
(152 M)
A
B
C
D
WEST 23RD STREET

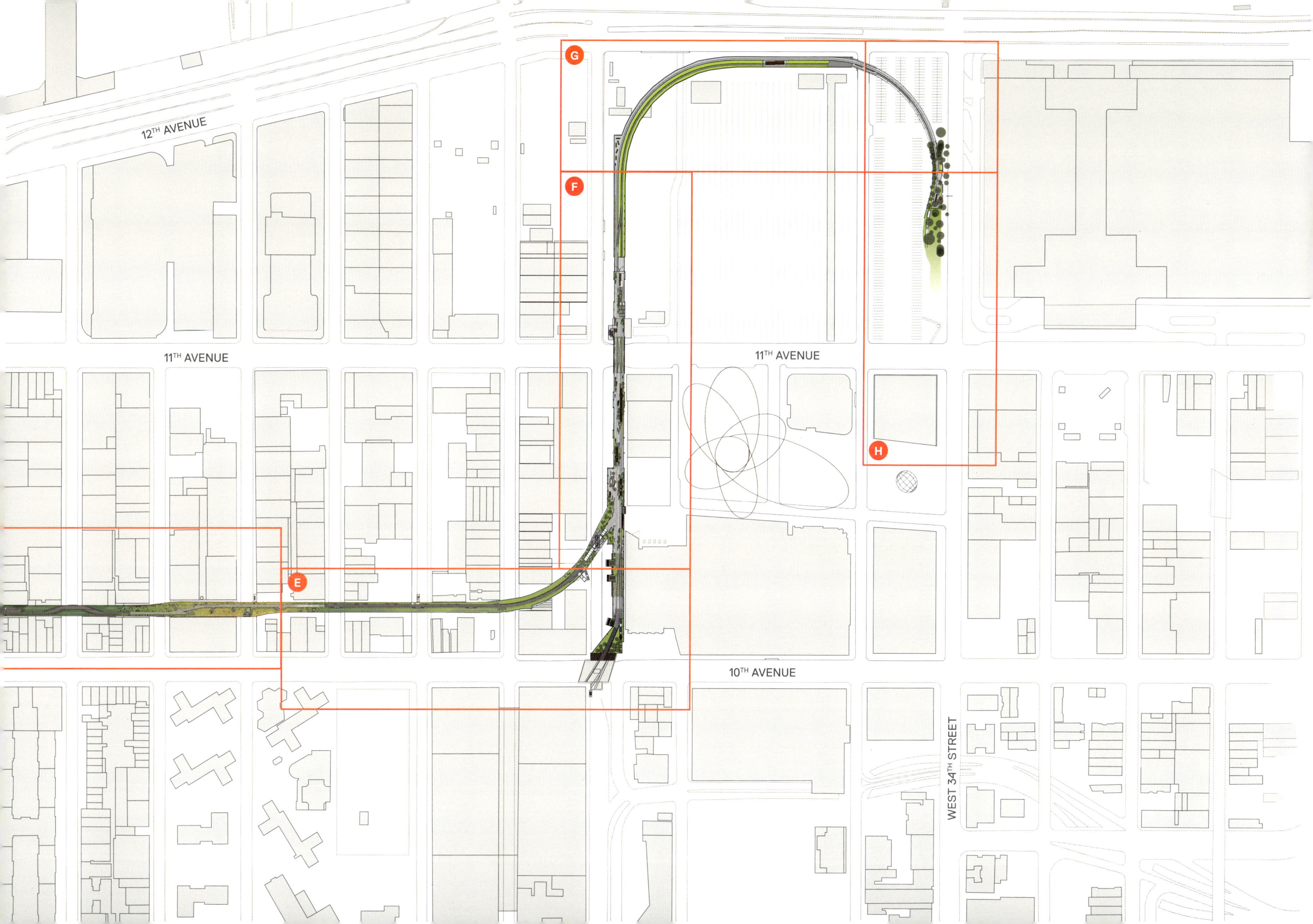

12TH AVENUE
11TH AVENUE
11TH AVENUE
10TH AVENUE
WEST 34TH STREET
G
F
H
E

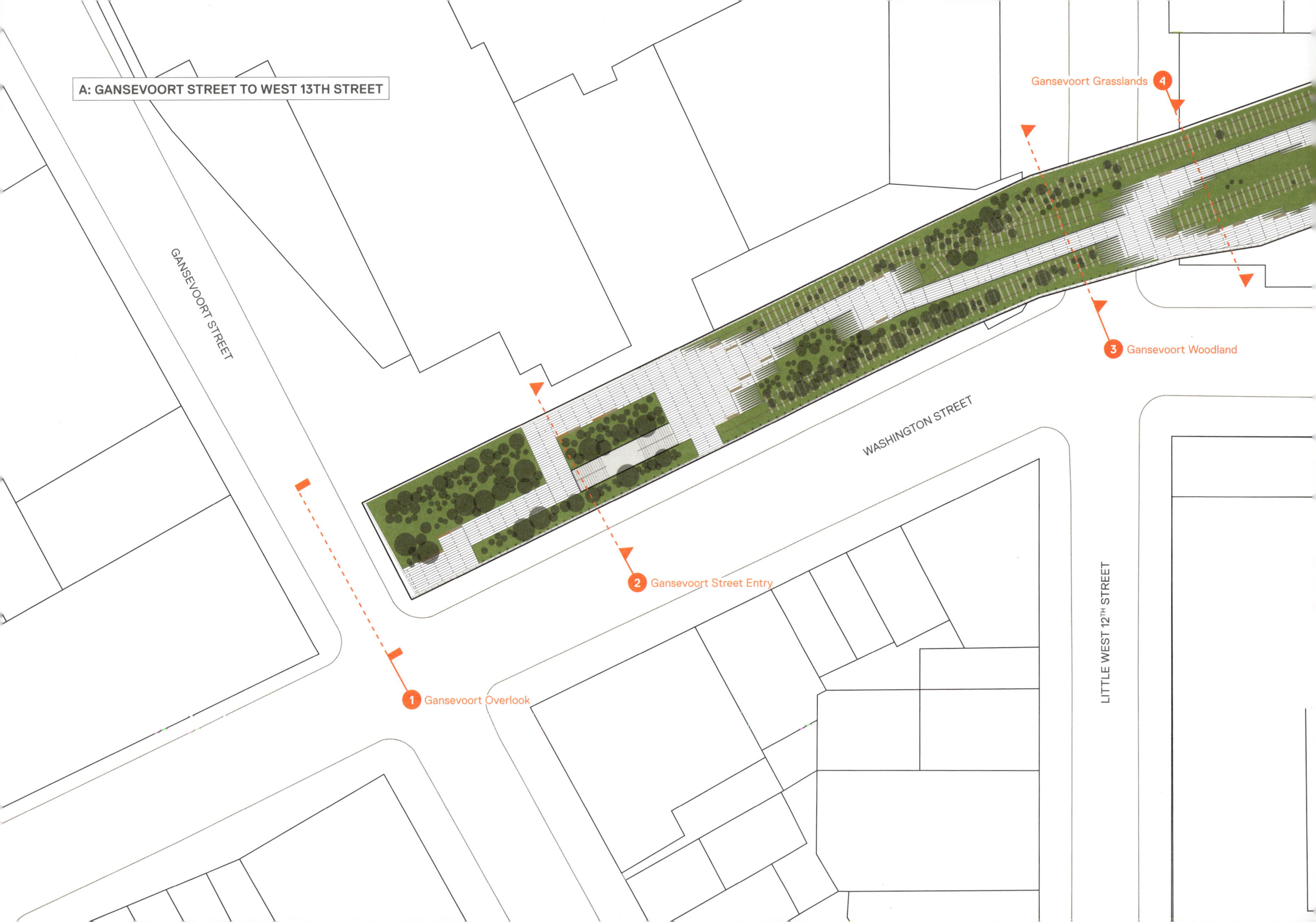
A: GANSEVOORT STREET TO WEST 13TH STREET
GANSEVOORT STREET
WASHINGTON STREET
LITTLE WEST 12TH STREET
1 Gansevoort Overlook
2 Gansevoort Street Entry
3 Gansevoort Woodland
4 Gansevoort Grasslands

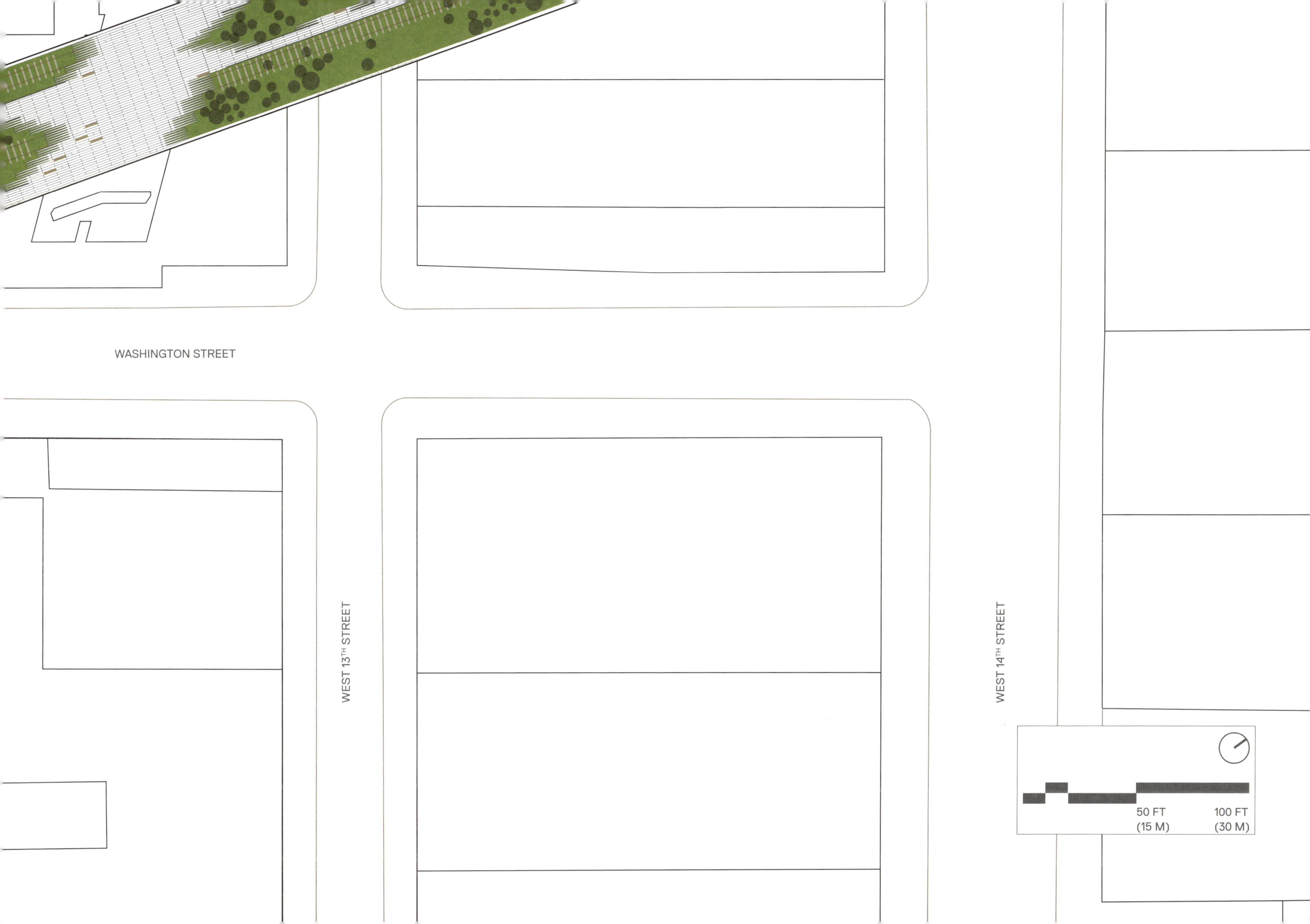
WASHINGTON STREET
WEST 13TH STREET
WEST 14TH STREET
50 FT
(15 M)
100 FT
(30 M)

1 Gansevoort Overlook

3 Gansevoort Woodland

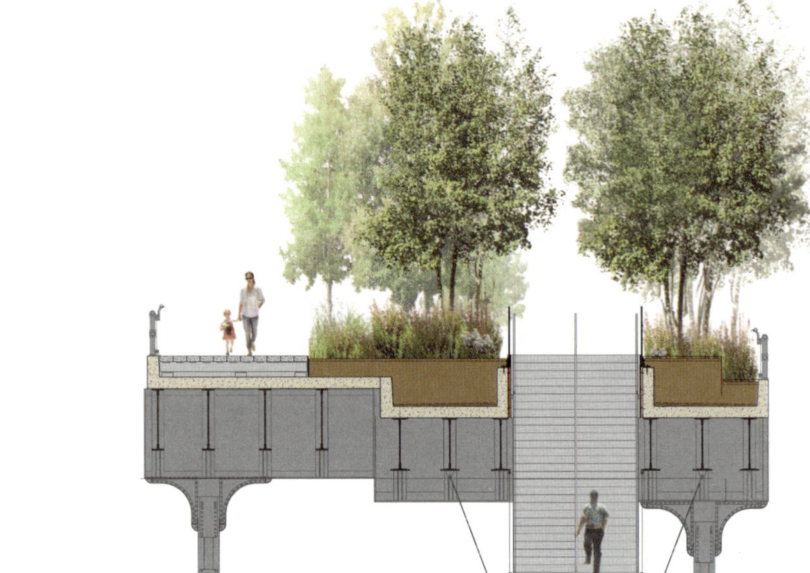

2 Gansevoort Street Entry

4 Gansevoort Grasslands

10 FT (3M) 50 FT (15M)

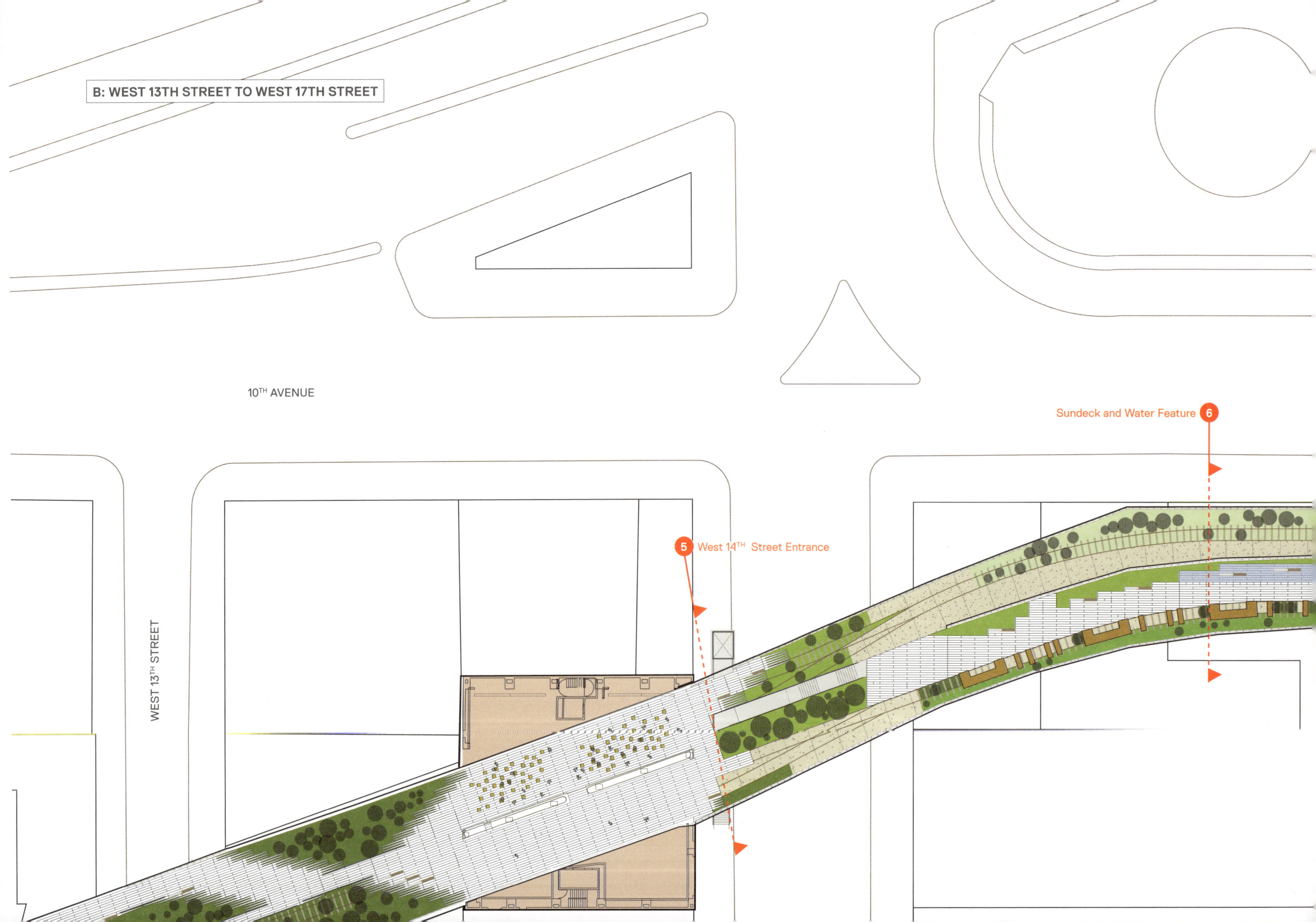
B: WEST 13TH STREET TO WEST 17TH STREET
10TH AVENUE
Sundeck and Water Feature
6
5
West 14TH Street Entrance
WEST 13TH STREET

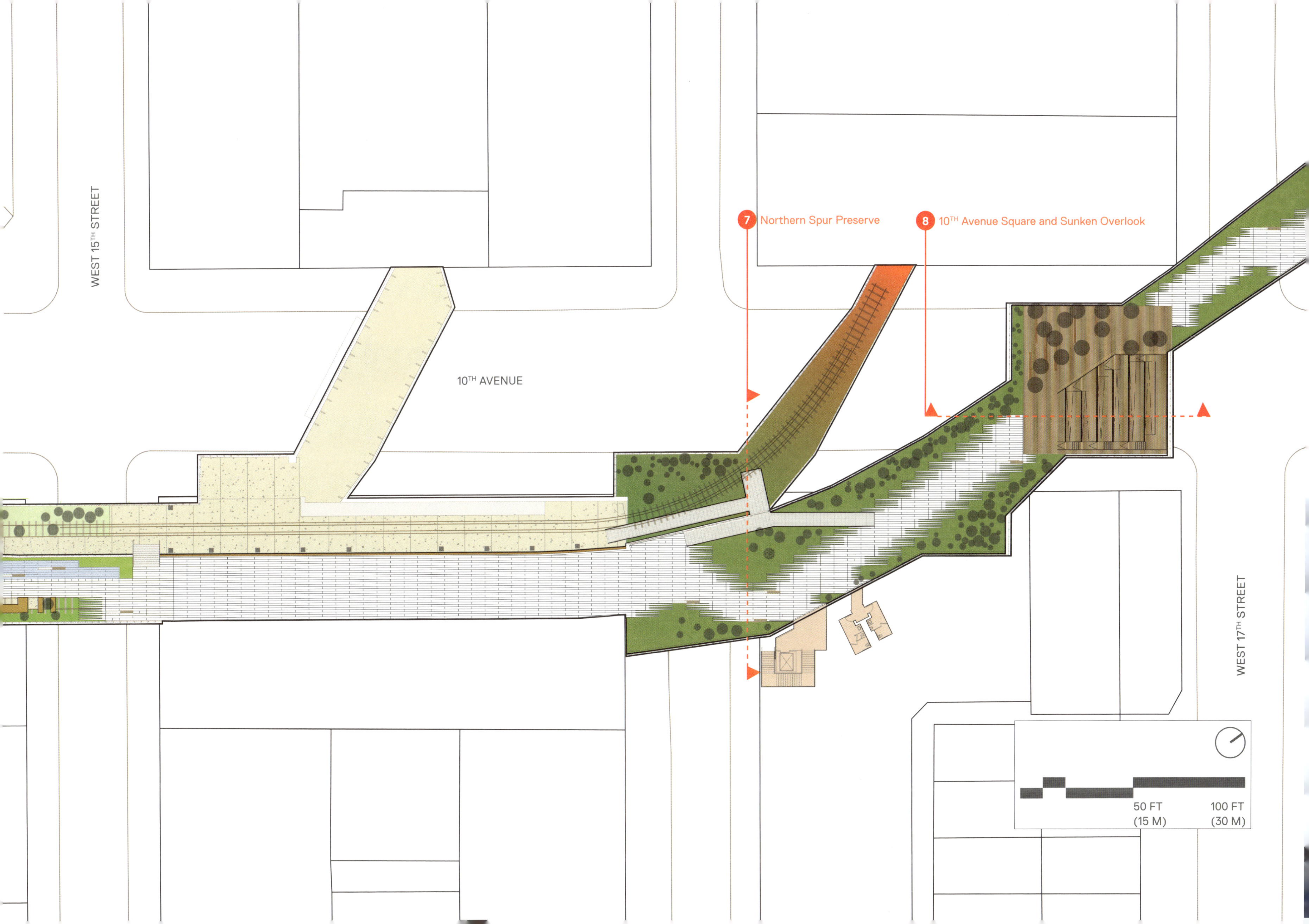

WEST 15TH STREET
10TH AVENUE
7 Northern Spur Preserve
8 10TH Avenue Square and Sunken Overlook
WEST 17TH STREET
50 FT
(15 M)
100 FT
(30 M)

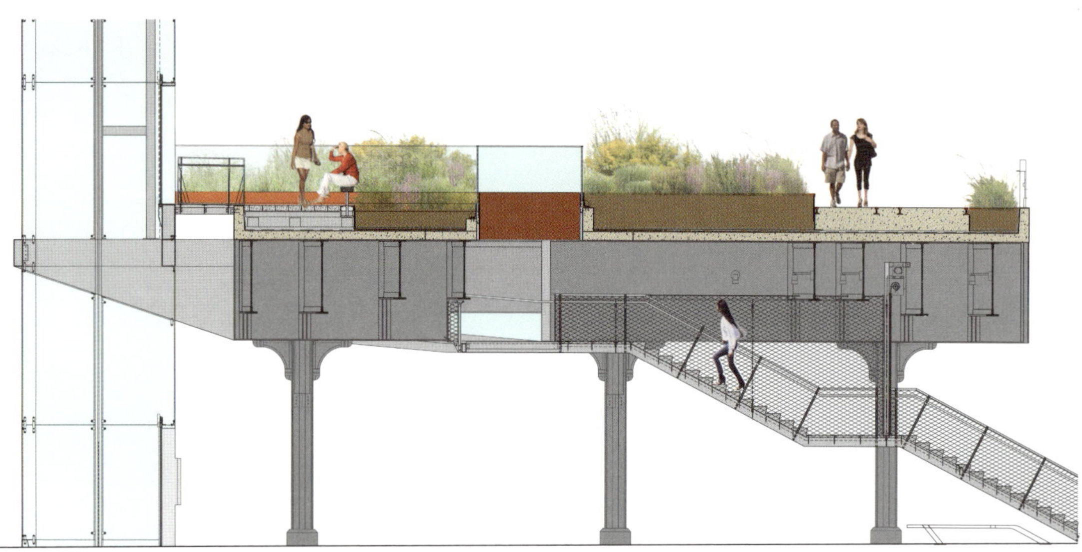

5 West 14TH Street Entrance

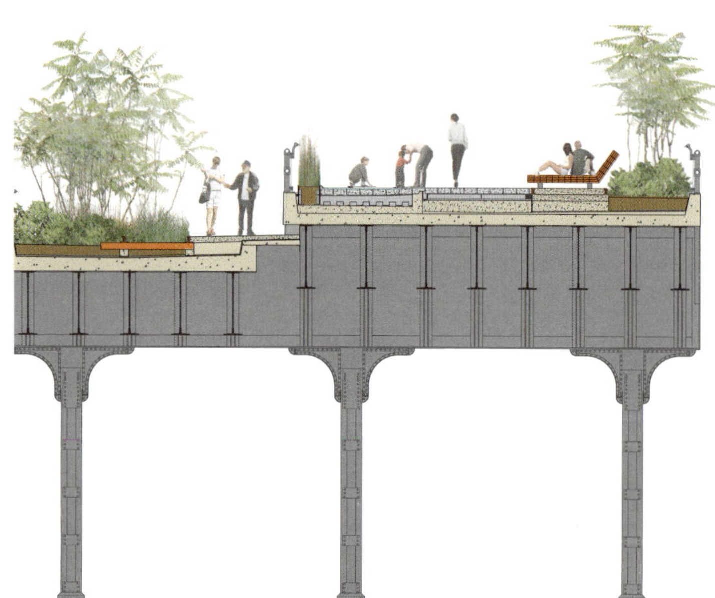

6 Sundeck and Water Feature

7 Northern Spur Preserve

8 10TH Avenue Square and Sunken Overlook

C: WEST 17TH STREET TO WEST 22ND STREET
WEST 18TH STREET
WEST 19TH STREET
9 West 18TH Street Seating Alcove
10 Chelsea Grasslands
10TH AVENUE

WEST 20TH STREET
WEST 21ST STREET
Chelsea Thicket 11
12 Chelsea Thicket
50 FT
(15 M)
100 FT
(30 M)

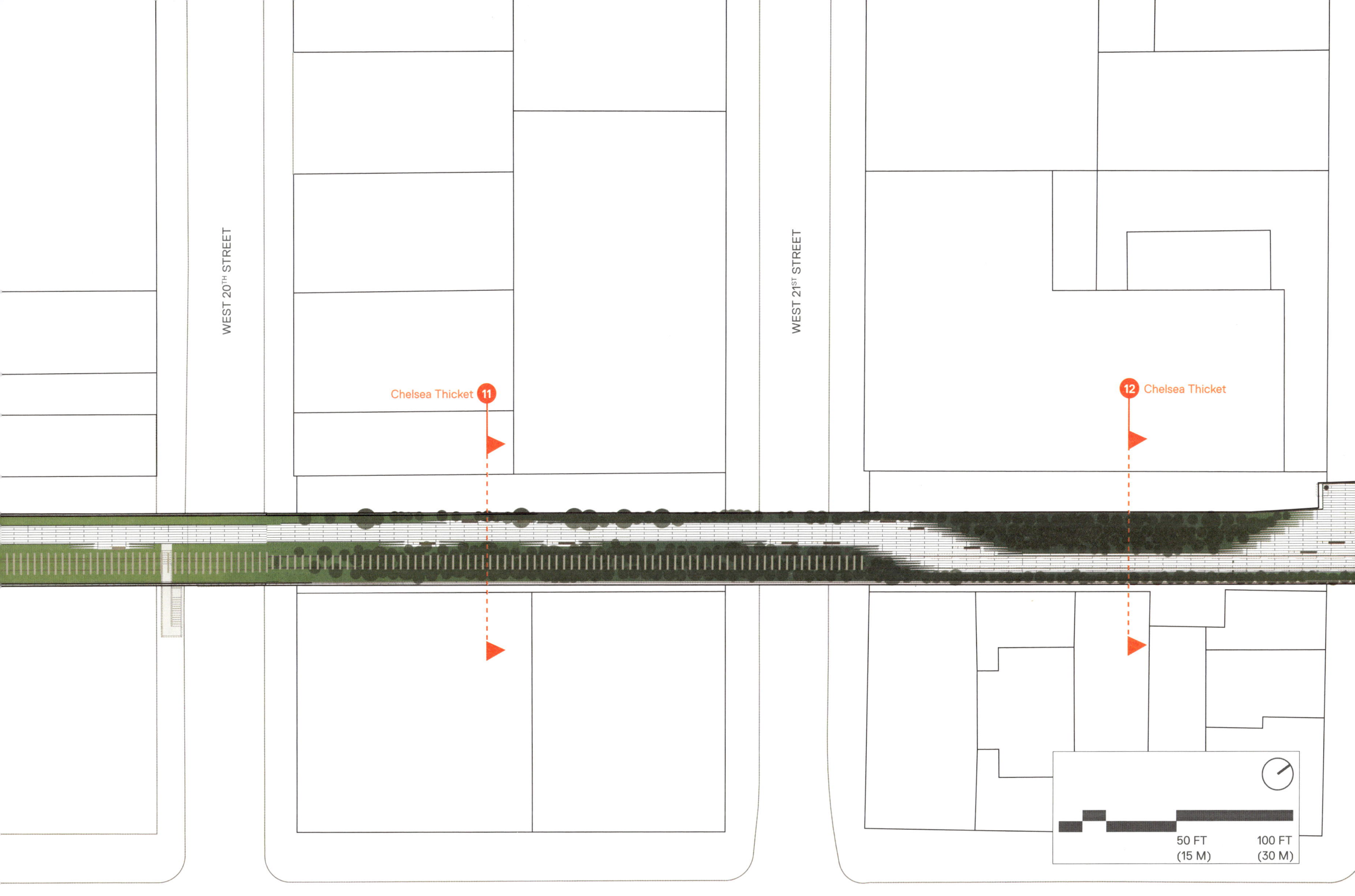

10TH AVENUE

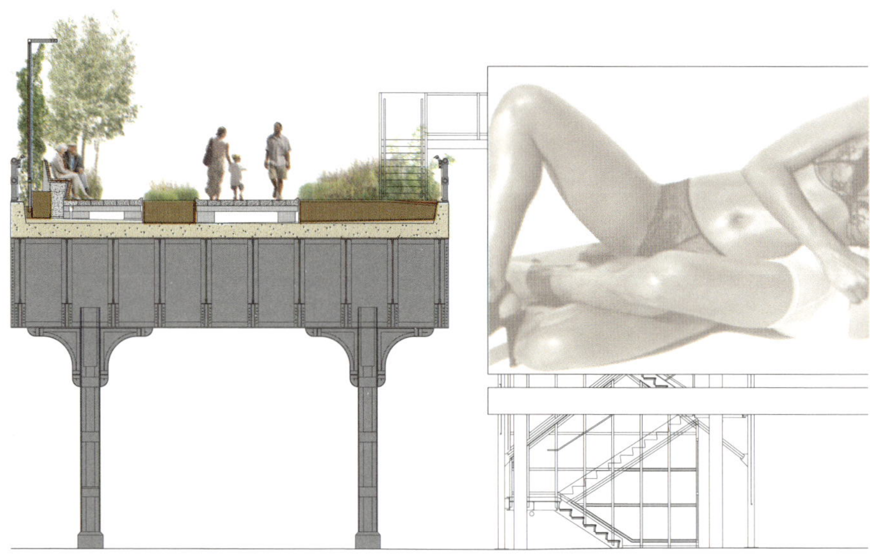

9 West 18TH Street Seating Alcove

11 Chelsea Thicket

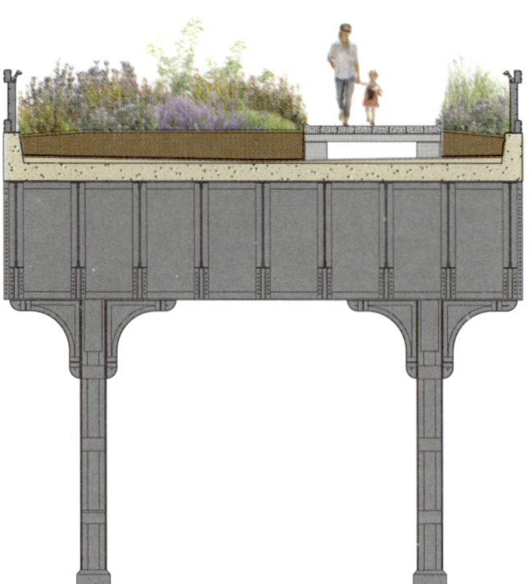

10 Chelsea Grasslands

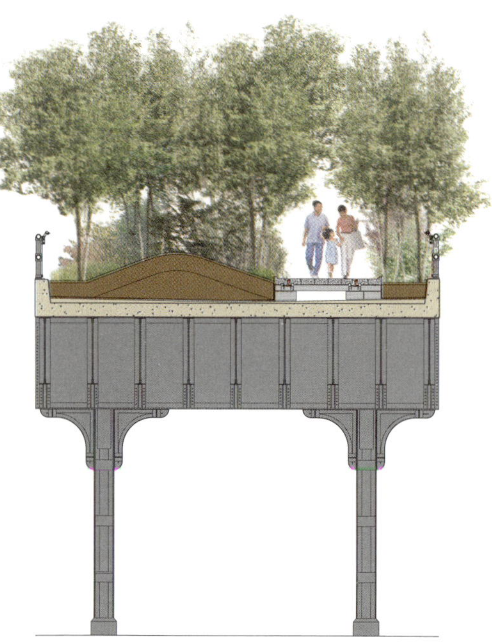

12 Chelsea Thicket

10 FT (3M) 50 FT (15M)

Self Storage

D: WEST 22ND STREET TO WEST 26TH STREET
WEST 23RD STREET
WEST 24TH STREET
13 West 22ND Street Seating Steps and Lawn
14 West 23RD Street Entrance
10TH AVENUE

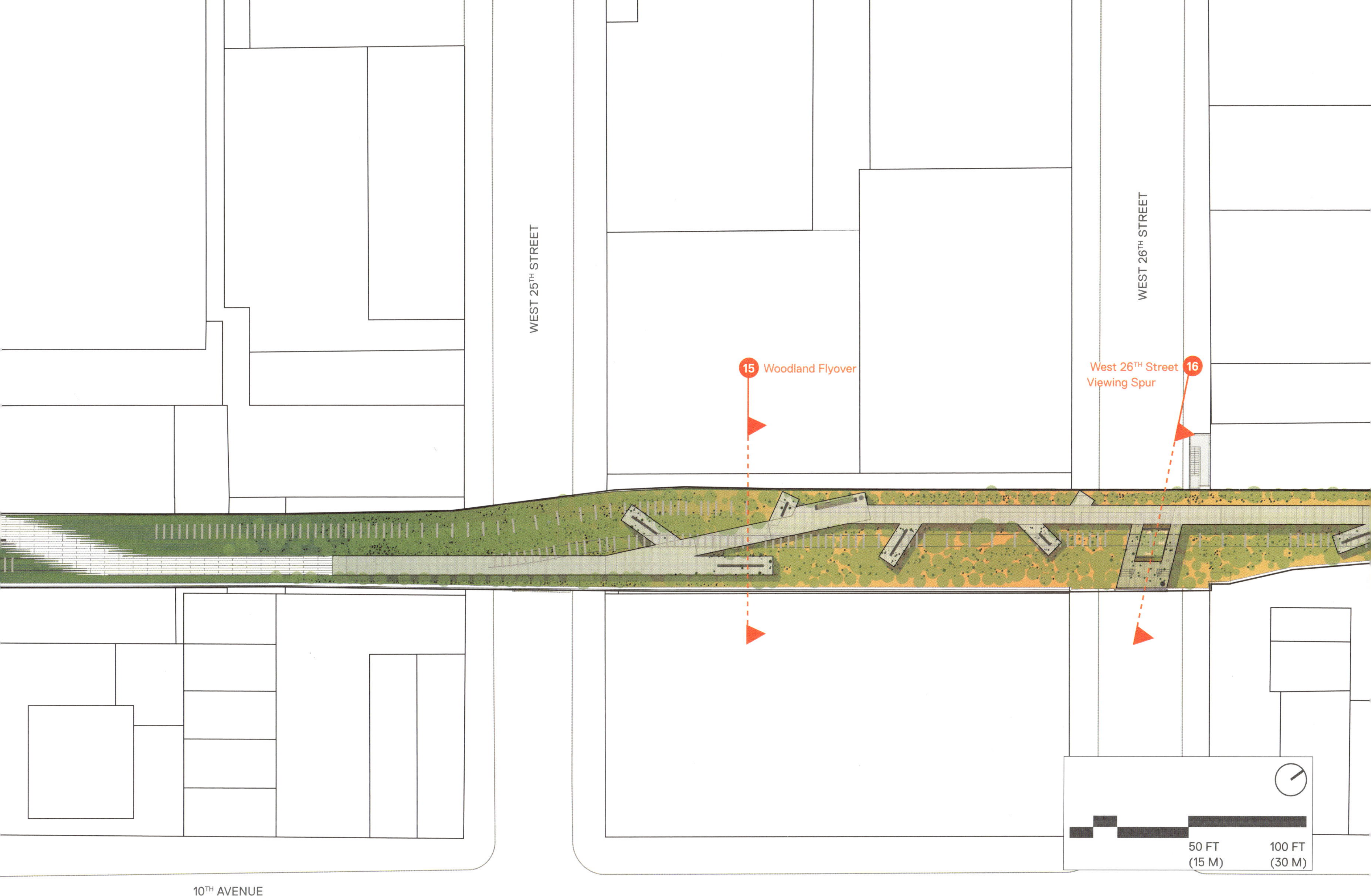

WEST 25TH STREET
WEST 26TH STREET
15 Woodland Flyover
West 26TH Street 16
Viewing Spur
50 FT
(15 M)
100 FT
(30 M)
10TH AVENUE

13 West 22ND Street Seating Steps and Lawn

15 Woodland Flyover

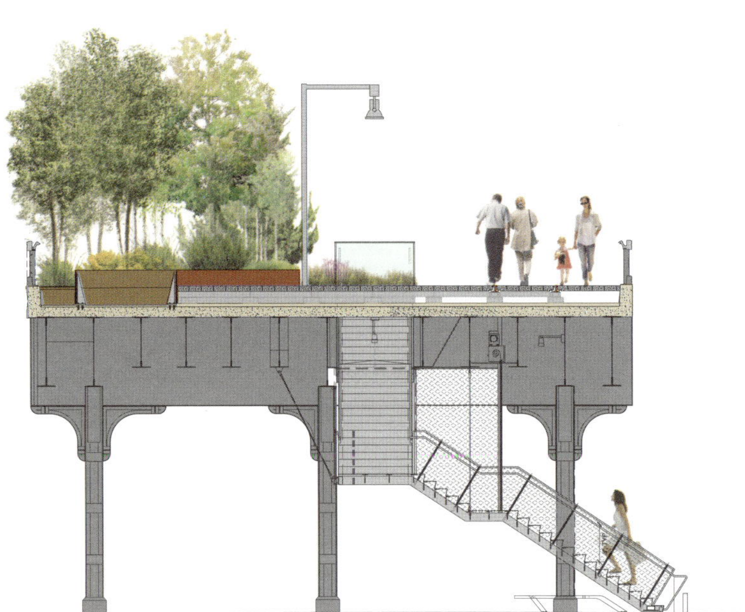

14 West 23RD Street Entrance

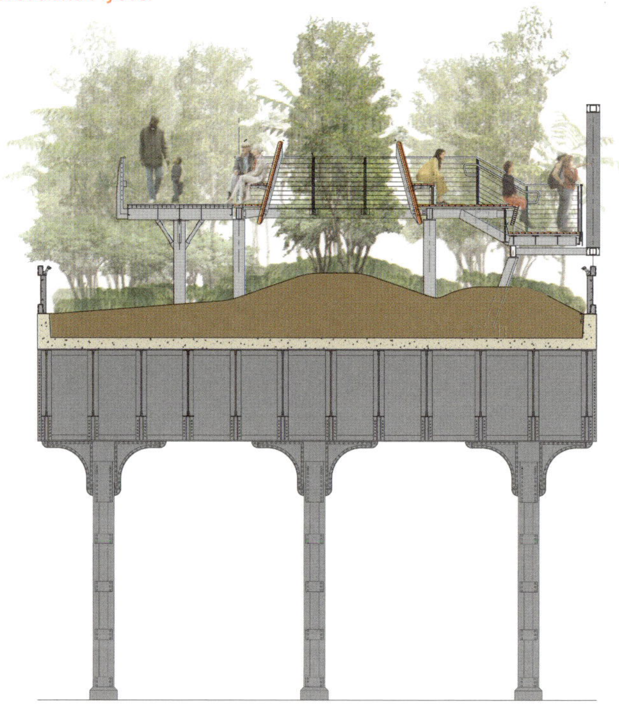

16 West 26TH Street Viewing Spur

10 FT (3M) 50 FT (15M)

E: WEST 27TH STREET TO WEST 30TH STREET
17 Wildflower Straightaway
WEST 27TH STREET
WEST 28TH STREET
10TH AVENUE
10TH AVENUE

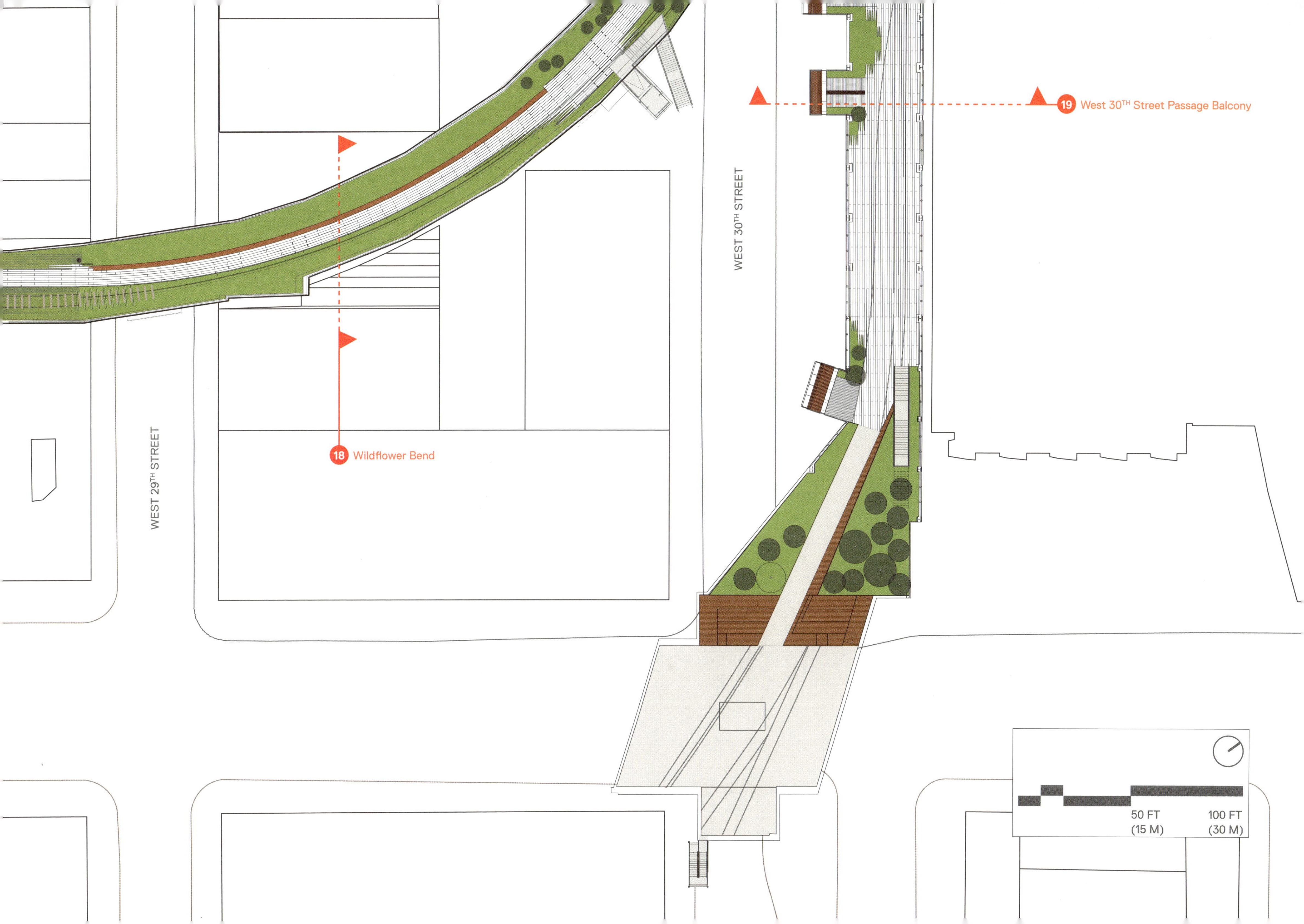

19 West 30TH Street Passage Balcony
WEST 30TH STREET
18 Wildflower Bend
WEST 29TH STREET
50 FT
(15 M)
100 FT
(30 M)

17 Wildflower Straightaway

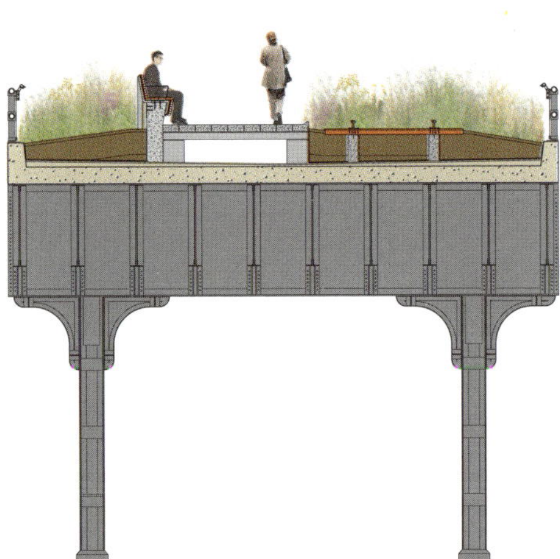

18 Wildflower Bend

19 West 30TH Street Passage Balcony

10 FT (3M) 50 FT (15M)

F: 30TH STREET
20 Crossroads
21 Grasslands Grove at West 30th Street
WEST 30TH STREET
HUDSON YARDS

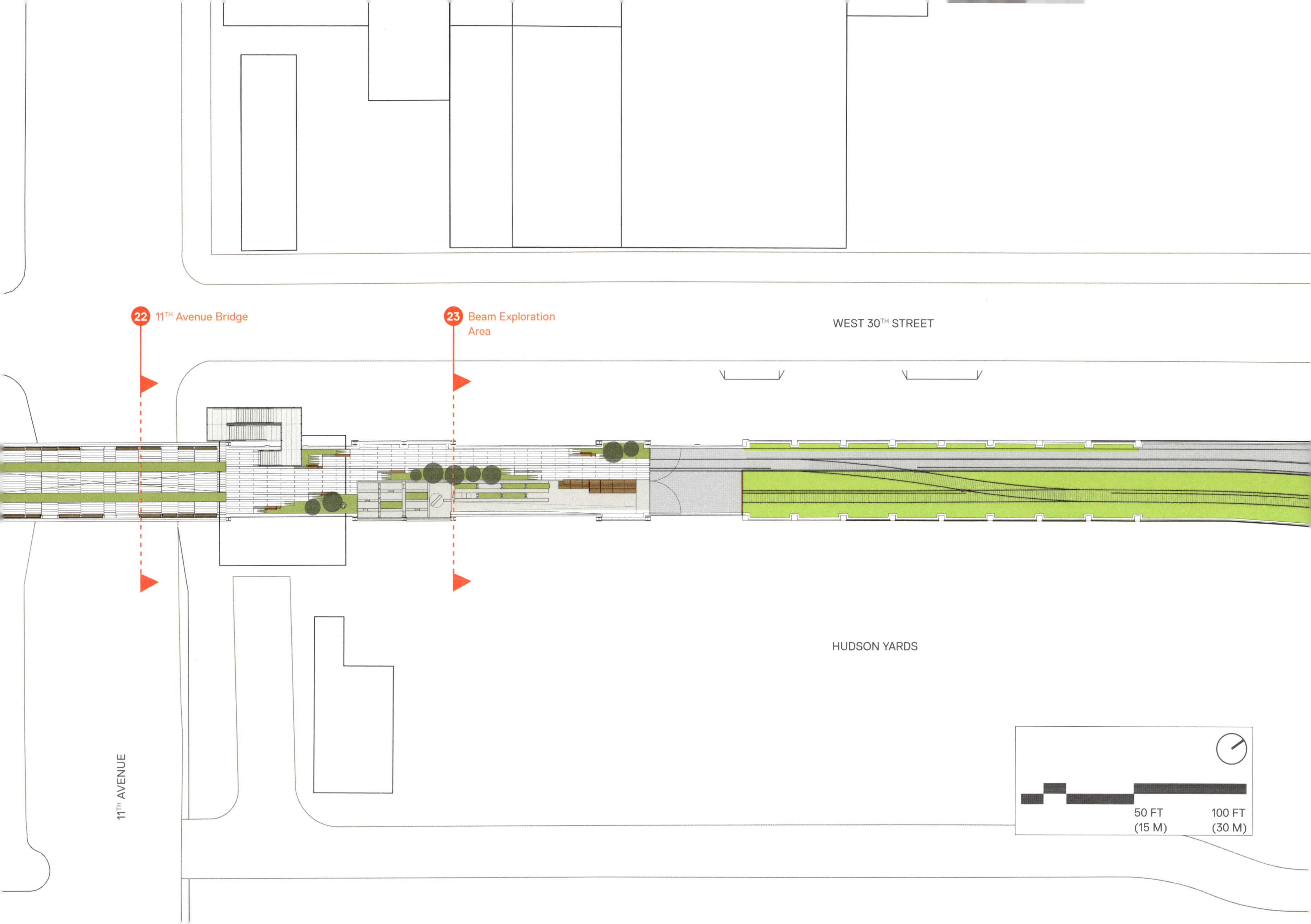

22 11TH Avenue Bridge
23 Beam Exploration Area
WEST 30TH STREET
HUDSON YARDS
11TH AVENUE
50 FT (15 M)
100 FT (30 M)

20 Crossroads

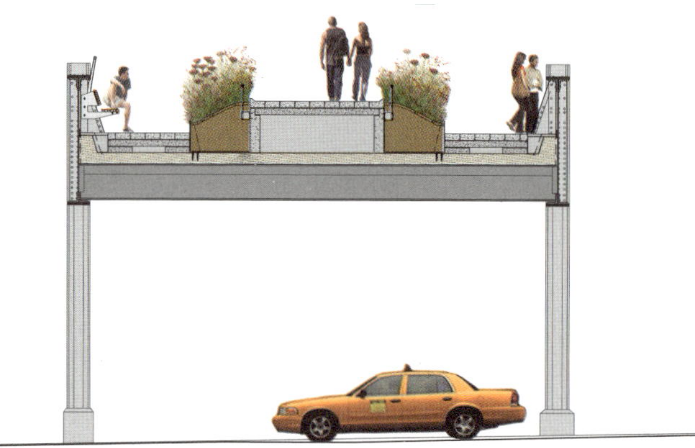

22 11TH Avenue Bridge

21 Grasslands Grove at West 30TH Street

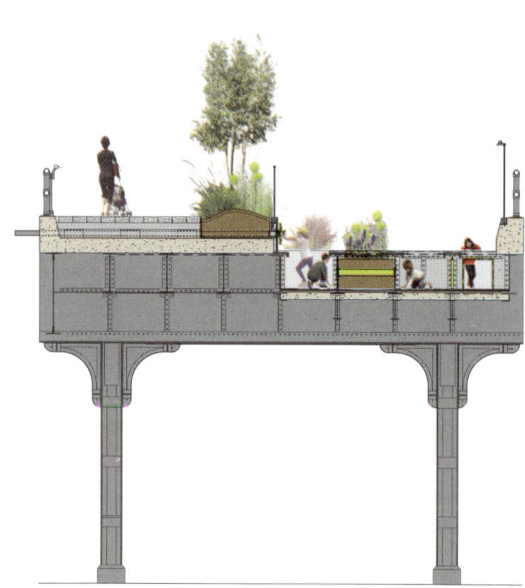

23 Beam Exploration Area

10 FT (3M) 50 FT (15M)

G: 12TH AVENUE
12TH AVENUE
WEST 30TH STREET
24 Interim Walkway

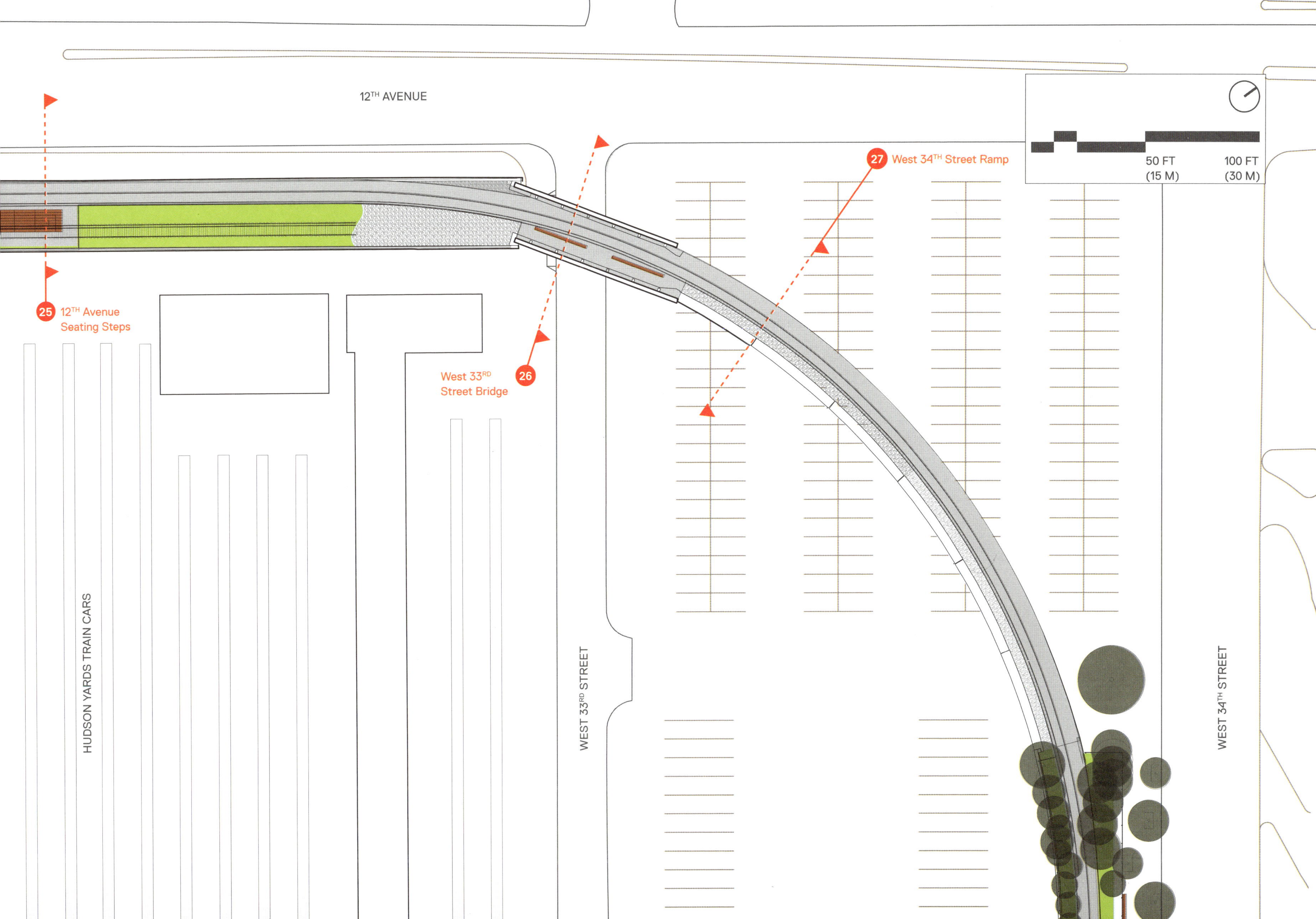

12TH AVENUE
25 12TH Avenue Seating Steps
26 West 33RD Street Bridge
27 West 34TH Street Ramp
50 FT (15 M)
100 FT (30 M)
HUDSON YARDS TRAIN CARS
WEST 33RD STREET
WEST 34TH STREET

24 Interim Walkway

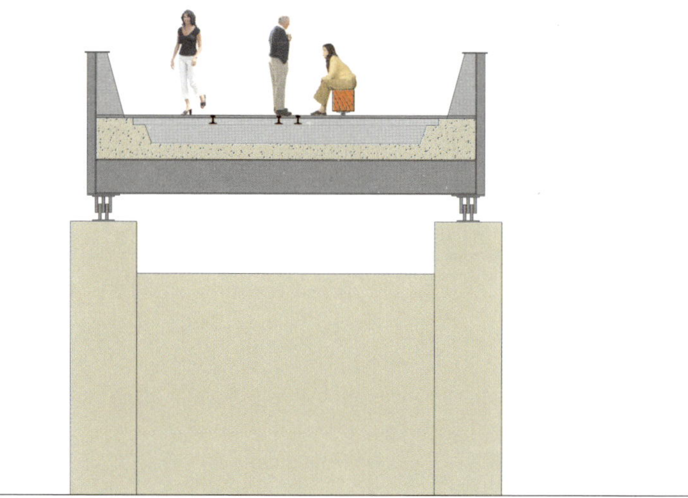

26 West 33RD Street Bridge

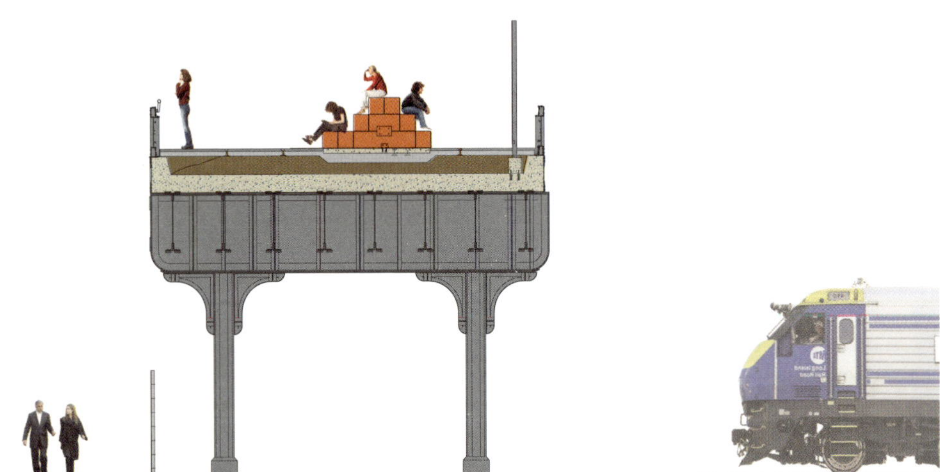

25 12TH Avenue Seating Steps

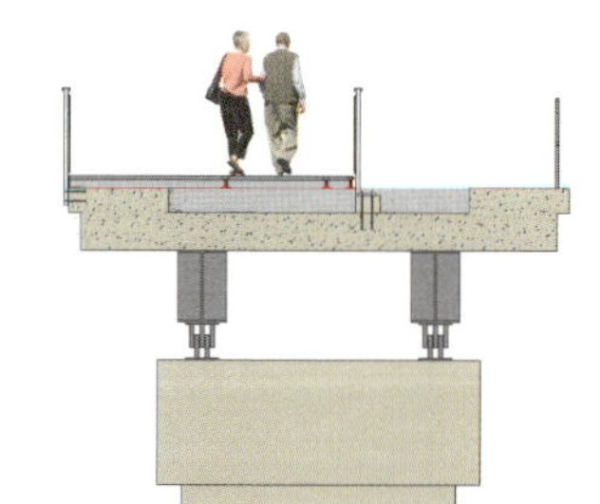

27 West 34TH Street Ramp

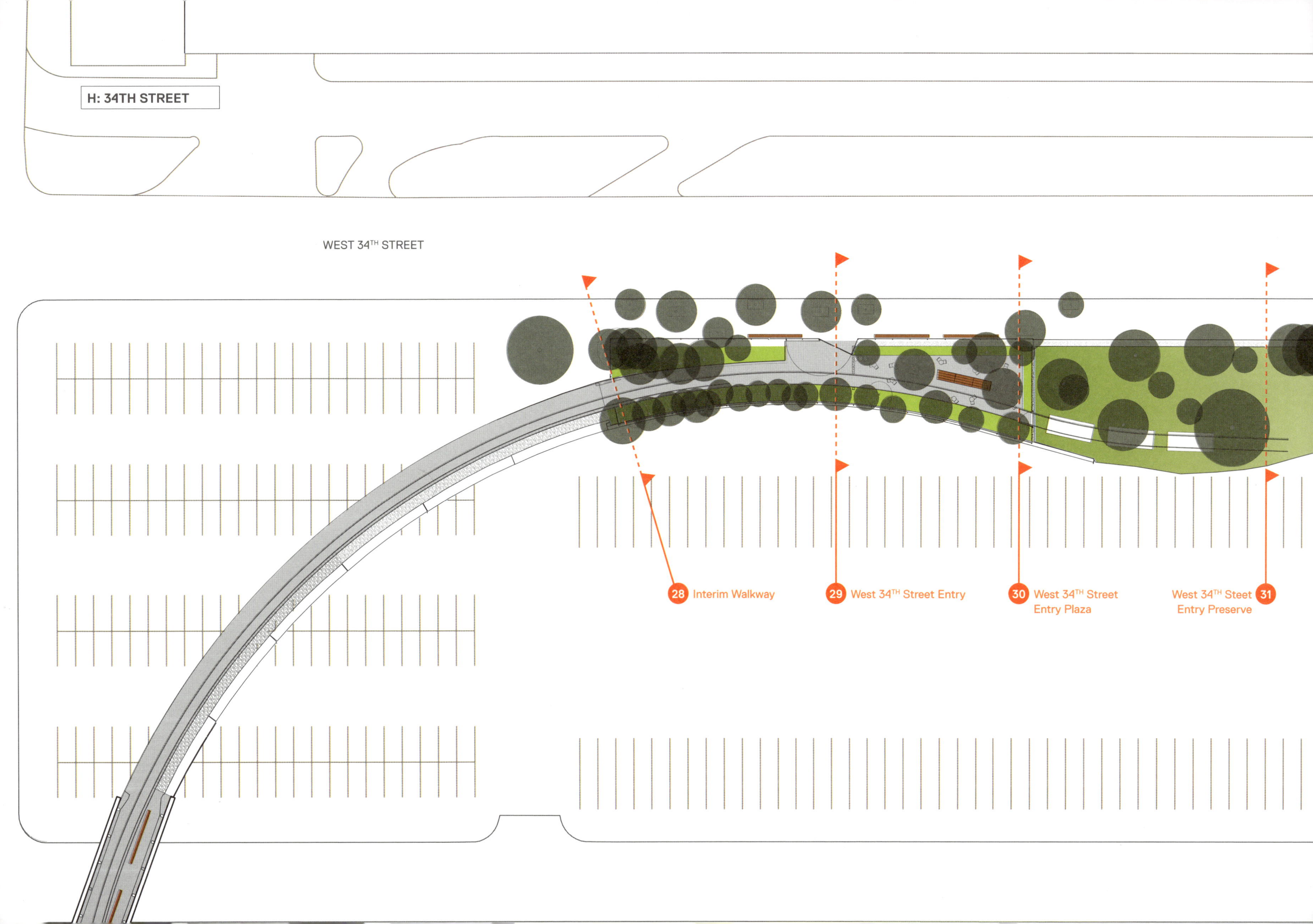

H: 34TH STREET
WEST 34TH STREET
28 Interim Walkway
29 West 34TH Street Entry
30 West 34TH Street Entry Plaza
West 34TH Steet Entry Preserve 31

WEST 34TH STREET
11TH AVENUE
50 FT
(15 M)
100 FT
(30 M)

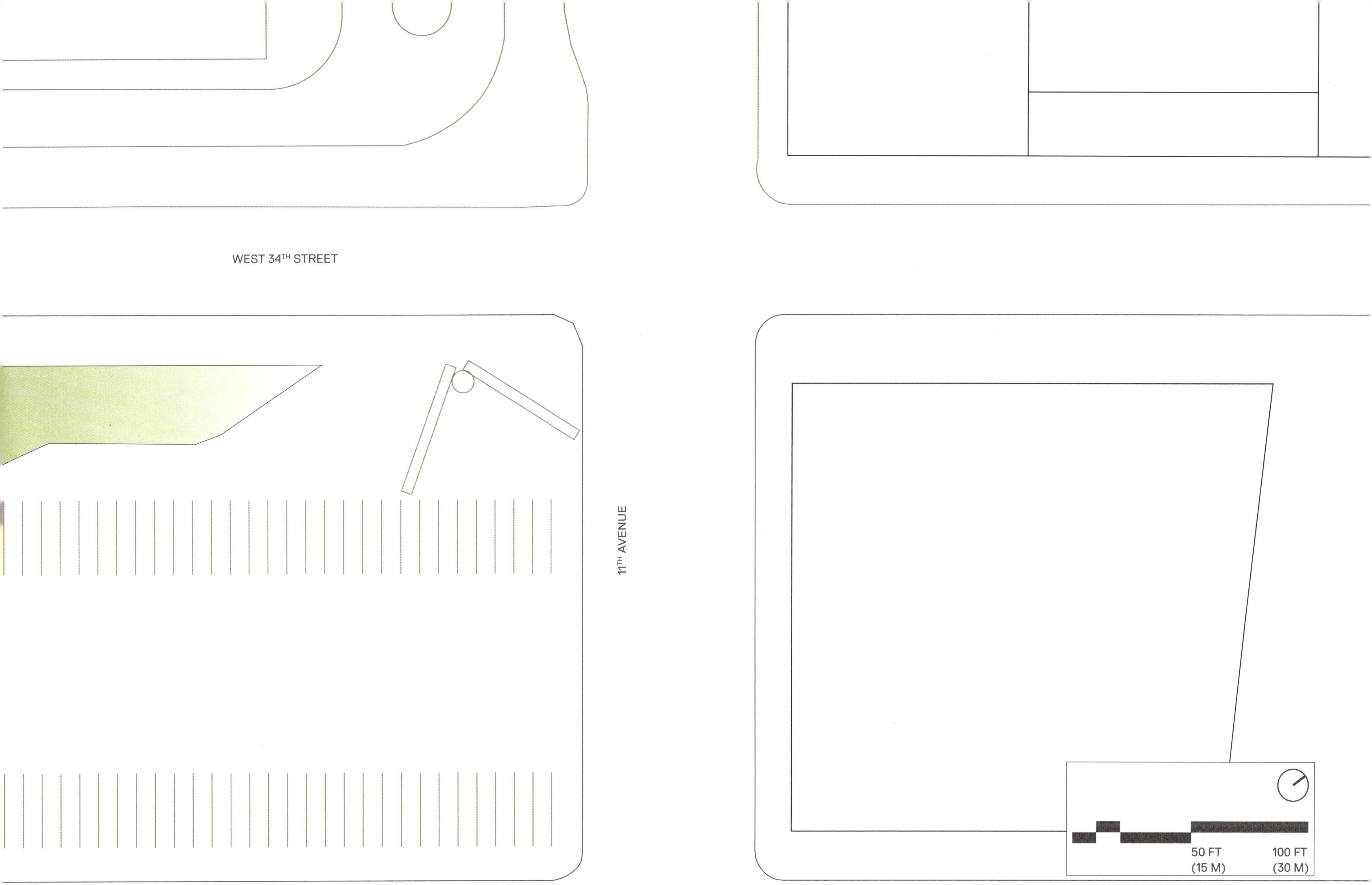

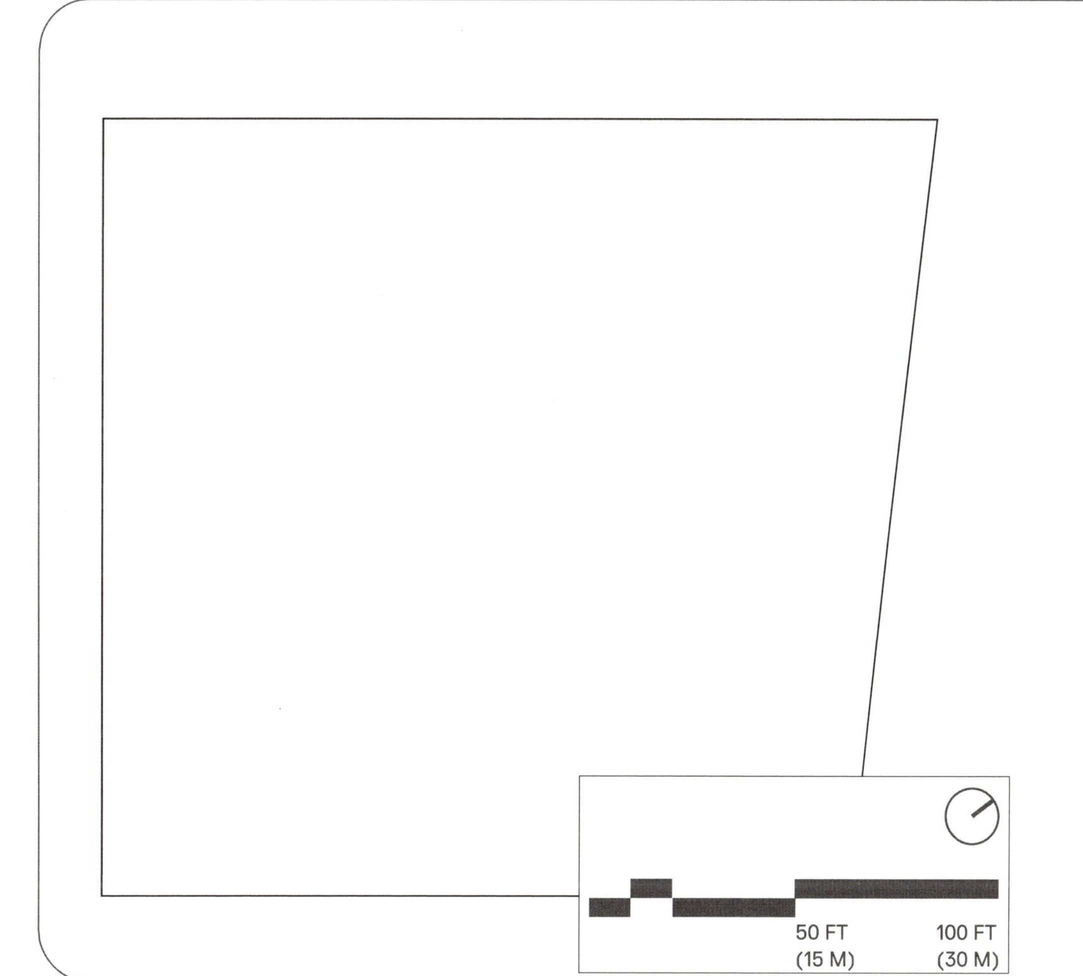

28 Interim Walkway

29 West 34TH Street Entry

30 West 34TH Street Entry Plaza

31 West 34TH Street Entry Preserve

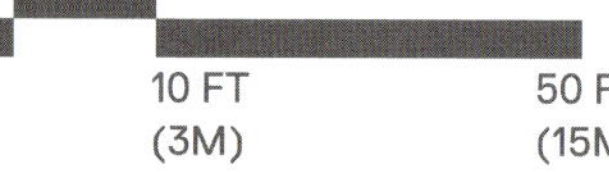

SPACE FOR RENT
HELMSLEY-NOYES CO
924-3880
CHELSEA
MINI-STORAGE
564-7735
CHELSEA
MINI
STORAGE
564-
7735

The shallow depth of the High Line's existing concrete tub required that all planting and landscape components—including planking, planters, soil, and mechanical, electrical, and drainage systems—be contained within an average build-up of only eighteen inches (460 mm). Every element, including the soil mix, was carefully engineered to fit. Throughout the park, the proportion of hardscape to softscape adjusts to the spatial needs of particular locations: the width of the planting beds increases as that of the planking tapers off, and vice versa. The planting beds have raised curbs to discourage the public from walking into plantings, and adjacent planks are spaced with a slight gap to allow rainwater to drain freely into the soil beneath. Over time, grasses and other plantings can emerge through these gaps, suggesting the wild, overgrown condition of the site before it became a park.

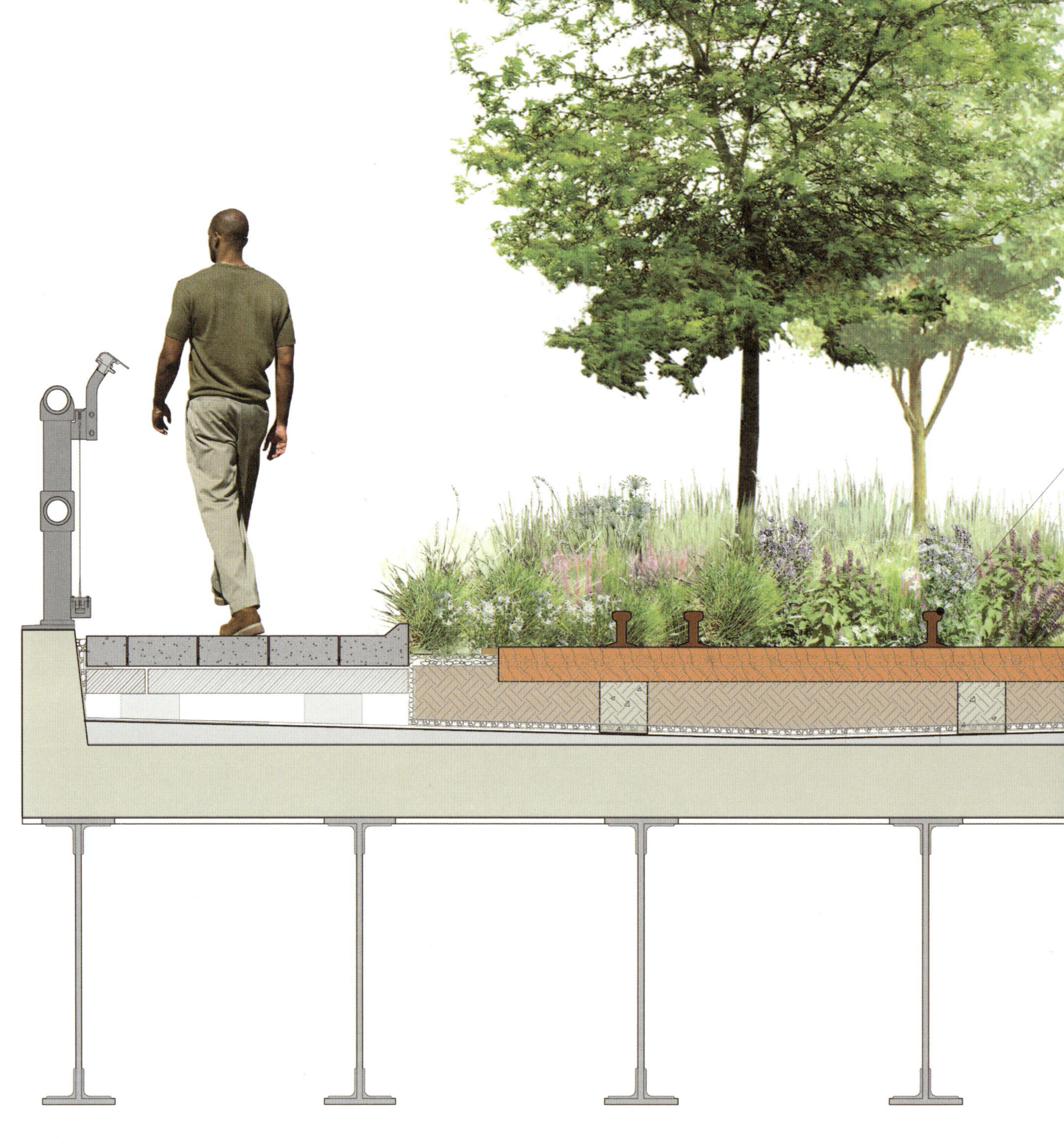

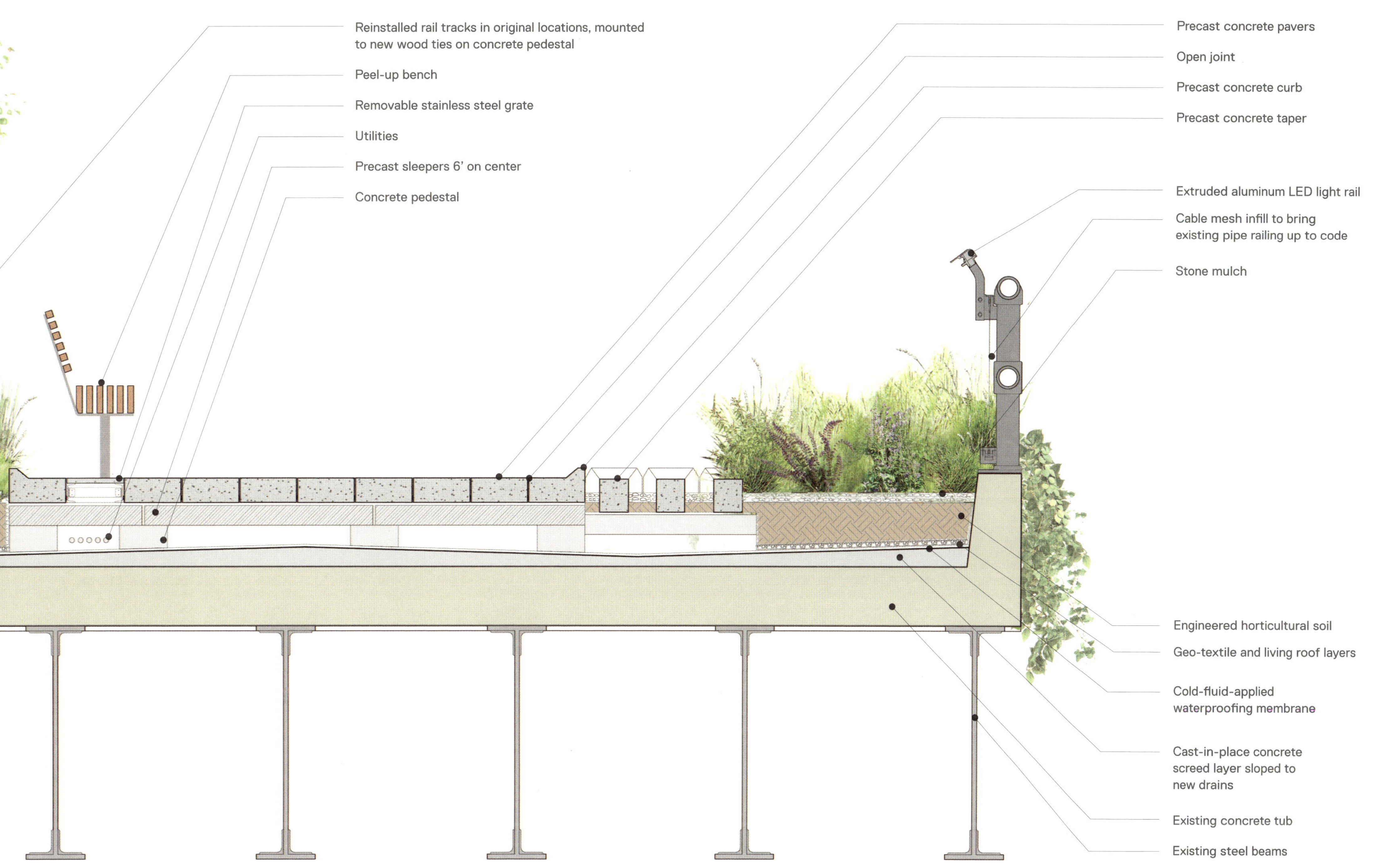

Reinstalled rail tracks in original locations, mounted to new wood ties on concrete pedestal
Peel-up bench
Removable stainless steel grate
Utilities
Precast sleepers 6' on center
Concrete pedestal
Precast concrete pavers
Open joint
Precast concrete curb
Precast concrete taper
Extruded aluminum LED light rail
Cable mesh infill to bring existing pipe railing up to code
Stone mulch
Engineered horticultural soil
Geo-textile and living roof layers
Cold-fluid-applied waterproofing membrane
Cast-in-place concrete screed layer sloped to new drains
Existing concrete tub
Existing steel beams

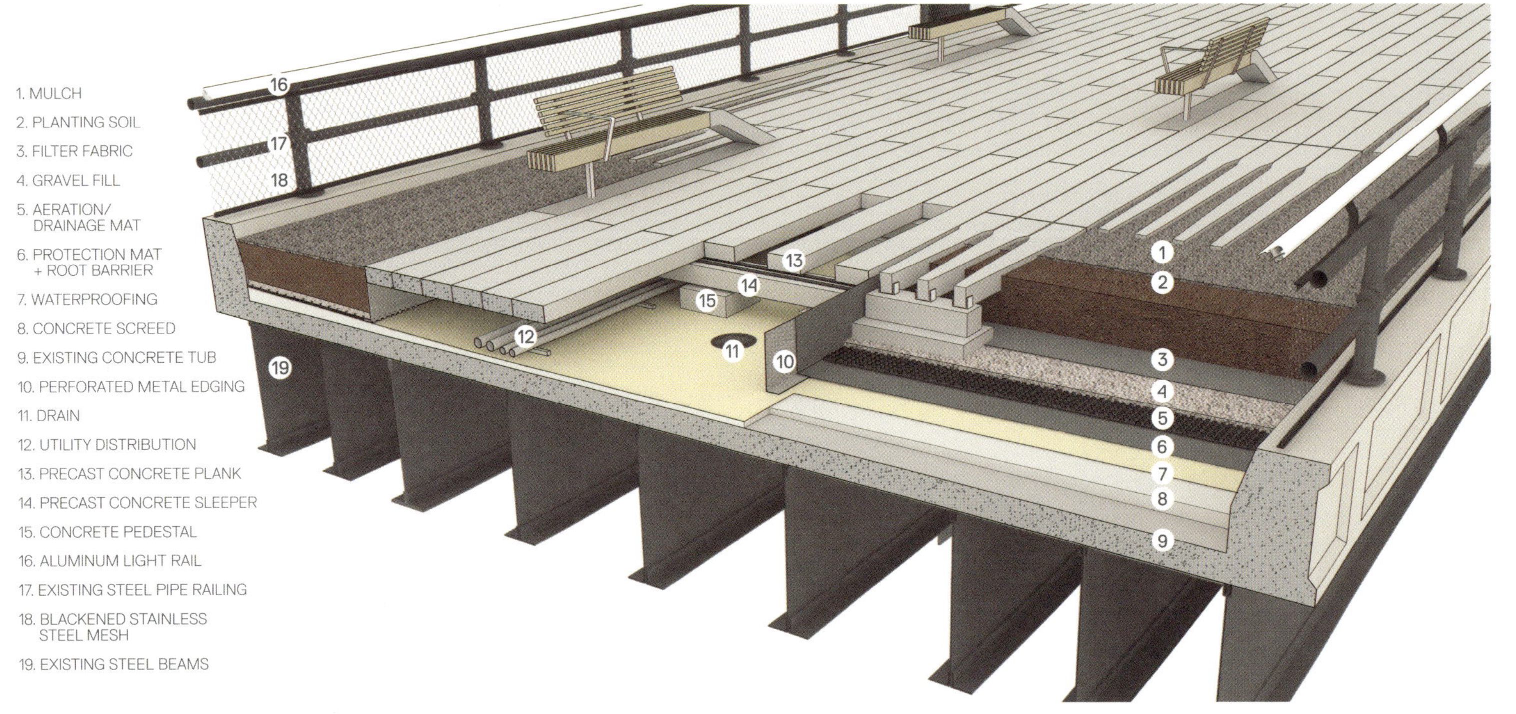

Typical High Line Buildup (Section Perspective)

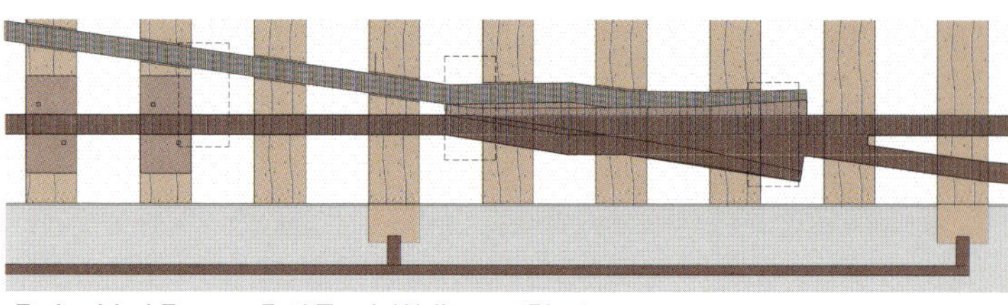

Embedded Frog at Rail Track Walkway (Plan)

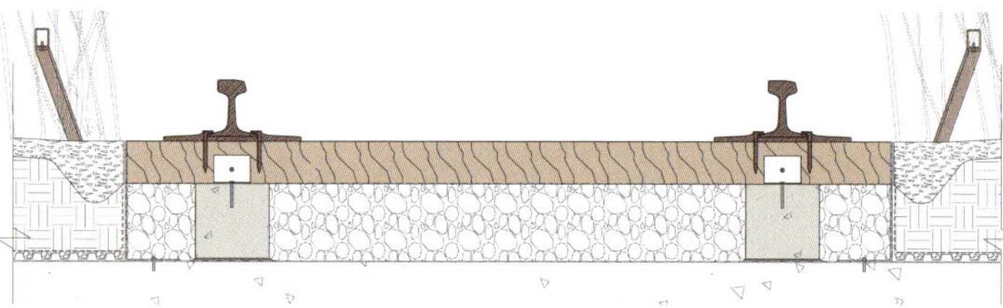

Rail Track Walkway (Section)

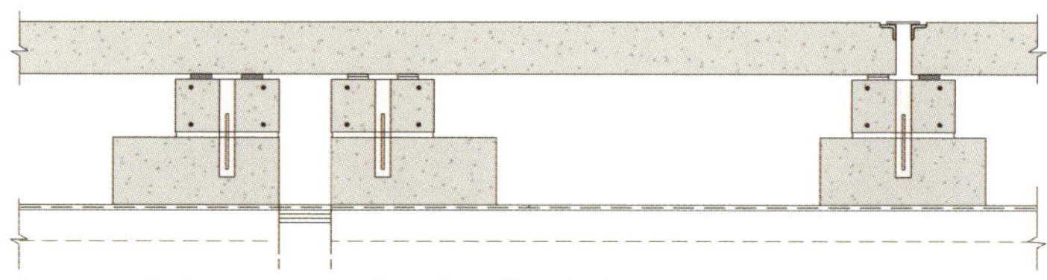

Concrete Substructure at Planking (Section)

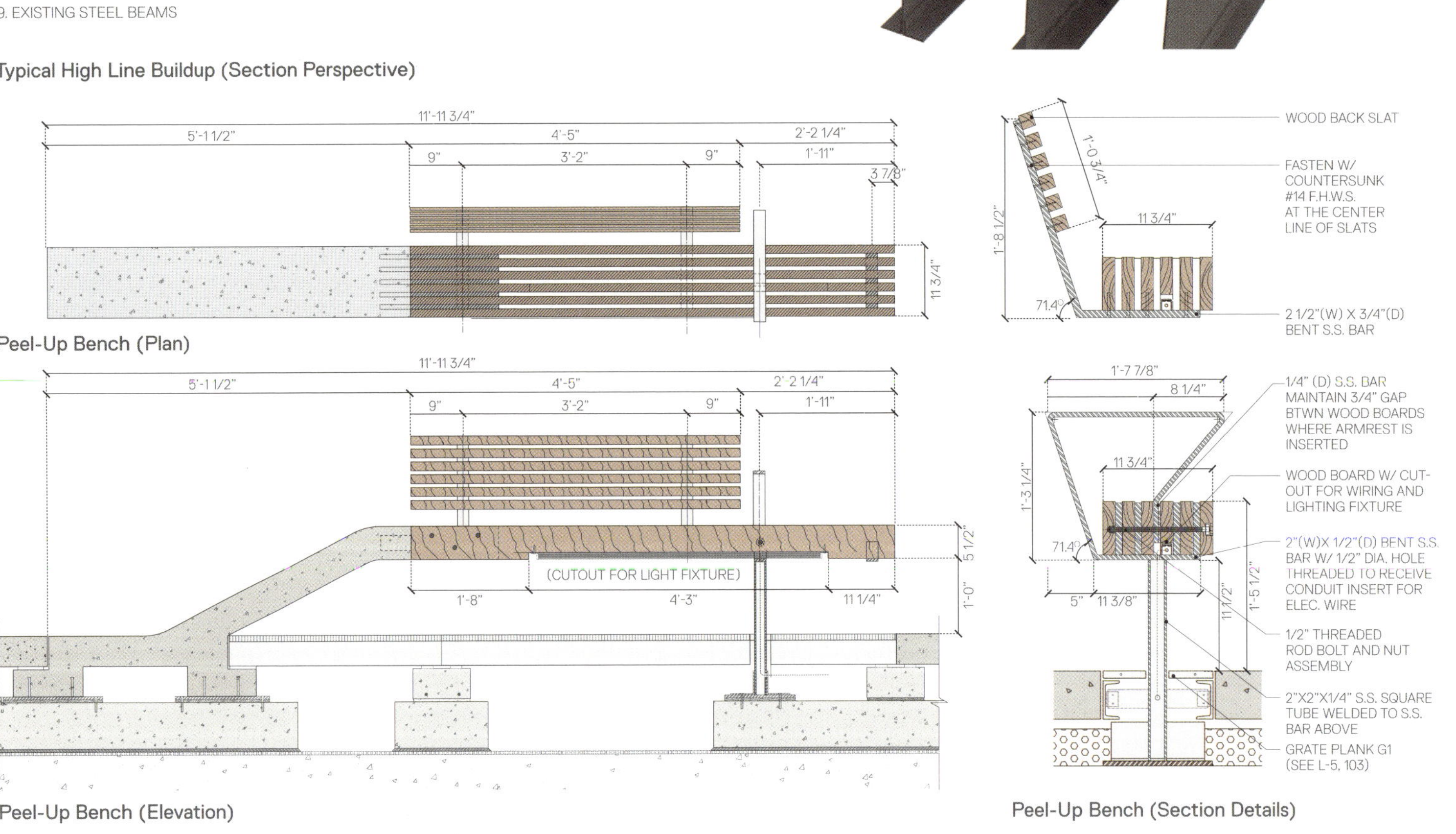

Peel-Up Bench (Plan)

Peel-Up Bench (Elevation)

Peel-Up Bench (Section Details)

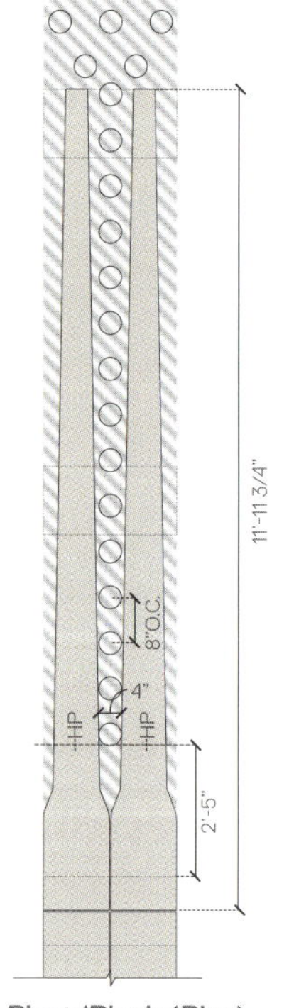

Plant/Plank (Plan)

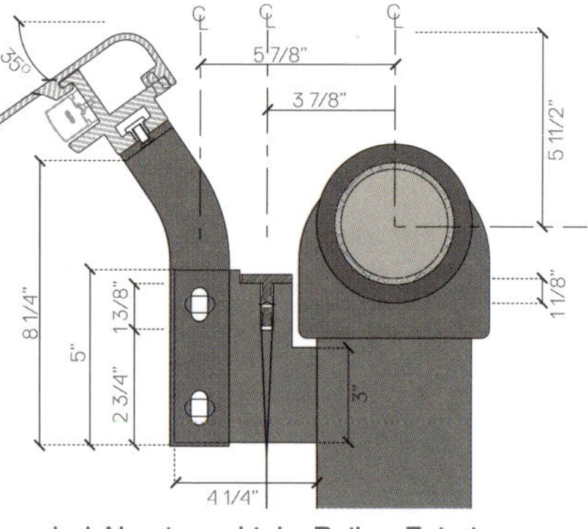

Extruded Aluminum Light Rail at Existing Pipe Railing (Section Detail)

Guardrail (Axonometric)

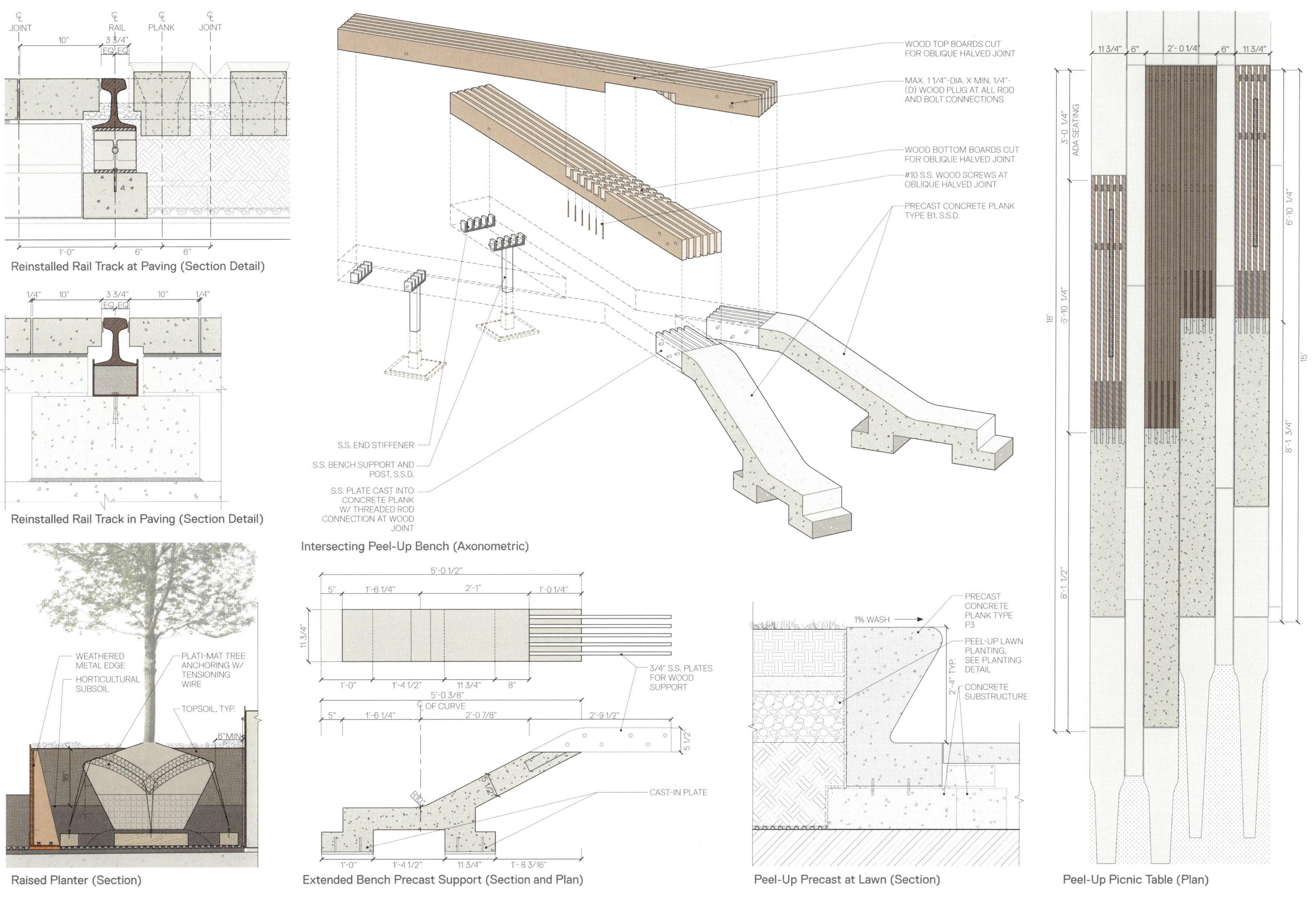

Reinstalled Rail Track at Paving (Section Detail)

Reinstalled Rail Track in Paving (Section Detail)

Raised Planter (Section)

Intersecting Peel-Up Bench (Axonometric)

Extended Bench Precast Support (Section and Plan)

Peel-Up Precast at Lawn (Section)

Peel-Up Picnic Table (Plan)

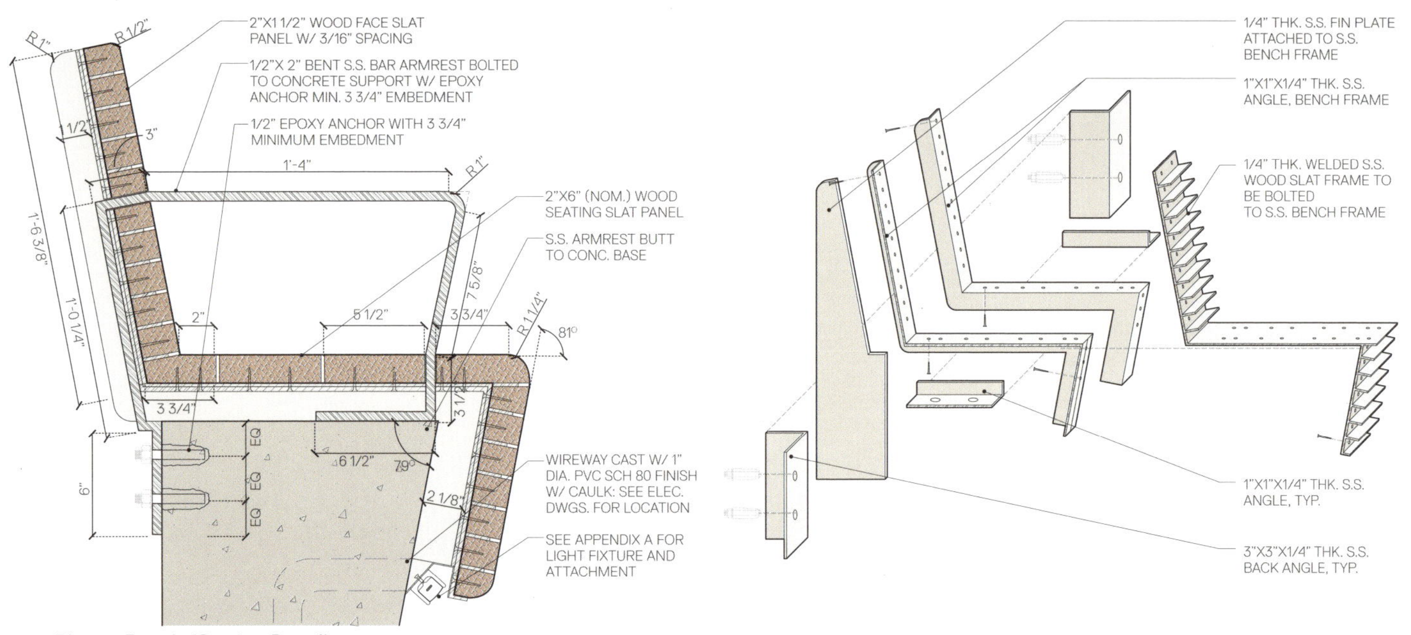

Planter Bench (Section Detail)

Bench Support (Exploded Axonometric)

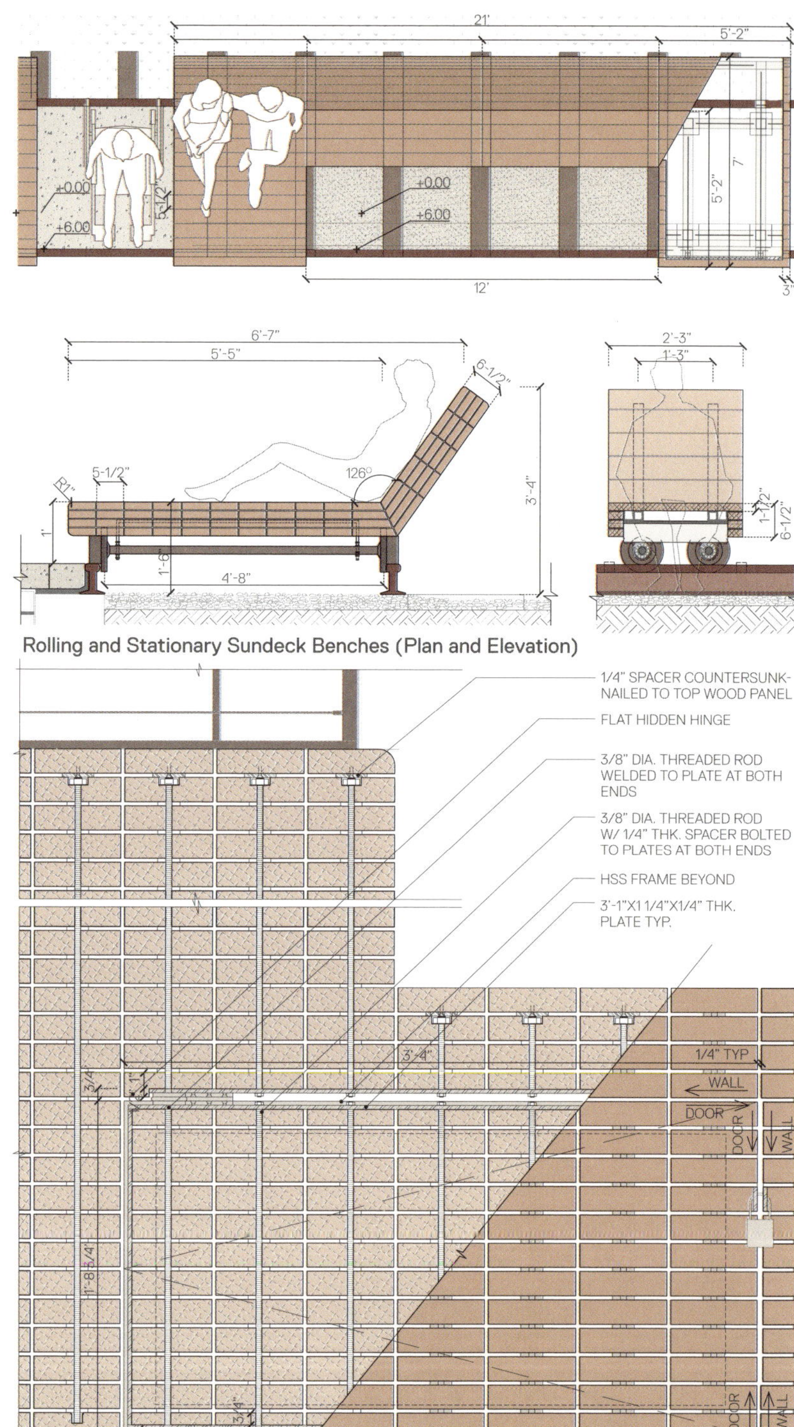

Rolling and Stationary Sundeck Benches (Plan and Elevation)

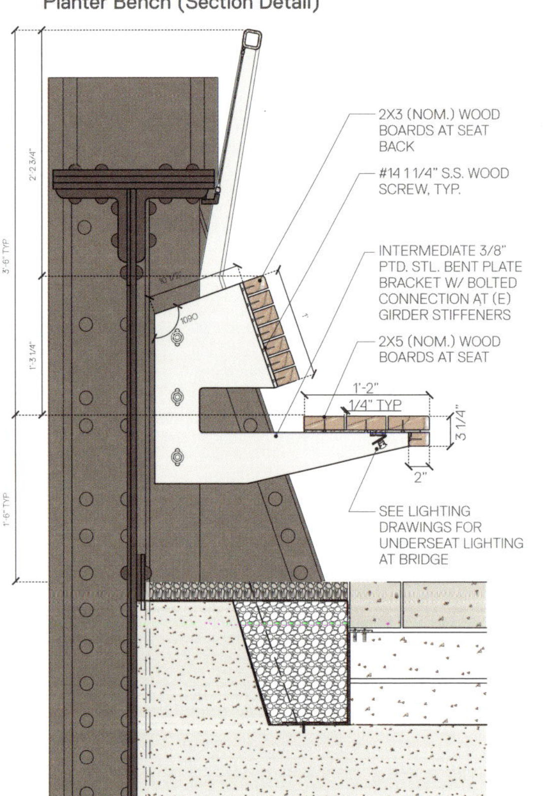

11TH Avenue Bridge Buttress Bench (Section)

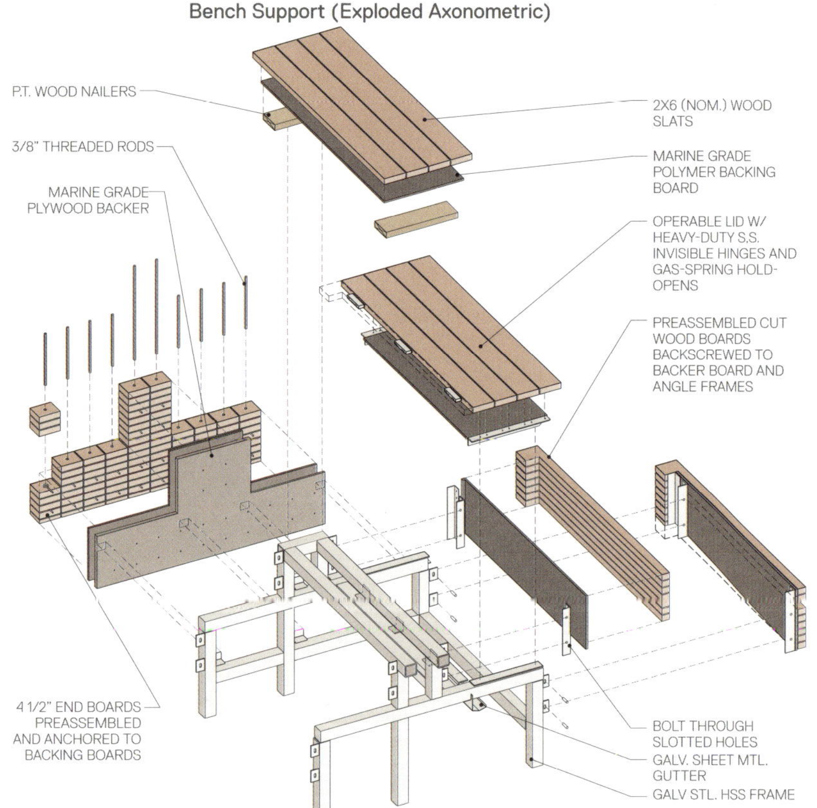

Stepped Bench with Storage (Exploded Axonometric)

Storage at Seating Steps (Section and Elevation)

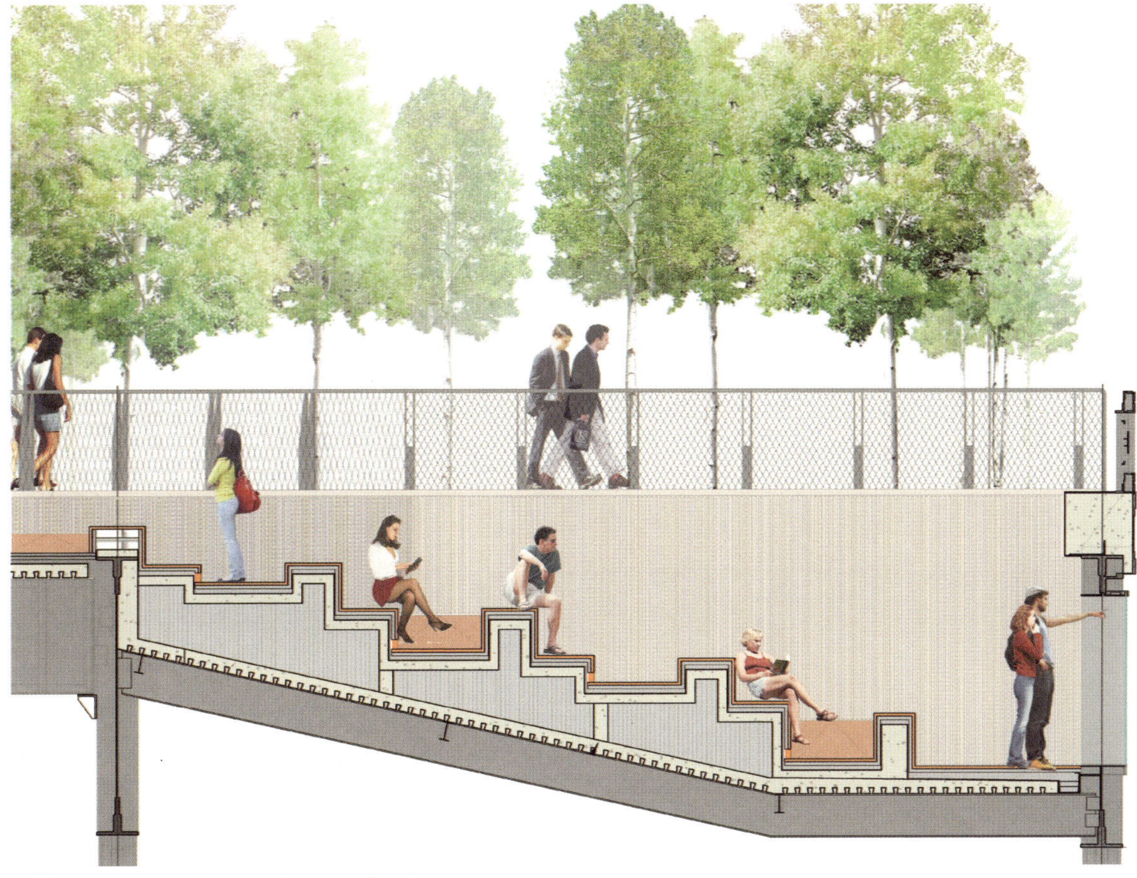

10TH Avenue Square Sunken Overlook (Section)

West 26TH Street Viewing Spur (Section)

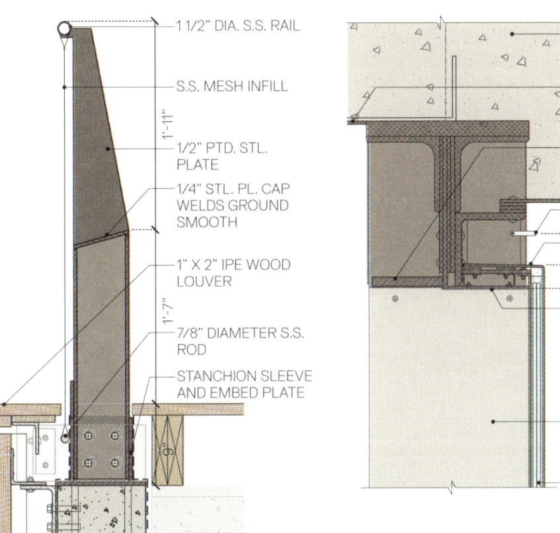

10TH Avenue Square Railing Deck Interface (Section)

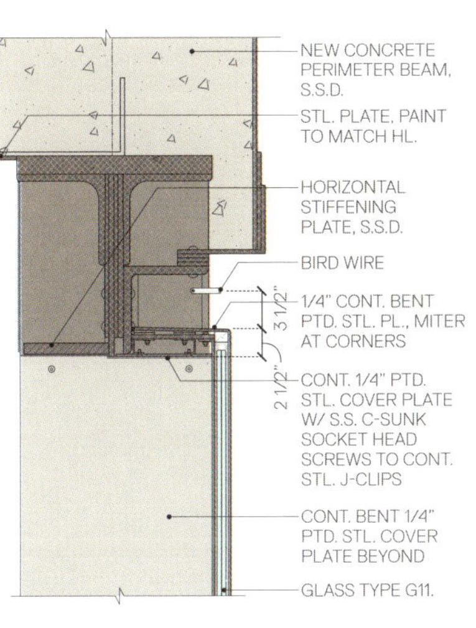

10TH Avenue Square Window Head (Section Detail)

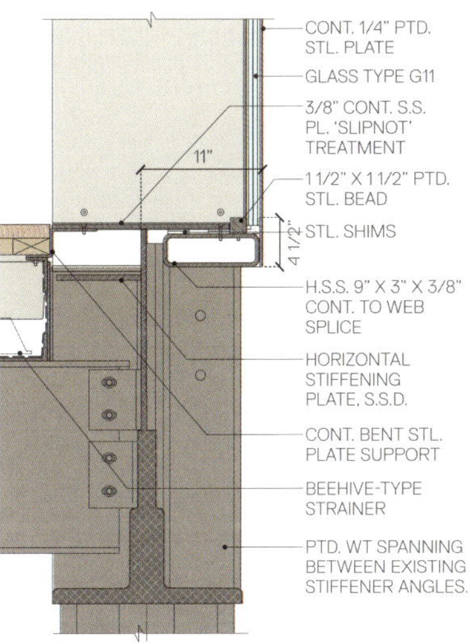

10TH Avenue Square Window Sill (Section Detail)

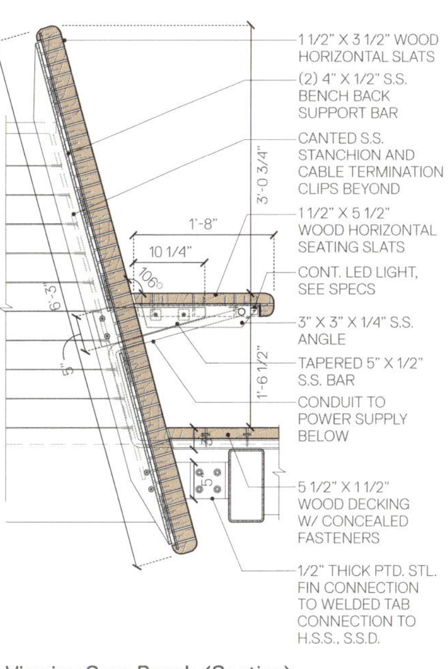

Viewing Spur Bench (Section)

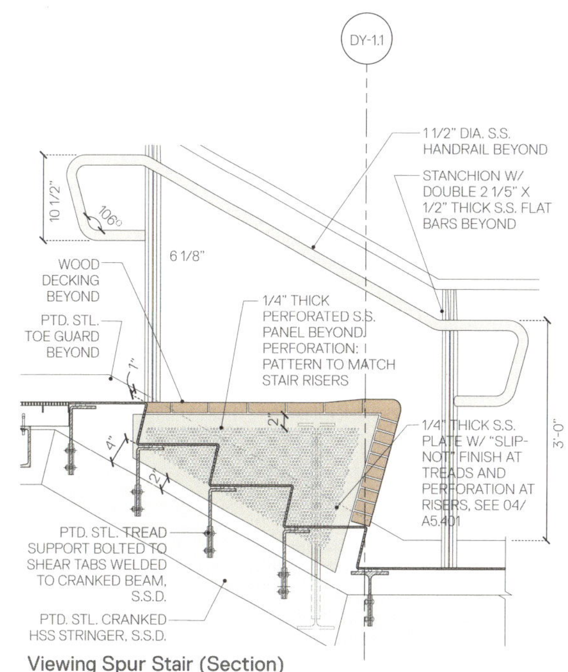

Viewing Spur Stair (Section)

Gopher Hole at Beam Exploration Area (Section Perspective)

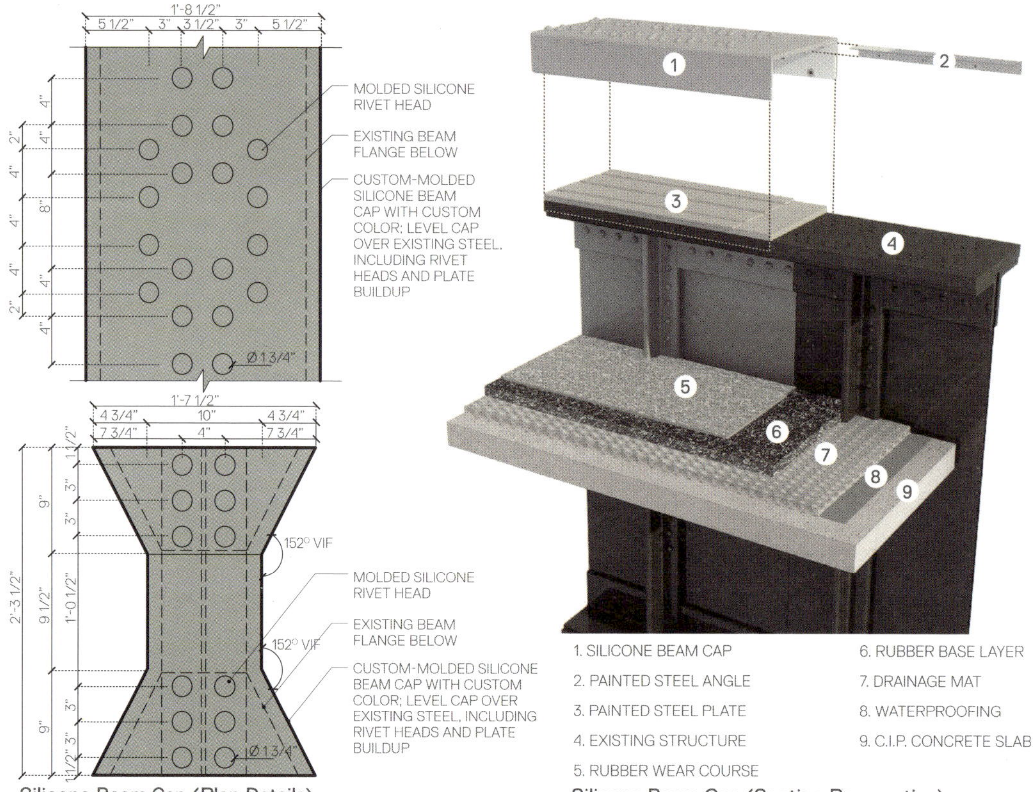

Silicone Beam Cap (Plan Details)

Silicone Beam Cap (Section Perspective)

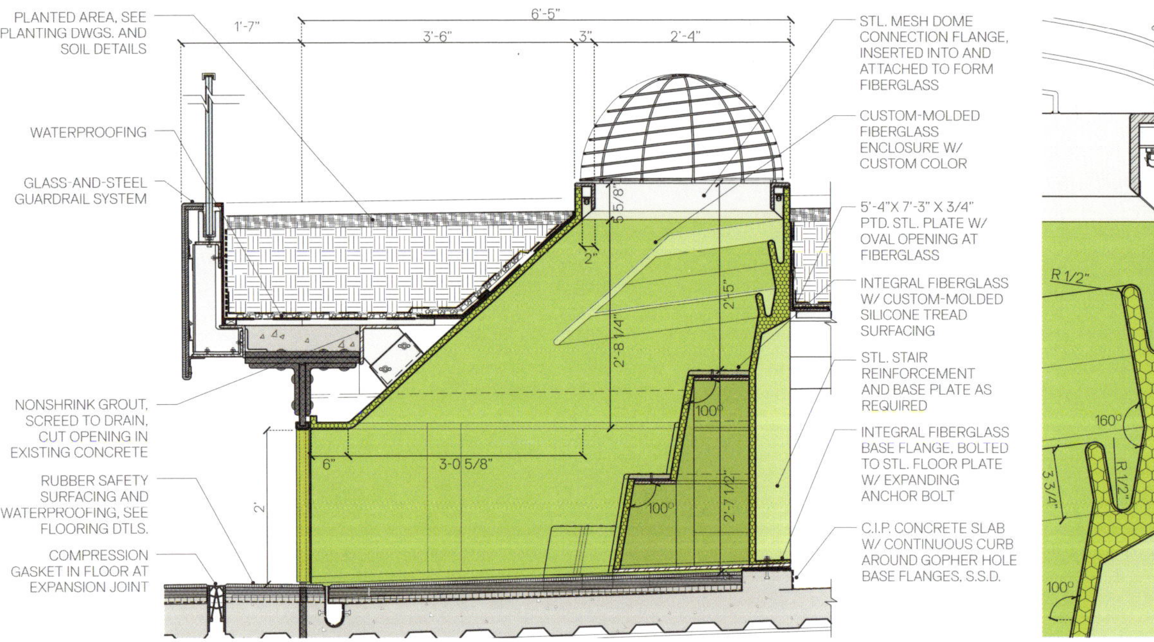

Gopher Hole at Beam Exploration Area (Section)

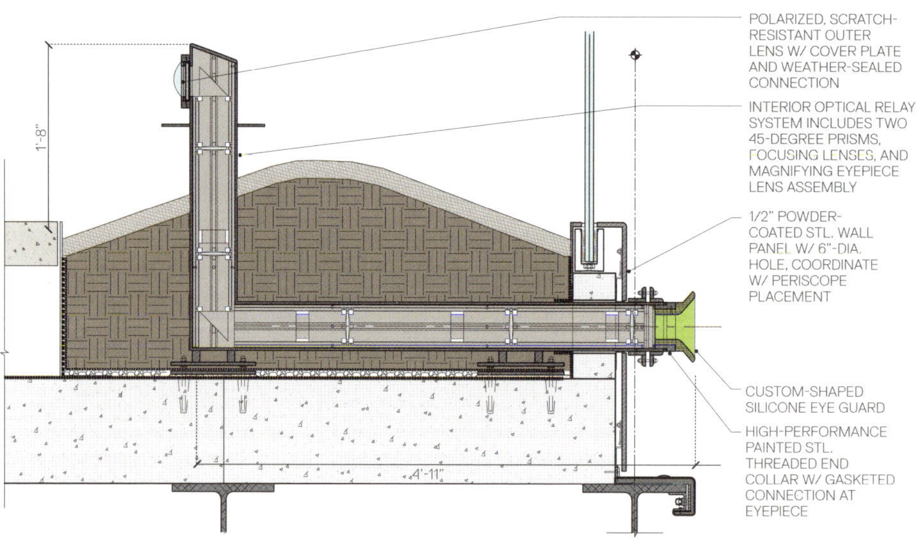

Planter Periscope at Beam Exploration Area (Section)

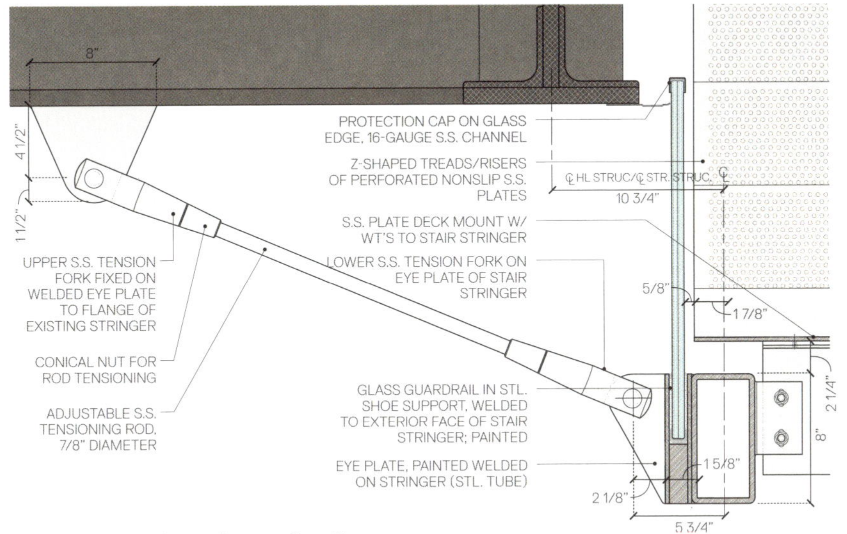

Tension Rod at Stair (Section Detail)

3/4" STIFFENER PLATES, BOTH SIDES, PLATES TO BE CUT AROUND ANGLE PLATES AND WELDED CONTINUOUSLY

7/8"-DIA. MEDIUM-STRENGTH HEAT-TREATED STAINLESS HANGER TO STAIR STRINGER

ALL RIVETS AT KNEE BRACE TO BE INSPECTED FOR REDUCED CAPACITY AND REPAIRED ACCORDINGLY

Structural Attachment at Existing Column (Axonometric)

1/4" JOINT

1 3/4"

1/4" S.S. "SLIPNOT" LANDINGS, TREADS, AND RISERS W/ PERFORATION AT RISERS, SEE 05/5.401

5/16" STL. PL. SHIM WELDED TO ANGLE, OFFSET FROM ANGLE EDGE BY 1/4"

2"

PTD. STL. STAIR STRINGER

S.S. TORX IN PIN SCREW THROUGH DECK AND SHIM TO UNDERSTRUCTURE, S.S.D.

DOUBLE SHEAR TABS WELDED TO STRINGER, S.S.D.

PTD. STL. WT/ANGLE BOLTED TO SHEAR TABS W/ SLOTTED HOLES FOR ADJUSTMENT, S.S.D.

1" TYP

4 1/2"

Stair Treads (Section Detail)

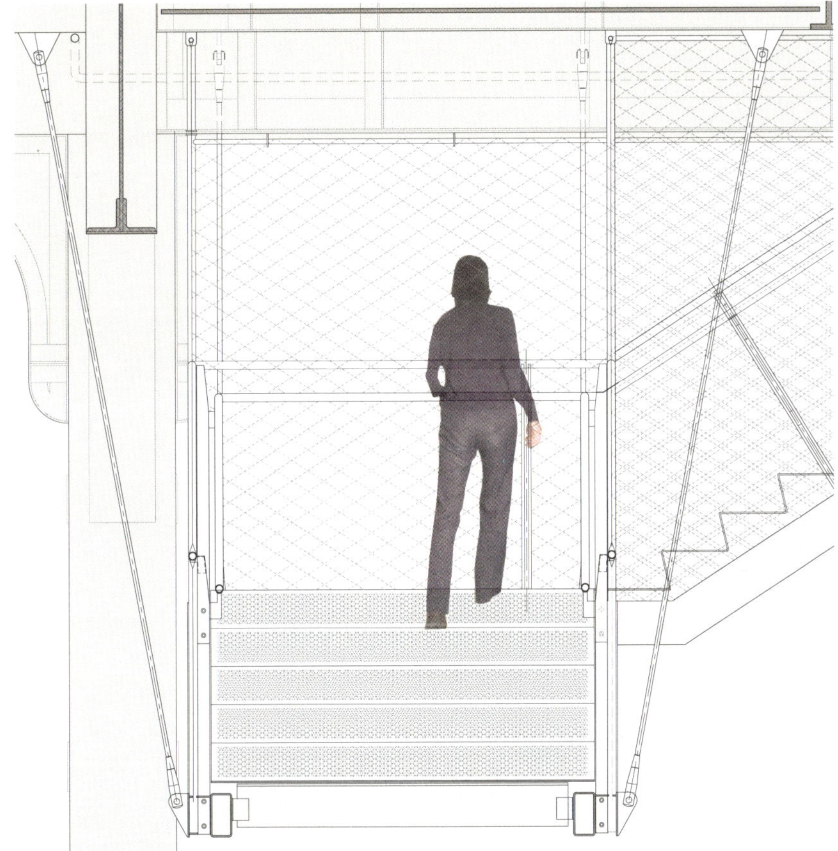

West 23RD Street Stair (Section)

3/4"

MOUNTING BRACKET BELOW

3/4"

MESH ABOVE SUPPORT ROD, WHERE OCCURS

S.S. 1 1/2" DIA. SUPPORT TUBE FOR MESH

1 3/8"

6"

3/8" X 3/4" LONG S.S. TORX PIN-IN TAMPER-PROOF FLATHEAD SCREWS COUNTERSUNK BOTH SIDES, TYP.

1 1/2" DIA. S.S. HANDRAIL

3/4"

1 3/4"

3/4"-THICK S.S. BRACKET

3"

S.S. X-TEND MESH

2 1/4" 2 1/4"

1/2"-DIA. S.S. ROD BEYOND AT ALL CORNERS AND END CONDITIONS U.O.N.

3'-0"

TYP. STANCHION: (2) 1/2"-THICK S.S. PLATES

3/4"-THICK S.S. KNIFE PLATE - DRILL AND TAP TO RECEIVE SCREWS BOTH SIDES, TYP.

3"

1'-1 1/2"

T.O.TREAD AT NOSE

Stair Stanchion and Railing (Plan and Section)

S.S. GUARDRAILS AND STANCHIONS W/ X-TEND MESH INFILL

PAINTED STEEL SECURITY FENCE SUPPORT FRAMING

PAINTED STEEL COLUMN W/ ARCHITECTURAL COVER PLATES

CONCRETE FOOTINGS

PRECAST CONCRETE PLANKS W/ NONSLIP FINISH

PAINTED STEEL STRINGER AND FASCIA PLATES

PRECAST CONCRETE TREADS

West 30TH Street Stair (Axonometric)

The park's precast concrete planking system is based on a modular unit that is one foot wide by twelve feet long (0.3 x 3.7 m). This unit is adapted to create a series of over one hundred variations, including planks with tapered ends, curbs, and radial curves. The peel-up benches rest on special supports that appear to grow out of the walkway planking. The system allows the walking surface to be materially consistent and spatially variable, calibrated to accommodate a variety of uses and environments along the length of the High Line.

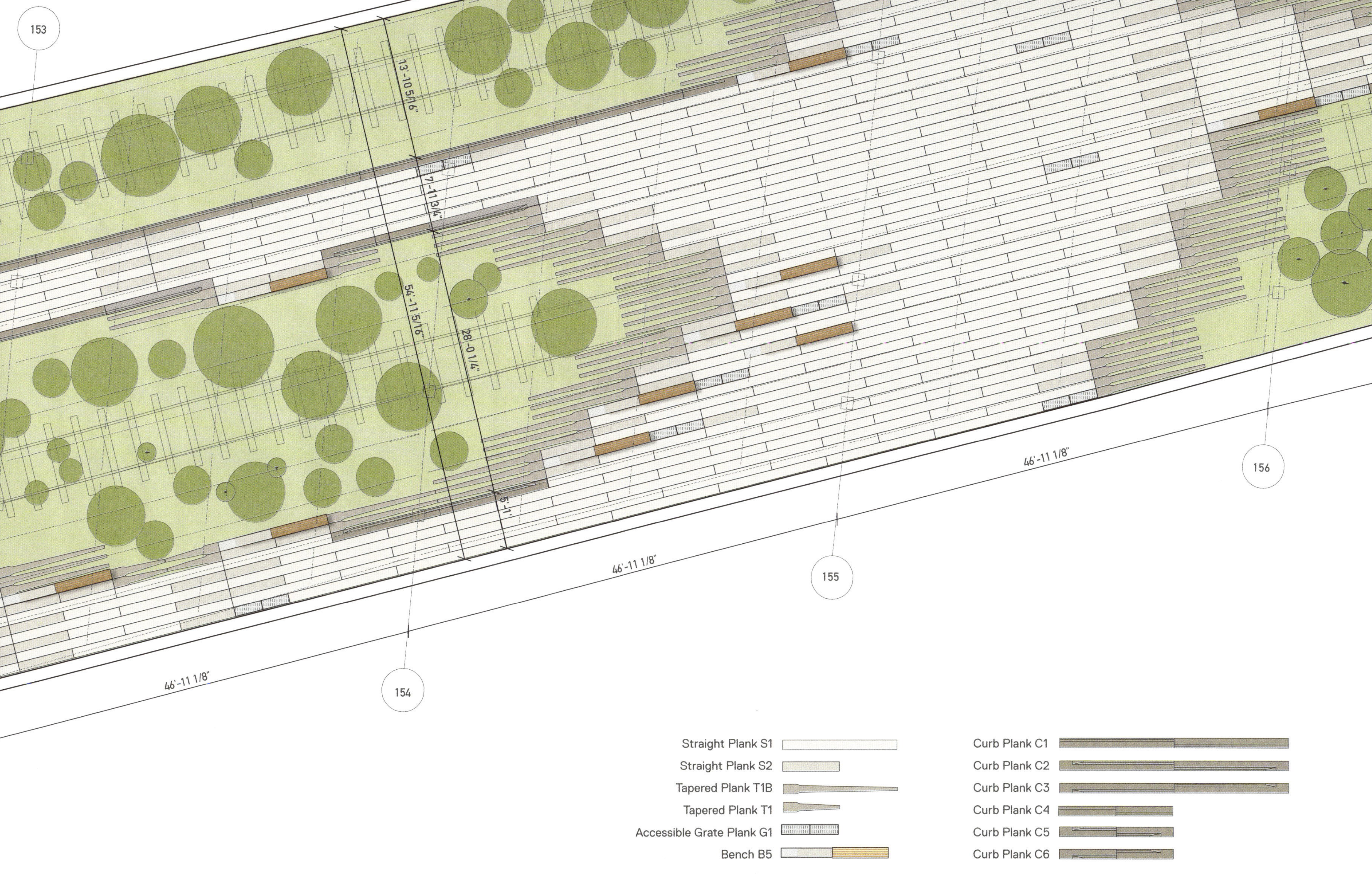
153
154
155
156
13'-10 5/16"
7'-11 3/4"
54'-11 5/16"
28'-0 1/4"
5'-1"
46'-11 1/8"
46'-11 1/8"
46'-11 1/8"
Straight Plank S1
Straight Plank S2
Tapered Plank T1B
Tapered Plank T1
Accessible Grate Plank G1
Bench B5
Curb Plank C1
Curb Plank C2
Curb Plank C3
Curb Plank C4
Curb Plank C5
Curb Plank C6

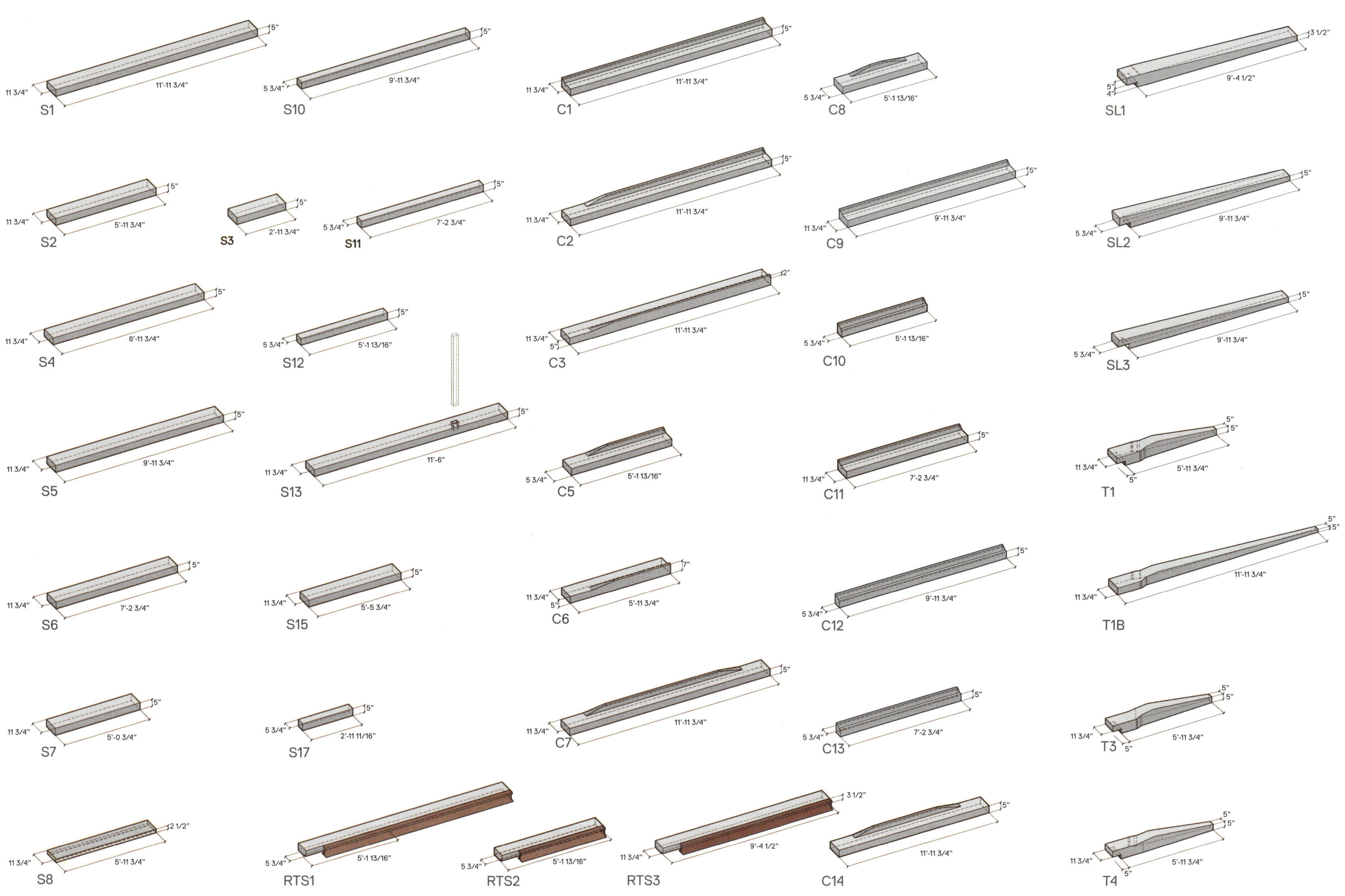

S1
11 3/4"
11'-11 3/4"
5"
S10
5 3/4"
9'-11 3/4"
5"
C1
11 3/4"
11'-11 3/4"
5"
C8
5 3/4"
5'-1 13/16"
SL1
5"
4"
9'-4 1/2"
3 1/2"
S2
11 3/4"
5'-11 3/4"
5"
S3
2'-11 3/4"
5"
S11
5 3/4"
7'-2 3/4"
5"
C2
11 3/4"
11'-11 3/4"
5"
C9
11 3/4"
9'-11 3/4"
5"
SL2
5 3/4"
9'-11 3/4"
5"
S4
11 3/4"
8'-11 3/4"
5"
S12
5 3/4"
5'-1 13/16"
5"
C3
11 3/4"
5"
11'-11 3/4"
2"
C10
5 3/4"
5'-1 13/16"
SL3
5 3/4"
9'-11 3/4"
5"
S5
11 3/4"
9'-11 3/4"
5"
S13
11 3/4"
11'-6"
5"
C5
5 3/4"
5'-1 13/16"
C11
11 3/4"
7'-2 3/4"
5"
T1
11 3/4"
5"
5'-11 3/4"
5"
5"
S6
11 3/4"
7'-2 3/4"
5"
S15
11 3/4"
5'-5 3/4"
5"
C6
11 3/4"
5"
5'-11 3/4"
7"
C12
5 3/4"
9'-11 3/4"
5"
T1B
11 3/4"
11'-11 3/4"
5"
5"
S7
11 3/4"
5'-0 3/4"
5"
S17
5 3/4"
2'-11 11/16"
5"
C7
11 3/4"
11'-11 3/4"
5"
C13
5 3/4"
7'-2 3/4"
5"
T3
11 3/4"
5"
5'-11 3/4"
5"
5"
S8
11 3/4"
5'-11 3/4"
2 1/2"
RTS1
5 3/4"
5'-1 13/16"
RTS2
5 3/4"
5'-1 13/16"
RTS3
11 3/4"
9'-4 1/2"
3 1/2"
C14
11'-11 3/4"
5"
T4
11 3/4"
5"
5'-11 3/4"
5"
5"

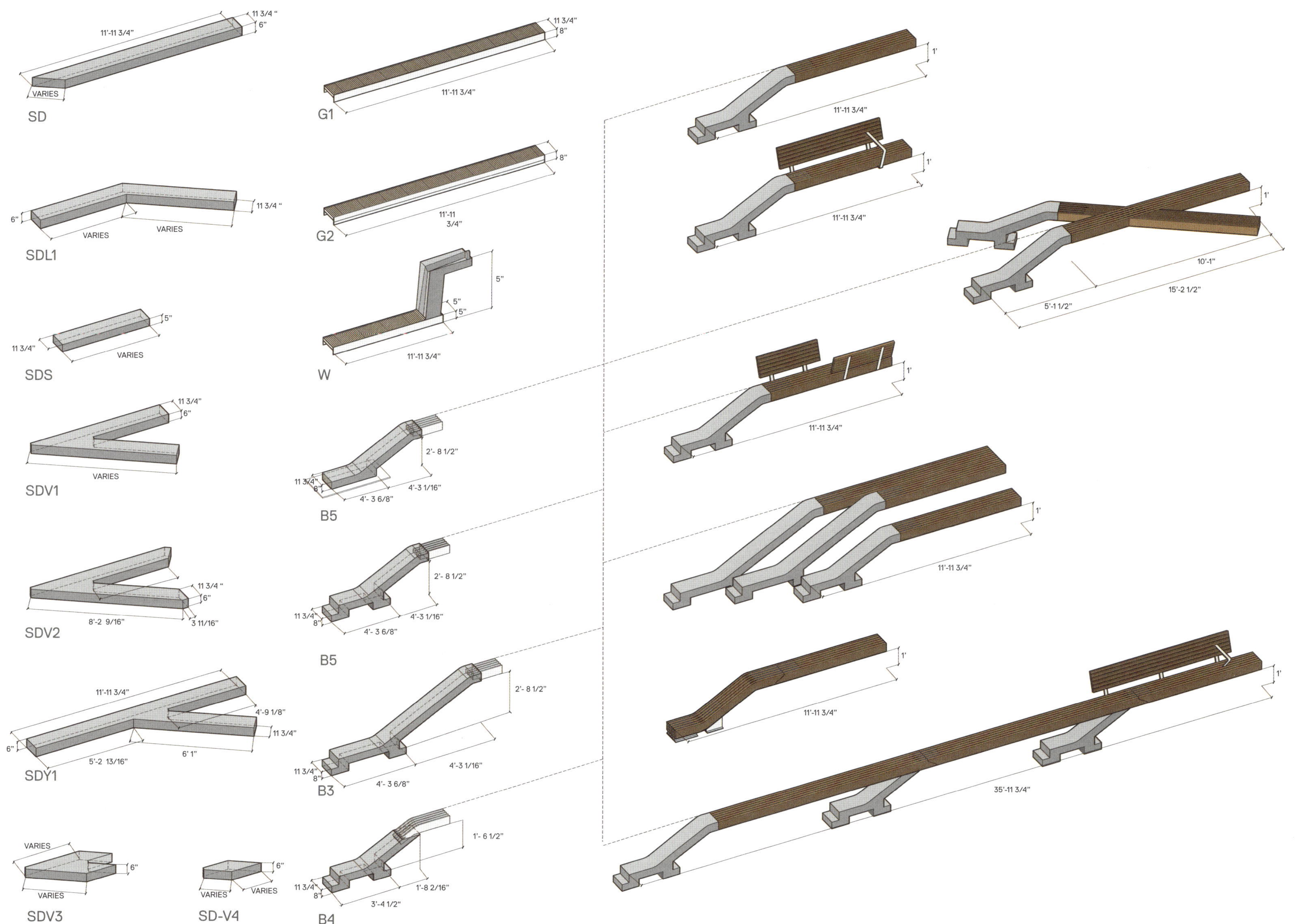
SD
SDL1
SDS
SDV1
SDV2
SDY1
SDV3
SD-V4
G1
G2
W
B5
B5
B3
B4
11'-11 3/4"
VARIES
35'-11 3/4"
15'-2 1/2"
10'-1"
5'-1 1/2"

The landscape of the High Line was designed to celebrate plants in all seasons, from fragrant summer meadows to sculptural winter brush. Plants are left to their natural growth patterns year-round. Throughout the year, new forms, colors, smells, shadows, and textures emerge as others subside. The Chelsea Grasslands area (below) showcases this seasonal variation.

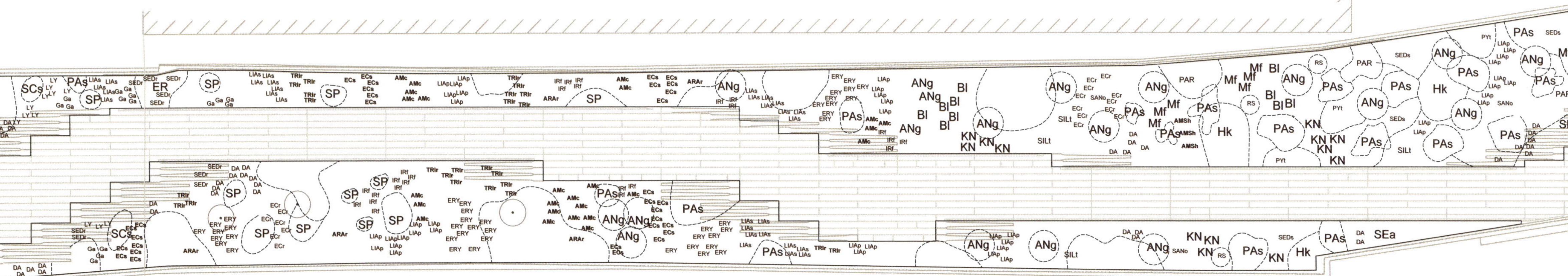

Technical Groundcover Planting Plan

January/February

March/April

May/June

Legend

AMc: *Amorpha canescens*
AMSh: *Amsonia hubrichtii*
ANg: *Andropogon gerardii*
ARAr: *Aralia racemosa*
Bl: *Baptisia leucantha*
DA: *Dalea purpurea*
ECr: *Echinacea purpurea* 'Sunset'
ECs: *Echinacea purpurea* 'Sunset'
ER: *Eragrostis spectabilis*
ERY: *Eryngium yuccifolium*
Ga: *Gentiana quinquefolia*
Hk: *Helenium* 'Rubinzwerg'
IRf: *Iris fulva*
KN: *Knautia macedonia*
LIAp: *Liatris pycnostachya*
LIAs: *Liatris spicata*
LY: *Lythrum alatum*
Mf: *Monarda fistulosa* 'Claire Grace'
PAs: *Panicum virgatum* 'Shenandoah'
PAR: *Parthenium integrifolium*
PYt: *Pycnanthemum muticum*
RS: *Rudbeckia subtomentosa*
SANo: *Sanguisorba officinalis* 'Red Thunder'
SEa: *Sesleria autumnalis*
SEDs: *Sedum* 'Sunkissed'
SILt: *Silphium terebinthinaceum*
SP: *Sporobolus heterolepis*
TRIr: *Trifolium rubens*

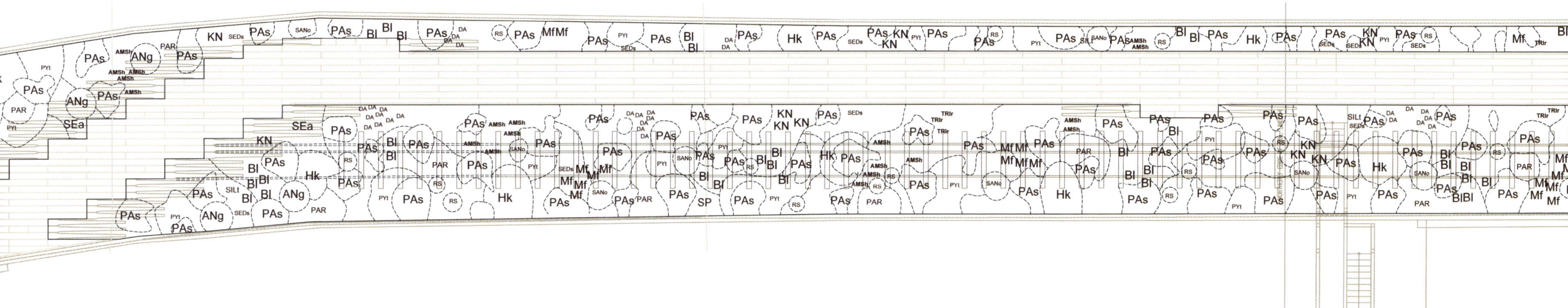

July/August

September/October

November/December

While the park appears wild, its planting layout relies on a measured system of layering, spacing, and repetition. This framework is particularly evident in the Woodland Flyover (below), where three layers of plantings rise from the ground below the elevated path.

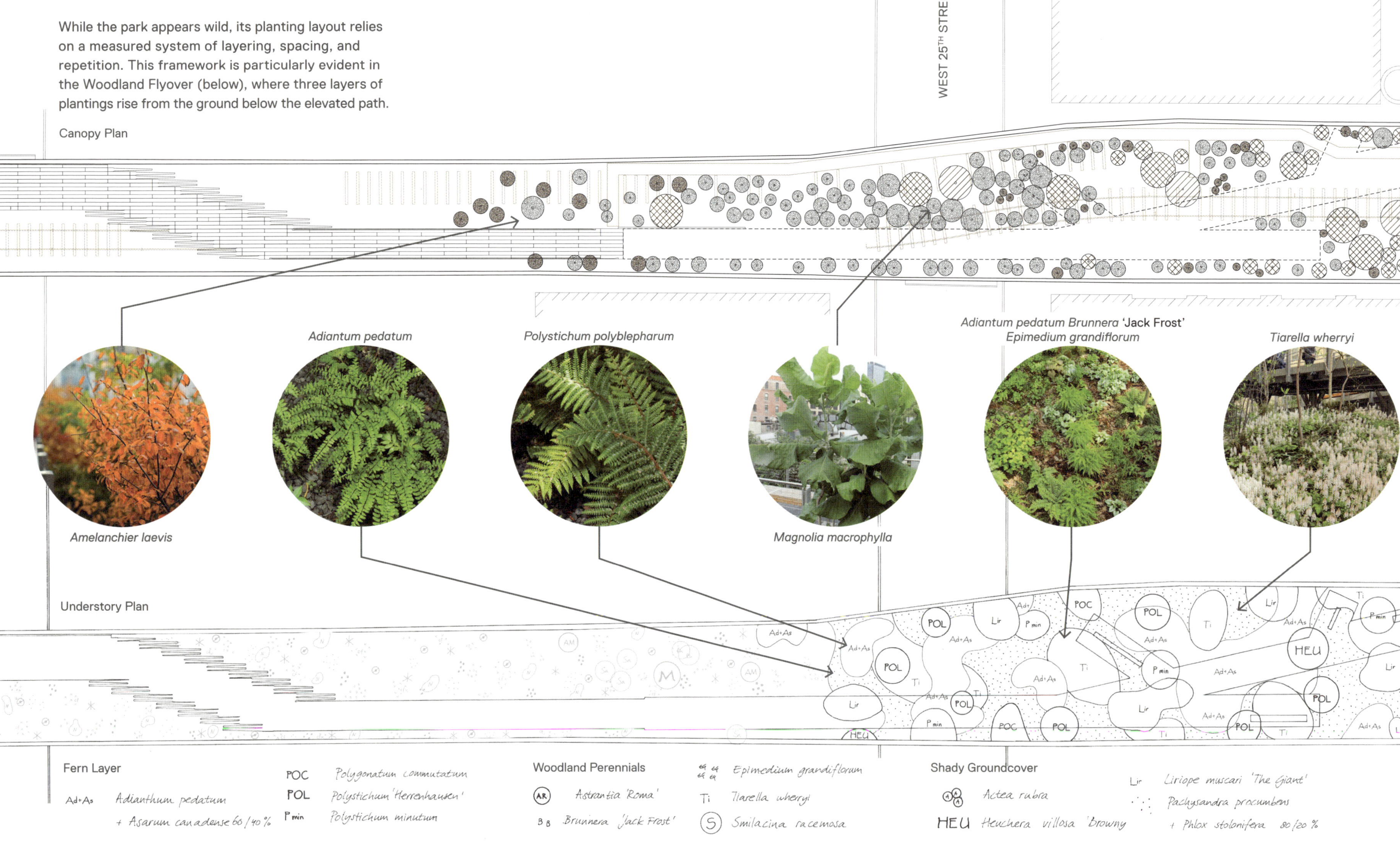

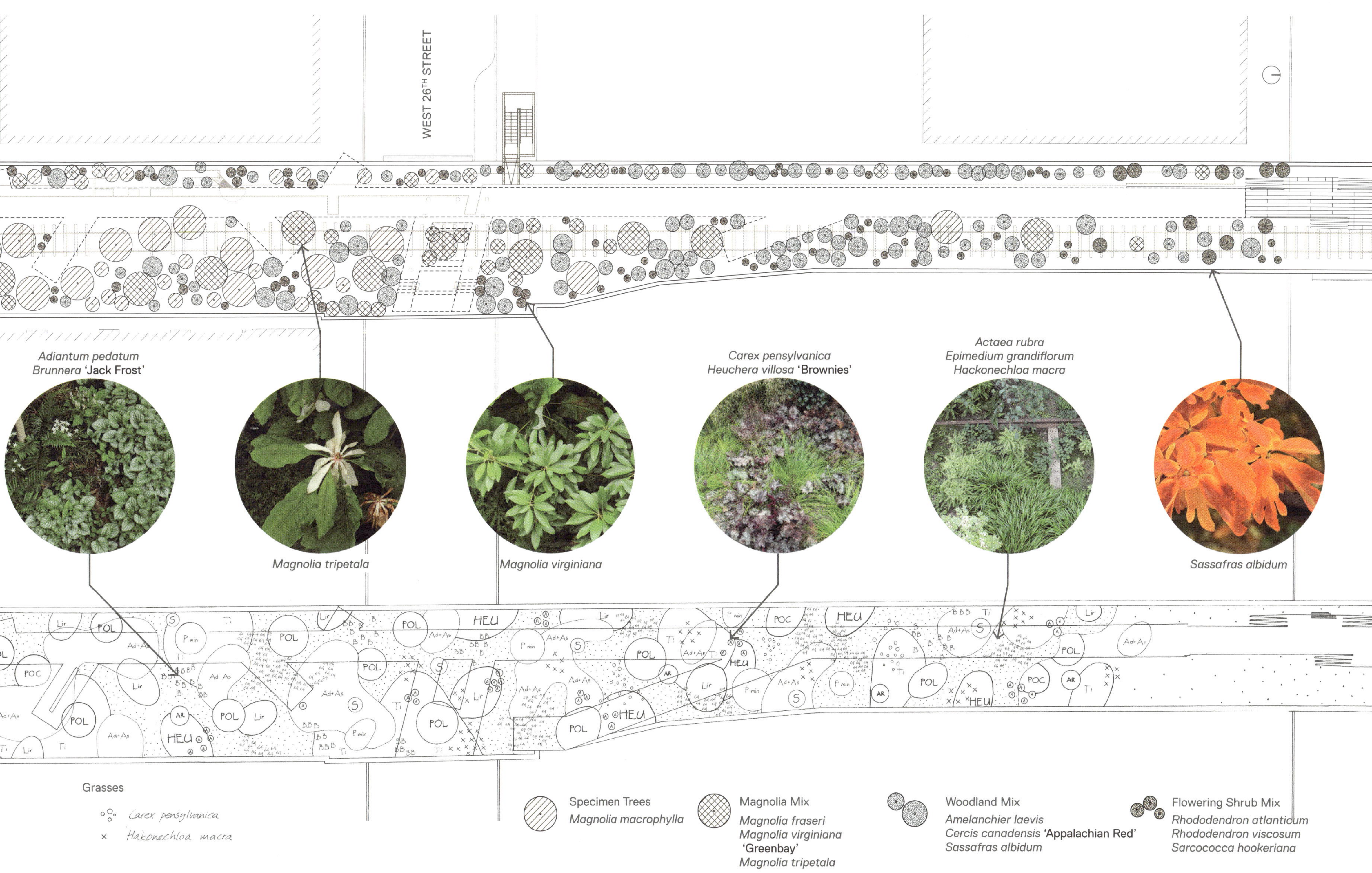

WEST 26TH STREET
Adiantum pedatum
Brunnera 'Jack Frost'
Magnolia tripetala
Magnolia virginiana
Carex pensylvanica
Heuchera villosa 'Brownies'
Actaea rubra
Epimedium grandiflorum
Hackonechloa macra
Sassafras albidum
Grasses
Carex pensylvanica
Hakonechloa macra
Specimen Trees
Magnolia macrophylla
Magnolia Mix
Magnolia fraseri
Magnolia virginiana 'Greenbay'
Magnolia tripetala
Woodland Mix
Amelanchier laevis
Cercis canadensis 'Appalachian Red'
Sassafras albidum
Flowering Shrub Mix
Rhododendron atlanticum
Rhododendron viscosum
Sarcococca hookeriana

Piet Oudolf, the team's planting expert, developed a "matrix" style for the High Line, in which a mix of dominant grass species—the "matrix" plants—supports clusters of plants chosen specifically for color or form, including perennials, bulbs, trees, and shrubs. In order to create a dynamic landscape experience, a wide spectrum of plant species, which collectively exhibit a striking variety of effects, was selected.

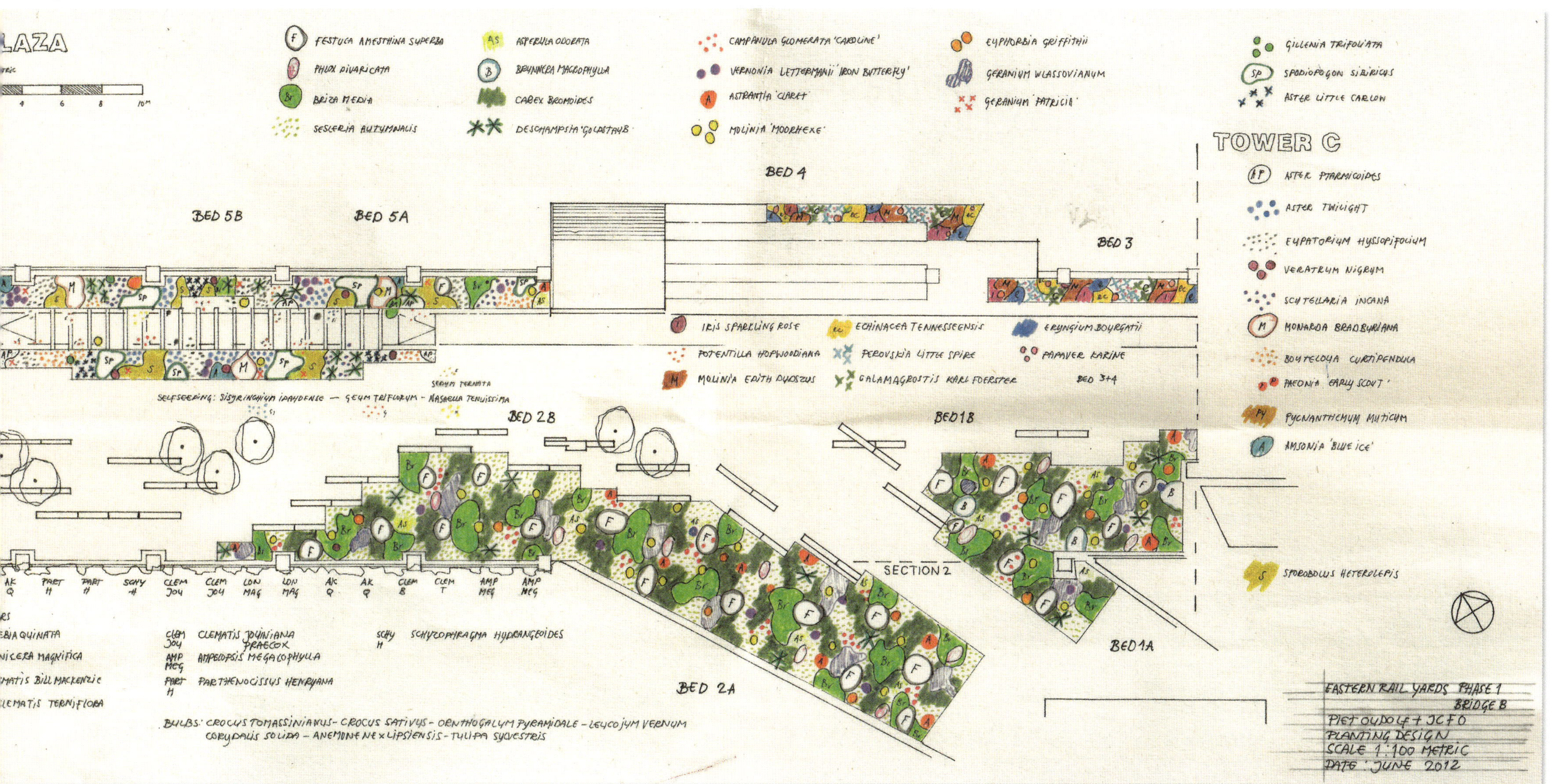

At the time of publication, there are 400 plant species on the High Line, including over 200 perennials, 36 grasses, 12 vines, nearly 50 bulbs, and over 100 varieties of trees and shrubs.

Acer triflorum; *Aesculus parviflora*; *Amelanchier laevis*; *Amorpha fruticosa*; *Aronia melanocarpa* 'Viking'; *Cercis canadensis* 'Pauline Lily'; *Chaenomeles x superba* 'Jet Trail'; *Chaenomeles speciosa* 'Toyo Nishiki'; *Chimonanthus praecox*; *Chionanthus retusus*; *Chionanthus virginicus*; *Clerodendrum trichotomum*; *Clethra alnifolia*; *Clethra barbinervis*; *Fothergilla x intermedia* 'Mount Airy'; *Gaultheria procumbens*; *Gaylussacia baccata*; *Hamamelis x intermedia*; *Hamamelis x intermedia* 'Jelena'; *Hamamelis x intermedia* 'Pallida'; *Hamamelis x intermedia* 'Sunburst'; *Hamamelis virginiana*; *Hydrangea paniculata* 'Limelight'; *Magnolia tripetala*; *Magnolia* 'Green Shadow'; *Mahonia x media* 'Winter Sun'; *Malus floribunda*; *Malus* 'Gold Russet'; *Nyssa sylvatica*; *Philadelphus* 'Natchez'; *Pinus sylvestris*; *Populus tremuloides*; *Rhus typhina*; *Rhus typhina* 'Laciniata'; *Rosa* 'Ausorts'; *Rosa* 'F.J. Grootendorst'; *Rosa* 'Sally Holmes'; *Rosa glauca*; *Rosa moyesii* 'Geranium'; *Rosa virginiana*; *Rosa x odorata* 'Mutabilis'; *Syringa laciniata*; *Syringa oblata* 'Cheyenne'; *Viburnum lentago*; *Viburnum prunifolium*; *Viburnum x bodnantense* 'Dawn'; *Viburnum x burkwoodii*; *Viburnum nudum* 'Winterthur'; *Vitex agnus-castus* 'Abbeville Blue'; *Amsonia tabernaemontanta* 'Blue Ice'; *Anaphalis margaritacea*; *Anemone cylindrica*; *Aralia racemosa*; *Aruncus* 'Horatio'; *Asarum canadense*; *Asclepias incarnata ssp. pulchra*; *Asclepias purpurascens*; *Asclepias tuberosa*

Baccharis halimifolia · *Betula nigra* · *Betula populifolia* · *Betula populifolia* 'Whitespire' · *Calycanthus floridus* 'Michael Lindsey' · *Cercis canadensis* · *Cercis canadensis* 'Ace of Hearts' · *Cercis canadensis* 'Appalachian Red' · *Cercis canadensis* 'Forest Pansy'

Cornus x 'Rutban' · *Cornus florida* 'Jean's Appalachian Snow' · *Cornus sanguinea* 'Midwinter Fire' · *Corylopsis spicata* · *Cotinus* 'Grace' · *Cotinus coggygria* 'Pink Champagne' · *Cotinus coggygria* 'Young Lady' · *Cotinus obovatus* · *Fothergilla gardenii*

Ilex opaca 'Dan Fenton' · *Ilex verticillata* · *Ilex verticillata* 'Red Sprite' · *Juniperus virginiana* 'Corcorcor' · *Indigofera amblyantha* · *Indigofera heterantha* · *Lespedeza thunbergii* 'Gibraltar' · *Lindera glauca var. salicifolia* · *Magnolia macrophylla*

Prunus virginiana · *Ptelea trifoliata* · *Quercus macrocarpa* · *Rhododendron atlanticum* · *Rhododendron viscosum* · *Rhus aromatica* 'Gro-low' · *Rhus copallinum* · *Rhus glabra* · *Rhus lanceolata*

Rubus calycinoides · *Salix chaenomeloides* · *Salix discolor* · *Salix eleagnos* · *Salix gracilistyla* 'Melanostachys' · *Sambucus nigra* 'Eva' · *Sarcococca hookeriana var. humilis* · *Sassafras albidum* · *Styrax japonicus* 'Emerald Pagoda'

Achillea filipendulina 'Parker's Variety' · *Achillea millefolium* 'Terracotta' · *Actaea pachypoda* · *Actaea rubra* · *Adiantum pedatum* · *Agastache foeniculum* · *Ageratina altissima* 'Chocolate' · *Amorpha canescens* · *Amsonia hubrichtii*

Astilbe chinensis 'Visions in Pink' · *Astrantia major* 'Roma' · *Athyrium filix-femina* 'Minutissimum' · *Athyrium niponicum* · *Baptisia alba* · *Baptisia x* 'Purple Smoke' · *Brunnera macrophylla* · *Campanula glomerata* 'Caroline' · *Ceratostigma plumbaginoides*

Chelone glabra
Clinopodium nepeta ssp. nepeta
Coreopsis tripteris
Coreopsis 'Full Moon'
Corydalis cava
Corydalis solida
Corydalis solida 'George Baker'
Dalea purpurea
Desmodium canadense
Echinacea 'Magnus'
Echinacea 'Evan Saul Big Sky Sundown'
Echinacea 'Vintage Wine'
Echinacea 'Virgin'
Epimedium grandiflorum 'Lilafee'
Epimedium x perralchicum 'Fröhnleiten'
Equisetum hyemale
Eryngium yuccifolium
Eupatorium altissimum
Eutrochium dubium 'Baby Joe'
Eutrochium dubium 'Little Joe'
Eutrochium maculatum 'Gateway'
Eutrochium maculatum 'Purple Bush'
Galium odoratum
Geranium macrorrhizum 'Spessart'
Geranium maculatum
Geranium sanguineum 'Max Frei'
Geranium soboliferum
Helianthus salicifolius
Helleborus argutifolius
Heuchera americana 'Dale's Strain'
Heuchera villosa 'Amethyst Mist'
Heuchera villosa 'Autumn Bride'
Heuchera villosa 'Brownies'
Hibiscus dasycalyx
Hibiscus moscheutos ssp palustris
Iris cristata 'Powder Blue Giant'
Liatris spicata
Limonium platyphyllum
Liriope muscari 'Densiflora'
Lythrum alatum
Maianthemum racemosum
Monarda bradburiana
Monarda fistulosa 'Claire Grace'
Nepeta racemosa 'Walker's Low'
Nepeta sibirica
Perovskia atriplicifolia 'Little Spire'
Persicaria amplexicaulis 'Alba'
Persicaria amplexicaulis 'Firetail'
Phlomis russeliana
Phlox divaricata 'Blue Moon'
Phlox paniculata 'Tracy's Treasure'
Phlox pilosa 'Lavender Cloud'
Phlox stolonifera 'Blue Ridge'
Phlox stolonifera 'Sherwood Purple'
Rudbeckia subtomentosa
Ruellia humilis
Salvia azurea
Salvia pratensis 'Pink Delight'
Salvia x sylvestris 'Rhapsody in Blue'
Sanguisorba canadensis
Sanguisorba officinalis 'Red Thunder'
Scutellaria incana
Sedum acre

Dianthus carthusianorum
Dodecatheon meadia
Doellingeria umbellatus
Echinacea pallida
Echinacea pallida 'Hula Dancer'
Echinacea paradoxa
Echinacea purpurea
Echinacea 'Fatal Attraction'
Echinacea 'Jade'
Eupatorium hyssopifolium
Eupatorium perfoliatum
Euphorbia amygdaloides ssp. robbiae
Euphorbia corollata
Euphorbia griffithii 'Fireglow'
Eurybia divaricata 'Eastern Star'
Eurybia macrophylla 'Twilight'
Eurybia spectabilis
Euthamia graminifolia
Geranium wlassovianum
Geranium x oxonianum 'Claridge Druce'
Geum triflorum
Helenium x 'Coppelia'
Helenium 'Mardi Gras'
Helenium 'Moerheim Beauty'
Helenium x 'Rubinzwerg'
Helenium 'Waltraut'
Helianthus angustifolius
Iris fulva
Iris siberica 'Steve'
Kalimeris incisa
Knautia macedonica 'Mars Midget'
Lathyrus vernus
Lavandula angustifolia 'Munstead'
Liatris aspera
Liatris pycnostachya
Liatris scariosa var. scariosa
Oenothera biennis
Oenothera pilosella
Oenothera speciosa
Oxalis violacea
Pachysandra procumbens
Papaver orientale 'Mandarin'
Parthenium integrifolium
Penstemon cobaea
Penstemon digitalis 'Husker Red'
Polygonatum biflorum
Polystichum acrostichoides
Polystichum munitum
Polystichum polyblepharum
Porteranthus stipulatus
Porteranthus trifoliatus
Pycnanthemum incanum
Pycnanthemum muticum
Rubeckia missouriensis
Sedum 'Bertram Anderson'
Sedum 'Maestro'
Sedum 'Matrona'
Sedum 'Red Cauli'
Sedum ternatum 'Larinem Park'
Silphium laciniatum
Silphium terebinthinaceum
Sisyrinchium angustifolium
Solidago caesia

Solidago juncea
Solidago ohioensis
Solidago ptarmicoides
Solidago sempervirens var. sempervirens
Solidago speciosa
x Solidaster luteus 'Lemore'
Stachys officinalis 'Hummelo'
Stokesia laevis 'Peachie's Pick'
Symphyotrichum ageratoides 'Adustus Nanus'

Symphyotrichum tataricus 'Jindai'
Tellima grandiflora
Tiarella cordifolia
Tiarella cordifolia var. collina
Tradescantia ohiensis 'Mrs. Loewer'
Tricyrtis 'Sinonome'
Trifolium rubens
Verbascum thapsis
Vernonia glauca

Briza media
Calamagrostis arundinacea var. brachytricha
Calamagrostis x acutiflora 'Karl Foerster'
Carex bromoides
Carex eburnea
Carex laxiculmis 'Hobb'
Carex pensylvanica
Chasmanthium latifolium
Deschampsia caespitosa 'Goldtau'

Molinia caerulea 'Transparent'
Muhlenbergia capillaris
Nasella tenuissima
Panicum amarum 'Dewey Blue'
Panicum virgatum 'Cheyenne Sky'
Panicum virgatum 'Heiliger Hain'
Panicum virgatum 'Rehbraun'
Panicum virgatum 'Shenandoah'
Pennisetum alopecuroides 'Foxtrot'

Clematis pitcheri
Clematis tangutica 'Bill MacKenzie'
Clematis x triternata 'Rubromarginata'
Clematis virginiana
Clematis viticella 'Carmencita'
Lonicera sempervirens 'Major Wheeler'
Passiflora edulis
Schizophragma hydrangeoides 'Moonlight'
Wisteria frutescens 'Amethyst Falls'

Anemone blanda 'Blue Shades'
Anemone blanda 'White Splendor'
Anemone nemorosa
Crocus ancyrensis 'Golden Bunch'
Crocus chrysanthus 'Ard Schenk'
Crocus pulchellus
Crocus sieberi ssp. sublimis 'Tricolor'
Crocus speciosus 'Albus'
Crocus tommasinianus

Narcissus 'Jenny'
Narcissus 'Sailboat'
Narcissus poeticus ornatu
Ornithogalum umbellatum
Puschkinia scilloides ssp. libanotica
Scilla luciliae
Scilla mischtschenkoana
Scilla sardensis
Scilla siberica

Symphyotrichum cordifolius 'Little Carlow'

Symphyotrichum ericoides

Symphyotrichum lateriflorum 'Lady in Black'

Symphyotrichum laevis 'Bluebird'

Symphyotrichum novi belgii

Symphyotrichum oolentangiense

Symphyotrichum 'Raydon's Favorite'

Symphyotrichum patens var. patens

Symphyotrichum shortii

Vernonia novaboracencis

Veronica longifolia 'Icicle'

Veronica longifolia 'Sonja'

Veronicastrum virginicum

Andropogon gerardii

Bouteloua curtipendula

Bouteloua gracilis

Bouteloua gracilis 'Blonde Ambition'

Deschampsia flexuosa

Eragrostis spectabilis

Festuca amethystina 'Superba'

Festuca mairei

Hakonechloa macra

Koeleria macrantha

Molinia caerulea 'Dauerstrahl'

Molinia caerulea 'Moorflamme'

Molinia caerulea 'Moorhexe'

Schizachyrium scoparium

Schizachyrium scoparium 'The Blues'

Sesleria autumnalis

Spodiopogon sibiricus

Sporobolus heterolepis

Celastrus 'Bailumn' Autumn Revolution™

Clematis 'Miss Bateman'

Clematis 'Gipsy Queen'

Allium atropurpureum

Allium cristophii

Allium nigrum

Allium obliquum

Allium oreophillum

Allium siculum ssp. dioscoridis

Allium sphaerocephalon

Allium stipitatum 'Mount Everest'

Darmera peltata

Eranthis hyemalis

Eremurus himalaicus

Eremurus stenophyllus

Erythronium 'Pagoda'

Galanthus nivalis

Muscari armeniacum 'Valerie Finnis'

Narcissus 'Hawera'

Narcissus 'Intrigue'

Tulipa clusiana 'Lady Jane'

Tulipa humilis

Tulipa humilis 'Liliput'

Tulipa humilis 'Odalisque'

Tulipa linifolia 'Red Hunter'

Tulipa saxatilis 'Lilac Wonder'

Tulipa sylvestris

Tulipa tarda

Tulipa turkestanica

KAESER

05_CONSTRUCTION

Construction began in 2006 and was executed in three sections: from Gansevoort Street to 20th Street, from 20th Street to 30th Street, and from 30th Street to 34th Street along the perimeter of the rail yards. For each of the sections, the construction process began with the rehabilitation of the structure. Remediation required the removal of all materials above the concrete deck, including soil, plantings, ballast, and rail ties. Each section of rail track was removed and tagged so that it could be returned later to its original location. Site preparation continued with structural steel and concrete repair, lead paint abatement, and repainting. Following this initial work, new waterproofing and drainage systems were installed. Railings were upgraded, and selective cuts in the structure were made for the installation of stairs and special features. The concrete planking system was set using precise surveying equipment. Precast concrete pedestals and sleepers were placed between the structural deck below and the planking and rail tracks above to allow rainwater to drain into the future planting beds. Utilities were laid below the planking. Stairs, elevators, and special features were then integrated into the railway structure. Planting beds were installed last: once the green roof system and engineered soil were in place, tens of thousands of plants were distributed according to a detailed planting scheme.

November 2006

March 2007

May 2007

January 2008

May 2008

October 2008

August 2007

November 2007

December 2007

December 2008

May 2009

June 2009

1A1
1·C2
1A2
1·B3
1B1
1·B2

784-1776
ABLE

CAT

Manhattan
Mini Storag
NO STANDING
ANYTIME
DON'T
HONK

MEDS

RTSIE
SIE
SIW
P3-19
10-7-13
SL-2
P4

MB21
MILLER
SCOOT-CRETE
718-937-7977
Liberty Farms

We Deliver For You.

JOHN W. WILLIAMS
VEAL CO., INC
212-243-1293
Weichsel
WHOLESALE
BEEF &
TOYOTA
TOYOTA

YOU BELONG H
FROM BLOO
TO LEATHER, TO F
NO PARKING

06_WALK

The first section of the High Line opened in June 2009. The second section followed two years later. While the final stretch faced the threat of demolition to make way for the thirty-four-acre (13 ha) Hudson Yards development, the park's advocates eventually convinced the City to protect the tracks, and by 2014—a decade after our team began work on the project—public access extended the entire length of the line, from Gansevoort Street to 34th Street. As of the publication date of this book, selective work remains. In the coming years, permanent stairs will replace temporary access points, the passages at 14th Street and Chelsea Market will be completed, an at-grade plaza on Tenth Avenue between 17th and 18th Streets will be designed and built, and the spur of track at 30th Street above Tenth Avenue will be integrated with the rest of the park. Above 30th Street, the northernmost stretch of the High Line will retain its relatively unaltered character into the foreseeable future. Today, the full mile-and-a-half (2.4 km) walk along the High Line reveals a cross-section of New York, its people, and its history.

MEET
WAYNE
THIEBAUD
5A52

25 ft. (7 m)

35 ft. (11 m)

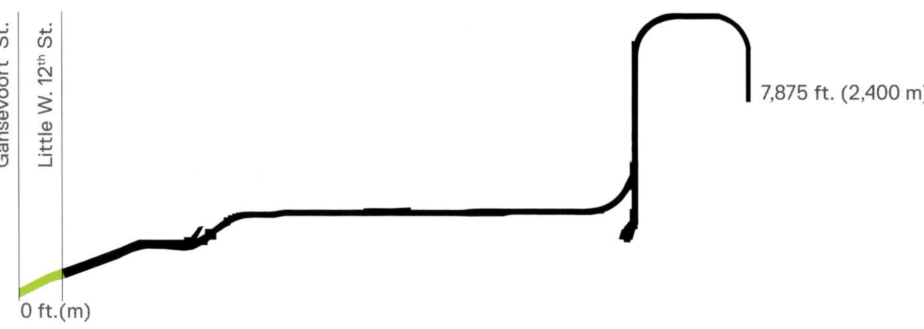

45 ft. (14 m)

230 ft. (70 m)

445 ft. (136 m)

460 ft. (140 m)

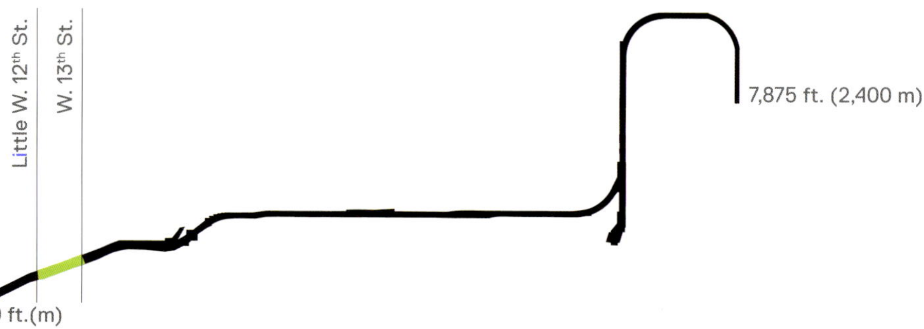

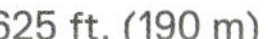

625 ft. (190 m)

750 ft. (229 m)

ONKEY
BEER
GARDE

815 ft. (248 m)

925 ft. (282 m)

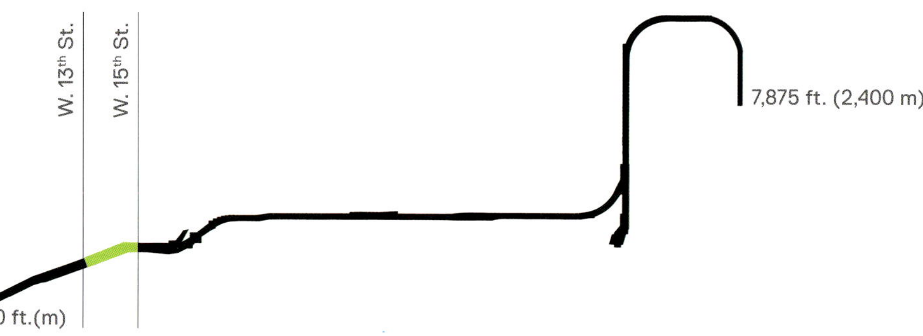

970 ft. (296 m)

1,045 ft. (319 m)

LUXURY RENTALS
POSTO
FIRE

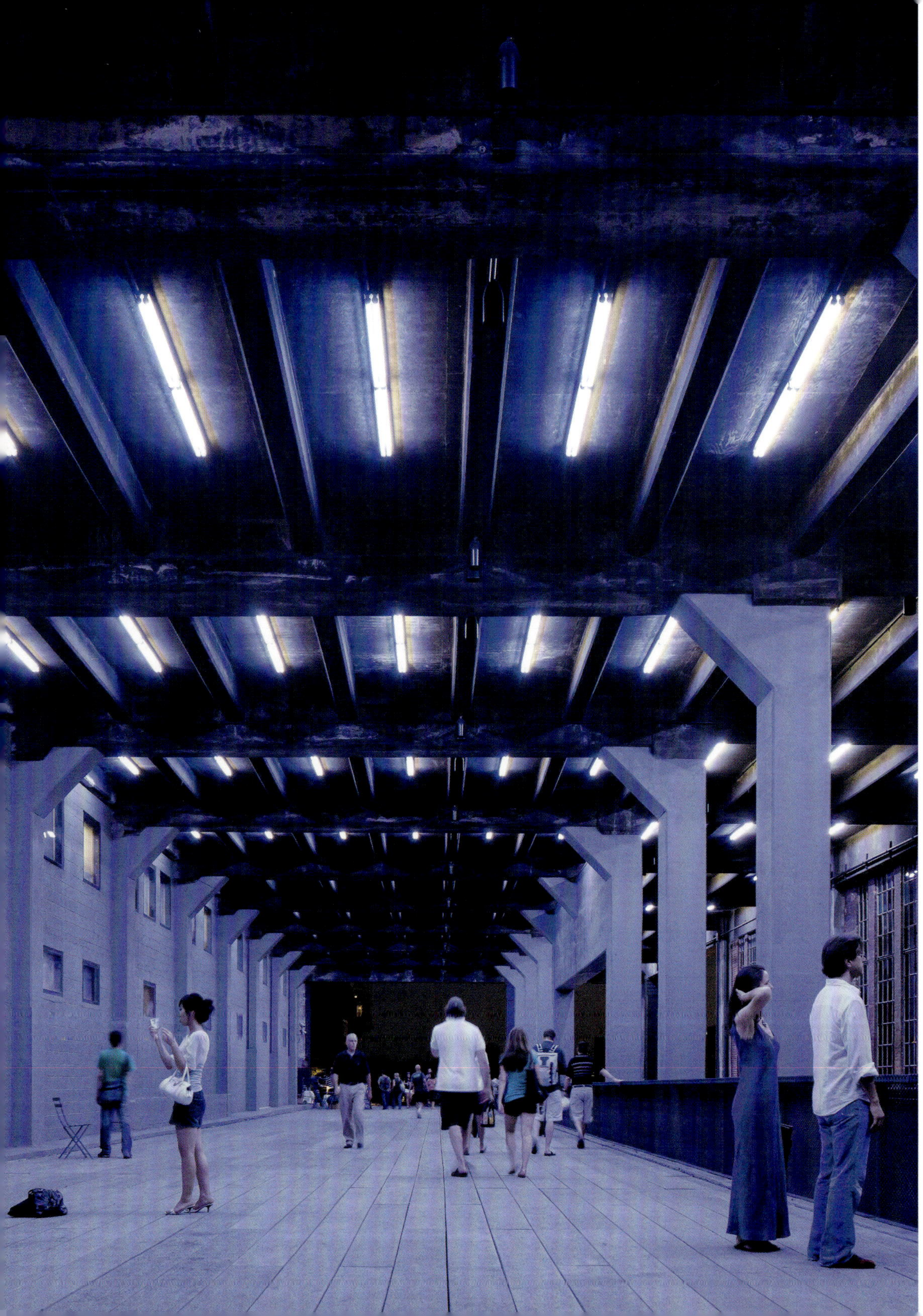

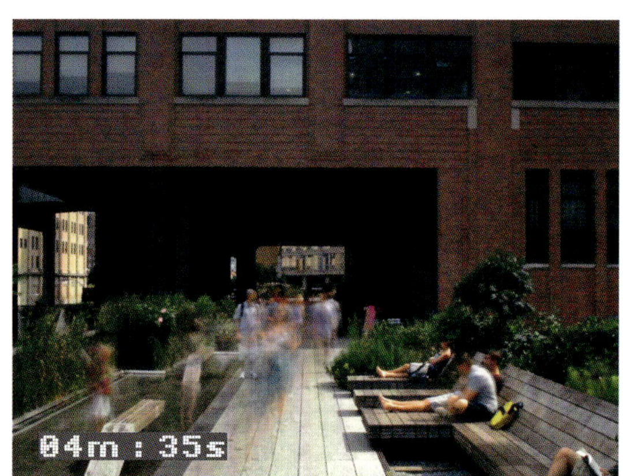

04m : 35s
1,150 ft. (351 m)

05m : 15s
1,295 ft. (395 m)

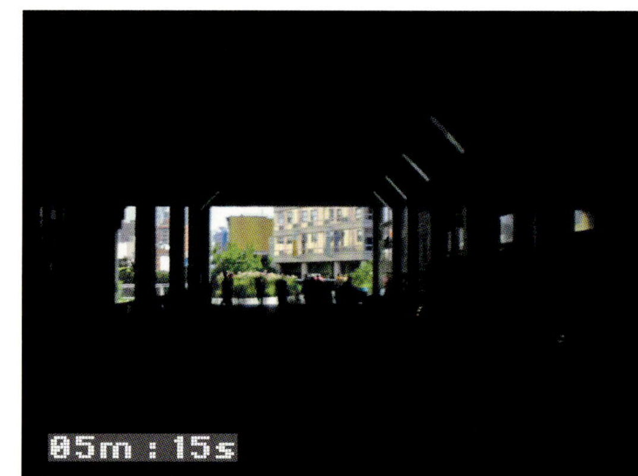

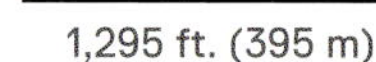

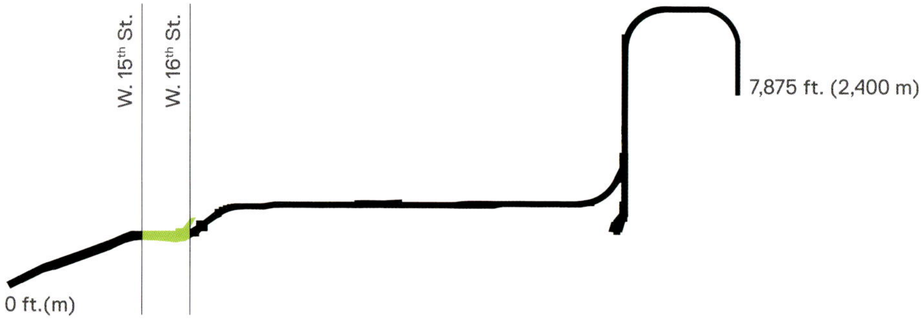

W. 15th St.
W. 16th St.
7,875 ft. (2,400 m)
0 ft.(m)

1,345 ft. (410 m)

1,465 ft. (447 m)

So you can't parallel park.
It'll be our little secret.
parkfast.com
888-parkfast
Edison
PARK
FAST
هذا الكتاب يخص صاحبه فتح الله سعد
اشتراه من ماله غرة آذار سنة ١٨٩٢
Love a Tortoise
Today!

1,680 ft. (512 m)

1,685 ft. (514 m)

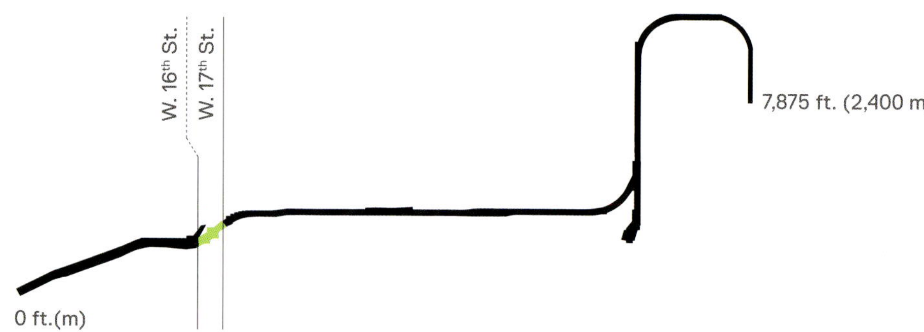

1,690 ft. (515 m)

1,695 ft. (517 m)

99 Tenth Avenue

FAST
ONE WAY
ONE WAY
West 17th St
Tenth Av
LIFE

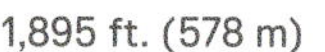
1,895 ft. (578 m)

1,960 ft. (597 m)

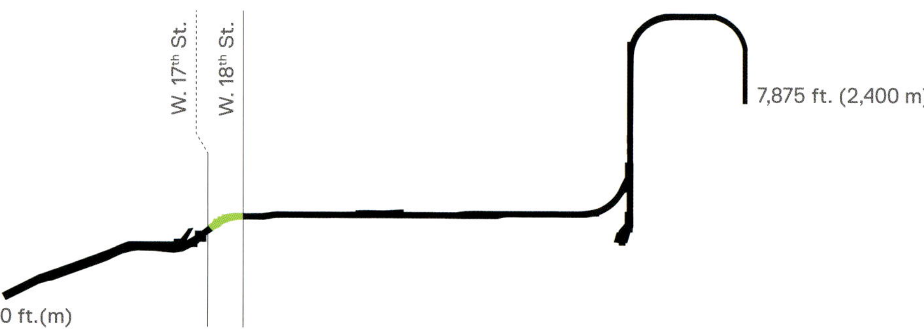

2,025 ft. (617 m)

2,115 ft. (644 m)

ALL I
a brand
SHOP,
415 WEST 13TH

STAFF
SOLINE

IZOD
PARK
FAST

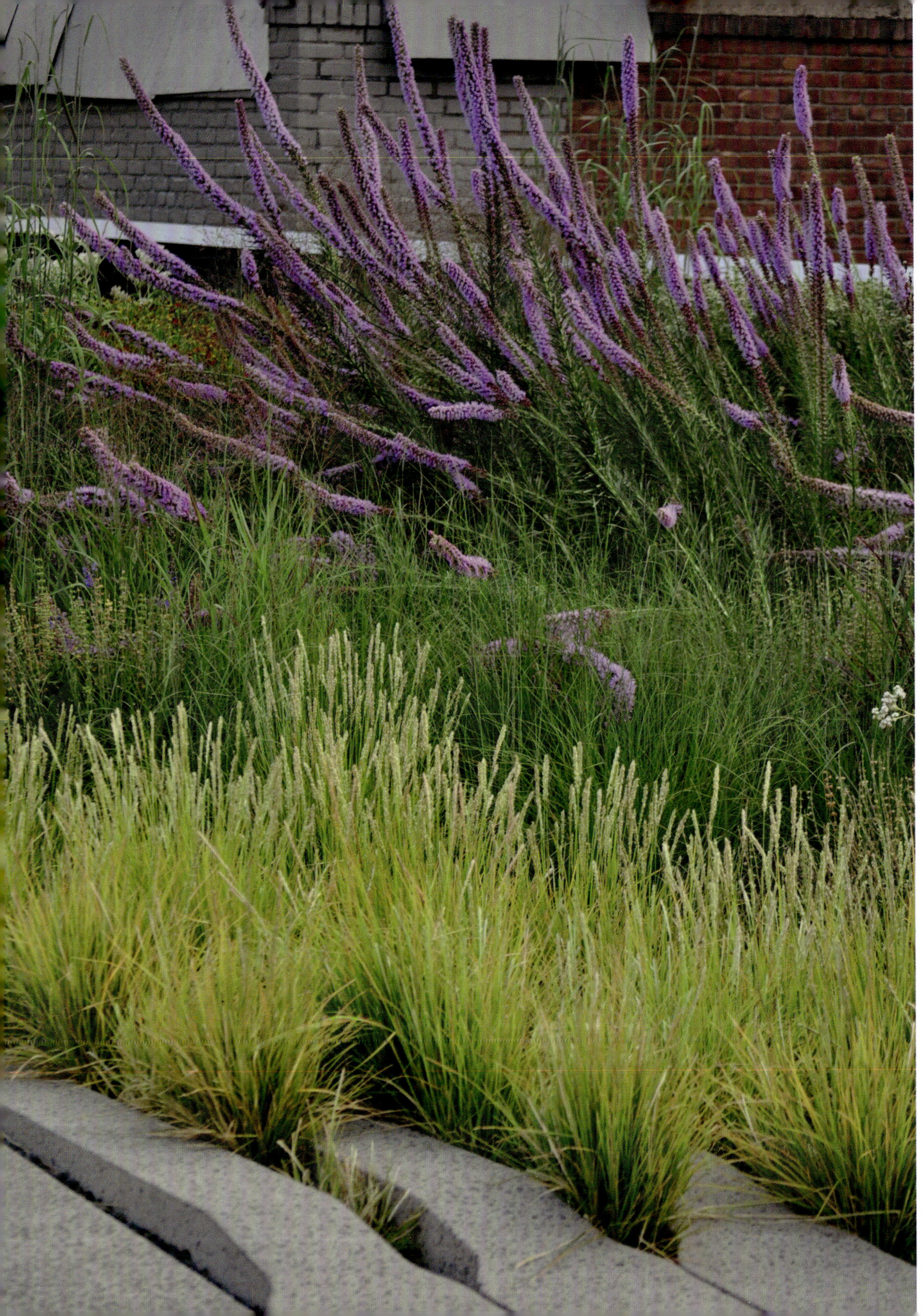

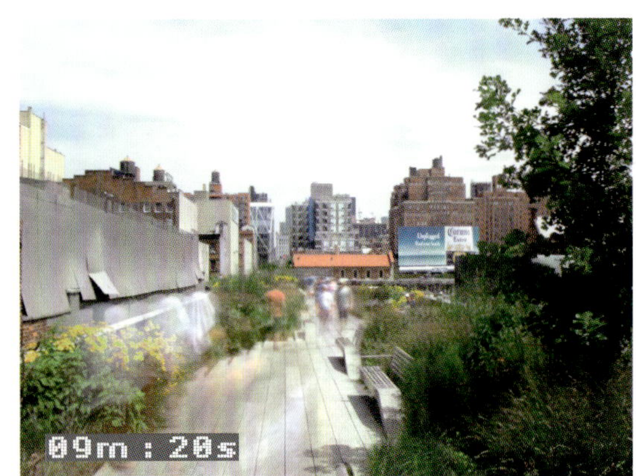

09m : 20s
2,350 ft. (716 m)

09m : 50s
2,470 ft. (753 m)

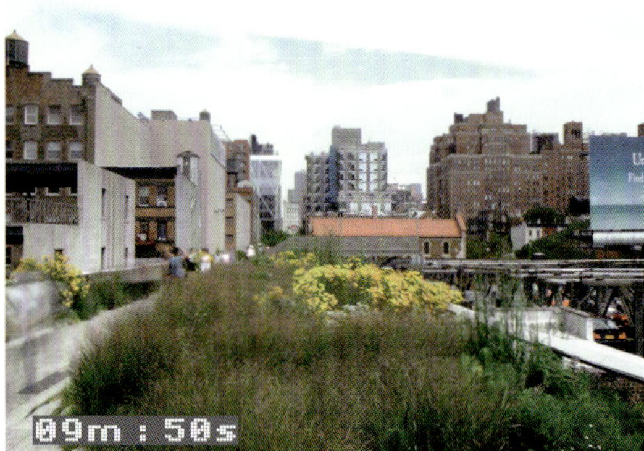

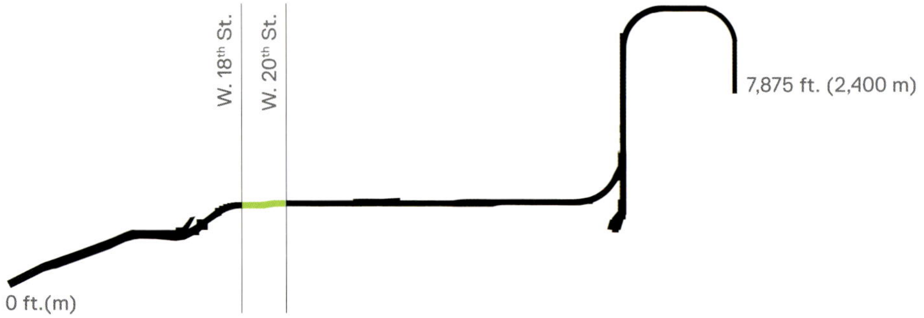
W. 18th St.
W. 20th St.
7,875 ft. (2,400 m)
0 ft.(m)

2,690 ft. (820 m)

2,750 ft. (838 m)

2,835 ft. (864 m)

3,025 ft. (922 m)

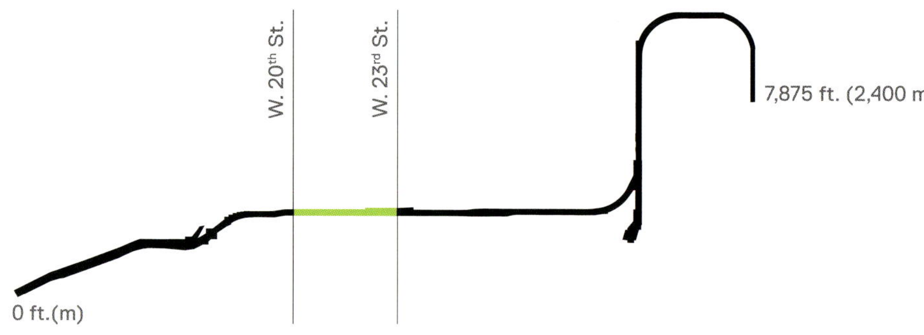

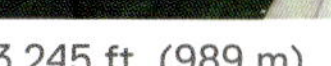
3,245 ft. (989 m)

3,375 ft. (1,029 m)

INC.
& BONDED

Manhattan Mini Storage.com
LOVE MEANS NEVER HAVING TO SAY, "I'M SORRY MY KICKBALL TROPHY FELL ON THE BABY AGAIN."
$29
FREE MOVE
Manhattan Mini Storage.com
212-storage

YORK STATE
SPECTION
O CENTER

Associates
ANDREA MEISLIN

4,010 ft. (1,222 m)

4,065 ft. (1,239 m)

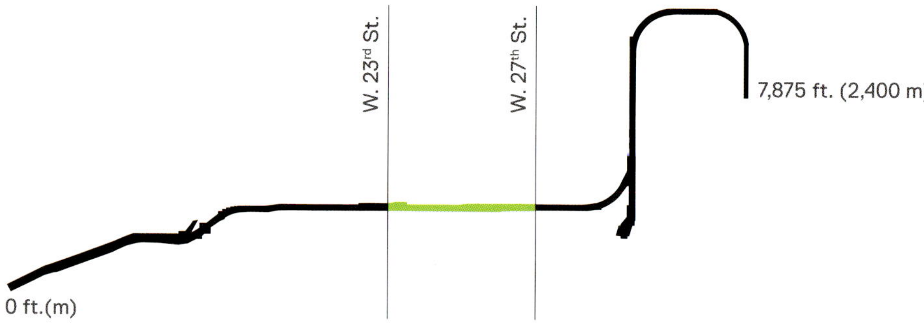

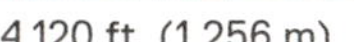
4,120 ft. (1,256 m)

4,225 ft. (1,288 m)

4,815 ft. (1,468 m)

4,995 ft. (1,522 m)

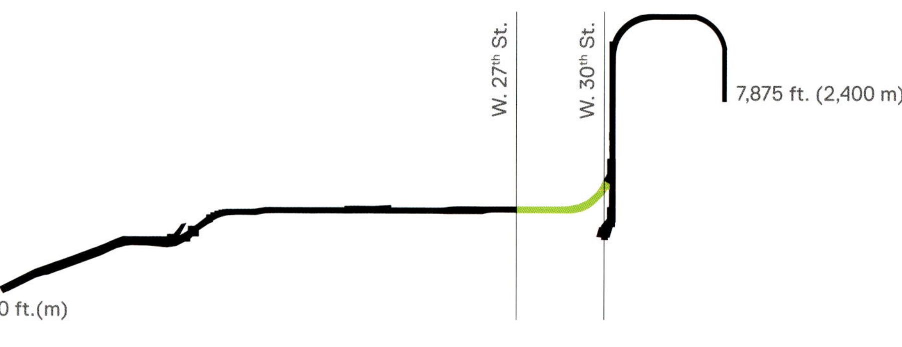

5,150 ft. (1,570 m)

5,190 ft. (1,582 m)

5,245 ft. (1,599 m)

5,385 ft. (1,641 m)

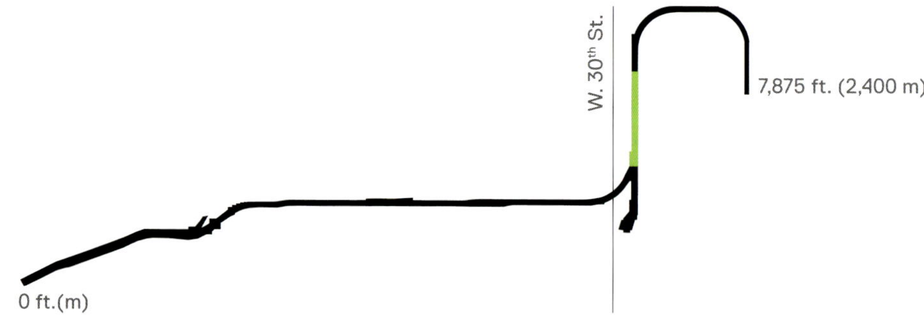

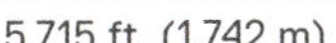
5,715 ft. (1,742 m)

5,910 ft. (1,801 m)

C2-DO
A2-DO

6,320 ft. (1,926 m)

6,655 ft. (2,028 m)

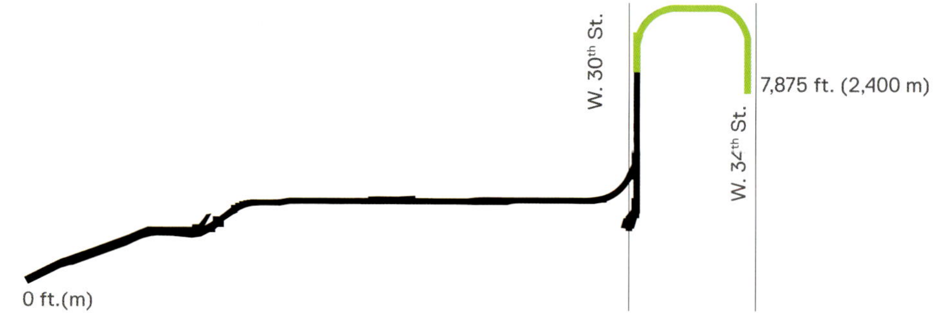

7,285 ft. (2,196 m)

7,815 ft. (2,382 m)

Ricardo Scofidio
Diller Scofidio + Renfro

James Corner
James Corner Field Operations

Lisa Switkin
James Corner Field Operations

Elizabeth Diller
Diller Scofidio + Renfro

Matthew Johnson
Diller Scofidio + Renfro

CONVERSATION PART THREE: AFTERTHOUGHTS

MODERATOR: It took you ten years to design and build the High Line. What were the surprises you encountered along the way?

ELIZABETH DILLER (ED): Well, that it actually happened. I was skeptical from the start—that we could win, that the project was even real.

LISA SWITKIN (LS): We were all skeptical, but once we stepped onto the High Line, we fell in love with the place and knew we had to do it.

RICARDO SCOFIDIO (RS): Funny; maybe the unnaturally positive response from the community at the beginning was so positive because no one believed it could actually happen.

JAMES CORNER (JC): Our skepticism was useful; it made us assume a very thoughtful and thorough design approach, one that seemed both compelling and feasible.

ED: Even after we knew it was going to be built, we never anticipated its popularity. That was another major surprise. When we first started, the High Line was projected to receive three hundred thousand visitors a year. Last year, over six million people came. We didn't expect this in our wildest dreams.

JC: And we never foresaw the sheer diversity of visitors. There are people of all ages and walks of life. There are individuals, couples, families, groups, some in wheelchairs, some in strollers, some from the neighborhood and New York, but many others from across the country and the world. It's a cosmopolitan place where people come and enjoy an unusual public experience. This mosaic of different users is what makes the High Line so extraordinary.

RS: The diverse types of visitors are interestingly stratified throughout the day: joggers at dawn, young urbanites on their way to work in the morning, then the lunch crowd, tourists speaking in every conceivable language and nannies ambling with young kids in the afternoon, then the urbanites returning home at dusk, then couples strolling in the evening, and cruisers in pursuit at night. There's a totally different crowd on the weekends.

ED: We have heard more and more complaints about the High Line being overly popular. People say that it's overcrowded, and it no longer feels like it's their own. Unfortunately, the dimensions of the park were a given. It has narrow boundaries, and the walking surface is shared with vegetation. In early design sessions, when we laid out the landscape plan, we studied the pinch points and how many people could walk side by side in one direction with their counterparts passing the other way on a crowded day. We wanted to optimize planting surface but were concerned about bottlenecks. Our planning worked well in the first years when there were fewer visitors, but the situation is changing. The park's intense popularity, coupled with the growth of mass tourism and increased visitors to New York, has unexpectedly made the High Line one of the city's top tourist attractions. We produced something that, inadvertently, may have fallen victim to its own success.

LS: People always ask if we would have changed the path widths had we known how popular the High Line was going to be. I think not. The balance of paving and planting is essential to the design. It could have been paved from edge to edge, but that wasn't the point.

MATTHEW JOHNSON (MJ): Perhaps part of the problem is that each time we open a new segment of the park, there's another major opening-day celebration that draws lots of press coverage. In the past five years, there have been three of these ceremonies. Each generates new excitement and larger crowds.

LS: Attendance never fully drops off before it picks up again.

With the unexpected level of attendance, is there anything about the behavior of visitors that has surprised you?

ED: Many things. We hoped the design would foster a sense of magical disorientation and freedom from the city. For instance, we wanted to encourage walking. Not with the aim of burning calories, but walking with others as a slow, mobile form of socializing. But we never imagined that the High Line would become a place of romantic intimacy. Recently, a website named it the city's number one date spot. It's considered the make-out park in New York City—I took a walk on a nice night recently and counted twenty-three couples passionately kissing.

RS: It's astonishing to me that people are able to engage in such private activities in public space. Does the High Line make people feel sufficiently comfortable to be so publicly intimate, or are we less concerned about privacy in the age of social media?

JC: Romance has always been associated with the promenade. In many ways, the High Line is a romantic promenade, albeit an unusual one, given its context.

ED: On the High Line, the close proximity of others and the guarantee of an audience attracts a strange sort of public intimacy. The voyeur and the exhibitionist have a consensual relationship. The pleasure of watching people is matched and perhaps exceeded by the pleasure of being watched. The layers recess endlessly: I watch you, you watch me, and they watch you watching me. It's fascinating to see how the centuries-old promenade typology aligns so perfectly with this contemporary drive for self-celebrity. It's the perfect match for a generation raised on reality television and obsessive self-documentation.

JC: Perhaps people are so enveloped in their own relationship that they're not aware of how public the High Line really is.

ED: Or maybe when people come to a place that feels truly new it acts as an unexpected aphrodisiac, independent of the fact that many people are sharing the experience with you.

MJ: When we started out, in 2004, the walls of the industrial buildings lining the High Line were mostly windowless, and there weren't as many residential buildings that looked onto it. There were very few eyes on the High Line, which contributed to its secret, intimate, and illicit atmosphere. It was a place to which you could escape and feel off the grid. It made sense that so many people went there for romantic encounters. Now, with so much of the adjacent development designed to face the High Line, any experience of romance there is automatically in full view of all these surrounding buildings.

ED: During its industrial heyday, adjacent residential buildings recoiled from the High Line, which was then considered a loud, rumbling eyesore. It remained a blight when it fell into disuse. But since it became an attraction, new condos within eyeshot of the High Line have been craning to catch a view of it, like the phototropic effect of plants orienting to a source of light.

MJ: And in spite of that, people still act as if they're in a secluded place. Encouraged by the many extra eyes on the High Line, exhibitionism seems more publicly embraced than ever. I don't get it. Some blog called the lawn area the new Plato's Retreat because so many couples are rolling around, kissing and fondling each other. The writer snidely suggested that the grass be sanitized daily or covered in latex.

ED: And then there are the guests at the Standard Hotel who have sex against the floor-to-ceiling glass windows in full view of people strolling below.

LS: We designed for a certain level of spontaneity and unexpectedness, but public behavior could never really be anticipated. I think that part of what we're seeing is an inevitable reaction to that strangeness of hovering over the streets in this liminal space. Our task was to turn an unofficial space into an official space, but our aim was to still encourage unofficial conditions and behaviors to surface.

ED: And its strange beauty. Unlike Central Park, the High Line eludes most common definitions of beauty. Maybe it's a beautiful ugliness that people respond to. In its semi-dilapidated context, perched between the past and the future, there's a feeling that hits you: the past is really past. It's gone. These industrial buildings are never going to come back; these tunnels, once used for hauling meat into buildings, no longer carry any meaning. It's this ambivalent moment in a postindustrial culture—watching luxury towers rise where manufacturing warehouses once stood—that elicits a sense of unease. You're standing on this artifact from a bygone era that no longer makes sense. You're in a place caught in time, and you get a momentary sense of your place in the bigger picture.

JC: You might be right that there's a certain psychological condition prompted by the High Line. The new life and optimism spawned from dereliction and neglect may very well provide a stimulating setting for new forms of interaction. It's this liberating sense of displacement that allows people to see themselves, one another, and the city in new ways.

ED: Take the impromptu performances of the Renegade Cabaret, for instance. A construction lamp was accidentally bumped so that its light fell on a well-positioned fire escape, illuminating Patty Heffley's living room. From the window of her apartment, she took full advantage of a captive audience with time on its hands. The spontaneous nightly concerts were better than anything we could have conceived as designers.

LS: In designing the High Line, we wanted to create a dialogue with the street, but I don't know if at the time we actually thought about creating a dialogue with adjacent buildings and their occupants.

MJ: Since we didn't know how the adjacent properties would develop, there was no way to anticipate a meaningful dialogue, except with the locations we knew could sustain a timeless relationship to the street, like the Tenth Avenue Overlook. Otherwise, we intentionally maintained an indifference to adjacent properties.

JC: It's the displacement from the everyday that somehow prompts a wide range of completely unforeseen activities, like astronomy buffs congregating to stare at the night sky, bird-watchers meeting in the early morning, sexual encounters in adjacent windows, outward displays of affection, and public speech and protest.

The High Line's popularity has led to unanticipated cultural effects. Can you speak about some of these?

ED: Like a scientist experimenting in the laboratory, something starts bubbling out of the test tube when you least expect it. Sometimes you're pleased by your discovery, and sometimes it blows up in your face. Sometimes you don't even know how to read the results: I'm still trying to understand how the High Line achieved such instant pop-culture status.

JC: Born of something found, the High Line has evolved a unique new identity and brand.

LS: People spend millions of dollars to create a brand. The High Line never even had a marketing department, and yet it has become a brand that so many businesses have latched onto for their own success.

JC: We've been surprised by the amount of entrepreneurship triggered by the High Line: businesses, products, buildings, pop-ups. You now have all the official High Line merchandise, but also the unofficial things: the High Line perfume, the High Line pressed juice, the High Line Hotel, the High Line Pizzeria, the High Line cocktail at the High Line Ballroom. Some of the businesses named after the park are nowhere near the High Line; there's a High Line Deli II on the Lower East Side.

MJ: David Bowie's High Line Festival at Radio City Music Hall and Madison Square Garden had only the vaguest connection to the High Line. They said in interviews that the festival was inspired by the "aesthetics" of the park. We were still two years away from building the first section.

MJ: When Josh and Robert first founded Friends of the High Line, they tried to copyright the High Line name but failed — it was too generic. Because of this, anyone can use the High Line name without permission from the park. There's no way to protect the identity of the park from appropriation by other entities or businesses.

ED: Despite these side effects, the High Line brand is reaching a new high. Location shots are becoming more and more frequent: fashion shoots, TV shows, comic books. The High Line has been absorbed into pop culture; it's part of our new cultural ecosystem. I keep wondering; how did it make that leap from that melancholic place we found a decade ago to a scene on *The Simpsons*?

MJ: An establishing shot at the High Line was used for a scene in *Family Guy* within the first year of the park's opening. It's odd because the High Line is not an identifiable icon on the level of, say, the Empire State Building, especially as it's captured in a cartoon. It's just a low, long, narrow structure that's mostly buried in the urban fabric. As soon as the park opened, it began to attract lots of fashion shoots, but in most of the initial photos, the only giveaway detail was the historic railing. Otherwise, the photos could have been shot anywhere in the city.

RS: Bill Cunningham did a great piece about the High Line as an urban catwalk — a place to see and be seen before a steady and wide-eyed audience.

ED: This evolution from eyesore to pop icon happened in stages. When we first came to the project, it was this beautiful, surreal place that nobody knew about. We wanted to share it with everyone. After it opened, there was a widespread love for the park. It happened post-9/11, when there was a sense of community and shared civic-mindedness in New York as well as a collective realization that we're all citizens of a vulnerable city. The High Line was a gift that no one expected. With its popularity, the park's identity has changed once again to celebrity status, which has triggered resentment.

Let's discuss the High Line's role in the past decade's urban growth.

ED: The High Line was thought to be a catalyst for urban development. The thinking was, if this hulking piece of rusty, obsolete infrastructure could be made into a park, it would attract visitors who had to be served by restaurants and other businesses that ultimately would raise the value of surrounding property and prompt more real estate investment.

JC: It's like putting energy into a slow-moving ecosystem — a new stimulant that creates an accelerating cascade of effects. As designers, we take the position that we're not going to try to control how those effects play out, but rather focus on providing stimuli and settings for action. And, indeed, the High Line has proved very effective in stimulating significant investment, development, and improvements in the surrounding neighborhood.

RS: We did not foresee the speed of the growth. The city spent $123.2 million on the project, with $20.3 million from the federal government and $400,000 from the state. The Friends of the High Line raised $44 million. In return, the High Line has generated billions of dollars in private investment surrounding the park, with tax revenues expected to exceed $900 million in the next decades.

MJ: But we all knew what the endgame was. Let's discuss urban growth in relation to the city's vision and the rezoning of West Chelsea. Amanda Burden, the New York City planning commissioner under Bloomberg, set up specialized zoning for this area. Historically, the city mostly had generic zoning restrictions for every neighborhood. Under Amanda's tenure, the city started to identify areas that could be revitalized, like West Chelsea and the Meatpacking District. In the case of the High Line, the city had to negotiate a complex air-rights transfer agreement to placate property owners around the High Line and to encourage developers to support the project. There was a lot of behind-the-scenes work that went into making the High Line happen. When people ask me about new park initiatives inspired by the High Line, I always explain that, in fact, it was a set of intricate policy changes that paved the way.

LS: The preservation of the High Line and the rezoning of the surrounding neighborhoods were deeply intertwined. People always ask if there's tension between the original vision of the park and the new development that's sprouted up around it. Actually, at the municipal government level, they were conceived together. The new zoning regulations helped the Friends of the High Line save the structure, but they also changed much of the neighborhood from exclusively industrial to partly commercial and residential as well.

MJ: The High Line was a piece of a larger calculus. We were aligned with the city in its goal to improve the quality of life in this area. There was very little open public space in West Chelsea and the Meatpacking District, apart from a handful of athletic fields and neighborhood playgrounds. The High Line provided an opportunity to distribute a new kind of public space that would connect the two neighborhoods.

LS: In all of Manhattan, not just Chelsea and the Meatpacking District, market-rate housing has become astronomically expensive. Hudson Yards, the most expensive real-estate deal in the history of the city, and the final frontier of massive-scale development in the borough, is now rising at the northern end of the High Line. This citywide process of transformation was well under way by the time the High Line opened in 2009. If we step back and say that we, as designers, could not control this trajectory, is it valid to argue that we're trying to do something special within this narrative? Rather than accepting the status quo, we're giving the neighborhood a slice of well-designed public space.

RS: True. If Giuliani had succeeded in demolishing the High Line, there would have been the same wave of new construction with a bit more density, and the real-estate prices would still have been sky-high — but it would not have attracted a better quality of architecture in the area. Within the orbit of the High Line are buildings by Frank Gehry, Jean Nouvel, Shigeru Ban, Zaha Hadid, Neil Denari, and Lindy Roy, and I hear BIG and Rem Koolhaas will be adding to the architectural menagerie.

MJ: The area is red hot. There are people buying apartments next to the High Line for investment with no intention of living in them. These people will never walk on the High Line; they're only buying the address.

LS: While the speculation is out of control, there are holdouts in the neighborhood, like the Gansevoort Meat Market, Manhattan's only meat cooperative since 1974, with a new lease that extends to 2031. Other survivors include the famed rowdy-times biker bar Hogs and Heifers, established in 1992; Hector's Place diner, one of New York City's oldest nonprofit art spaces, dating to 1962; and the Kitchen, since 1971. There are also over 2,400 residents living in the New York City Housing Authority Chelsea-Elliot Houses between West 25th Street and West 27th Street. So while there is more and more expensive retail and residential space, there is still a mix.

ED: There's a lot of anxiety around urban development right now, especially in cities like New York: mass tourism, expensive housing, loss of control, loss of community, loss of intimacy. These are valid concerns. But the response prompted by this anxiety often errs on the side of nostalgia.

The same people who criticize Manhattan for becoming a playground for the rich openly yearn for their own version of exclusivity with a uniform hostility to the popular, which is itself a form of elitism. People often draw the conclusion that design prompts gentrification, when really the only thing that can actively control the affordability of housing is policy and regulation — not the buildings themselves. Take the commercial development around the High Line: should we condemn the proliferation of innovative architecture there? Hiring high-profile architects allows developers to sell apartments at a higher rate, but, at the same time, the neighborhood is spared the development of these buildings into generic, characterless glass boxes. The apartments might have gone for a few dollars less, but they still would have been developed for the one percent, because in the New York of today, this is the market that offers the highest profit margins. The major difference is that the streetscape and skyline would have been much less interesting. It's a double-edged sword.

JC: We did not foresee the High Line becoming a target for critics of the current economic development of the neighborhood. We thought of our design as a kind of public service, as creating something good for all, although some like to criticize that effort because of perceived gentrification and development.

With its generally popular reception and urbanizing effects, the High Line has been a model for other cities. Are you proud of that?

ED: The High Line went viral, and cities worldwide have been rushing to turn their obsolete infrastructure into public space, trying to spur a revitalizing "High Line effect" of their own. Unwittingly, we inspired policy makers to think sustainably and imagine a second life for highways and railway beds beyond their original uses. However, the catalytic effect of the High Line on the New York economy is hard to replicate.

JC: Although, of course, not all abandoned infrastructure warrants adaptive reuse. There are plenty of instances where old infrastructures are best removed. But there are many other examples where it makes good sense to creatively revitalize postindustrial structures and lands for new uses. The strongest argument for this is economic: public investment in the revitalization of abandoned parts of the city produces catalytic effects on economic growth. The High Line demonstrates this brilliantly and is a large part of the reason other cities look to it as a model — a model of significant return on investment and a model that demonstrates how an economic development strategy can create value for cultural experience, societal benefits, ecological enhancement, and community building.

RS: Here is the standard model for any revitalization process: the city buys abandoned buildings and extends cheap rent to artists. When artists move in, an art gallery usually pops up. Then a coffee shop. A boutique follows, and slowly the neighborhood changes, until a developer finds the area interesting, and up go the condos.

ED: And then the artists are out in the street because they can't afford the rents.

JC: Was that your fear for the High Line and its environment?

RS: Yes, but there's a strange feedback loop now that short-circuits the process. Cities are looking to launch urban renewal efforts specifically in sites that they previously thought were immune to revitalization because they were by railroad tracks, which is what made them depressed in the first place. Because defunct railroad tracks now mean something else — something chic — cities think: if we can turn this into a High Line, then developers will move in, and we can watch our tax base increase.

MJ: Without the deeper objective of truly urbanizing a city, these projects often are driven by profit alone.

JC: From our point of view, that's a negative unforeseen condition of the High Line.

LS: I understand when people are inspired by the High Line and propose converting an abandoned rail track, embankment, or freeway into a public park. But we also get calls from cities that don't even have a piece of infrastructure analogous to the High Line. They just want to build a brand-new High Line.

ED: The High Line has strangely become a reference point for new infrastructure projects like the Garden Bridge in London, a new pedestrian walkway filled with vegetation that crosses the Thames. It might be true that improving pedestrian circulation is needed in that part of London and that building a park-bridge is a good idea, but it has little to do with the adaptive reuse concept of the High Line, even though it's branded in the same vein.

RS: Serious revitalization projects are almost always in industrial areas —

neighborhoods with factories, warehouses, and railroad lines that have slipped out of step with the postindustrial global culture.

ED: The Guggenheim Bilbao was a critical precedent for this phenomenon. An iconic building was introduced to a depressed port town with the intention of stimulating the economy. A strong piece of architecture was paired with a global brand.

RS: Not easily repeatable.

ED: No, but the so-called Bilbao effect traveled around the globe to many cities, prompting iconic buildings and trying to achieve the same ends. The problem is that there's no formula. Unprecedented success was achieved in Bilbao by intersecting that particular town with that particular architect and that particular brand. In a more modest way, a similar thing happened at the High Line: a certain set of circumstances produced an effect that many cities are trying to emulate. But it's very difficult to replicate a phenomenon created by the singular confluence of economic, geographical, political, and architectural conditions.

JC: Yes, and I would add that another important ingredient in that confluence was a relatively optimistic approach toward design innovation. Most public clients are hesitant to move forward with new design approaches until ideas are somehow tested and validated with predictive scenarios for future programming and use. What is unique to the High Line is that so many aspects were new and unprecedented. We also didn't try to assert control or certainty over everything. We weren't overly anxious about how it would be used, how it would later be appropriated, or how things would change around it. We knew that the park would stimulate new effects and that it would create a new energy in the neighborhood, but we were never particularly certain as to what all of these various effects would actually be.

RS: There was no science applied to the redevelopment of the High Line and no risk-assessment analysis. Everyone took their best guess.

LS: The best projects are those that learn from the High Line but don't aim to create a replica. The public-private partnership and nonprofit organization behind the park is also very important. Friends of the High Line started out as an advocacy group that went on to oversee the fundraising, design, and construction process with the city. Now they manage maintenance, operations, events, and programming. They are the stewards of the High Line. Their goal now is to figure out how to keep it fresh, exciting, and engaging. They want to integrate local communities as much as possible. If you look at their calendar, the programming is highly creative. A lot of their creativity has come from the founding spirit of the organization — to work with what they have. They have always had to think outside of the box.

MJ: If a city expects the same results with an initiative inspired by the High Line without the grassroots effort, it won't succeed. Each project has to be honest about its context and its constituents. The great hope is that this new crop of initiatives around the world will bring a diversity of design approaches, each precise to its site and situation.

ED: Aside from the impact we may have had on stimulating new initiatives in public spaces abroad, there may be a feedback loop that alters the High Line's identity once again. Perhaps the proliferation of High Line-inspired projects will soften the novelty of our park and make it less of a tourist destination. I can imagine a natural popularity-cycle stabilizing or winding down in the near future with the park totally absorbed into the everyday life of the city. The next generation will think that the High Line is a just a place for ambling. They won't even associate it with an abandoned railway.

RS: Maybe centuries from now people will ask what the High Line was, and someone will say: "A perfume!"

Have the unanticipated effects of the High Line altered your conception of what a designer's role is?

RS: In terms of urban transformation, the change has happened so fast that it's been hard to process. As architects, we have to be involved in the city's past and future, and as such, we're constantly engaged in decisions like: tear it down or keep it? Preserve it or find an adaptive reuse? Who gets to choose what history is worth saving? How much change can a city endure? Should we let the city go in the direction of *Blade Runner* or face mummification? How do we reinterpret the past going forward? The High Line, of course, deals with a lot of these issues. While it was saved, its new leisure use is ironically disjunctive from its productive past.

JC: In urban planning, the principle is to invest in transformational projects like the High Line in order to catalyze economic development. There's nothing wrong with this — capital growth is the basis of all cities — but how do you do so in a way that produces a uniquely varied set of opportunities, distinct from the prototypical urban development scenario? What is successful about the High Line urbanistically is the way in which the design and subsequent development have leveraged and built upon the unique attributes of the historical context — the old railroad, the industrial and manufacturing character of Chelsea and the West Side, and the mix of residential communities with commerce, art, and culture. This cumulative collage has come to inspire and inform the subsequent transformation of the district as a whole, building upon the unique identity and character of the neighborhood.

ED: But is it all good? Cities, like organic tissue, go through life cycles — birth, growth, decline, death, decay, and rebirth. The metabolism of a city can be accelerated by a catalyst in the form of a building or another urban asset. But how fast should acceleration be? How fast is too fast? The High Line was once a place of tranquility and introspection and has now become a social hub and an agent of rapid urbanization. What are the ethics of entering into and altering a city's life cycle? What's the measure of success for an architectural catalyst? What is the responsibility of the architect in shaping the aftermath of urban change? Is there a role for the architect in a post-occupancy site? If we can accelerate change, can we also slow it down? These are the questions I ask myself daily.

LS: People ask if the prospect of rapid growth entered our thought process as we developed the High Line and if we considered ways to reorient or change its effects to neighborhood-scale transformation. It's difficult, even with the team's cumulative knowledge, to understand the real-time role the High Line is playing.

MJ: Clearly we all knew that this area was going to transform dramatically based on the rezoning that made the High Line viable in the first place, though I don't think any of us thought it would happen so fast. We knew that the distinctive toughness of Chelsea and the Meatpacking District might give way to new construction that would feel sterile in comparison. There was nothing we could do about that. The only thing we could do was to ensure that the High Line retained a bit of its scruffiness and make sure that its edges didn't blur with those of the new development. There are no private building connections to the High Line for exactly that reason. All connections to the High Line are required to be public. Over time, the neighborhood and the High Line can, by design, evolve at a different pace.

ED: The city is growing very fast around the High Line. That the park stimulated so much growth and so many unanticipated consequences is a fact. Consciously or not, we have impacted the urban life-cycle. Who are we to say that the unanticipated effects, both social and economic, are good or bad? Take a new plant shooting up between concrete planks on the High Line and a new restaurant opening next door. The plant grows on a steel structure thirty feet (9 m) in the air; the restaurant spawns to serve the new attraction and to feed into the economy that keeps it going. Is one more natural than the other? Both are organically intertwined and thrive opportunistically on one another. This is the new "urban natural."

JC: When we started, we asked the question: what will grow here? We meant this in two ways: first in terms of natural ecosystems — soils, plants, birds, butterflies, and entire habitats — and second in terms of communities — programs, activities, economies, and buildings. In retrospect, it was smart that we left the question open, because we never could have answered it properly. Most of what has grown on and around the High Line has been out of our control. The High Line was a catalyst for open and dynamic things to happen. It continues to be a stimulant in a larger and still-evolving urban ecology.

07_UNFORESEEN

Unexpectedly, the High Line has become an icon of pop culture and a landmark on the world tourist map. Initially imagined to provide a modest boost to neighborhood economic growth and optimistically predicted to attract 300,000 people annually, the park exceeded expectations exponentially, drawing over six million visitors in 2014. With this unanticipated audience comes a wide range of unexpected activities—from anonymous exhibitionism to political protest—each taking advantage of the rare conditions of the urban promenade. The neighborhood, already in flux when we began the project, has transformed rapidly. What was once an unlikely community of butchers, auto mechanics, drag queens, and artists is now a cosmopolitan mélange of locals, tourists, gallerists, executives, families, socialites, club kids, cruisers, retirees, and fashionistas amid crumbling factories and new condo towers. The U.S. government's contribution of $143 million has repaid itself many times over, stimulating billions of dollars in urban development in the surrounding neighborhoods. Beyond New York, the High Line has gone viral. From Seoul to Mexico City, cities worldwide have rushed to turn their obsolete infrastructure into public space, aspiring to a "High Line effect" of their own. This diverse array of projects embodies a new global consciousness about the need for public space in growing postindustrial cities and the possibilities for sustainable reuse of underutilized and overlooked urban spaces.

Finding her apartment window spotlit by a stray High Line construction light, artist Patty Heffley transformed her fire escape into the Renegade Cabaret. On opening night, she introduced the performance as a response to the evisceration of her privacy: “Ladies and gentlemen—invaders of my private space—after thirty-one years, this is what I have to live with, so we are going to exploit it.”

BUSHNELL

The floor-to-ceiling glass windows of the Standard Hotel, a new building specifically designed to straddle the High Line, offers long vistas of the park to the north and south. Hotel guests with exhibitionist tendencies have been known to take advantage of the captive audience on the High Line.

The High Line quickly earned a reputation for merging romance with spectacle. Local press dubbed the park the Thigh Line and named it the city's premier make-out park. A matchmaking website announced it was the number one dating spot in New York, and bridal-trend publications listed it as a top destination for guerrilla weddings, even though the park's official policy prohibits marriage celebrations.

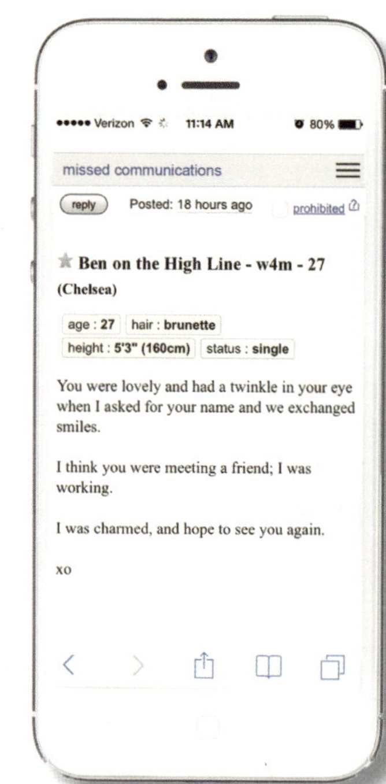

$29
212-storage

The park's narrow borders have created a charged space where activists can openly challenge the restricted use of public space. Since 1993, Robert Lederman, founder of A.R.T.I.S.T. (Artists' Response to Illegal State Tactics), has protested the city's practice of banning art vendors on sidewalks. Following his 2009 arrest on the High Line, Lederman sued the city, arguing that the park's policy on artist-vendors, which restricts their operations to less trafficked areas, violates the First Amendment.

In summer 2013, members of the Outdoor Co-ed Topless Pulp Fiction Appreciation Society gathered at the Sunken Overlook for their monthly seminude meeting. In full view of the park and the street below, the group's topless meeting combined performance and activism, taking a stand for the right of New Yorkers of all genders to bare their chests in public. ››

LANE
FIRE

Designed to be open and flexible—without any use-specific gathering spaces—the High Line hosts a variety of programs, from stargazing clubs to fitness classes to community meals. The High Line art program features a wide array of site-specific installations, performances, and screenings. Throughout the day, these official events share space with the spontaneous, unofficial interventions brought to the High Line by the public.

HOMU
THE HOMELESS MUSEUM OF ART

24 HRS
DRIVE THRU
10 AV.
34 ST.
PARK!

THE CITY OF
DEPARTMENT

In everything from comic books to TV shows, the High Line has been embraced as a pop culture icon and an avatar for the postmillennial Manhattan, recognizable to local, national, and global audiences. Below: excerpt from *Daredevil*, issue 2. Right: establishing shot of the Standard Hotel from *Family Guy*, season 9, episode 6.

Writers have adopted the High Line as both setting and inspiration. Ben Lerner's 2014 novel *10:04* opens with a description of the narrator's transfixed gaze as he watches traffic from the Sunken Overlook, capturing a contemporary New York moment in all its poetic complexity. *The Curious Garden*, a best-selling children's book, imagines a postindustrial fantasy in which the boy protagonist intervenes, rescues, and cultivates a garden on an abandoned bridge.

The city had converted an elevated length of abandoned railway spur into an aerial greenway and the agent and I were walking south along it in the unseasonable warmth after an outrageously expensive celebratory meal in Chelsea that included baby octopuses the chef had literally massaged to death. We had ingested the impossibly tender things entire, the first intact head I had ever consumed, let alone of an animal that decorates its lair, has been observed at complicated play. We walked south among the dimly gleaming disused rails and carefully placed stands of sumac and smoke bush until we reached that part of the High Line where a cut has been made into the deck and wooden steps descend several layers below the structure; the lowest level is fitted with upright windows overlooking Tenth Avenue to form a kind of amphitheater where you can sit and watch the traffic. We sat and watched the traffic and I am kidding and I am not kidding when I say that I intuited an alien intelligence, felt subject to a succession of images, sensations, memories, and affects that did not, properly speaking, belong to me: the ability to perceive polarized light; a conflation of taste and touch as salt was rubbed into the suction cups; a terror localized in my extremities, bypassing the brain completely.

The Curious Garden
PETER BROWN

As the weeks rolled by, Liam began to feel like a real gardener,
and the plants began to feel like a real garden.

The High Line began construction one year before the first iPhone was released. By the time the third section opened in 2014, 58% of adults in the U.S. owned a smartphone. Photo apps have carved a place in the social habits of most visitors, prompting both locals and tourists to stage self-edited scenes and portraits throughout the park. Alexander Dunkel's data maps visualize the transformation of the area surrounding the High Line by analyzing the density of location-tagged Flickr photos before and after the opening of the park. This page: Dunkel's spatial pattern analysis of Flickr photo distribution near the High Line. Right page: official New York Flickr meetup, February 18, 2012.

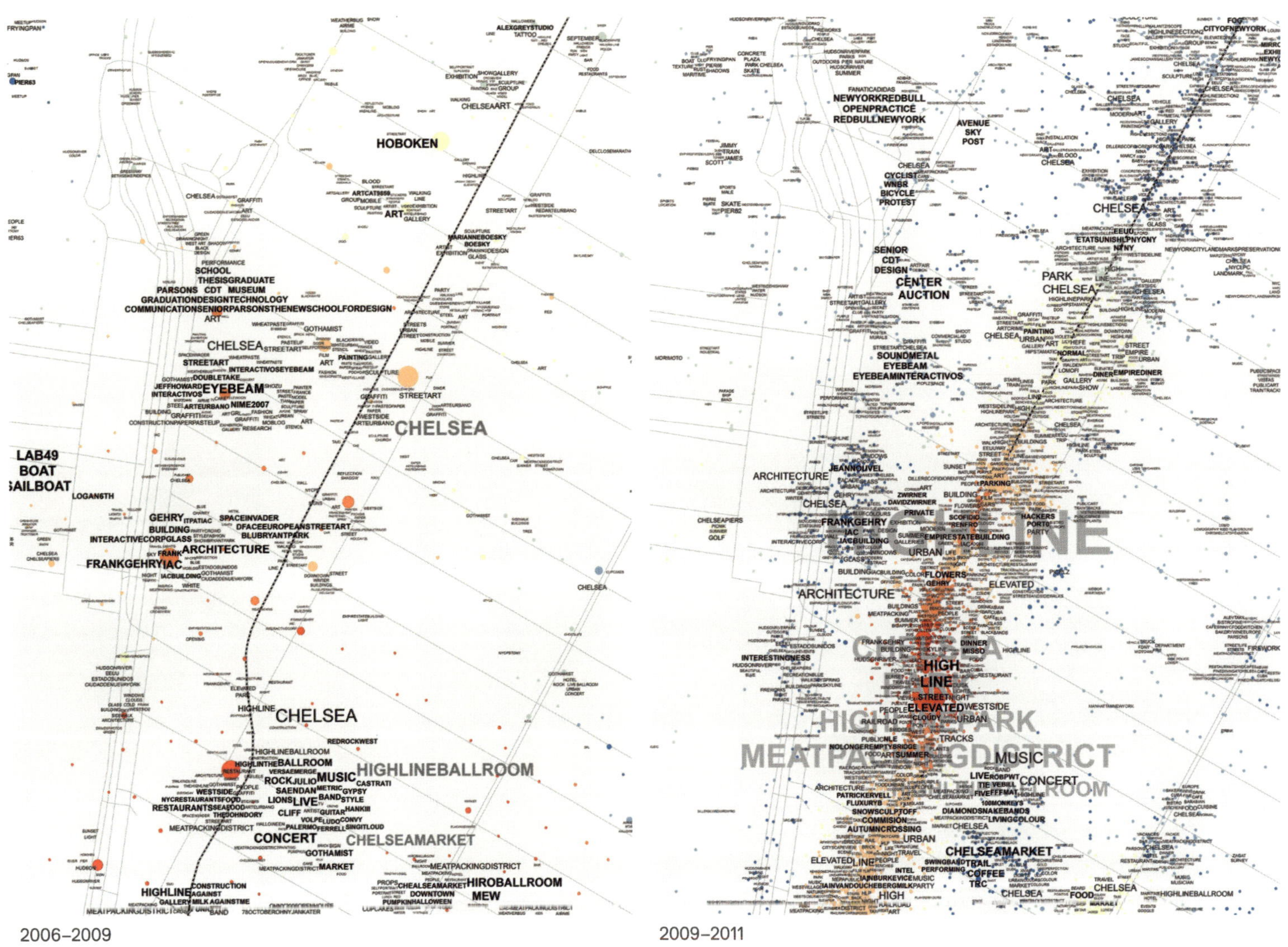

2006–2009

2009–2011

Although the Friends of the High Line commissioned Pentagram to create a logo for the future park in 1999, the founders could not legally copyright the name itself. As the popularity of the park continues to grow, appropriation of the High Line name has become ubiquitous, branding everything from luxury perfumes (left) to illegal drugs (right). Bond No. 9, a SoHo-based fragrance company, introduces its High Line scent as "the world's first railroad perfume."

High Line Eau De Parfum

The scent of wildflowers, green grasses... and urban renewal.

The scent starts off with a prairie grazing weed-purple love grass-mixed with citrusy bergamot and zesty Indian rhubarb. The perfume's floral heart is red-leaf rose, Lady Jane tulips, and grape hyacinth. Its lingering base notes combine bur oak-from the sheltering tree that thrives here-with imported sea moss, to evoke the Hudson's River proximity, along with musk and teakwood, to remind us that Bond No. 9 High Line is a metro-perfume.

The daily rush of park-goers confirmed the immense popularity of the new promenade. Local businesses and building projects took notice, and the High Line became a common namesake.

A McDonald's in Tokyo replicated a well-known wall of High Line graffiti above the 22nd Street Lawn. In New York, a SoHo clothing store created a High Line store display, complete with peel-up benches and fake plantings.

March 3, 1997: "Historically the most decadent of New York's decadent streets, the Meatpacking District is Manhattan's last frontier—a pocket of sin caught in a vise of hipness" (Matt Pincus, *New York Magazine*).

Chelsea Enters Its High Baroque Period

The art scene is booming like never before. A guide to understanding the madness, bracing for the backlash and enjoying it while it lasts.

FOR the throngs who pack its streets on any reasonably dry Saturday, the sprawl of art galleries known as Chelsea is one of the hot spots of cool. But for art-world professionals, it is the place they love to loathe.

After a decade of rapid growth, the neighborhood now harbors more than 230 galleries within its borders, which stretch from West 13th to West 29th Streets and from 10th Avenue to the West Side Highway in Manhattan. That's twice the number of galleries SoHo had at its zenith in the early 1990's. The notion of spending a day "doing" the Chelsea galleries now seems downright quaint, since it would take at least a week to see them all.

As a result of this explosion, the inevitable anti-Chelsea backlash has been on the rise, too. The rap against Chelsea is that it is too big, too commercial, too slick, too conservative and too homogenous, a monolith of art commerce tricked out in look-alike white boxes and shot through with kitsch. This litany is recited by visitors from Los Angeles and Europe, by dealers with galleries in other parts of Manhattan or in Brooklyn and often by Chelsea dealers themselves. As the Lower East Side gallerist Michele Maccarone put it recently in an interview: "The Chelseafication of the art world has created a consensus of mediocrity and frivolousness."

Two of the city's most highly respected small art museums, the Drawing Center and the New Museum for Contemporary Art, both recently rejected the idea of relocating to Chelsea, in part because they felt they would be lost among so many galleries. Christian Haye, who has a gallery on 57th Street and who once memorably described Chelsea as

Continued on Page 33

November 28, 2004: "A contemporary art scene on this scale has never happened before, and it's hard to imagine it ever happening again. Catch it now, because in a few years, Chelsea nostalgia will have replaced SoHo nostalgia, and the current state of affairs will have become the good old days" (Roberta Smith, *New York Times*).

March 10, 2007: The Roxy closes after 28 years.

June 29, 2008: Restaurant Florent closes after 22 years.

May 15, 2010: the original Empire Diner closes after 34 years

May 7, 2007: "The High Line is...the end-product of a perfect confluence of powerful forces: radical dreaming, dogged optimism, neighborhood anxiety, design mania, real-estate opportunism, money, celebrity, and power. In other words, it's a 1.45-mile, 6.7-square-acre, 30-foot-high symbol of exactly what it means to be living in New York right now" (Adam Sternbergh, *New York Magazine*).

April 2007: "The Great Rock N Roll Swindle/Gentrification of the High Line Area" (M. Wartella, *Village Voice*).

Along with the popularity of the High Line, the designation of the Gansevoort Market Historic District in 2003 and the rezoning of West Chelsea in 2005 catalyzed a wave of development that transformed the area, bringing new businesses, luxury condominiums, and crowds of visitors.

BIG DEAL

SARAH KERSHAW

A High Line Boomlet

PHOTOGRAPHS BY CHESTER HIGGINS Jr./THE NEW YORK TIMES

NEO-EDGY The condo +aRt, above, is half a block from the 28th Street entrance of the High Line, the park's second phase.

THE view of West Chelsea from the roof of 540 West 28th Street, a new condominium at 11th Avenue, prompts a somewhat irrational question: what housing crash?

All around, construction is buzzing and the landscape is filling up with new buildings and warehouse conversions, funky and sleek condominiums, hotels, galleries and public spaces designed by big-name architects like Frank Gehry, Jean Nouvel, Richard Meier and Annabelle Selldorf. And other projects once trapped in limbo by the mortgage and construction financing crises are moving ahead.

In the last four years, 27 residential projects have come on the market in West Chelsea, a submarket of Chelsea that runs from 14th to 30th Street, west of Ninth Avenue, according to an analysis by Streeteasy.com. A building boomlet that began a decade ago intensified after the rezoning for residential use of a 15-block area and the beginning phases of the High Line park.

Many of these properties struggled after the collapse of Lehman Brothers two years ago. But the market is coming back, developers and brokers say — through a combination of timing (the opening of the popular High Line), chic (art galleries) and edginess (the rezoning of an industrial area).

West Chelsea's growth came during a period of almost unheard-of building development citywide. In 2007, for example, 25,659 new units were completed. But in 2009 building permits — a measure of future building activity — fell by 90 percent, to 3,275 from 30,947 in 2008, and the decline has persisted in 2010, according to data compiled by the Furman Center for Real Estate and Urban Policy at New York University.

A relative lack of inventory in Chelsea is also sustaining demand in West Chelsea. There are 126 available units in Chelsea as a whole, from 14th Street to 30th Street, west of Fifth Avenue, according to Halstead Property. That is three more than were available last May.

But even in West Chelsea, there are pockets of hot and cold. The High Line will eventually run from Gansevoort Street to 34th Street. The first segment, stretching to 20th Street, is open. The second, extending to 30th Street, is expected to open next spring, and likely to have a similar effect on apartments in that area.

At 540 West 28th Street, a 12-story building called +aRt, developers have so far had a hard time selling condos. Preconstruction sales of the 91 units began in September 2008, but sales were suspended from December 2008 until last May.

Since the units at +aRt — half a block from the 28th Street High Line entrance — recently returned to the market, with prices from $500,000 to $2.3 million, about 20 percent of them have sold, though most for 10 to 15 percent below asking prices.

Across 28th Street, AvalonBay Communities, a national developer, had signed a 99-year lease on about 60,000 square feet of land in 2007. A rental building with 600 to 700 units had been planned but stalled, although according to someone with knowledge of the plans who was not authorized to speak publicly, ground-breaking is anticipated for the middle of 2011.

Erik T. Ekstein, the principal of Ekstein Development and one of the developers of +aRt, said he was encouraged by the current pace of sales and did not regret setting his sights on West Chelsea. The first buyers are moving into the building this week, he said, and he is also developing a 30-unit rental building at 537 West 27th Street.

"We saw what was coming north, we saw the High Line coming, we saw the art galleries," said Mr. Ekstein, who has also developed properties in TriBeCa and in Long Island City, Queens.

Among the first developers to march into West Chelsea in the last 10 years was Cary Tamarkin, the architect and the developer of 456 West 19th Street, where 16 of 22 duplexes, ranging in price from $1.5 million to $7.9 million, are in contract or closed. Mr. Tamarkin focused his marketing efforts on the proliferation of art galleries and exhibits of globally acclaimed painters and sculptors.

"Art was huge," Mr. Tamarkin said. "It was the whole tag line of our building," which is modeled after artist studios of the early 20th century.

"When we first started thinking about this four years ago," he said, "the High Line was just kind of a dream and the area was scary; it had a scary component to it at night. But it has just flourished on a straight line up from that moment."

He also designed and developed a building at 491-495 West Street in the West Village. But he said, "The West Village remains great, but it's, like, done. It's like living in the suburbs. It's not edgy."

While the art district always had cachet, art alone was not enough to sell West Chelsea, said Leonard Steinberg, a broker with Prudential Douglas Elliman who specializes in West Chelsea.

But then came the High Line, the elevated park that is, in phases, transforming an old trestle that snakes through the West Side of Manhattan into a tourist attraction. "Having an art gallery on your street doesn't necessarily imply quality of life," Mr. Steinberg said. "Art galleries are the first indicators of a turning neighborhood, but what's happening now in West Chelsea is the perfect storm."

THE NEW YORK TIMES **NEW YORK** MONDAY, JUNE 6, 2011

The High Line Isn't Just a Sight to See; It's Also an Economic Dynamo

By PATRICK McGEEHAN

Mayor Michael R. Bloomberg and the City Council speaker, Christine C. Quinn, on Friday touring Segment 2 of the High Line, which is to open this week. In one building along Segment 1, the price of apartments has doubled since the park opened.

A decade ago, so many moneyed interests were united against saving the elevated freight tracks that cut through the West Side of Manhattan that the idea appeared to be doomed. Owners of land and buildings throughout Chelsea wanted the decaying High Line viaduct razed, and the administration of Mayor Rudolph W. Giuliani supported their feelings.

But on Friday afternoon, there was Mr. Giuliani's successor, Michael R. Bloomberg, proclaiming that preserving the High Line as a public park revitalized a swath of the city and generated $2 billion in private investment surrounding the park.

The mayor pointed to the deluxe apartment buildings whose glass walls press up against the High Line and the hundreds of art galleries, restaurants and boutiques it overlooks. All of that commerce more than makes up for the $115 million the city has spent on the park and the deals it has made to encourage developers to build along the High Line without blocking out the sun, Mr. Bloomberg said. On top of the 8,000 construction jobs those projects required, the redevelopment has added about 12,000 jobs in the area, the mayor said.

Indeed, what started out as a community-based campaign to convert an eyesore into an asset evolved into one of the most successful economic-development projects of the mayor's nine years in office. The co-founders of Friends of the High Line, a group that operates the city-owned park, said the mayor and his staff deserved credit for having embraced the park and rezoned the neighborhoods it passes through to help it flourish.

Robert Hammond, one of the founders, said the organization commissioned a study of the potential economic benefits of the project in 2002. "We talked about a High Line district and that it would be good for the local economy," Mr. Hammond recalled. But, he added, "we had no idea that it would happen this fast. If you had said then that 10th Avenue would be a location for some of the world's best chefs, it would

Amanda Burden, the city's planning director, emphasized the boost to property values, saying that in one building that abuts the lower section of the High Line, the price of apartments had doubled since the park opened, to about $2,000 a square foot. Ms. Burden called the area "Architects Row" as she ticked off the roster of designers of nearby buildings, including Jean Nouvel, Annabelle Selldorf and Neil Denari.

Yet those exclusive accommodations are wedged in within a block of huge brick complexes of public housing, where sheets serve as curtains and dented air-conditioners list toward the earth. A seating area on the second half-mile segment of the High Line, which is to open this week, offers visitors a pigeon's-eye view of a Firestone auto-repair shop on 26th Street.

The second segment bisects

Avenues from 20th Street to 30th Street. If the third section is completed, it will end near the terminus of the extended No. 7 subway line, said Robert K. Steel, the deputy mayor for economic development. People could ride the subway from Queens, then walk the High Line through Chelsea to the meatpacking district, said Mr. Steel, who recently became a resident of Chelsea, just a block from the High Line.

In a way, the High Line has done for those neighborhoods what new subway lines have done in other parts of the city, Mr. Hammond said. "Normally, the farther you get from the subway the less expensive the housing is," said Mr. Hammond, who confessed that he rents an apartment in the West Village. "But the closer you are to the High Line, the farther you are from the subway, and still, the closer the apartments are to the High Line,

The New York Times

Sunday, December 18, 2005

Special:
Westchester/Connecticut
Real Estate Offerings

Real Estate

WC Section 11

Turning the High Line Into . . .
The High Life

Developers have already begun work on buildings that will add a planned 5,500 apartments along the park that is to grow on the elevated railroad tracks in Chelsea.

By CLAIRE WILSON

SAY bye-bye to the parking lots along 10th Avenue, between 14th and 30th Streets, and maybe a few of the chaotic clubs and bars on the side streets. Bid adieu to the rough-and-tumble allure of taxi garages and the fringe of weeds running the length of the High Line, the derelict but irresistibly charming dinosaur of an elevated railroad that is the backbone of West Chelsea's thriving gallery scene.

Say hello to designer buildings, valet parking, concierges, meditation gardens and, oh yes, lines of limos jockeying for position outside the borough's trendiest new restaurants branded by celebrity chefs like Mario Batali, Tom Colicchio and Masaharu Morimoto.

The heady grit-and-glamour cocktail that New Yorkers so love about the meatpacking district is about to expand northward — although perhaps with more glamour than grit in the final equation — as the city's major developers snatch up any and all available parcels along the High Line and start work on a planned 5,300 units of housing, all but 1,100 of them for the fabulously well-heeled.

Zoning changes made final last summer have won praise for how they put the spotlight on the elevated 22-block park the High Line is to become and protect the estimated 200 galleries while allowing extensive luxury residential development. Height limitations and required setbacks on some new buildings will complement the [illegible]-year-old structure and conserve views of it, while preserving some of the light and open spaces that have defined the neighborhood. Work on

Continued on Page 8

GOING UP
The High Line, above, looking north from 19th Street. Frank Maresca, from left, a partner in the Ricco/Maresca Gallery; Melva Max, the owner of La Luncheonette; and the developers Craig D. Wood of Cape Advisors Inc. and Alf Naman of Alf Naman Real Estate Advisors.

D1

Home

THURSDAY, AUGUST 2, 2012

The New York Times

WHO LIVES THERE

Close Quarters

On the most intimate stretch of the High Line, new residents adjust to a life on display.

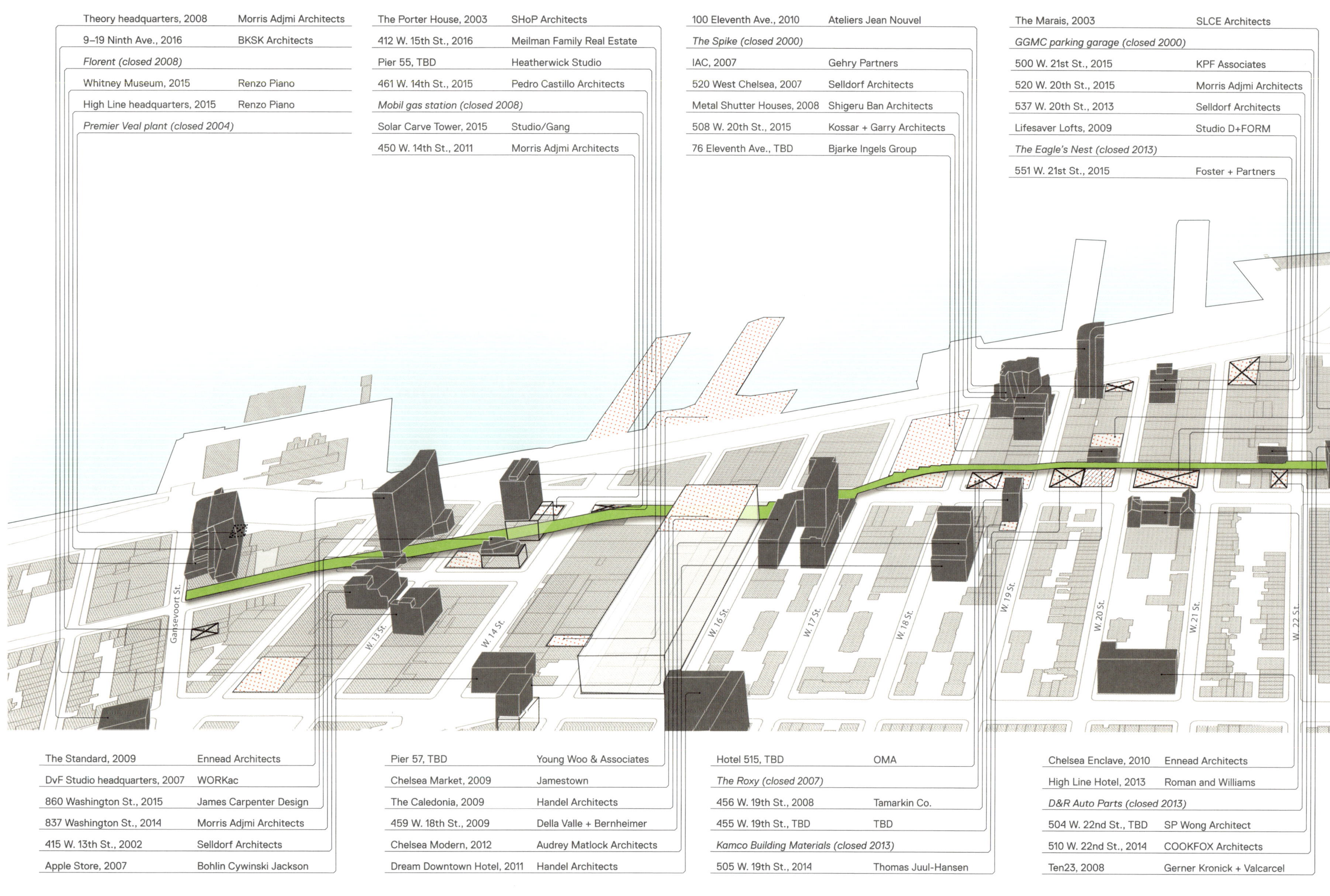

Theory headquarters, 2008 Morris Adjmi Architects
9–19 Ninth Ave., 2016 BKSK Architects
Florent (closed 2008)
Whitney Museum, 2015 Renzo Piano
High Line headquarters, 2015 Renzo Piano
Premier Veal plant (closed 2004)
The Porter House, 2003 SHoP Architects
412 W. 15th St., 2016 Meilman Family Real Estate
Pier 55, TBD Heatherwick Studio
461 W. 14th St., 2015 Pedro Castillo Architects
Mobil gas station (closed 2008)
Solar Carve Tower, 2015 Studio/Gang
450 W. 14th St., 2011 Morris Adjmi Architects
100 Eleventh Ave., 2010 Ateliers Jean Nouvel
The Spike (closed 2000)
IAC, 2007 Gehry Partners
520 West Chelsea, 2007 Selldorf Architects
Metal Shutter Houses, 2008 Shigeru Ban Architects
508 W. 20th St., 2015 Kossar + Garry Architects
76 Eleventh Ave., TBD Bjarke Ingels Group
The Marais, 2003 SLCE Architects
GGMC parking garage (closed 2000)
500 W. 21st St., 2015 KPF Associates
520 W. 20th St., 2015 Morris Adjmi Architects
537 W. 20th St., 2013 Selldorf Architects
Lifesaver Lofts, 2009 Studio D+FORM
The Eagle's Nest (closed 2013)
551 W. 21st St., 2015 Foster + Partners
Gansevoort St.
W. 13 St.
W. 14 St.
W. 16 St.
W. 17 St.
W. 18 St.
W. 19 St.
W. 20 St.
W. 21 St.
W. 22 St.
The Standard, 2009 Ennead Architects
DvF Studio headquarters, 2007 WORKac
860 Washington St., 2015 James Carpenter Design
837 Washington St., 2014 Morris Adjmi Architects
415 W. 13th St., 2002 Selldorf Architects
Apple Store, 2007 Bohlin Cywinski Jackson
Pier 57, TBD Young Woo & Associates
Chelsea Market, 2009 Jamestown
The Caledonia, 2009 Handel Architects
459 W. 18th St., 2009 Della Valle + Bernheimer
Chelsea Modern, 2012 Audrey Matlock Architects
Dream Downtown Hotel, 2011 Handel Architects
Hotel 515, TBD OMA
The Roxy (closed 2007)
456 W. 19th St., 2008 Tamarkin Co.
455 W. 19th St., TBD TBD
Kamco Building Materials (closed 2013)
505 W. 19th St., 2014 Thomas Juul-Hansen
Chelsea Enclave, 2010 Ennead Architects
High Line Hotel, 2013 Roman and Williams
D&R Auto Parts (closed 2013)
504 W. 22nd St., TBD SP Wong Architect
510 W. 22nd St., 2014 COOKFOX Architects
Ten23, 2008 Gerner Kronick + Valcarcel

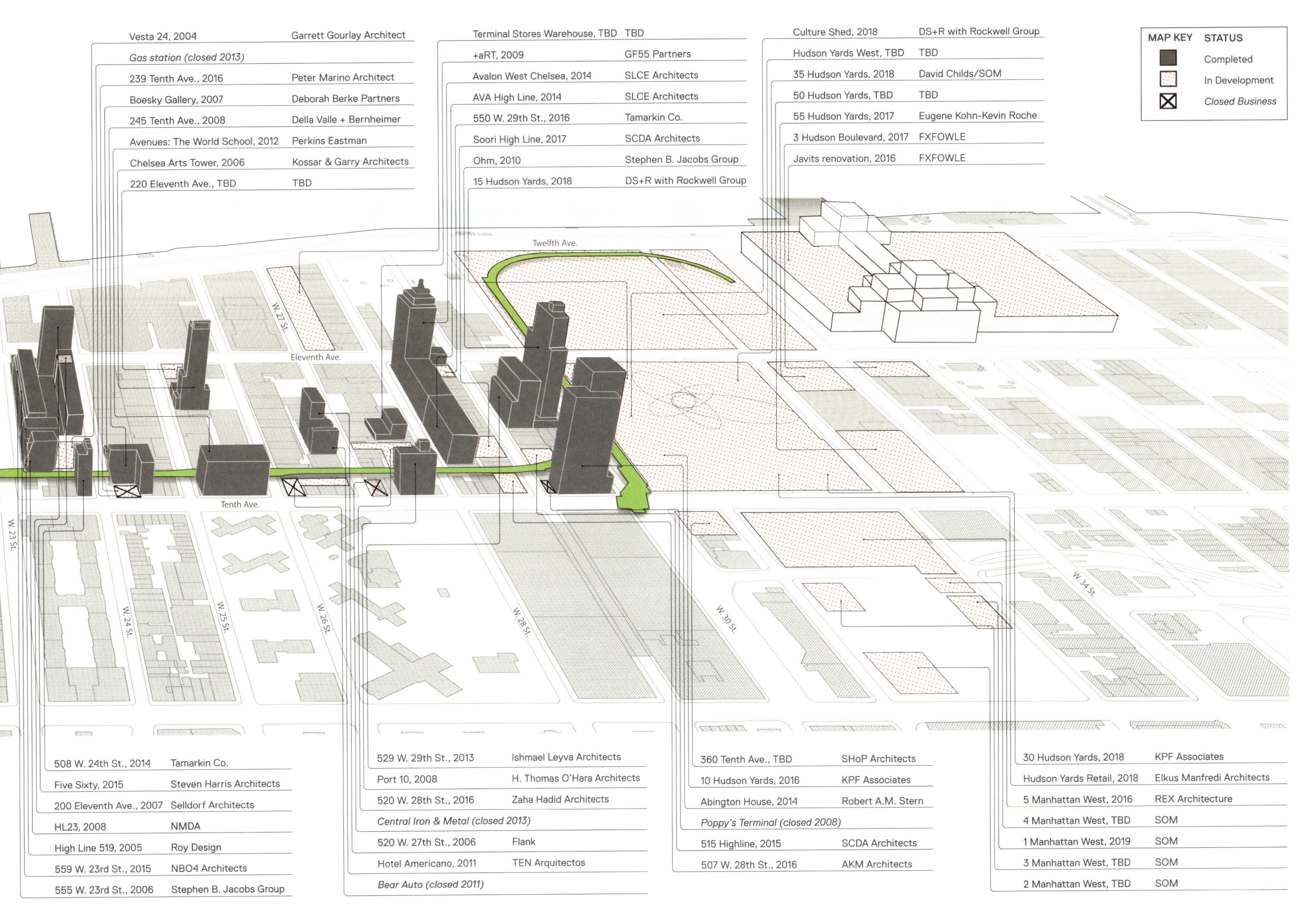
Vesta 24, 2004 Garrett Gourlay Architect
Gas station (closed 2013)
239 Tenth Ave., 2016 Peter Marino Architect
Boesky Gallery, 2007 Deborah Berke Partners
245 Tenth Ave., 2008 Della Valle + Bernheimer
Avenues: The World School, 2012 Perkins Eastman
Chelsea Arts Tower, 2006 Kossar & Garry Architects
220 Eleventh Ave., TBD TBD
Terminal Stores Warehouse, TBD TBD
+aRT, 2009 GF55 Partners
Avalon West Chelsea, 2014 SLCE Architects
AVA High Line, 2014 SLCE Architects
550 W. 29th St., 2016 Tamarkin Co.
Soori High Line, 2017 SCDA Architects
Ohm, 2010 Stephen B. Jacobs Group
15 Hudson Yards, 2018 DS+R with Rockwell Group
Culture Shed, 2018 DS+R with Rockwell Group
Hudson Yards West, TBD TBD
35 Hudson Yards, 2018 David Childs/SOM
50 Hudson Yards, TBD TBD
55 Hudson Yards, 2017 Eugene Kohn-Kevin Roche
3 Hudson Boulevard, 2017 FXFOWLE
Javits renovation, 2016 FXFOWLE
MAP KEY STATUS
Completed
In Development
Closed Business
Twelfth Ave.
Eleventh Ave.
Tenth Ave.
W. 23 St.
W. 24 St.
W. 25 St.
W. 26 St.
W. 27 St.
W. 28 St.
W. 30 St.
W. 34 St.
508 W. 24th St., 2014 Tamarkin Co.
Five Sixty, 2015 Steven Harris Architects
200 Eleventh Ave., 2007 Selldorf Architects
HL23, 2008 NMDA
High Line 519, 2005 Roy Design
559 W. 23rd St., 2015 NBO4 Architects
555 W. 23rd St., 2006 Stephen B. Jacobs Group
529 W. 29th St., 2013 Ishmael Leyva Architects
Port 10, 2008 H. Thomas O'Hara Architects
520 W. 28th St., 2016 Zaha Hadid Architects
Central Iron & Metal (closed 2013)
520 W. 27th St., 2006 Flank
Hotel Americano, 2011 TEN Arquitectos
Bear Auto (closed 2011)
360 Tenth Ave., TBD SHoP Architects
10 Hudson Yards, 2016 KPF Associates
Abington House, 2014 Robert A.M. Stern
Poppy's Terminal (closed 2008)
515 Highline, 2015 SCDA Architects
507 W. 28th St., 2016 AKM Architects
30 Hudson Yards, 2018 KPF Associates
Hudson Yards Retail, 2018 Elkus Manfredi Architects
5 Manhattan West, 2016 REX Architecture
4 Manhattan West, TBD SOM
1 Manhattan West, 2019 SOM
3 Manhattan West, TBD SOM
2 Manhattan West, TBD SOM

As of the publication of this book, there are dozens of building projects around the globe either in the planning stages, under construction, or already built that have cited the High Line as a precedent. Some of these projects involve adaptive reuse of postindustrial infrastructure such as highways, bridges, and railroads; others emulate only the idea of the linear promenade, building brand-new structures to create an elevated park.

1 Abu Dhabi
2 Atlanta
3 Chicago
4 Detroit
5 Edinburgh
6 Florida Keys
7 Bari
8 Jersey City
9 Rotterdam
10, 17, 18, 19, 50 New York
11 Copenhagen
12, 13, 35 London
14 Mexico City
15, 33 Washington, DC
16 Liverpool
20 Bethlehem
21 Philadelphia
22 Poughkeepsie
23 Jerusalem
24, 25, 53 Seoul
26 Shenzhen
27 Singapore
28 St. Louis
29, 30, 57 Toronto
31 Montreal
32 Mumbai
34 Leeds
36, 58 Santiago
37, 55 São Paulo
38 Cleveland
39 Madrid
40 Lake Pertusillo
41 Miami
42, 52 Sydney
43 Medellin
44 Buenos Aires
45 Milwaukee
46 Rio de Janeiro
47 Seattle
48 Lima
49 Cape Town
51 Helsinki
54 Paris
56 Summit
59 New Haven
60 Los Angeles

5
34
16
11
51
9
12
13
35
54
7
40
39
23
1
32
26
24
25
53
27
49
42
52

1 UAE Abu Dhabi | Urban Oasis Rooftop Park, unrealized

2 USA Atlanta | Beltline, exp. 2030

3 USA Chicago | The 606 Bloomingdale Trail, 2015

4 USA Detroit | Dequindre Cut Greenway, 2014

5 UK Edinburgh | Leith Walk, 2013

6 USA Florida Keys | Overseas Heritage Trail, exp. 2017

7 ITALY Bari | Baricentrale, unrealized

8 USA Jersey City | Harsimus Stem Embankment, unrealized

9 THE NETHERLANDS Rotterdam | Hofbogen, unrealized

10 USA New York | The Dry Line, 2017

11 DENMARK Copenhagen | Superkilen, 2012

12 UK London | Garden Bridge, exp. 2018

13 UK London | Promenade of Curiosities, unrealized

14 MEXICO Mexico City | Chapultepec Project, unrealized

15 USA Washington, DC | Dupont Underground, exp. 2015

ADAPTIVE REUSE
ELEVATED PARKS
LINEAR PARK
SPECULATIVE

16 UK Liverpool | Churchill Flyover, 2012

17 USA New York | Hunter's Point South Waterfront Park, 2013

18 USA New York | The Low Line, exp. 2018

19 USA New York | Queensway, unrealized

20 USA Bethlehem | Hoover Mason Trestle, exp. 2015

21 USA Philadelphia | Rail Park Phase 1, exp. 2015

22 USA Poughkeepsie | Walkway over the Hudson, 2009

23 ISRAEL Jerusalem | Train Track Park, 2014

24 SOUTH KOREA Seoul | Skygarden, 2017

25 SOUTH KOREA Seoul | Cheonggyecheon Park, 2005

26 CHINA Shenzhen | Hua Qiang Bei Road, unrealized

27 SINGAPORE | Green Corridor, 2010

28 USA St. Louis | Trestle, 2013

29 CANADA Toronto | Green Line, unrealized

30 CANADA Toronto | West Toronto Railpath, 2009

31 CANADA Montreal | Chemin Qui Marche, 2012

32 INDIA Mumbai | Greenway Project, unrealized

33 USA Washington, DC | 11th Street Bridge Park, exp. 2018

34 UK Leeds | Holbeck Viaduct, exp. 2015

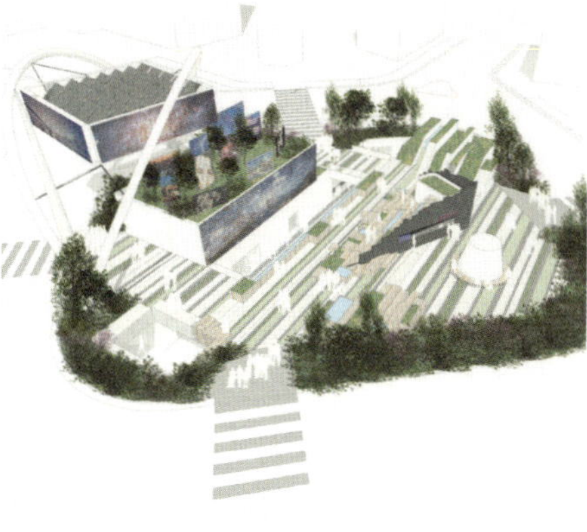

35 UK London | Old Street Green, unrealized

36 CHILE Santiago | Rio Mapocho Pedaleable, 2010

37 BRASIL São Paulo | Rio Tiete Park, unrealized

38 USA Cleveland | Red Line, unrealized

39 SPAIN Madrid | Parque Elevado de La Cebada, exp. 2017

40 ITALY Lake Pertusillo | Green Bridge, unrealized

41 USA Miami | The Underline, 2018

42 AUSTRALIA Sydney | The Goods Line, exp. 2015

43 COLOMBIA Medellín | Parque Rio, unrealized

44 ARGENTINA Buenos Aires | Playa Ferroviaria de Liniers, unrealized

45 USA Milwaukee | Erie Street Plaza, 2010

46 BRASIL Rio de Janeiro | Parque Madureira, 2012

47 USA Seattle | Olympic Sculpture Park, 2007

48 PERU Lima | Ghost Train Park, 2010

49 SOUTH AFRICA Cape Town | High Line Park, unrealized

50 USA New York | Harlem River Promenade, unrealized

51 FINLAND Helsinki | "Baana" Bike Corridor, 2012

52 AUSTRALIA Sydney | High-Lane, unrealized

53 SOUTH KOREA Seoul | Elevated Motorway, exp. 2016

54 FRANCE Paris | Le Petite Ceinture, unrealized

55 BRASIL São Paulo | Minhocao Park, unrealized

56 USA Summit | Rahway Valley Railroad, unrealized

57 CANADA Toronto | King High Line, 2017

58 CHILE Santiago | FFCC Tunnel, unrealized

59 USA New Haven | Farmington Canal Heritage Trail, 2012

60 USA Los Angeles | Park 101, unrealized

07.15.2010

The New York Times

The High Line, a Pioneer Aloft, Inspires Other Cities to Look Up

By KATE TAYLOR

Phone calls and visitors and, yes, dreams from around the world are pouring into the small offices of the Friends of the High Line on West 20th Street in Manhattan these days.

Detroit is thinking big about an abandoned train station. Jersey City and Philadelphia have defunct railroad beds, and Chicago has old train tracks that don't look like much now, but maybe they too . . .

The High Line's success as an elevated park, its improbable evolution from old trestle into glittering urban amenity, has motivated a whole host of public officials and city planners to consider or revisit efforts to convert relics from their own industrial pasts into potential economic engines.

In many of these places there had already been some talk and visions of what might be, but now New York's accomplishment is providing ammunition for boosters while giving skeptics much-needed evidence of the potential for success. The High Line has become, like bagels and CompStat, another kind of New York export.

"There's a nice healthy competition between big American cities," said Ben Helphand, who is pushing to create a park on a defunct rail line in Chicago. "That this has been done in New York puts the onus on us to do it ourselves and to give it a Chicago stamp."

In Chicago, Jesse Davila visits the elevated Bloomingdale Trail. A design master plan has been commissioned for that trail.

The High Line, an elevated freight spur that runs along the West Side of Manhattan and overlooks the Hudson River, was also nothing more than a crumbling eyesore 10 years ago. But since it opened as a park last year, its plantings and vistas, tasteful design and intricate weave through the redbrick bastions of New York's meatpacking past and contemporary buildings by Frank Gehry and Jean Nouvel have been a hit. Though the High Line is not fully completed — plans have it potentially extending as far north as West 34th Street — more than two million people have already visited.

Developers from Rotterdam and Hong Kong have come looking for ideas. Officials from Jerusalem are hoping to visit. Recently a team from Singapore (Is there really anything old and rusty in Singapore?) spent time on the landscaped walkways that stretch from Gansevoort Street to West 20th Street.

03.17.2014

The Sydney Morning Herald

New South Wales

Railway goods line reborn as New York-style high line

Pedestrians should be able to walk the first section of Sydney's version of New York's "High Line" by the end of the year with construction due to start this month.

But the latest plans for the goods line walkway - a redevelopment of a little-used rail corridor between Central station and Darling Harbour - show it is expected to be much more than a pedestrian thoroughfare.

Pop-up bars, cafes, performance stages, "study pods" and electronic screens are all planned to line the border of the goods line, a 500-metre stretch linking Central with Haymarket, Ultimo and Darling Harbour.

The line - part of which will consist of raised walkways - is to be built in two stages.

The first, and northern, section of the line runs from the Frank Gehry-designed Dr Chau Chak Wing Building being built at the University of Technology, Sydney to the Powerhouse Museum.

Artist impression of The Goods Line.

And on Saturday, Planning Minister Brad Hazzard released new images of the southern section of the line, which will run past the ABC at Ultimo and link with the pedestrian walkway under Central and Railway Square.

"The goods line south has already generated interest in redevelopment from landowners in the surrounding area, who can see the great advantages this new facility will offer for economic and property development," Mr Hazzard said.

The goods line was originally billed as a pedestrian and cycling thoroughfare. But the images of the southern section of the goods line raise the question of how well cyclists will fit in what is shown as a busy thoroughfare, flanked by pockets for retail and live entertainment.

The president of advocacy group BIKESydney, David Borella, said the group supported the creation of places that led to good outcomes for both walkers and cyclists. But he said the design should cater for the passage of low-speed cyclists.

"Like water, cyclists will find the path of least resistance and will tend to want to use the corridor," Mr Borella said.

Work will begin on the northern section of the goods line this month, and is expected to be finished by November, soon after the Gehry building is due to open.

A spokeswoman for Mr Hazzard said the south section of the line would go to tender late this year, with construction starting early next year.

LA NACION | DOMINGO 28 DE SEPTIEMBRE DE 2014

9.28 2014

Alma de valija

Horacio de Dios

La High Line, una idea importada de Francia

¿Qué hay de nuevo para un visitante frecuente de Manhattan? Mi respuesta es la terraza jardín para caminar más de 20 cuadras, con el río Hudson a un lado y un catálogo de rascacielos, tiendas, galerías de arte, restaurantes y bares de onda al otro.

Es la High Line que comienza en la 18 Street, en el corazón del Meatpacking District, el de Sex and the City (aunque la serie haya terminado). Es un living roof system, un parque público por donde corrían las vías del elevado, que se fue remodelando en tres etapas desde 2009 y que terminó el 21 de septiembre, en el otoño de ellos y la primavera nuestra.

Ahora llega hasta la 34 Street, con el portaaviones Intrepid en su muelle y muy cerca del Centro de Convenciones, el Madison Square Garden y Penn Station. Al borde de Hell's Kitchen (la Cocina del Infierno), es el escenario real de las peleas entre pandillas que retrató West Side Story (Amor sin barreras en español). Desde la película ha pasado medio siglo y nada es igual en Nueva York, donde los barrios, como la gente y las costumbres, cambian continuamente. Lo comprobamos en cada viaje, lo mismo que el aumento del precio de sus hoteles, los más caros de Estados Unidos.

Para subirnos a esta terraza usamos las escaleras en el extremo de Gansevoort, al norte del Village y Tribeca. Hay un ascensor y hasta baños públicos, lo que no es frecuente en NYC.

Allí empieza un paseo formidable y muy económico, con plantas y árboles de sombra que tienen hasta magnolias, pájaros y mariposas de visita. Frente al agua pasan cruceros y ferries, y los jardines son ideales para picnics al paso, aptos para chicos (lo único prohibido son los perros), accesibles para sillas de ruedas y muy seguro porque nunca estamos solos, y cuando oscurece hay iluminación con LED.

Igual que en un city tour elegimos las escalas, callejeamos curioseando hoteles de lujo o las últimas obras de Frank Gehry, el mismo de Bilbao, el francés Jean Nouvel y el nuevo museo Whitney, del italiano Renzo Piano (todos premios Pritzker, el Nobel de Arquitectura).Para conocedores de las entretelas de la Gran Manzana está el complejo Westbeth, donde funcionaron los laboratorios de la Bell (1866-1966) transformados por Richard Meier (otro Pritzker) en viviendas, estudios y talleres para 384 artistas de mil disciplinas, por un alquiler de unos 800 dólares mensuales, tres veces menos que el promedio de Manhattan. Allí vivieron Robert De Niro y la legendaria coreógrafa Merce Cunningham ensayaba con su ballet.

Mi parada preferida es Chelsea Market, con restos de todo tipo haciendo juego con sus productos, igual que el mercado de Chueca en Madrid. En las calles transversales, en especial en torno de la 9» Avenida, se multiplican las galerías de arte que emigraron desde el SoHo. Y una variedad de comercios, cafés pequeños. bares y pizzerías mezclados con chefs famosos como Mario Batali o Vongerichten. Incluso, si quiere hablar español está el mexicano Dos Caminos o puede elegir en Internet los que más le convengan.

La idea del High Line, la inteligencia de utilizar un ramal inactivo, no es una creación norteamericana, sino francesa que es una maravilla. Doy fe porque me encanta caminar entre sus jardines con rosas (como en nuestro Palermo) de la Ópera de la Bastilla y el Viaducto de las Artes. Lo llaman Promenade Plantée o Coulée Verte y lo abrieron en 1993. Aunque han pasado 20 años, todavía hay muchos turistas que nunca lo visitaron.

No creo que pase lo mismo con la High Line, que es éxito por su público creciente y ya aparece en películas de Julianne Moore y Will Smith, en temas de hip hop dedicados, y hasta Bart la visitó en un episodio de los Simpson.

La High Line será seguida como ejemplo en St Louis, Filadelfia, Nueva Jersey, Chicago y Rotterdam en Holanda. Otra de las lecciones de este paseo, sobre todo en familia, es aprender que copiar de los que saben no es un pecado, sino una virtud.

¿Para qué inventar la rueda si ya está inventada?

10.11.2014

LA STAMPA TUTTOGREEN

High Line a Roma? Ci prova il Viadotto dei Presidenti

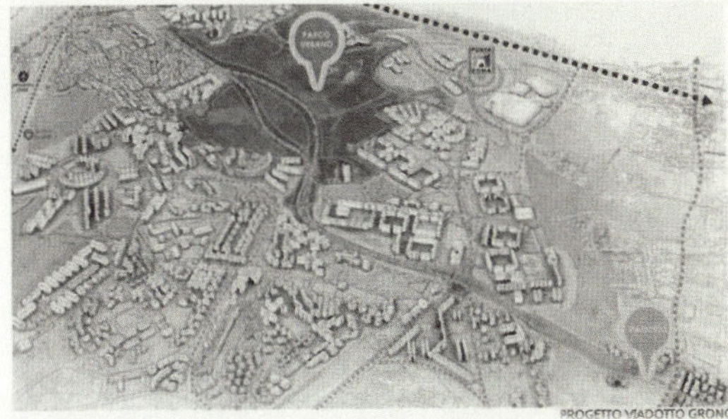

Progetto Viadotto Gronchi

Periferie urbane? Una risorsa da valorizzare in un'ottica decisamente verde. Parte da quest'idea "Sotto il Viadotto", manifestazione romana che dell'11 e il 12 ottobre presso il Viadotto dei Presidenti, quartiere Nuovo Salario, ripensa l'hinterland in versione città-friendly. L'evento nasce da un grande disegno di sostenibilità che da mesi aleggia sulla capitale e sulle rispettive politiche di mobilità. L'idea di creare anche per Roma un progetto gemello a quello della **High Line** di New York; un parco ricavato da un binario ferroviario in disuso.

Si parlava di una prima ipotesi di progettazione all'interno del tratto della Tangenziale Est, da Batteria Nomentana alla nuova stazione Tiburtina, ma adesso anche la partnership tra il G124 di Renzo Piano, l'associazione Greenapsi e il III Municipio nell'ambito del progetto TUTUR, si muove in questa direzione e mette la prima pietra per creare il parco sopraelevato in un quartiere interessato da un forte degrado urbanistico. Il Viadotto Gronchi nasce negli anni'90 come asse che avrebbe dovuto collegare **Roma** Nord a Roma Sud, da Saxa Rubra fino al Laurentino, attraverso l'impiego di una ferrovia leggera. Il progetto rimase incompiuto e oggi l'intera area è un luogo di accumulazione di rifiuti e di degrado cittadino. Trasformarla però in un parco verde e totalmente ecosostenibile è il sogno dei suoi abitanti e degli architetti che hanno dato vita per primi alla scintilla necessaria a mettere in moto l'utopia metropolitana. Sono Alessandro Lungo e Massimiliano Foffo, due **architetti** romani che nella tesi intitolata "Il riciclo dei vuoti urbani come strategia per la città" hanno immaginato una destinazione diversa per quella che oggi rappresenta una spina nel fianco del III Municipio. Da questo sabato quindi verrà seminata la prima ondata verde che dovrebbe portare nel giro di due anni alla costruzione di una pista ciclabile e di un parco, al posto del mostro di cemento. Un progetto lungo e diviso in tre fasi. La prima vede la riattivazione del viadotto attraverso il recupero della struttura esistente, in un secondo momento la realizzazione del percorso ciclo-pedonale e infine il collegamento dell'intera zona con il piano della mobilità che interesserà l'area circostante, compreso il collegamento con la metro B1 prevista entro il 2020. Per questo motivo il weekend si aprirà con la sistemazione di un manto erboso provvisorio e la creazione di un'area verde per i più piccoli. Durante le giornate della manifestazione sarà possibile prendere parte a una gita in bicicletta lungo il percorso del viadotto, fare un giro nel nuovo spazio green e partecipare alla tavola rotonda dal titolo Spazio Pubblico Bene Comune. Due piccole grandi giornate pensate per coinvolgere la comunità e per ripensare la città in un'ottica più collettiva e verde.

12.19.2014

theguardian
Winner of the Pulitzer prize

London garden bridge: the Thames is now a playground for private fantasies

The news that Boris Johnson has rubber-stamped the garden bridge should come as no surprise. Since taking office he has become the self-styled tsar of novelty infrastructure projects, bestowing London with an empty cable-car (the Emirates Airline doesn't see a single regular user according to recent TfL figures) , a fleet of sweltering buses and misty renderings of a glowing airport floating in the estuary. But what is staggering is quite how quickly a plan for a private tourist attraction planted in the centre of the city, at the whim of a celebrity, has been swept through the planning system - and taken £60m of public funding with it.

Joanna Lumley has been peddling her idea for "a chance to walk through woodlands over one of the greatest rivers in the world" for more than a decade, but Boris has been the first to take it seriously. She originally conceived the project as a Princess Diana memorial bridge and pitched it to Ken Livingstone in 2002. He had the good sense to turn it down, but she has now managed to seduce City Hall, Lambeth and Westminster councils alike with a liberal sprinkling of architectural fairy-dust, courtesy of "the Da Vinci of our day" Thomas Heatherwick - who also designed the Boris Bus.

It has since emerged that the miraculous garden bridge is neither a garden nor a bridge. It will provide a planted area less than half the size of a football pitch, will be closed to the public at night and will require advanced registration for groups, in order to discourage protesters. Nor will cyclists be allowed in. It is projected to attract crowds second only to Disneyland in Europe, at one of the busiest stretches of the South Bank, leading local critics to describe it as "another Hillsborough disaster in the making".

It has been vociferously opposed by residents on both sides of the river, by St Paul's cathedral and by the barristers of Middle Temple - who have declared Lambeth's planning decision unlawful. The Westminster committee reached the height of farce when the entire decision came down to a judgement over whether the joy brought by new views from the bridge would outweigh the damaged caused to existing cherished views; imaginary views that weren't even provided in the planning application.

The decision sends the signal that, like the rest of London, the Thames is now a playground for the construction of private fantasies - that will be furnished with public funds to achieve them.

04.01.2015

O GLOBO

High Line Park ensina outras cidades como abraçar seu passado industrial

Parque suspenso construído sobre uma plataforma ferroviária desativada em Nova York revitalizou região

POR O GLOBO

NEW YORK — Julian Hunt foi visitar o High Line Park, um parque suspenso no West Side, em Nova York, antes mesmo de ele ser aberto. O arquiteto de Washington fez a viagem como parte de um trabalho meticuloso. Durante a maior parte de uma década, ele vem tentando converter uma série de túneis de concreto abandonados sob a Dupont Circle, onde antes passavam bondes, em uma mistura de galerias de arte, cafés e espaços para apresentações.

Logo no início da jornada, Hunt visitou o High Line, construído sobre uma plataforma ferroviária desativada, perto do Rio Hudson, com vários espaços de lazer, exposições de arte, um jardim e o motor do que é hoje um dos bairros que mais cresce em Manhattan.

— Este foi o melhor exemplo americano que pudemos achar de reprogramação de uma infraestrutura industrial. E teve um impacto muito visível em Manhattan.

Ele está longe de ser o único a fazer uma peregrinação ao High Line Park. Como Washington vem tentanto acabar com seu próprio passado industrial, empresários locais e arquitetos vêm fazendo o mesmo caminho. Alguns projetos são de natureza comercial, outros públicos, alguns as duas coisas. No ano passado, Robin-Eve Jasper, presidente do NoMa Business Improvement District, em Washington, visitou o local e outros parques de Nova York que seguem a mesma linha.

— É realmente um bom exemplo de como as pessoas usam o espaço público como seu escritório, sua sala de estar — disse, sobre o High Line Park. — Eles querem aproveitar os espaços públicos com uma xícara de café ou um copo de vinho.

Quando o primeiro trecho foi inaugurado, em 2009, já não havia trem nos trilhos há quase 30 anos. Outras partes tinham sido demolidas e as que permaneceram de pé foram cercadas da vizinhança, que em grande parte consistia em armazéns de abastecimento e centros comerciais de estética. Em 1999, dois moradores da região formaram uma organização sem fins lucrativos que começou a planejar a reutilização da linha, e acabou convencendo o governo a adquirí-la e contratar arquitetos para repensar o espaço.

— Os designers sempre dizem que é o único lugar em Nova York onde você faz nada — brincou Peter Mullan, vice-presidente executivo da ONG.

Hoje, a ONG Friends of High Line conta com 70 funcionários, que incluem horticultores e curadores de arte, e um orçamento anual de US$ 8 milhões. O terceiro trecho do parque foi concluído em setembro, deixando o projeto quase completo. Grande parte evoca a história da linha de trem, com trilhos ao longo do caminho e longos trechos outrora precários que permanecem do jeito que estavam quando o espaço foi abandonado e fechado ao público.

Embora o grupo tenha lutado durante anos para conseguir investimento e aprovações para finalizar a obra, agora veem um boom de construções no bairro. Condomínios multimilionários são anunciados e um prédio de escritórios, que será a sede da Time Warner, está sendo finalizado nas proximidades.

Mullan contou que o parque é tão popular entre os visitantes que ele precisa se certificar constantemente de que o local continua a ser frequentado por moradores — embora isso às vezes tenha o efeito contrário, de torná-lo ainda mais popular para os turistas.

— Acho que essa é a sua singularidade. É uma maneira de ver Nova York. É uma maneira de saber como é viver em Nova York.

BE PART OF THE HIGH LINE'S NEXT CHAPTER

In 1999, when Joshua David and I stood on the abandoned rail tracks, surrounded by both wildflowers and the grit and vigor of New York City, we knew this was a once in a lifetime opportunity. Thanks to a fantastic community of advocates, supporters, and community members, as well as our partnership with the City of New York, we opened the first section ten years later in 2009.

Part of this community was the design team consisting of James Corner Field Operations, DS+R, and Piet Oudolf. When we interviewed them in 2004 to be the architects for the High Line, we were all impressed. Rather than talking about the beauty of the space, they talked about how the High Line could be a living, breathing part of the city. Their design created an exciting tension between opposites that reflected the structure's past—the hard and the soft, the old and the new, boldness and modesty, manmade and nature. Our beauty is in our complexity.

Through our donors and supporters, we continue to raise nearly 100% of the High Line's annual budget and program, maintain, and operate the park. We create and present hundreds of public programs every year. We curate annual public art installations and exhibitions, all for the public to experience, 365 days a year, for free.

We hope to continue to be an inspiration for how cities can transform industrial infrastructure into hybrid public spaces through our work with the High Line Network, a learning community of people-led projects all over North America.

We do all this while keeping our four-season gardens thriving by using sustainable practices, encouraging pollinators, and always experimenting with new techniques. And of course, we ensure park features are cared for at the highest standards so that everyone feels welcome and inspired.

I would love for you to join us for this next chapter. Come to one of our programs, learn more about our public art exhibits, check us out on social media, become a member, or take a walk on the park.

See you soon,

Robert Hammond
Co-Founder and Executive Director
Friends of the High Line

ACKNOWLEDGMENTS

There are hundreds of people who have contributed to the success of the High Line over the years. We cannot possibly recognize everybody here, but we would like to formally acknowledge and thank our primary collaborators. First, the indomitable Robert Hammond and Joshua David, the cofounders of the Friends of the High Line, whose pure passion drove this remarkable project forward against all odds. Mayor Michael Bloomberg and his director of city planning, Amanda Burden, were the essential catalysts who moved a grassroots vision toward an ambitious new level of realization. New York City parks commissioner Adrian Benepe grasped the once-in-a-lifetime significance of this project and put his full weight behind the vision. The dedication and support of city council speakers Christine Quinn and Gifford Miller; Manhattan borough president Scott Stringer; US Senators Charles Schumer, Hillary Rodham Clinton, and Kirsten Gillibrand; and US Representative Jerrold Nadler made the High Line possible through commitments in public funding. The project was guided by a dedicated project team at the Friends of the High Line—Peter Mullan, Adam Ganser, Louise Eddleston Lewis, and Patrick Hazari—and hardworking staff at City Hall: Patricia Harris; Dan Doctoroff; Robert Lieber and Robert Steel; EB Kelly, Angela Cavaluzzi, Andrew Winters, Marc Ricks, Zachary Smith, and Jennifer Sun-Vigoreaux; Joshua Laird, Charles McKinney, George Kroenert, Michael Bradley, Jennifer Hoppa, and Leslie Wolf of the New York City Department of Parks and Recreation; Vishaan Chakrabarti, Erik Botsford, Jamie Chan, Keith O'Connor, and Erika Sellke of the New York City Department of City Planning; and Len Greco and Michael Rem at the New York City Economic Development Corporation. Special thanks to CSX Transportation for the donation of the High Line structure to the city of New York. We also thank those who have provided moral, financial, and other forms of crucial support over the years: Philip E. Aarons and Shelley Fox Aarons; Bill and Karen Ackman; John Alschuler; Avenues: The World School; Elizabeth Belfer; Bloomberg Philanthropies; the Coach Foundation; Anisa Kamadoli Costa and The Tiffany & Co. Foundation; Sharon Davis; Barbaralee Diamonstein-Spielvogel; Barry Diller, Diane von Furstenberg, and the Diller–von Furstenberg Family Foundation; Philip A. and Lisa Maria Falcone; Google; Gary Handel; the Hanson family; Jamie and Jeffrey Harris; Hermine Riegerl Heller and David B. Heller; Jane Lauder; the Philip and Janice Levin Foundation; Adam and Brittany Levinson; the Christy and John Mack Foundation; Catie and Donald Marron; Goldman Sachs Gives, at the direction of Donald R. Mullen, Jr.; Alf Naman; Edward Norton; Michael and Sukey Novogratz; Sherry and Douglas Oliver; Mario Palumbo; Donald Pels and Wendy Keys; The Pershing Square Foundation; Jon L. Stryker and Slobodan Randjelović; Jennifer and Jonathan Allan Soros; Goldman Sachs Gives, at the direction of Susan and David Viniar; and many others who now serve on the board of the Friends of the High Line.

FIRM PROFILES

JAMES CORNER FIELD OPERATIONS (JCFO) is a leading-edge landscape architecture, urban design, and public-realm design practice based in New York City. JCFO works across a variety of types and scales, from large urban districts and complex postindustrial sites to small, well-crafted design projects. There is a special commitment to the design of a vibrant and dynamic public realm, informed by the interactive ecology between people and nature. In addition to New York's High Line, major projects include Race Street Pier in Philadelphia, Tongva Park in Santa Monica, Navy Pier in Chicago, South Park at Queen Elizabeth Olympic Park in London, Central Waterfront in Seattle, Presidio Parklands in San Francisco, Cornell University Tech Campus on Roosevelt Island in New York, Shelby Farms Park in Memphis, Lincoln Road, the Underline, and Knight Plaza in Miami, Qianhai Water City in Shenzhen, and Tsim Tsa Tsui Waterfront in Hong Kong. The work of James Corner Field Operations has received the National Design Award (2010), the American Academy of Arts and Letters Award for Architecture (2004), and the Daimler-Chrysler Design Excellence Award (2002). Projects have been published and exhibited internationally at such venues as the Museum of Modern Art, the Royal Academy of Art, the Venice Biennale, and the Rotterdam Biennale. JCFO was named one of the world's most innovative design companies by *Fast Company* (2012) and one of *Time* magazine's most influential landscape architecture firms (2010). James Corner is also professor of landscape architecture at the University of Pennsylvania School of Design. James Corner led the effort for the design of the High Line along with principal Lisa Switkin.

DILLER SCOFIDIO + RENFRO (DS+R) is an internationally acclaimed design firm that spans the fields of architecture, the visual arts, and the performing arts. The studio was recognized by the MacArthur Foundation with a "genius" award, the first given in the field of architecture, and has received the Brunner Prize from the American Academy of Arts and Letters (2003) and the National Design Award from the Smithsonian (2005). In 2003, the Whitney Museum of American Art mounted a major exhibition of the studio's work, the museum's first retrospective surveying the career of a living architect. In addition to the High Line, major projects include the redesign of Lincoln Center for the Performing Arts, including the Juilliard School, Alice Tully Hall, and the School of American Ballet; the Granoff Center at Brown University; Boston's Institute of Contemporary Art; The Broad museum in Los Angeles; Culture Shed and the Museum of Modern Art expansion, both in New York; the US Olympic Museum in Colorado Springs; the Museum of Image and Sound in Rio de Janeiro; and Zaryadye Park in Moscow. The studio's alternative projects include Blur, a building made of atomized lake water in Switzerland; *Musings on a Glass Box* at the Fondation Cartier in Paris; and *Charles James: Beyond Fashion* at the Metropolitan Museum of Art. *Time* magazine named DS+R in its annual list of the word's 100 most influential people (2009). Elizabeth Diller is professor of architecture at Princeton University, Ricardo Scofidio is professor emeritus at Cooper Union, and Charles Renfro teaches at the School of Visual Arts. Ricardo Scofidio led the design effort for the High Line with Elizabeth Diller, Charles Renfro, and Matthew Johnson.

PROJECT CREDITS

DESIGN TEAM

The design of the High Line is a collaboration between James Corner Field Operations (project lead), Diller Scofidio + Renfro, and Piet Oudolf. The design team comprised many individuals who all put in long hours and committed to nothing short of excellence on all fronts.

JAMES CORNER FIELD OPERATIONS

Partners: James Corner, Lisa Switkin
Project Leaders: Isabel Castilla, Nahyun Hwang, Tom Jost
Team Leaders: Sierra Bainbridge, Kimberly Cooper, Maura Rockcastle, Heeyoon Yoon
Full Team: Megan Born, Elizabeth Fain Labombard, Justine Heilner, Wookju Jeong, Trevor Lee, Ashley Ludwig, Danilo Martic, Tatiana von Pruessen, Karen Tamir, James Tenyenhuis, Lara Shihab-Eldin, Stephanie Ulrich, Yitian Wang, Hong Zhou

DILLER SCOFIDIO + RENFRO

Partners: Elizabeth Diller, Ricardo Scofidio, Charles Renfro
Partner in Charge: Ricardo Scofidio
Project Leader: Matthew Johnson
Team Leaders: Tobias Hegemann, Miles Nelligan, Ben Smoot
Full Team: Chiara Baccarini, Robert Condon, Hayley Eber, Trevor Lamphier, Gaspar Libedinsky, Jeremy Linzee, David Newton, Dan Sakai, Don Shillingburg, Flavio Stigliano, Brian Tabolt, Dustin Tobias

PLANTING DESIGN

Piet Oudolf

DESIGN CONSULTANTS

The design team was supported by a team of consultants whose expertise and dedication helped make the project a success.

Structural and MEP Engineering: BuroHappold (led by Craig Schwitter)
Structural Engineering and Historic Preservation: Robert Silman Associates (led by Joe Tortorella)
Lighting Design: L'Observatoire International (led by Hervé Descottes)
Signage: Pentagram (led by Paula Scher)

OTHER CONSULTANTS

Civil and Traffic Engineering: Philip Habib & Associates
Cost Estimating (Sections 1 and 2): VJ Associates
Cost Estimating (Section 3): Dharam Lally & Smith
Life Safety Engineering and Code Consulting (Section 1): Code Consultants
Public Space Management: ETM Associates
Irrigation: Northern Designs
Play Safety: Site Masters, Inc.
Environmental Engineering and Site Remediation (Sections 1 and 2): GRB Environmental Services
Environmental Consulting (Section 3): Roux Associates
Soil Science (Section 1): Pine & Swallow Associates
Soil Science (Sections 2 and 3): Craul Land Scientists
Elevator Consultant: Iros Elevator Design Services
Glass Engineering (Sections 1 and 2): Russell H. Davies
Glass Engineering (Section 3): BuroHappold
Expediting (Section 1): Municipal Expediting
Expediting (Section 2): KM Associates of New York
Expediting (Section 3): JAM Consulting
Site Surveyor: Control Point Associates
Custom Hardware Engineering: Perfection Electricks
Water Feature Engineering: CMS Collaborative
Security Design: MKJ Communications
Specifications (Section 1): Paul DiBona Specifications
Specifications (Sections 2 and 3): C/S Group

CONSTRUCTION TEAM
We wish to thank the contractors that helped to realize the physical building of the High Line.

The Section 1 team includes KisKA Construction as general contractor; the LiRo Group as resident engineer; Bovis Lend Lease; SiteWorks Landscape; Helen Neuhaus & Associates as community liaison; and subcontractors Delta Fountains, Kelco Landscaping and Construction, the Plant Group, USA Iron, Metalcrafters, Inc. (Hammersmith), and GrayGlass Co.

The Section 2 team includes CAC as general contractor; HDR and the LiRo Group as resident engineers; SiteWorks; Bovis Lend Lease; Helen Neuhaus & Associates as community liaison; and subcontractors Jersey Precast Corp, Kelco Landscaping and Construction, the Plant Group, Metalcrafters, Inc. (Hammersmith), and City Newark Glass.

The Section 3 team includes Sciame for construction management; the LiRo Group for construction management (site preparation); and subcontractors BPDL, CAC, Concrete Industries One, Steven Dubner Landscaping, Egg, L&L Painting, Sunny Border, Venture, FMB, Sawkill Lumber, SiteWorks, ATTA, Inc., Landscape Structures, Studio dell'Arte, Optical Mechanics, Inc., and VGS.

BOOK TEAM
We wish to thank the members of the book team at Diller Scofidio + Renfro and James Corner Field Operations for their great work and dedication to this book, which was a design project in its own right and true to the unique spirit of the High Line.

Project Leaders: Rodrigo Tisi with Margaret Jankowsky
Graphic Design: Forrest Jessee, Javier Moreno Sarrión
Editorial Lead: Hannah Wilentz
Research Assistant: Angela Estevez
Project Support: Aldo Cherdabayev, Swarnabh Ghosh, Trevor Lamphier, Lindsey May, Mac McAnulty, Houman Momtazian, David Richardson, Alessandro Scognamiglio, Dustin Tobias, Lexi Tsien, Manda Yakiwchuk, Yelena Zolotorevskaya

Special thanks to Barbara Clark, the book's literary agent; Rick Little, Patrick Hazari, Erika Harvey, and Amelia Krales from Friends of the High Line; and photographers Iwan Baan, Matthew Monteith, and Timothy Schenck.

This book would not have been possible without the extraordinary care and attention from the leadership and editorial team at Phaidon. Special thanks to Keith Fox, Emilia Terragni, Julia Hasting, Laura Loesch-Quintin, Sue Medlicott, and Nerissa Vales.

Thanks to all who helped to make the High Line a reality and continue to care for it.

IMAGE CREDITS

Rights to all photos, renderings, and drawings are held by James Corner Field Operations and Diller Scofidio + Renfro, unless otherwise noted.

FRONT MATTER

Courtesy of Kalmbach Publishing Company: 4.

CONVERSATIONS

Matthew Monteith: 12, 170, 338; RadicalMedia: 181; © Terra Lannoo Publishers: 177.

00_INTRODUCTION

Courtesy of USDA Farm Service Agency: 10.

01_FOUND

Jesse Chehak: 77; Courtesy of Friends of the High Line: 28, 76; Jason Kottke: 24, 25; Peter Mullan, courtesy of Friends of the High Line: 46; Barry Munger: 82; Piet Oudolf: 22; Michael Rogol: 29; Gino Scofidio: 26, 34, 42, 50, 58, 66, 74, 80; Timothy Schenck: 76; Stephen Sherman: 39, 39, 47, 63, 65.

02_ARCHIVE

Courtesy of Friends of the High Line: 84; Numbered archival materials (pages 86–114): (1) Courtesy of Columbia University, photo by Patrick Ciccone/Dan Fox; (2, 3) Courtesy of Kalmbach Publishing Company; (4, 5, 14) *New York World*; (6–9, 20–22, 31, 36, 49, 70, 75) © *The New York Times*, all rights reserved; (10) Associated Press; (11, 69) Courtesy of New York City Municipal Archives; (12) *Popular Science Monthly*; (13) *Harper's Weekly*; (15–16) Courtesy of *Scientific American* magazine; (17) Courtesy of New York Public Library; (18–19) Courtesy of the Railroad Enthusiasts of New York at the Williamson Library; (23–27, 30, 50–51, 54, 64, 66, 68, 74) Courtesy of Friends of the High Line; (28) Courtesy of Gerry Weinstein, binder photos by Gerardo Vizmanos; (29) Harry Brown/*The New Yorker*; (32) Courtesy of *National Geographic* magazine; (33) Jim Shaughnessy; (34–35) Michael Syracuse; (37–39) Efrain John Gonzalez; (40) © Pamela Greene, 2011, originally published in *Blood & Beauty: Manhattan's Meatpacking District*, Schiffer Publishing, Ltd.; (41) © Brian Rose; (42, 47) Courtesy of Florent Morellet; (43–46, 48) Courtesy of The Center; (52) Steven Holl; (53) *New York Post*; (55, 58) Joel Sternfeld; (56) Paula Scher/Pentagram; (57) Adam Gopnik/*The New Yorker*; (59) Courtesy of Regional Plan Association; (60) Courtesy of HR&A Advisors, Inc.; (61) New York City Department of City Planning, all rights reserved; (62) Courtesy of the Design Trust for Public Space; (63, 65) Courtesy of Manhattan Community Board 4; (67) Nathalie Rinne; (71) *The Villager*; (72–73) *Daily News*.

03_CONCEPT

Chris Campbell: 120, 128 (br); Courtesy of Center for Architecture: 129 (br); Courtesy of Friends of the High Line: 156–159, 162–163; 168 (m, r), 169; James Corner Field Operations and Diller Scofidio + Renfro, photos by Gerardo Vizmanos: 122–128, 151–165; Courtesy of Kalmbach Publishing Company: 122 (l); © The Museum of Modern Art/Licensed by SCALA/Art Resource, NY: 166–167; © *The New York Times*, all rights reserved: 129 (l), 150; *The Villager*: 129 (tr).

04_DESIGN

Gigi Altarejos: 234 (m), 235 (r); Elvert Barnes: 236 (fourth from left), 237 (fifth from left); Courtesy of Friends of the High Line: 240–245; Joan Garvin: 236 (first from left); Michael B. Gordon: 237 (fourth from left); Annik LaFarge: 234 (l); Lebasi Lashley: 240 (column 2, row 2), 241 (column 3, row 4); Cristina Macaya: 241 (column 4, row 1); Melissa Mansur: 235 (m); Piet Oudolf: 238; Reena Rose/NJ Advance Media/Landov Media: 235 (l); Steven N. Severinghaus: 234 (r), 235 (l), 236 (second, third, fifth, and sixth from left), 237 (first, second, third, and sixth from left), 243 (column 1, row 6).

05_CONSTRUCTION

Iwan Baan: 267; Earthcam, courtesy of Friends of the High Line: 248; Courtesy of Friends of the High Line: 252, 254, 256; Barry Munger: 272; Timothy Schenck: 246, 250, 253, 255, 257–263, 265, 268, 270 (r).

06_WALK

Iwan Baan: 277–278, 279–281, 287, 290–292, 293, 296–297, 298, 305, 309, 312–317, 320, 327–329, 332, 334, 337; Ludovic Bertron: 306; Will Chafkin: 276, 307; Benjamin Chiang: 311; Diane Cook and Len Jenshel/National Geographic Creative: 274; © Cameron Davidson/Corbis: 295; Andrew Frasz: 322, 323; Joan Garvin: 304; David Goodman: 321; J Graham: 308; Katherine Humphrey: 288; JaegerSloan Studio: 278–279, 282–283, 288–289, 292–293, 300–301, 306–307, 310–311, 318–319, 322–323, 330–331, 334–335; Matthew Monteith: 284, 286, 294, 296, 297, 299, 333, 336; Landon Nordeman: 310; Trey Ratcliffe: 302; Changwoo Ryu: 301; Timothy Schenck: 330, 331, 335; Steven N. Severinghaus: 282, 285, 300, 303, 324; Andrew St. Clair: 283; Sarah Tester: 318; Mike Tschappat: 319, 325, 326; Sébastien Uribarrena: 289.

07_UNFORESEEN

Iwan Baan: 361 (column 1, t), 377 (tl, tr); Artwork by Ericka Beckman, photo by Timothy Schenck, courtesy of Friends of the High Line: 359 (column 1, t); Bond No. 9, photo by Gerardo Vizmanos: 375 (l); Hortencia Caires, photo of Rachel Lynch: 363 (l); Krissa Corbett Cavouras: 354 (tr); Tony Cenicola/*The New York Times*/Redux: 378 (mr); Will Chafkin: 351, 362 (l,m); Chris Christian: 346; Kiersten

Chou: 350; Ashley Clark: 358 (l); Jessica Dimmock/*The New York Times*/Redux: 349; Alexander Dunkel: 370; eko/ekosystem.org: 377 (bl); Andrew Frasz: 354 (tl); Courtesy of Friends of the High Line: 358 (column 3, t), 361 (column 2, b); *Globo*: 391 (r); David Goodman: 360 (column 2, b), 361 (column 1, b); *The Guardian*: 391 (m); Kevin Hagen: 356 (l); Ayano Hisa: 360 (column 2, t); Krisanne Johnson/*The New York Times*/REDUX: 378 (tr); Allison Joyce/*New York Post*/Splash News: 353 (r); Lara Kleinschmidt: 352, 363; Ari Klickstein: 355; Artwork by Alison Knowles, photo by Liz Ligon, courtesy of Friends of the High Line: 359 (column 2, m); Josiah Lau: 360 (column 2, m); Robert Lederman: 356 (m, r); Yoav Lerman: 354 (br); Ben Lerner/Farrar, Straus and Giroux, photo by Gerardo Vizmanos: 368; Liz Ligon: 358 (column 2, t), 359 (column 3, b), 360 (column 3, t); Scott Lynch: 359 (column 2, b); Karin du Maire: 359 (column 2, t); David J. Martin: 378 (br); © MARVEL: 366; Matthew Monteith: 364; *La Nación*: 390 (r); *New York* Magazine: 378 (l), 379 (l); © *The New York Times*, all rights reserved: 478 (m), 380 (m, r), 381, 390 (l); NPZO: 348; Chelsea Ozeri: 365; Courtesy of Peter Brown Studio, photo by Gerardo Vizmanos: 369; Marco Pinna: 358 (column 3, b); David X Prutting/BFAnyc.com: 358 (column 2, b); Steven N. Severinghaus: 380 (l); Markus Spiering: 371; *La Stampa*: 391 (l); Artwork by Tomoaki Suzuki, photo by Austin Kennedy, courtesy of Friends of the High Line: 360 (column 3, b); *The Sydney Morning Herald*: 390 (m); Mario Tama, Getty Images: 359 (column 3, t); Topless Pulp Fiction: 357; FAMILY GUY © 2010 Twentieth Century Fox Television, all rights reserved: 367; Juan Valentin: 354 (bl), 358 (column 3, m), 359 (column 1, b), 360 (column 1, b), 361 (column 2, t), 361 (column 3, t), 373–374; Photos of binders and High Line Haze by Gerardo Vizmanos: 354, 375–377; M Wartella: 379 (r); Sharon Watt: 353 (l); Jonathan Ystad, photo of Elizabeth Fuller: 360 (column 1, t); Business cards (page 376): (column 1) High Line 519/Sleepy Hudson, HL23, Abington House Leasing, High Line Residential, The High Line Hotel; (column 2) Ava High Line, Soori High Line, The HighLine West Village, High Line Construction Group, Highline Ballroom; (column 3) Bubby's High Line, The Rail Line, Underline Coffee, Highline Pizzeria, The Highliner; (column 4) Highline Deli, Highline Deli 2, Highline Records/Masha Karpushina, Highline Stages, Morris Adjmi; Global projects (pages 386–389): (1) Abu Dhabi Department of Municipal Affairs, (2) James Corner Field Operations, (3) © Ross Barney Architects, Michael Van Valkenburgh Associates, Arup, (4) Smithgroup JJR, (5) Biomorphis, (6) Florida Department of Environmental Protection, (7) © Archivio Fuksas, (8) Roman Pohorecki and Mark Bonsignore, (9) DoepelStrijkers, (10) BIG, (11) Iwan Baan, courtesy of BIG, (12) Arup, Heatherwick Studio, (13) erect architecture with J & L Gibbons, (14) Ernesto Valero, Jimena García, Juan Pablo Espinosa, (15) Hunt Laudi, (16) Friends of the Flyover and We Make Places, (17) Weiss/Manfredi, Thomas Balsley Associates, Arup, (18) RAAD, (19) WXY Architects, (20) Wallace Roberts & Todd, (21) STUDIO | BRYAN HANES, (22) Bergmann Associates, (23) Yael Engelhart, (24) MVRDV, (25) Mikyoung Kim Design, (26) WORKac 2009, (27) Green Corridor, (28) Kiku Obata & Company, (29) Gabriel Wulf, (30) Brown Storey Architects, (31) Lemay, (32) Abraham John Architects, (33) OMA, (34) Bauman Lyons Architects and Estell Warren Landscape Architects, (35) Mailen, (36) Pedaleable, (37) Base3, (38) Greater Cleveland Regional Transit Authority, (39) Rubio Arquitectura and Estudio Alvarez-Sala, (40) Angelo Tomaiuolo, (41) James Corner Field Operations, (42) ASPECT Studios with CHROFI for the Sydney Harbour Foreshore Authority, (43) Latitud Taller, (44) Alberto Varas, Estudio Aisenson, (45) John December, courtesy of Stoss, (46) Ruy Rezende Arquitetura, (47) Weiss/Manfredi, (48) Basurama CC BY-NC-SA 3.0, (49) Tsai, (50) Starr Whitehouse Landscape Architects and Planners with Perkins+Will, (51) Ramboll, (52) David Vago of Habit8, (53) Jung Min-ho, (54) Nicolas Boutmy, (55) Tuca Vieira, (56) Carl Perelman, (57) Urban Strategies Inc., Kasian Architects, Scott Torrance Landscape Architect Inc., First Capital Realty Inc., Cumulus Architects Inc., TACT Architecture Inc., Hatch Mott MacDonald, RJ Burnside and Associates Inc., Bay Area Economics, (58) © Andrés Besomi, Plataforma Urbana, (59) Far North Endurance, (60) AECOM.

BACK MATTER
Iwan Baan: 398.

Every effort has been made to locate the owners of copyright and to ensure that the credit information supplied is accurately listed. Any errors or omissions are inadvertent and will be corrected in future printings.

Phaidon Press Limited
2 Cooperage Yard
London E15 2QR

Phaidon Press Inc.
111 Broadway
New York, NY 10006

Phaidon SARL
55, rue Traversière
75012 Paris

phaidon.com

First published 2015
This format published 2020
Reprinted 2025
© 2015 Phaidon Press Limited

ISBN 978 1 83866 077 2

A CIP catalogue record for this book is available from the British Library and the Library of Congress.

All rights reserved. No part of this publication may be reproduced, stored in a retrieval system or transmitted, in any form or by any means, electronic, mechanical, photocopying, recording or otherwise, without the written permission of Phaidon Press Limited.

Commissioning Editor: Emilia Terragni
Project Editors: Laura Loesch-Quintin, Emma Barton
Production Controllers: Nerissa Vales,
Sue Medlicott, Adela Cory
Design: Diller Scofidio + Renfro, James Corner
Field Operations
Cover Design: Julia Hasting
Cover and Endpapers Photography: Matthew Monteith

Printed in China

phaidon.com

978 1 83866 077 2